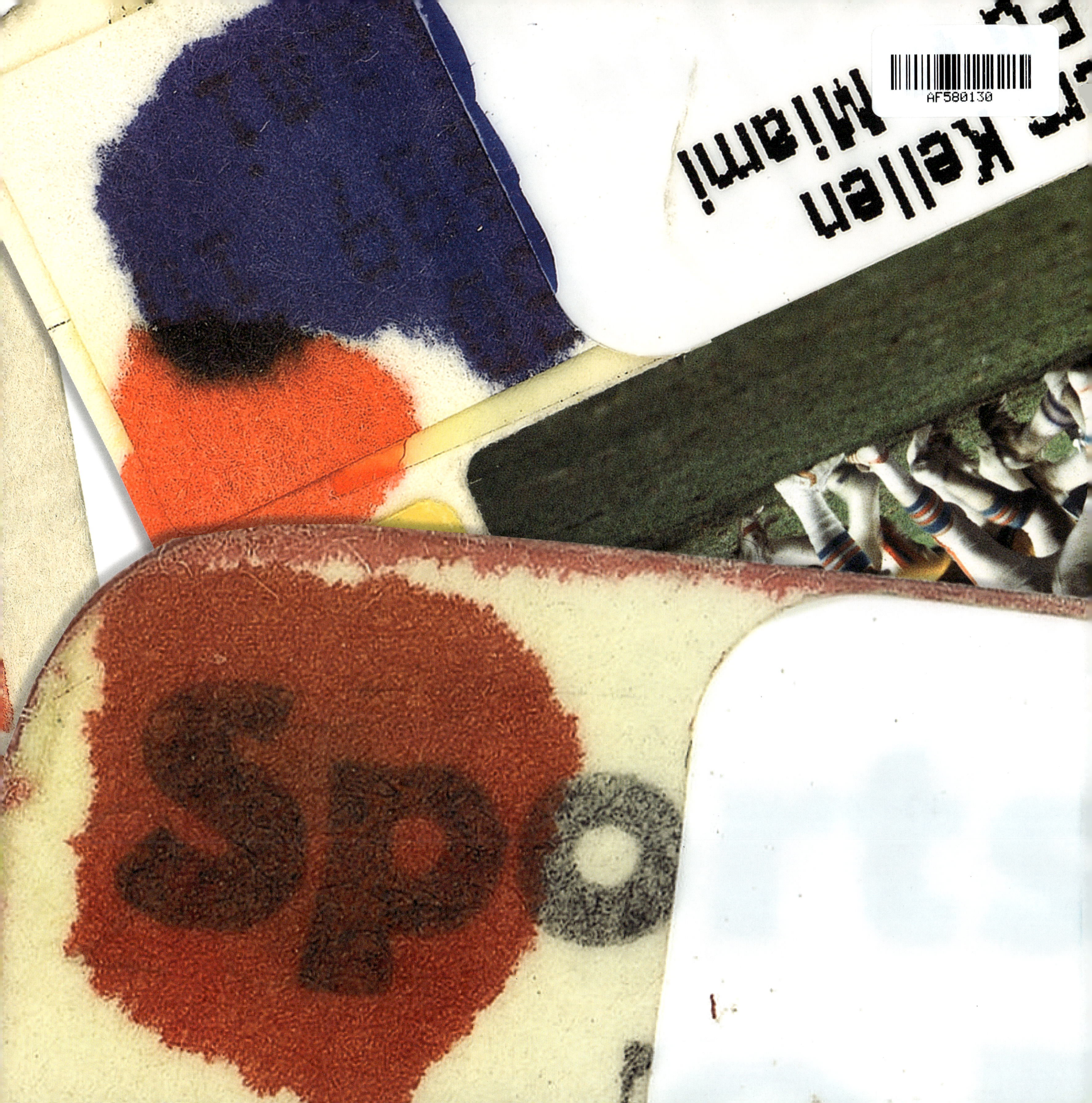
Kellen
Miami

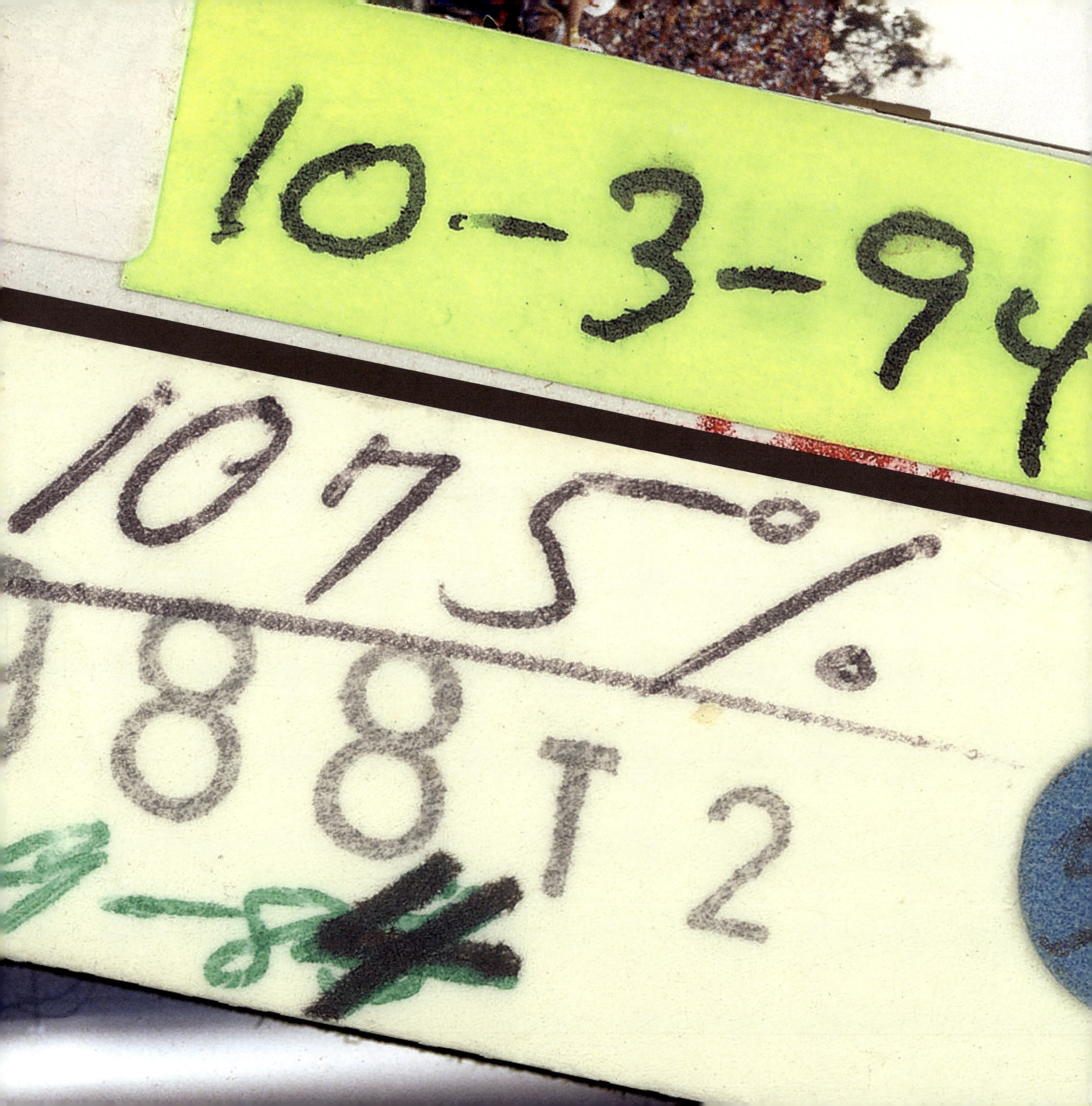
10-3-94
88T2

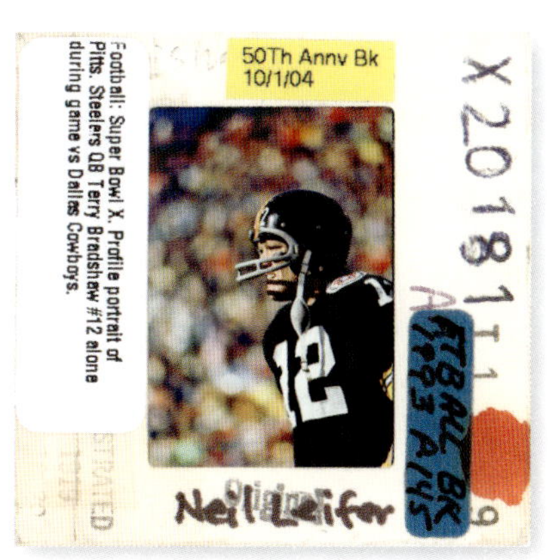
50Th Annv Bk
10/1/04
Football: Super Bowl X. Profile portrait of Pitts. Steelers QB Terry Bradshaw #12 alone during game vs Dallas Cowboys.
Neil Leifer

SLIDE SHOW

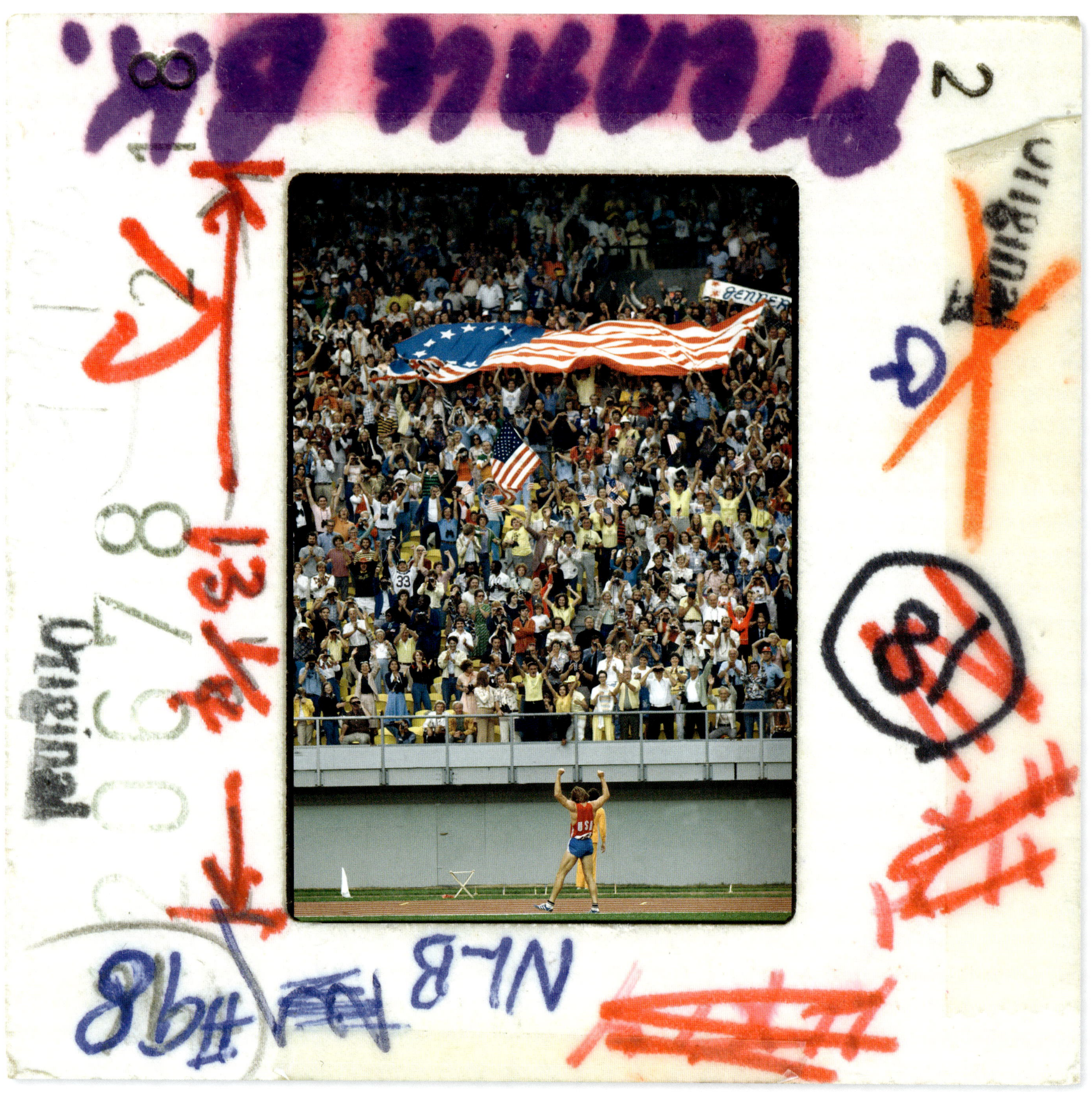

The slide mount around Bruce Jenner, winner of the 1976 Olympic decathlon, is fittingly bedecked in red, white and blue. • *Photograph by* NEIL LEIFER, July 30, 1976

Sports Illustrated

SLIDE SHOW

BY STEVEN HOFFMAN

Introduction by Terry McDonell

EDITED BY BILL SYKEN

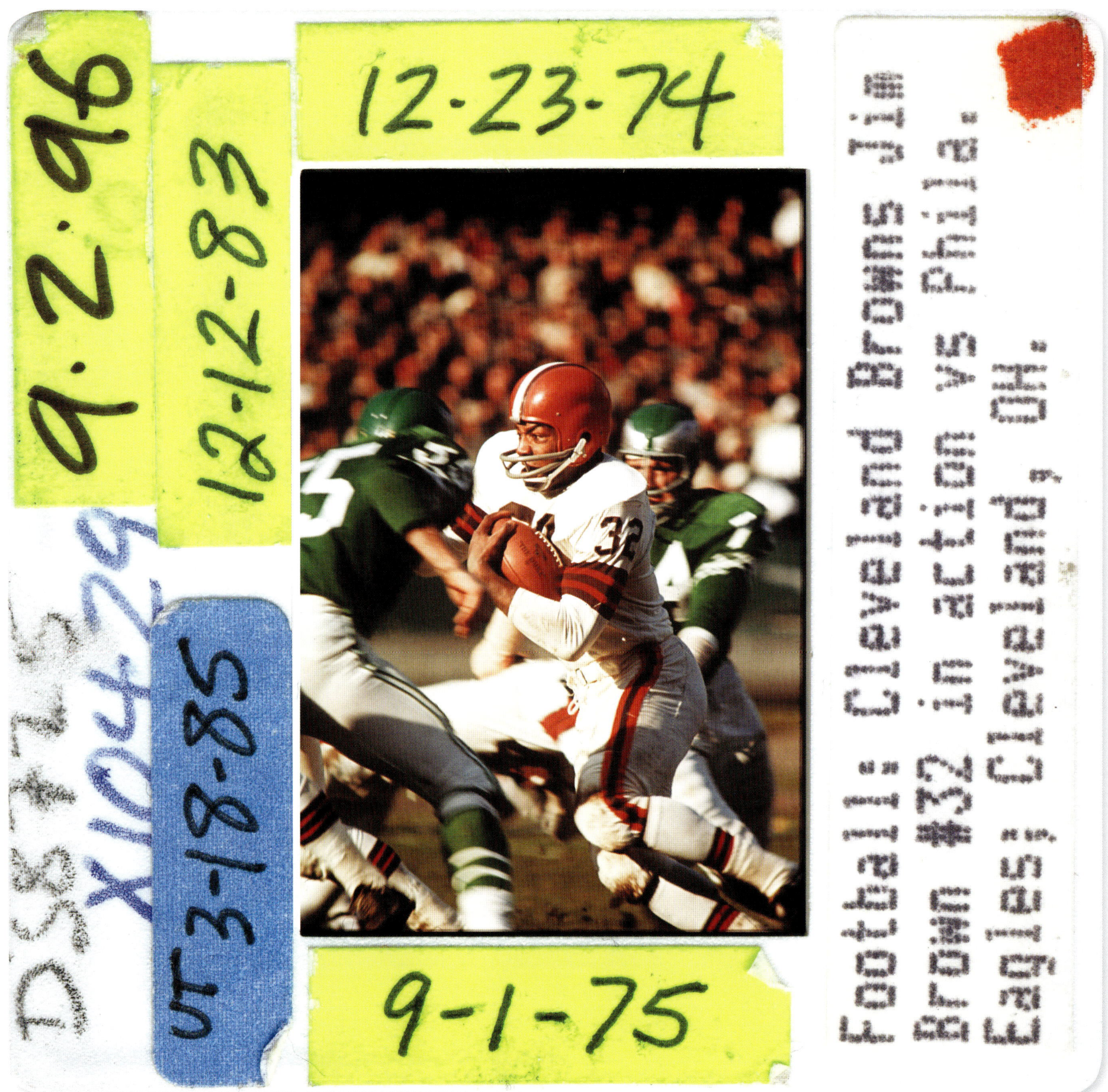

The dates on the stickers tell that this oft-published photo of the peerless Jim Brown was re-used long after his 1965 retirement. • *Photograph by* NEIL LEIFER, November 29, 1964

Contents

STEVEN HOFFMAN *Creative Director* / BILL SYKEN *Editor*

DAVID BAUER *Project Editor* / STEFANIE KAUFMAN *Project Manager* / CRISTINA SCALET *Photo Editor* / TED MENZIES *Photo Archivist* / KEVIN KERR *Copy Editor*
JOSH DENKIN *Associate Art Director* / REBECCA SUN *Reporter* / CHELSEA CARTABIANO *Design Assistant* / GEOFF MICHAUD *Imaging Group Director*

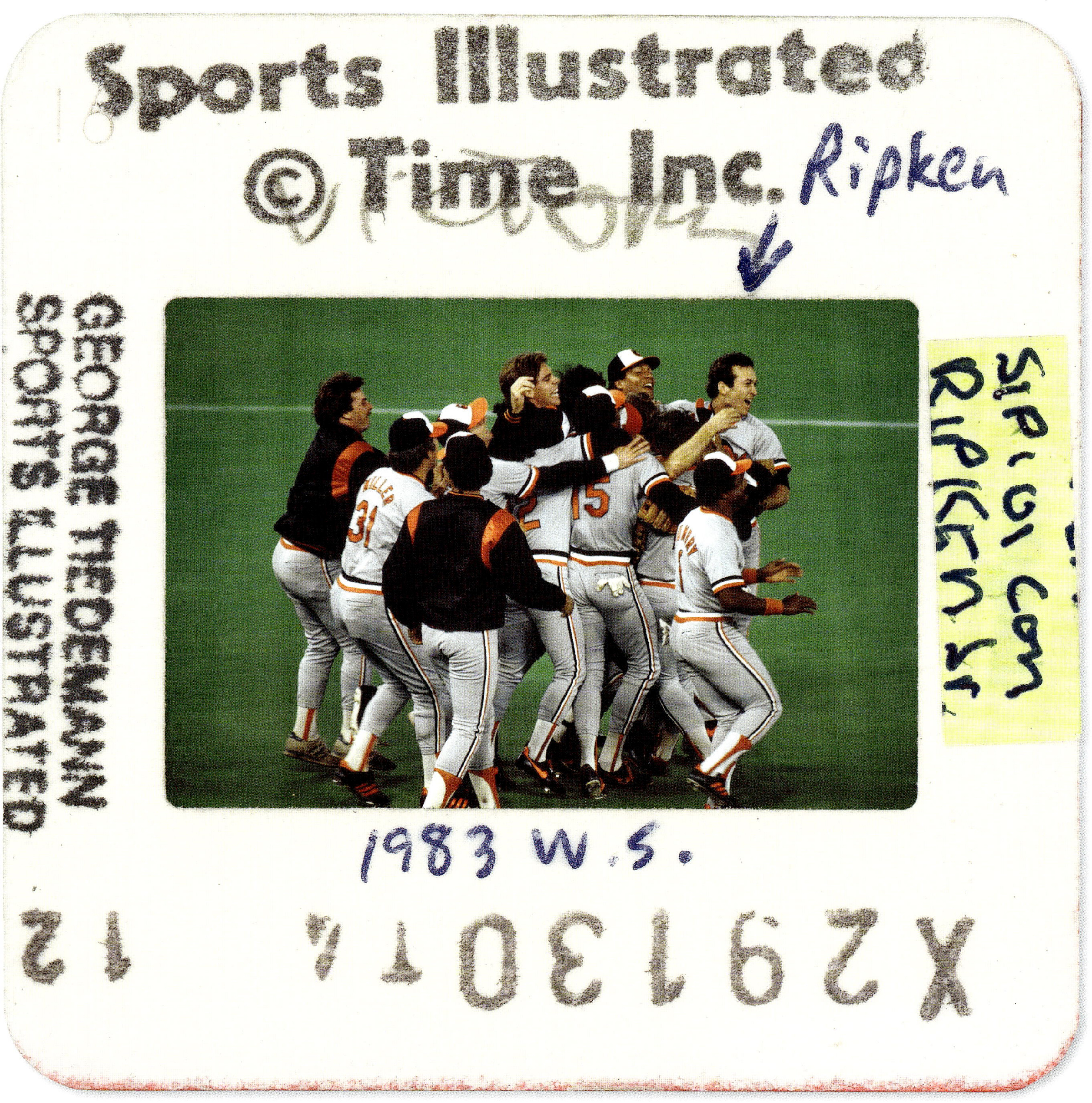

If in need of help finding the Orioles Hall of Famer in this World Series celebration, just follow the arrow. • *Photograph by* GEORGE TIEDEMANN, October 16, 1983

 • ISBN 10: 1-60320-053-3 ISBN 13: 978-1-60320-053-0 LIBRARY OF CONGRESS CONTROL NUMBER: 2008909718 • PRINTED IN CHINA

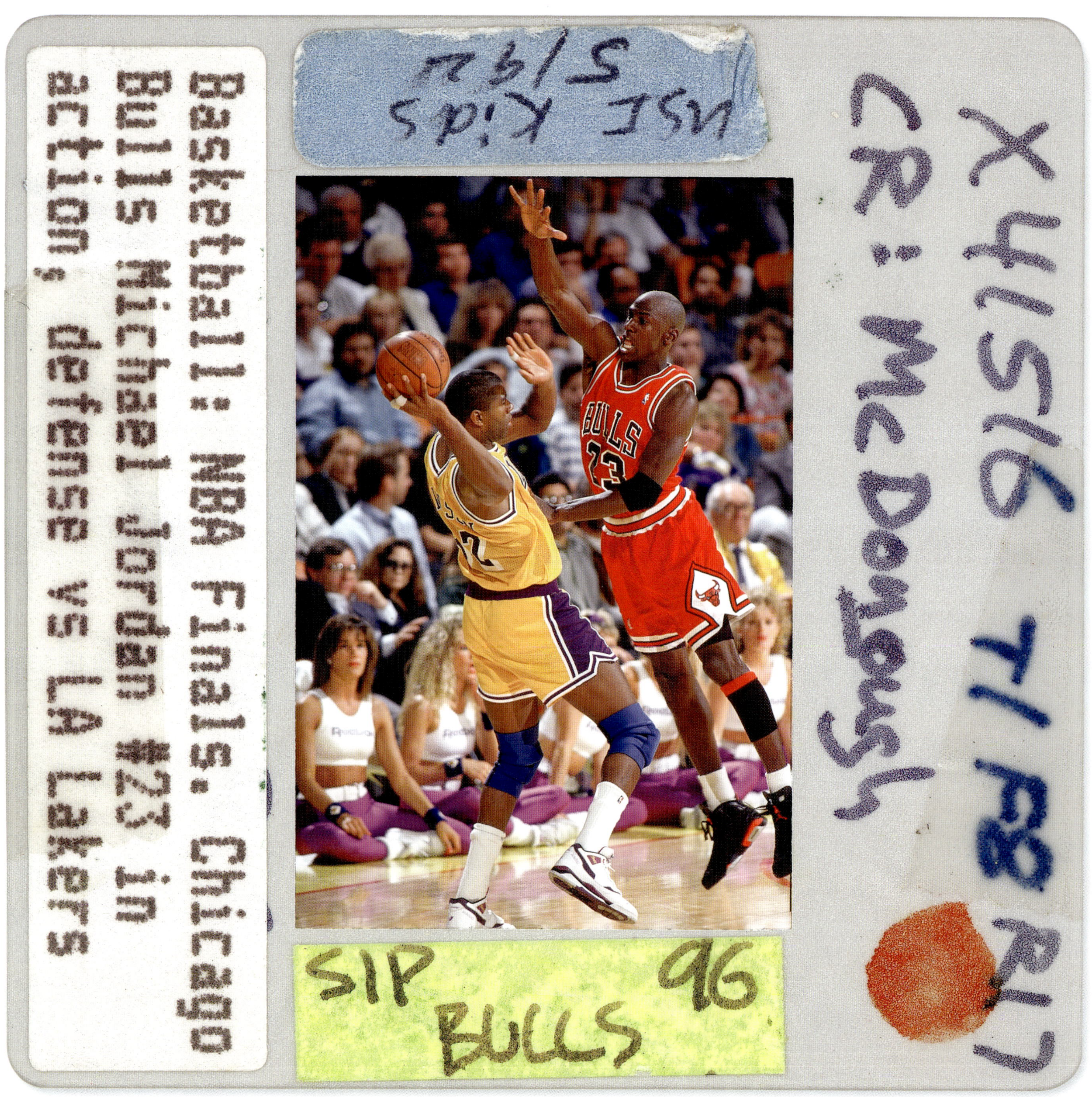

In an image capturing a battle of icons, the great Michael Jordan rose up to deny the great Magic Johnson. • *Photograph by* JOHN W. MCDONOUGH, June 7, 1991

Seeing The Light

The notes of photographer Marvin E. Newman tell us this picture (previously unpublished) is of a gathering of Yankee stars before a 1956 night game.

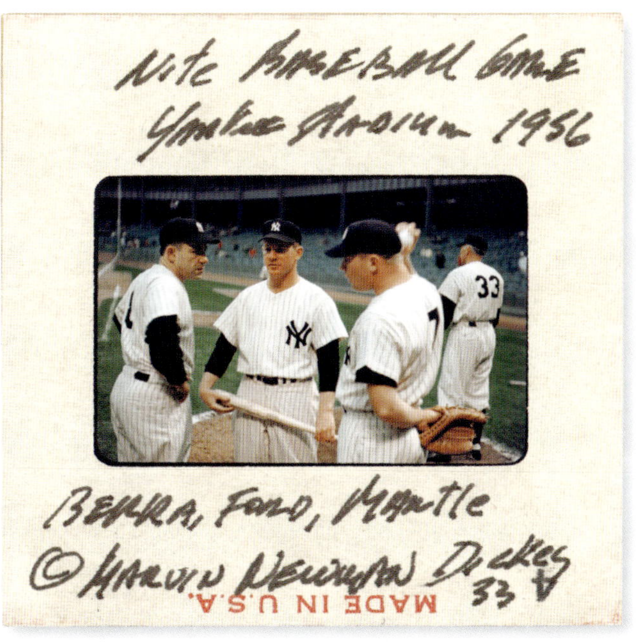

TO ENTER THE SPORTS ILLUSTRATED photo archive is to be immersed in a frame-by-frame chronicle of sports over the last half century. But if every picture in that archive tells a story, every slide tells an even deeper one. The stickers and scribblings along the cardboard borders are like tags on a streamer trunk, clues to the tale of each photo's journey from the playing field to the magazine page.

Inside those borders, some of the images are recognizable as classic SI cover shots (the Miracle on Ice celebration, Lynn Swann's leaping catch in Super Bowl X); others are those extraordinary photos that fire our memories (a Magic and Michael showdown in the NBA Finals, Joe Namath lounging poolside before Super Bowl III). Then there is that rare find—a poignant photo never before published (an impromptu gathering of Yankee heroes in 1956). The pictures themselves are iconic, but as slides they bear the embellishments of history.

Tiny objects of art, these slides have an unintended beauty of their own. On one, the marginalia dazzle with the color and movement of a Jackson Pollock drip painting. Another is reminiscent of a Robert Rauschenberg combine painting. They have an aesthetic both baroque and pop.

But if it is art, it is a lost art. These slides are vanishing. Images are no longer mounted in miniature frames and stuffed into cabinet drawers; rather, they are digitized and entered into a vast electronic database. Yes, it is more efficient to search: keyword > Tiger Woods > Masters; but is it as gratifying, or as much fun, as sorting through a stack of Arnold Palmer slides on a light box? For generations at SPORTS ILLUSTRATED, photographers, art directors and photo editors gathered around light tables, armed with eye loupes and marker pens, to spread out the day's haul of slides like jewelers evaluating precious gems. It is a practice—a ritual, really—that is gone.

The earliest slides, dating to the mid-19th century, were called lantern slides, viewed with a wondrous device called a Magic Lantern. We have new wonders now, but the slides in this book still seduce with an irresistible magic.

—STEVEN HOFFMAN *Creative Director,* SPORTS ILLUSTRATED

Slide Culture

by Terry McDonell

In the neo-olden days, tribes of magazine editors gathered to view slides, sometimes images of charging horses, in darkened, cavelike rooms.

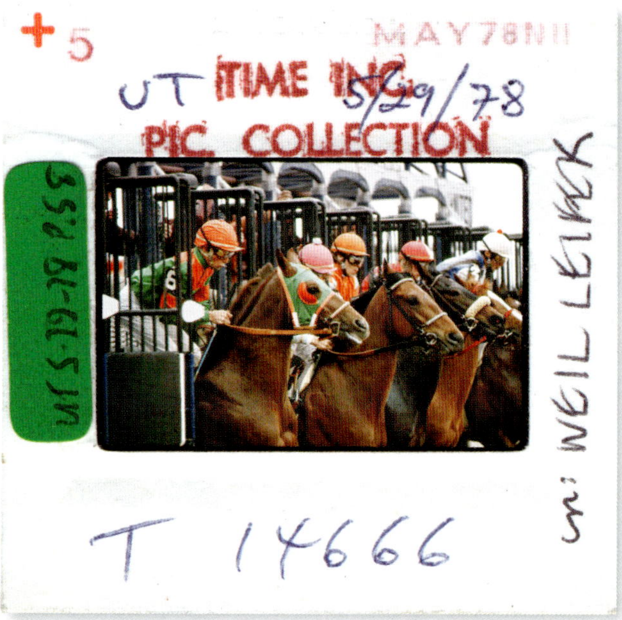

IT OCCURRED TO ME in the summer of 1988 that I needed my own light box. Had to have one. I was launching a magazine out of Jean Pagliuso's photo studio on West 16th Street in New York City, and that simple plastic and metal box with its translucent top and the light shining up from inside was crucial technology. *Tool* is actually a better word because my modest magazine startup was also a test site for the new Macintosh computers that Apple was just then bringing to market. Both were crucial but to see an Alvin Satin-Glow light box sitting on a worktable next to a Mac II was to see the past and future prankishly paired.

This was not lost on any of the handful of us who were, as far as we knew, "desktop" publishing a national magazine for the first time. The magazine was called *Smart*, and it lasted only a year and a half, but I still have the light box. It sits in storage, unused for two decades but too important to toss away—an artifact of a lost culture.

Call it Slide Culture, and in 1988 it was just peaking.

I already had my own loupe, which I had taken to wearing around my neck as an unconscious if unsubtle signal that I was spending much of my time looking at pictures—which, because of the great photographic work being done seemingly everywhere then, was the cool thing to be doing if you were a magazine editor. With a big nod to David Hemmings playing an ultracool fashion photographer in Michelangelo Antonioni's *Blowup* two decades earlier, I specifically remember an entire school of celebrity/art/rock photographers spreading out behind Annie Leibovitz; Sebastião Salgado's work from the mines of Serra Pelada, Brazil; and many surprises like the "sketchbook" photographs Eric Fischl used as studies for his disturbing paintings of middle-class leisure. I had already been acting like a photo editor, calling in submissions and looking at so many pictures that I came to realize I was spending much too much time walking between my desk and the light table in the art department, way at the other end of the studio, to look at slides.

A "slide," of course, was a positive image recorded on 35mm film—usually either Kodachrome or Ektachrome,

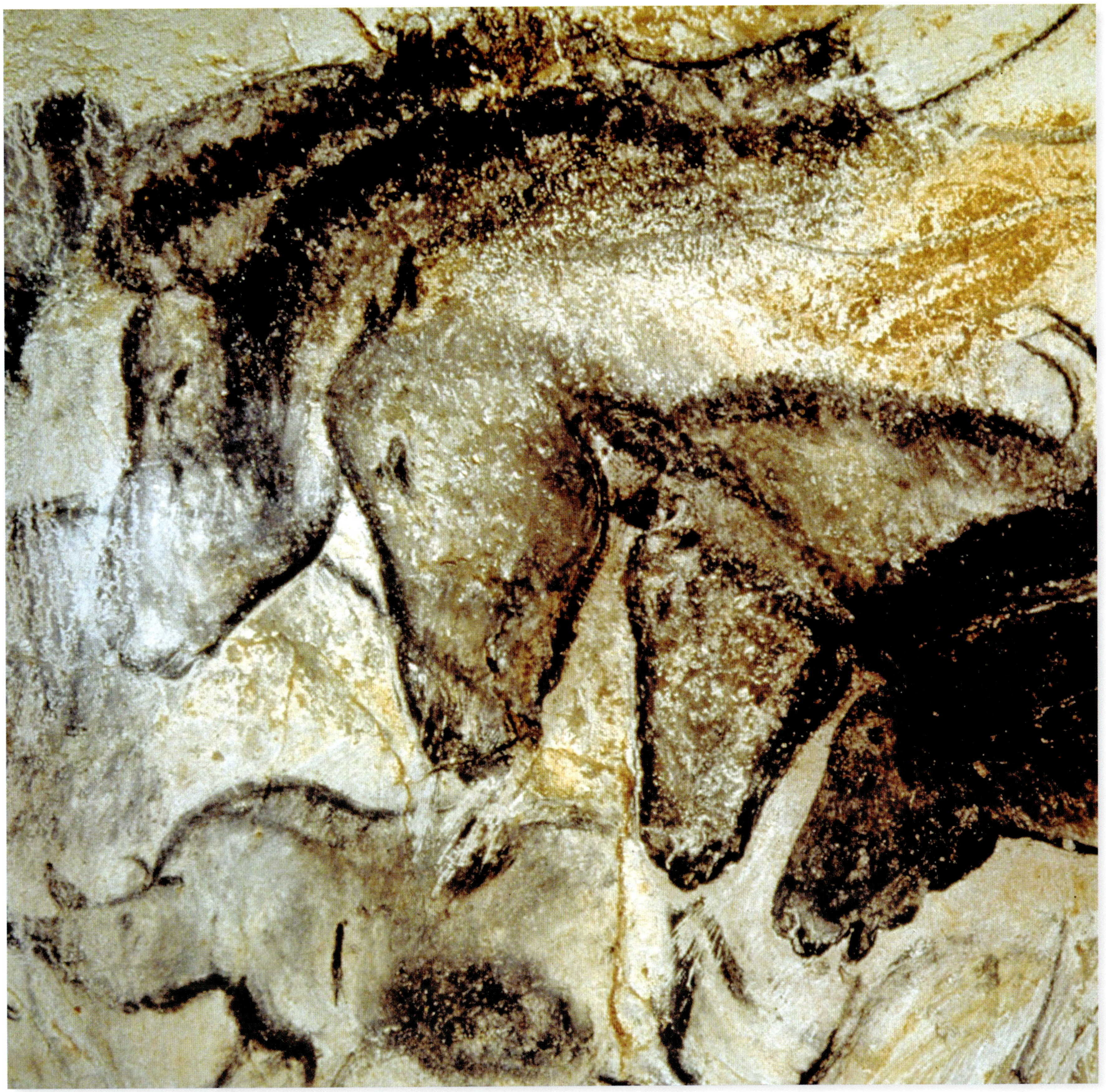

An estimated 30,000 years ago, in the Paleolithic era, artists rendered images of charging horses on the stone walls of their caves in southern France.

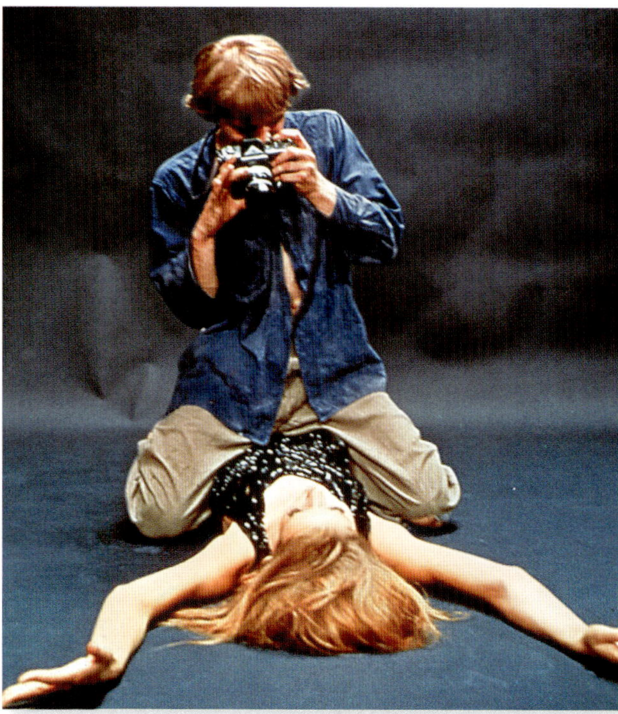

Michelangelo Antonioni's 1966 film *Blowup*, starring David Hemmings, reflected, or perhaps launched, the social ascent of the photographer as glamour figure.

which were simply the best films when it came to color accuracy, tonal range and sharpness. Kodachromes actually exhibited a visible "relief" image on the emulsion side. It was beautiful. Fujichrome came a little later and was also brilliant. Because Ektachrome and Fujichrome could also be processed faster (and on weekends) they became the film for sports action. One or another was what all the pros used, but everybody else could use them too. Every serious shooter I ever knew swore by this film. You could get technical and explain that when shot with a high quality lens, a 35-millimeter Kodachrome slide holds detail equivalent to 25 or more megapixels of image data, but you didn't need to know that to be blown away by what you saw through your loupe on your new light box.

The 2"-by-2" cardboard or plastic mounts both framed and protected the image. Photo editors at big magazines like SPORTS ILLUSTRATED, TIME and *Newsweek* spent much of their time sequencing images and dropping them into plastic carousels. The subsequent slide shows brought together various editors, researchers and designers working on a particular story. These shows could be shocking and disturbing, with thick silence in the room as you clicked through Jim Nachtwey's images of civil strife in Northern Ireland. You could also be moved viewing an old slide of a teenage Marvin Gaye the day after the singer, at age 44, had been shot dead by his father. It felt like theater in those so-called "color rooms."

And because magazine work is fundamentally collaborative—depending on time of day and proximity of deadline—the shows could also turn suddenly into boisterous impromptu captioning sessions, like one I remember at *Newsweek* when an image was shown of vice presidential candidate Dan Quayle holding up a golf club with a particularly stupid look on his face: "Tennis anyone?" It was all great fun, as long as it wasn't frustrated by stuck projectors and blown bulbs. Sometimes it also felt important.

I remember one Sunday night at *Newsweek*, sitting in that cool, dark room on the 19th floor at 444 Madison Avenue drinking lukewarm coffee and looking at academic slides of paleolithic cave paintings, when I made the connection between what I was doing and the 30,000-year-old art I was looking at. It went beyond that art history experience we have all had of sitting in a college lecture hall looking at Gothic cathedrals or whatever. It was tribal. And by that I mean it was what we did in my tribe. Prehistoric hunters squinted in the flickering firelight at shaman paintings of game on stone walls; we looked at slides. We even wrote notes on them to help us remember where they fit into our culture.

THE BURST of creative photography that popped in the 1960s and rolled through the second half of the 20th century had about it the sense of something coming and going very fast—like the so-called "climax culture" of the Plains Indians, to stay tribal here. From the early 1970s on, if you were working in or with any kind of media you could get hit simultaneously with the exhilaration of being too early and the dread of being too late. The good news is that we didn't have time to overthink it. By "we" I mean just about everyone having anything to do with magazine photography over those years.

What we understood was that slides themselves would be disappearing very, very fast, and that our unnamed slide culture would look increasingly sentimental in the rear-view mirror.

And we would find how much we missed it, almost everything about it. Slides had a physical reality that you could play with, move around and sequence and move around again on that light box. A short stack of slides even felt good in your hand, like poker chips. Some editors held slides up to overhead lights and blew on them as if that was a smart way to get rid of dust. Others wore thin white editing gloves all the time. The big light tables at magazines like *Rolling Stone* and *Esquire* became like editorial watering holes where people would meet to socialize, and the translucent surfaces got smudged with brie or worse. Lines of cocaine even. Wine was spilled on them. Slide Culture threw good parties. But then it was all over by the mid-1990s when Kodak abandoned Kodachrome research and development—even though a refrigerator full of the film lingers as instant status among the most eccentric pro shooters.

What became clear when SI's creative director Steven Hoffman came up with the idea for this book *(page 8)* is that in the same way that, say, the caves in southern France frame the importance of Paleolithic horse paintings, every slide mount collected in this book—and for that matter every one that saw any action at SI over the last half century—certainly has its own story to tell. Some of the markings on the mounts are lost filing codes in colored dots; other notes and dates and symbols should be read like graffiti, as the "tags" of the various photo editors who worked with them.

And all of the stories are haunted in their own way, and beautiful, all of them contextual stories, graphic and nuanced at the same time. You just have to look at the archaeology, or maybe it's closer to forensic photo editing *(page 14)*. That's the context of Slide Culture and what it left behind. Which is what this book is about.

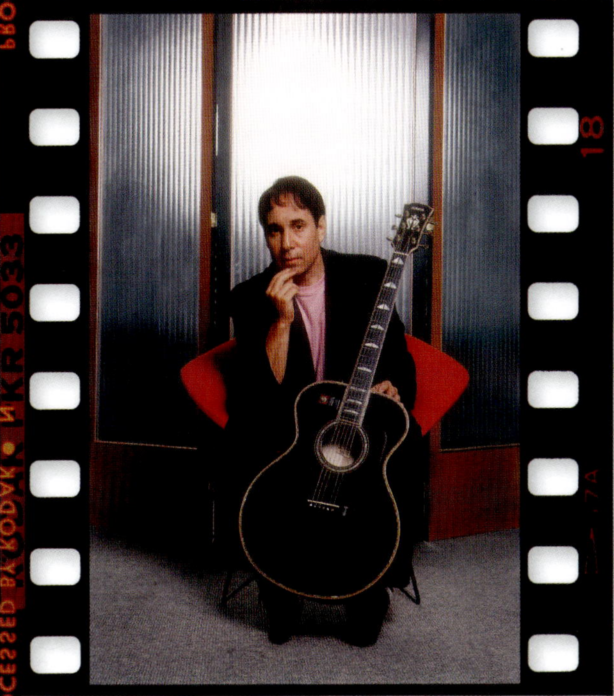

Kodachrome became the film of choice for professional and weekend photographers alike, as well as a fitting rhyme for a Paul Simon song.

PAUL SIMON will tell you that he came up with *Kodachrome* while trying to write "going home" into a melody he already had. But "going home" was much too square, and he already had that wonderfully defiant first line, the true one, as Simon puts it: "When I think back on all the crap I learned in high school/It's a wonder I can think at all." So he kept working, letting his mind wander until it slipped into something less familiar, a word that rhymed with "going home"—"Kodachrome," which would soon scale the *Billboard* charts.

That was 1973 and Simon's cultural pitch was perfect way beyond his music. It was just so *not* full of crap. Nikons were cool, so were the growing number of hardcore professional and semi-outlaw freelance photographers roaming the country and the world. Working at a light table in those days with a spread of slides glowing up at you under your loupe, the film was so rich and sharp that all the world could, in fact, look like a sunny day.

How to Read a Slide

by Bill Syken

A prelaunch prototype of SPORTS ILLUSTRATED concealed the real name of the new magazine—and led to an "X-rated" cataloging system for slides.

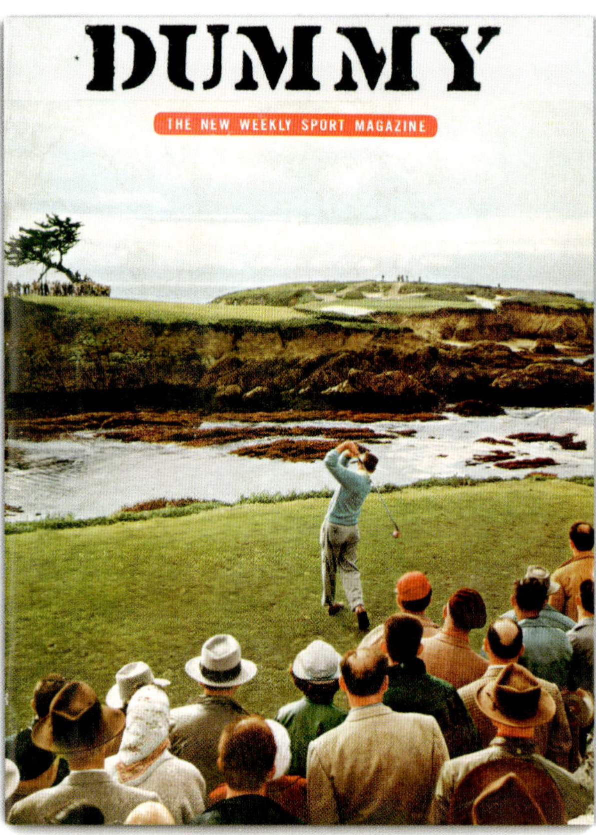

SOME OF THE GRAFFITI scribbled on the slide mounts in this book is in a language simple enough to understand. When you see a photo of golfer Payne Stewart kneeling on the green, gripping his putter in anguish, it's easy enough to figure out why someone might have written MISSED on the slide mount. But other, more obscure markings require some explanation.

The most common detail seen on these mounts is an X number, used by the magazine to track assignments. And there's a story behind SPORTS ILLUSTRATED's using an X, while its sister publications at Time Inc. use more obvious initials. (For instance, TIME magazine uses T numbers, and FORTUNE uses F numbers.) The editors at SI were making photo assignments a full year before the magazine officially launched in August 1954, but the company wished to keep the name and nature of the project secret. So, photographically, SPORTS ILLUSTRATED started as brand X, and never changed. As you can see at the left, that desire for secrecy extended to keeping the actual name and logo off the covers of the magazine's early prototypes. (Which, in this case, did not reflect well on the fellow teeing off in the photo of that 1953 golf tournament.)

Other frequently found markings are deconstructed on the opposite page. These, together with the captions throughout the book, will guide you through the hieroglyphs. But if you should study the slides in this book closely, you'll notice exceptions to the rules, a sign that over the decades the handlers of these slides have indulged their inevitable idiosyncrasies. Some photo editors put blue dots on slides they liked best. One put stars on his favorites. A generally redoubtable SI archivist was recently asked why one slide had a red sticker instead of the standard yellow; he e-mailed back that, among various possibilities, "there may have simply been a shortage of yellow stickers (they're very hard to find)."

In short, the markings upon these slides do not follow a rigid protocol, but they do add to the history, and the artistry, of these photographs.

THE BLUE STICKER

This indicates that a photograph has been used in either an SI book or in SPORTS ILLUSTRATED FOR KIDS. A green sticker would indicate the photo had run in TIME magazine.

CAPTION INFORMATION

Many slides carry printed labels detailing what is happening in the photo. These labels are more prose than poetry, usually limited to the who, what, where and when.

THE YELLOW STICKER

This identifies the issue in which the photo ran. In this case it was a 1996 Chicago Bulls championship commemorative, created by SI's specialty publications division, SPORTS ILLUSTRATED PRESENTS (SIP for short). More often these stickers carry an issue date from the regular weekly edition.

THE X NUMBER

Every photographer at every event is assigned a unique X number used for precise cataloging. So every shot John W. McDonough took at this game would be marked X41516. Another photographer at the same game would have a different X number.

TAKE, FRAME, ROLL

Shots are further cataloged by take (generally a commonsense grouping, such as all shots from the first half of a game), by frame and by film roll. This photo, therefore, is from Take 1, Frame 8, Roll 17.

INTO THE SYSTEM

A red dot means the photo has been scanned into SI's electronic photo library.

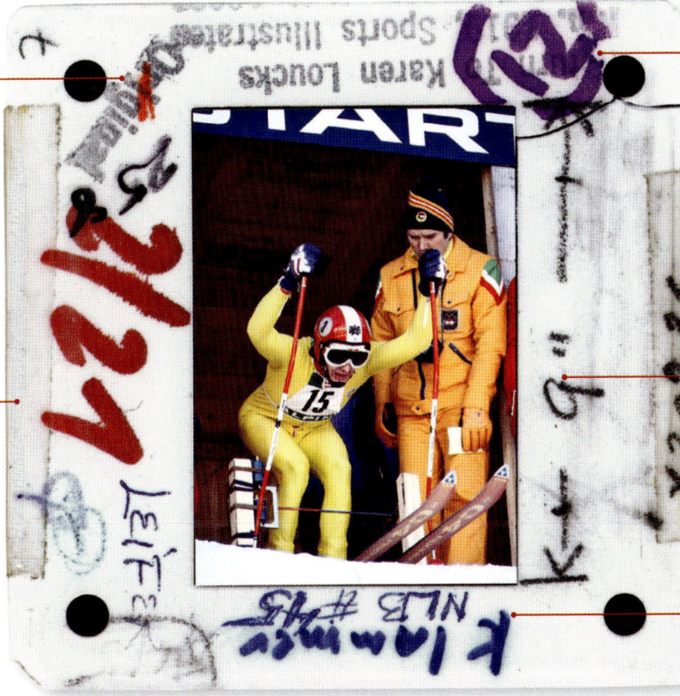

ON LOAN

Before digital images could be transported electronically, slides were mailed and messengered for outside use. Often duplicates were made. These stamps mark this slide as an original—with a concerned caretaker at home.

SURGICAL SCARS

Older slide mounts needed to be cut open when the image was scanned. The mounts would then be reassembled with scotch tape.

BOOK NOTES

Some photos in this book, most often those taken by Neil Leifer, have also appeared in other books and have been marked by those publishers with their own annotations.

FIT TO PRINT

The dimensions are a sizing instruction to the technician who is making a physical print from the photograph for framing or another use.

JOTTINGS

On slides with no printed label, the only caption information is often nothing more than an editor's quick scribble. That's the case for this shot of Austria's Franz Klammer, about to make a gold-medal run in the 1976 Olympics.

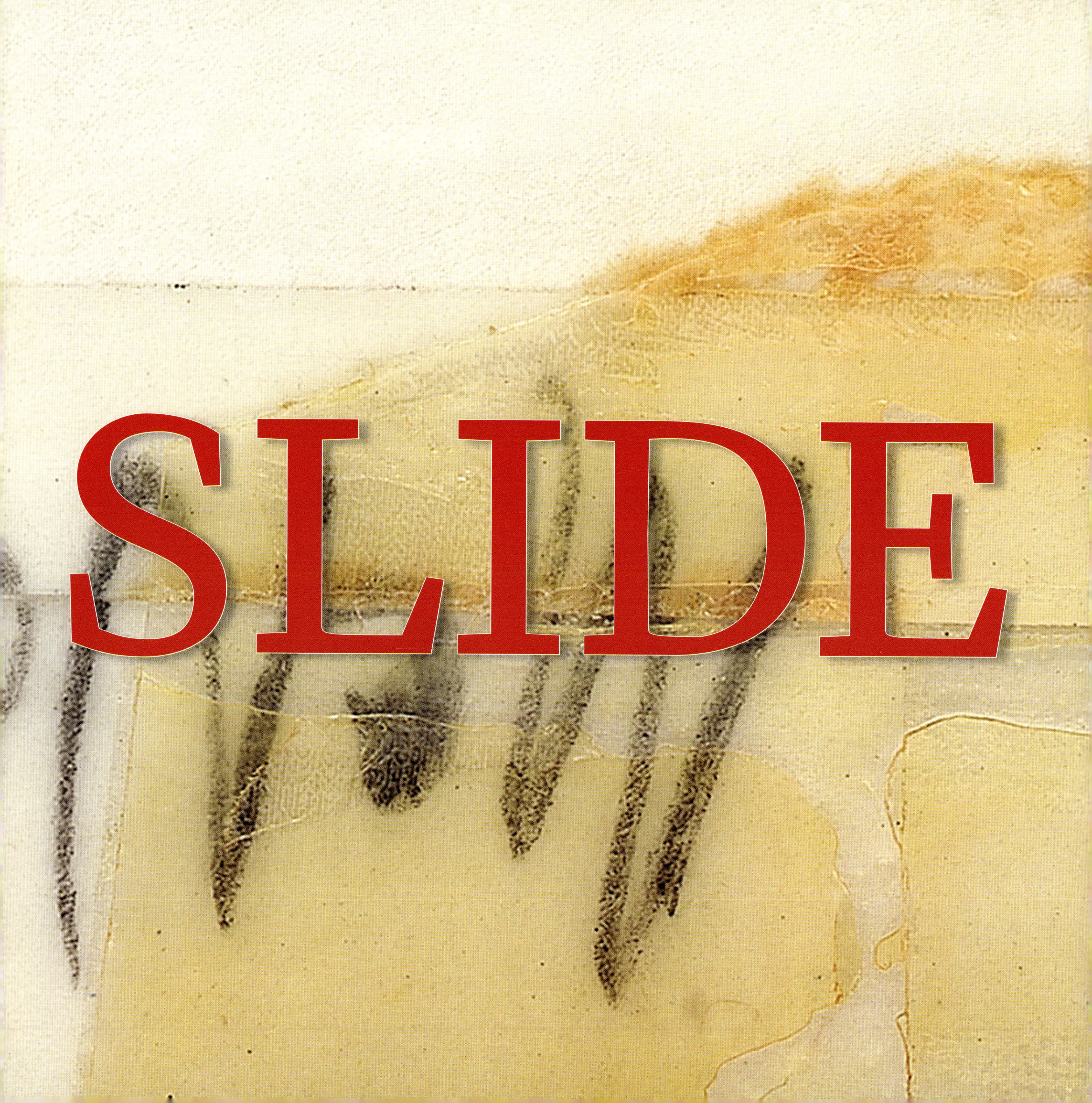
SLIDE

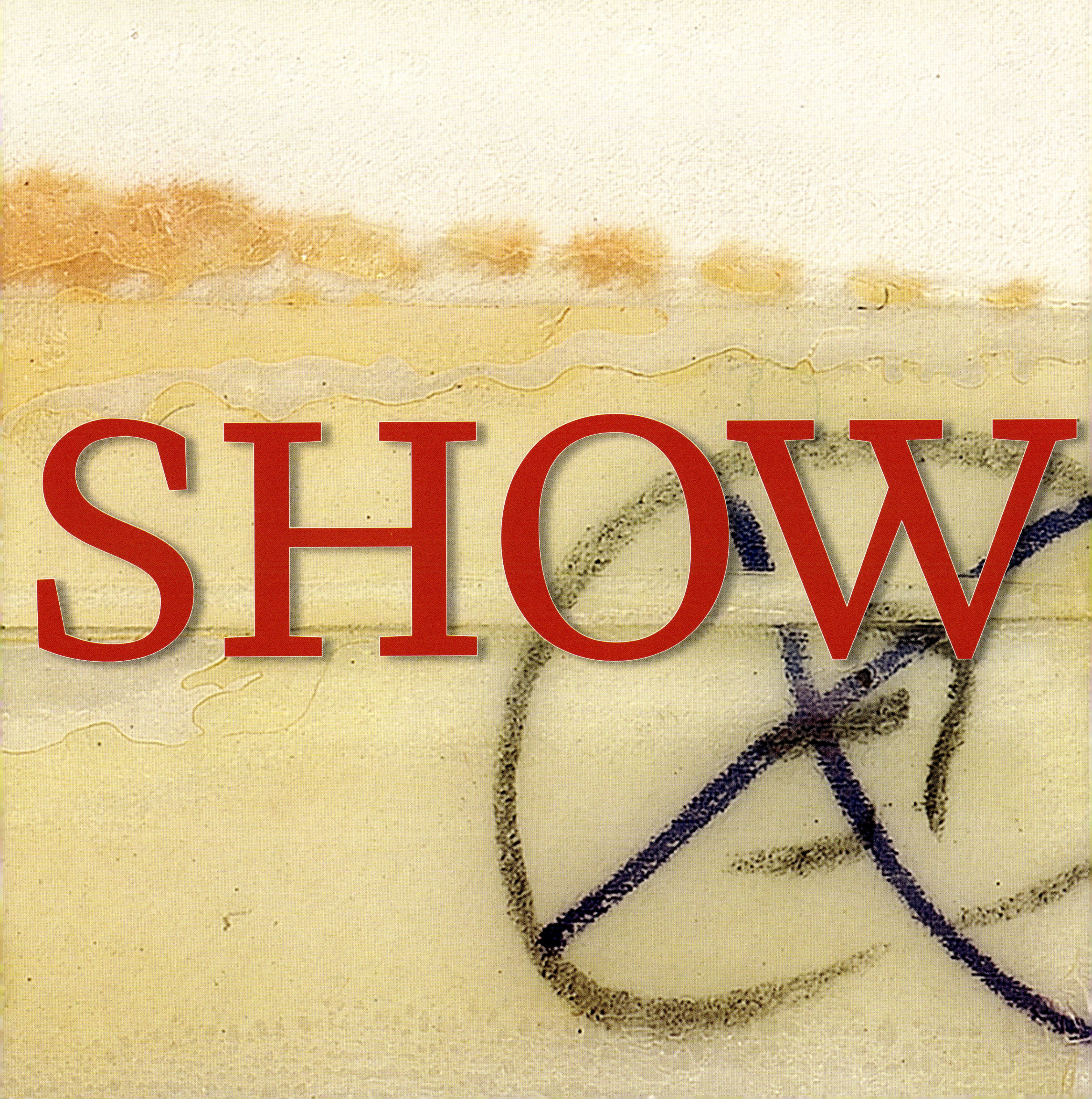
SHOW

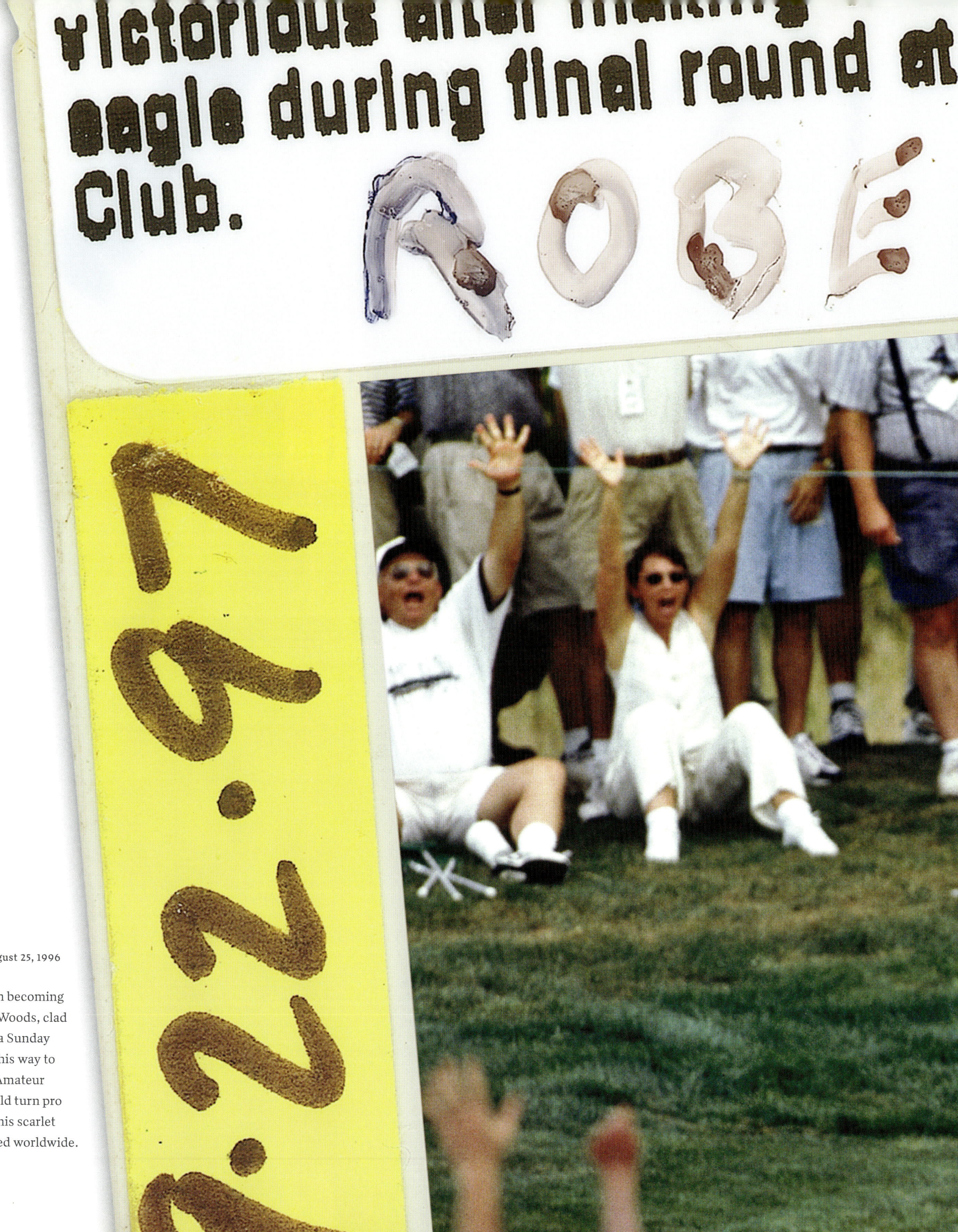

Red Dawn

TIGER WOODS

Photograph by ROBERT BECK, August 25, 1996

IT WAS A SIGHT just then becoming familiar to golf fans: Tiger Woods, clad in red, pumping his fist on a Sunday afternoon. Here he was on his way to his third consecutive U.S. Amateur championship. Woods would turn pro days later, and before long his scarlet Sundays would be celebrated worldwide.

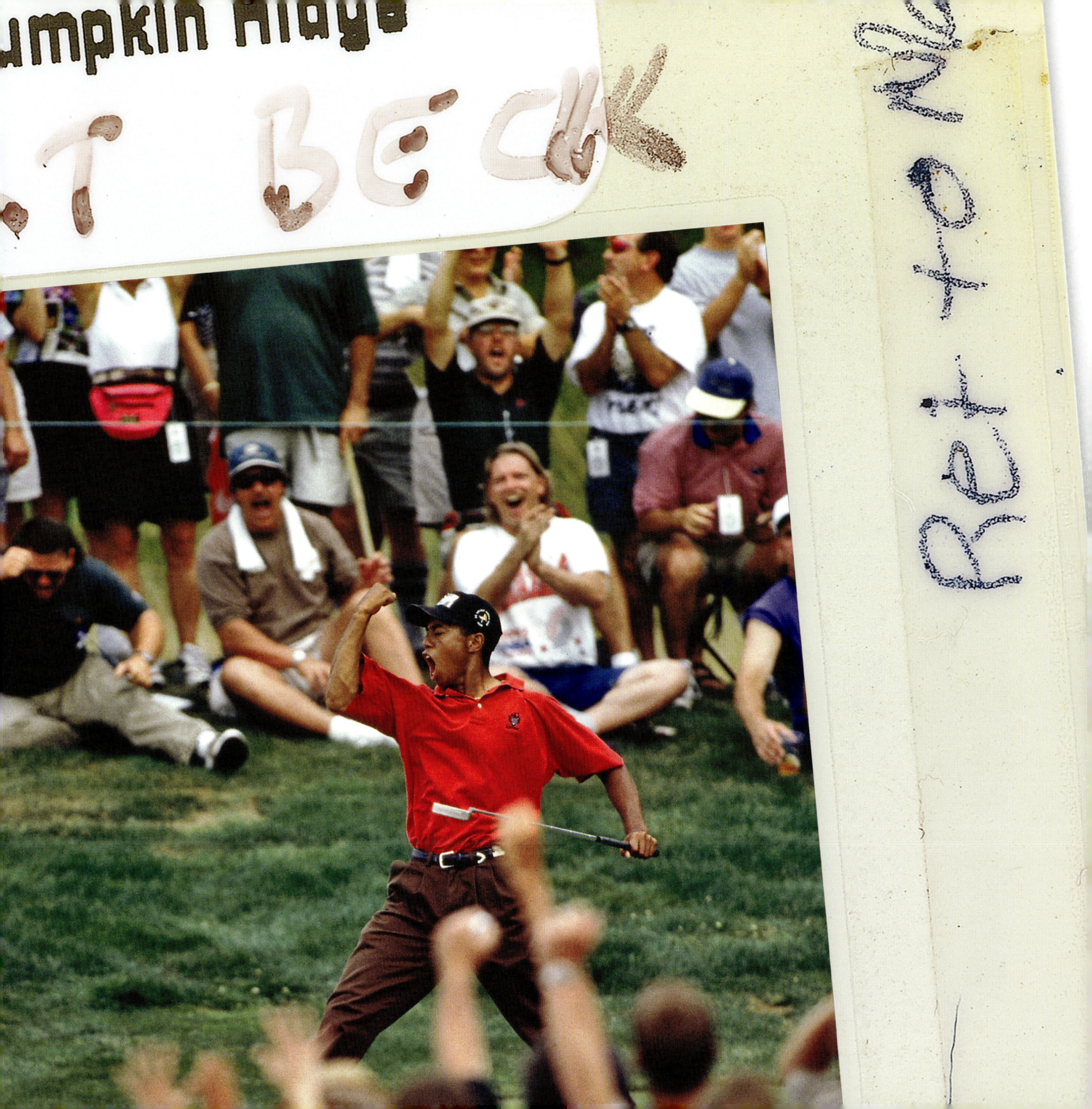

Football: Super Bowl X. Pitts. Steelers Lynn Swann #88 in action, making catch vs Dallas Cowboys. Cover.

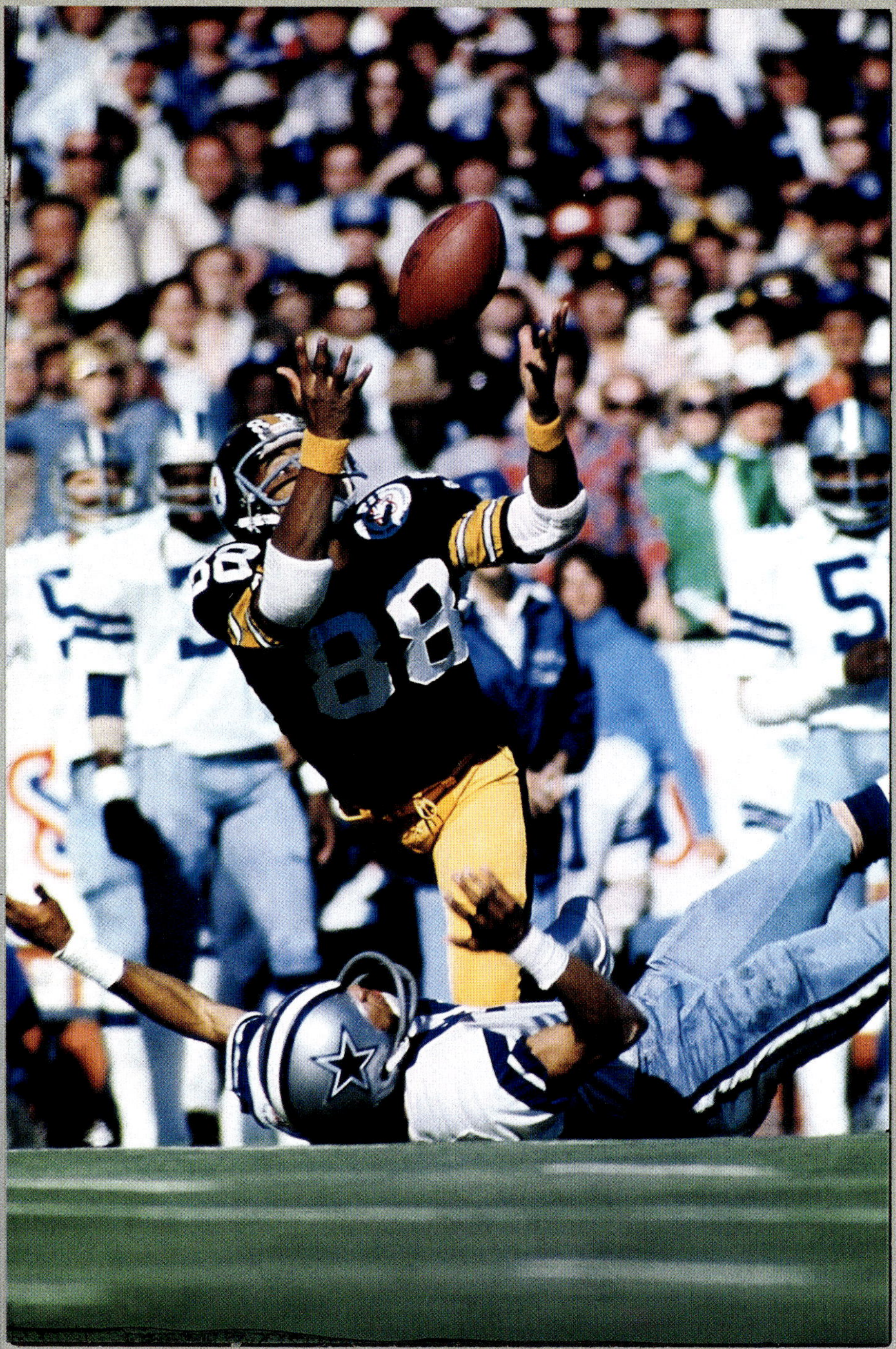

USI BOOK GREAT PICS

USI BOOK FB GAMES

1.26.76

SIP/COWBOYS 2.4.94

SIP/COWBOYS 2/93

X20183

Super Catches

LYNN SWANN HUNG IN THE AIR so long when making this catch that Heinz Kluetmeier had time to change lenses—twice. At least that's the joke the photographer tells when asked about this shot, which became the defining image of Swann's Hall of Fame career. (When Kluetmeier received a 2007 Lucie award, photography's equivalent of the Oscars, the Steelers great flew in to give a testimonial.) The stickers on the slide mount only hint at how often Kluetmeier's famous shot has been reused. Damian Strohmeyer's cover photo of David Tyree's catch in Super Bowl XLII (below) will surely have an equally active afterlife, but because it was shot digitally, it was never made into a slide and thus can't acquire that same sort of physical history.

SUPER BOWL X

Photograph by HEINZ KLUETMEIER, January 18, 1976

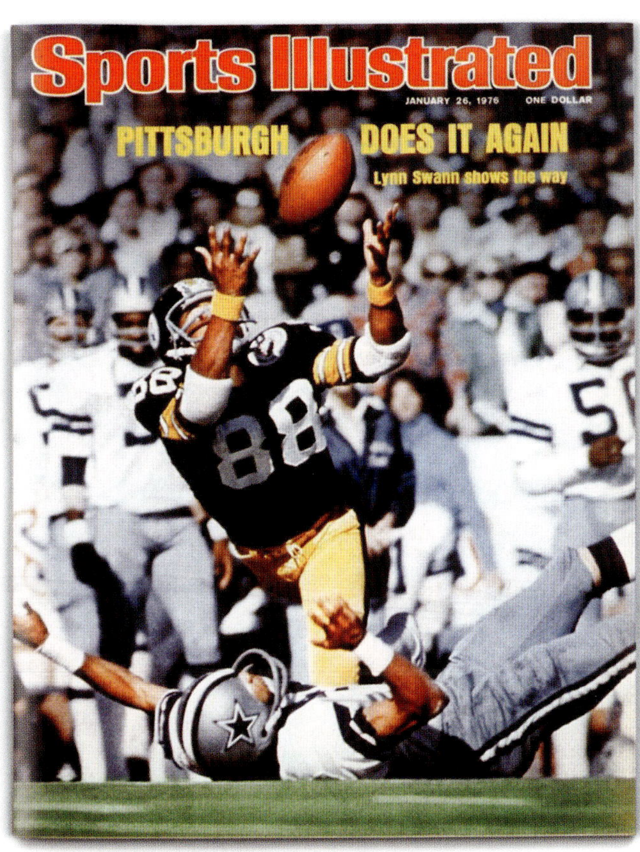

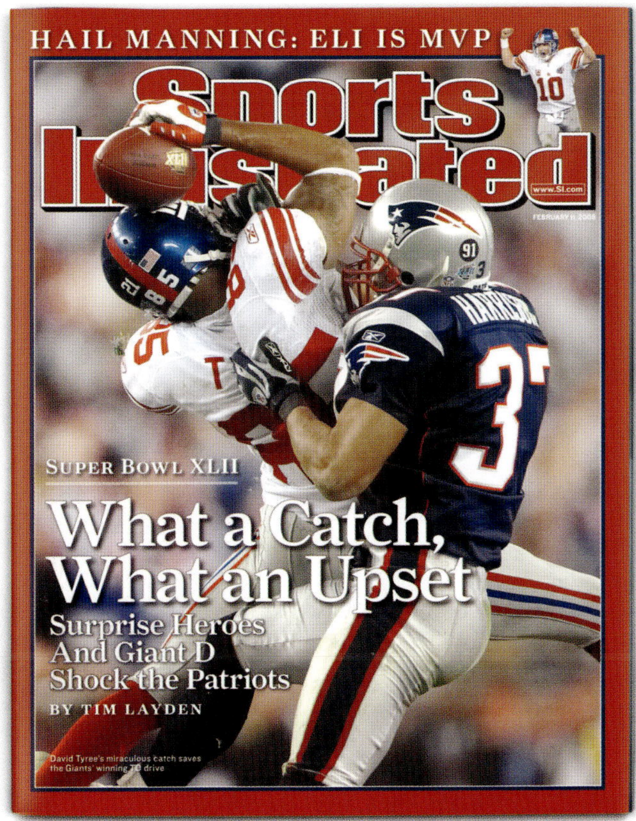

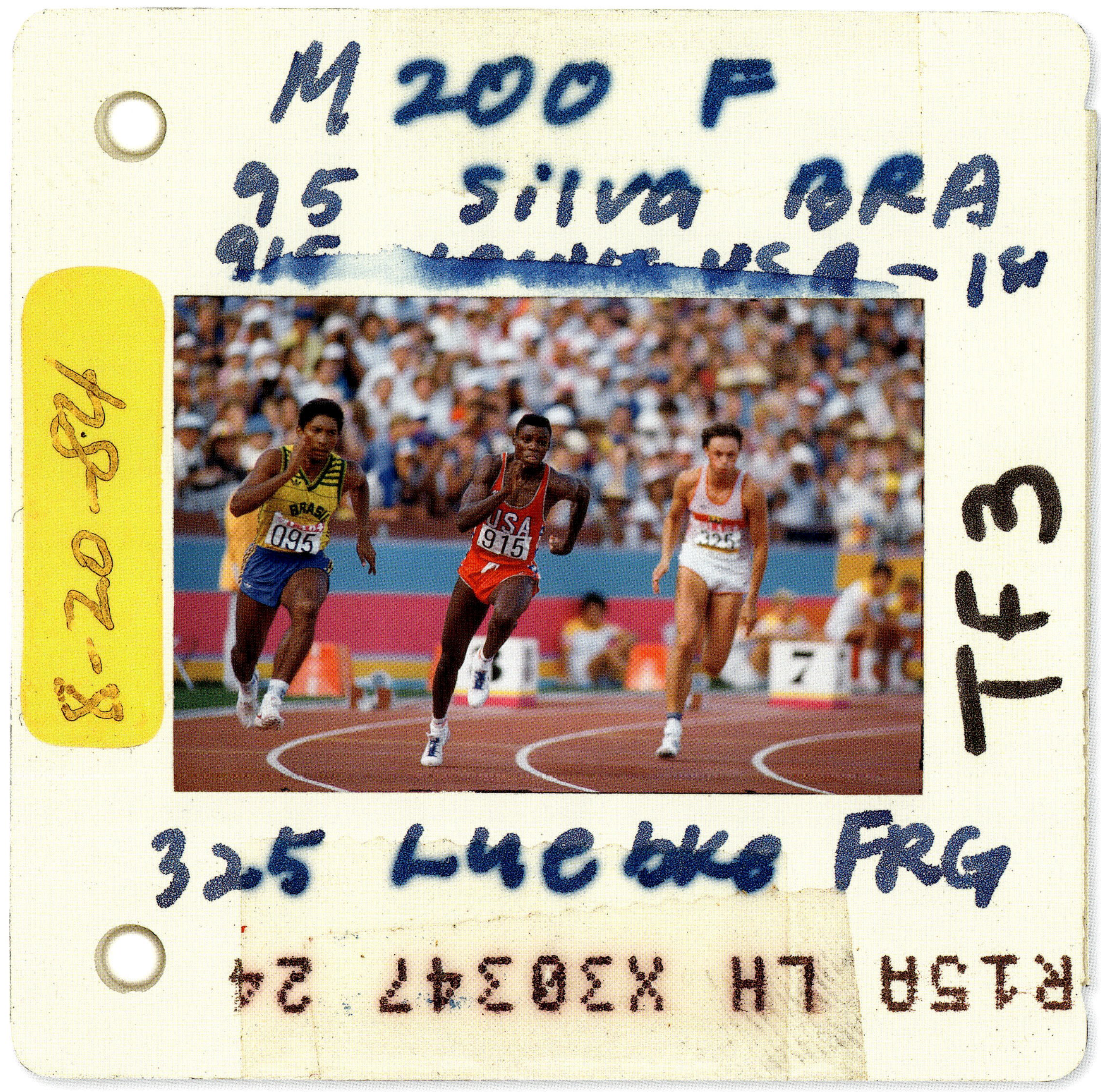

To Glory in a Hurry

CARL LEWIS *(above). Photograph by* JOHN W. McDONOUGH, August 8, 1984 • BO JACKSON *(opposite). Photograph by* RICHARD MACKSON, September 28, 1985

THEY WERE BOTH hard to catch. Carl Lewis sped toward one of his nine Olympic gold medals (this one the 200 meters, as the scribble indicates); Bo Jackson ripped off one of his many blazing runs for Auburn en route to the Heisman Trophy.

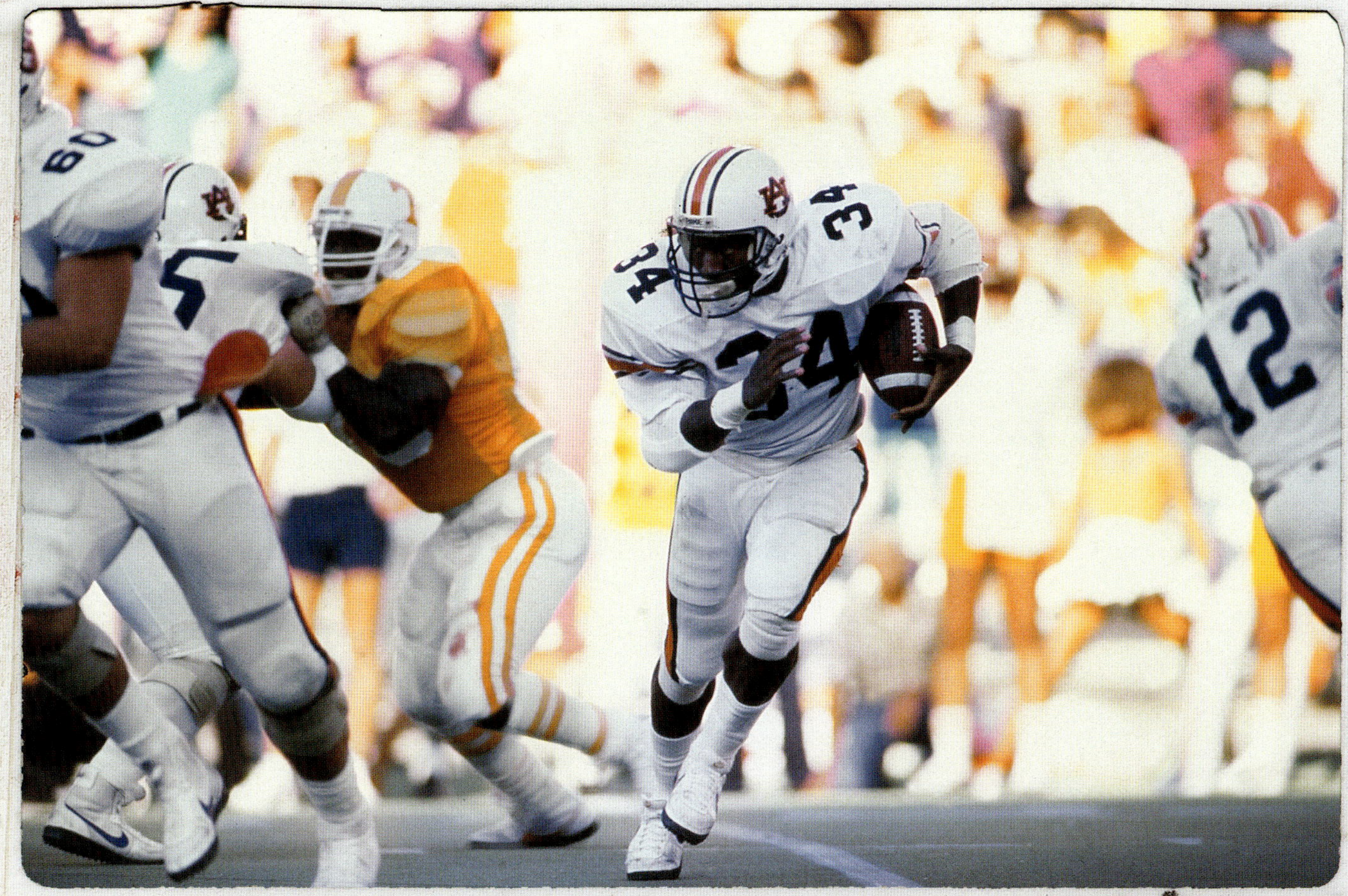
D20
32104
RICHARD MACKSON
SPORTS ILLUSTRATED
Bo Jackson
DUPLICATE
MACKSON
35th
Issue
3 #13
3760

Jim Beam 3/95

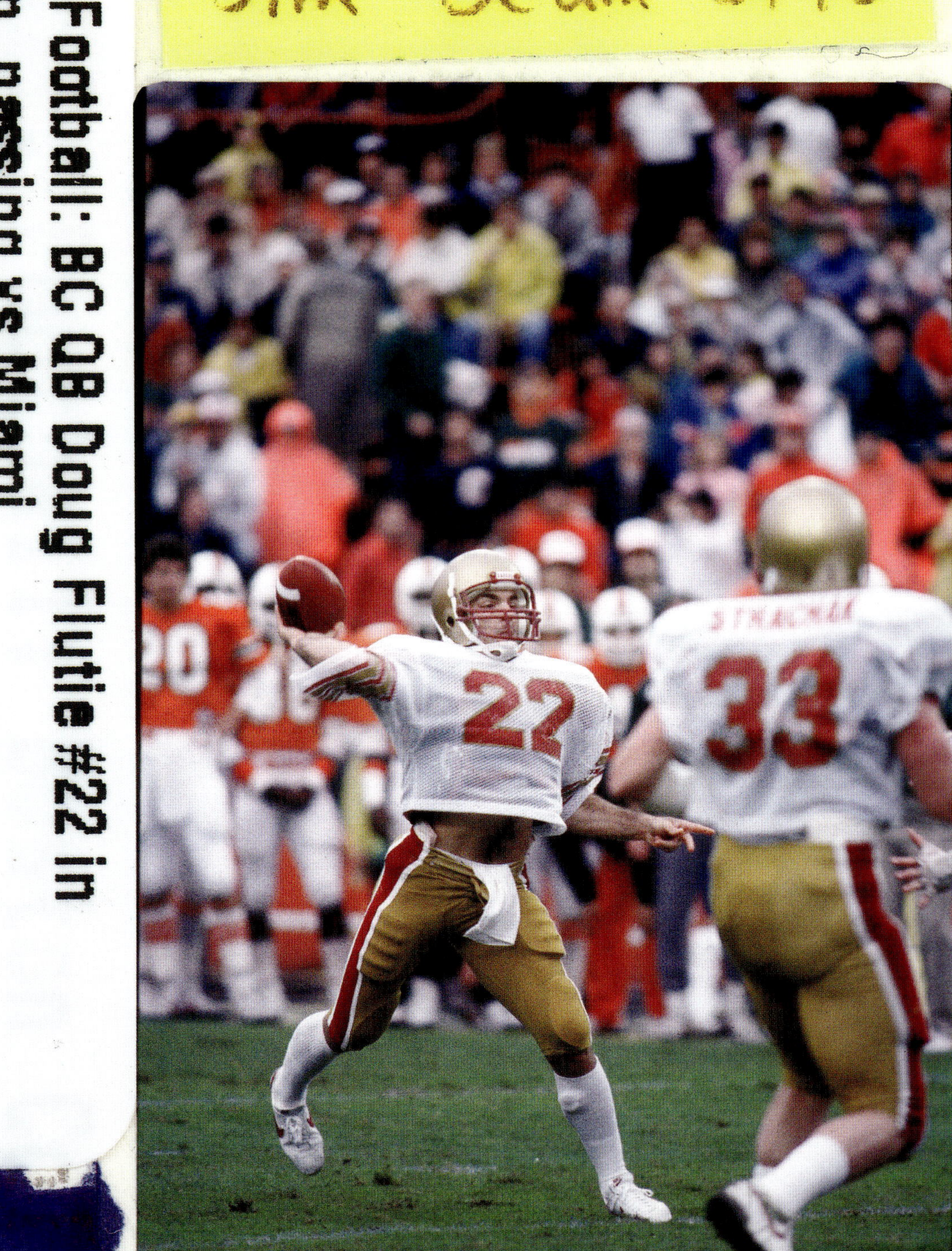

Coll. Football: BC QB Doug Flutie #22 in action, passing vs Miami.

X 30810 T1 19

Football

12-3-84

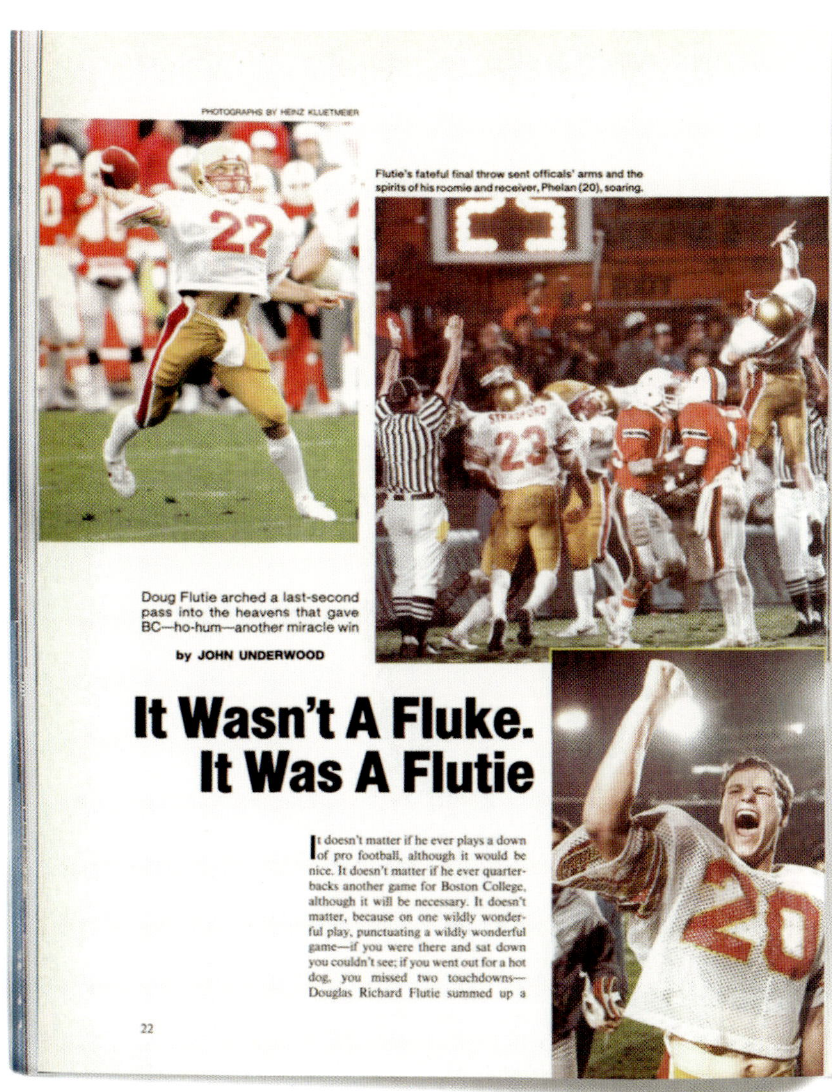

PHOTOGRAPHS BY HEINZ KLUETMEIER

Flutie's fateful final throw sent officials' arms and the spirits of his roomie and receiver, Phelan (20), soaring.

Doug Flutie arched a last-second pass into the heavens that gave BC—ho-hum—another miracle win

by JOHN UNDERWOOD

It Wasn't A Fluke. It Was A Flutie

It doesn't matter if he ever plays a down of pro football, although it would be nice. It doesn't matter if he ever quarterbacks another game for Boston College, although it will be necessary. It doesn't matter, because on one wildly wonderful play, punctuating a wildly wonderful game—if you were there and sat down you couldn't see; if you went out for a hot dog, you missed two touchdowns—Douglas Richard Flutie summed up a wildly wonderful college career last Friday in unsunny Miami. Never mind that he has two more games to play. They can only be anticlimactic.

Of course with Flutie you never know. Forty games into the most prolific passing career any college quarterback has ever had, you have to think in terms of "anything can happen" and other clichés. With Flutie, says Gil Brandt of the Dallas Cowboys, one of the few scouts who stands apart from the NFL's doubting Thomases and actually believes this outrageous little rascal can cut it as a pro, life is a magic show, and "Doug Flutie never loses, he only runs out of time." But pick your own cliché. With Flutie, they all apply.

"It's not over until the last play"? This was Friday's final play: From the line of scrimmage, a Flutieball arched high into that grieving Miami sky, covering 64 yards from toe to toe, to roommate Gerard Phelan—Flutie pushing off on his right toe and throwing into the gusting wind and rain. Phelan, in the end zone, falling directly behind and beneath the groping hands of two Miami defenders who were doing a stunning impersonation of an open door.

"It's the size of the fight in the man, not the size of the man in the fight"? At 5′ 9¾″—if you don't give him the three-fourths, Flutie complains—little Dougie is not much bigger than the Heisman Trophy he will most certainly be awarded this week, deserving as he is of every metallic ounce. Miami was the biggest team on his menu. And on a day better suited for ducks, the Eagles soared with Flutie, his passing alone accounting for 472 yards and three touchdowns, his running for nine yards and another TD. When the computers stopped humming, he had become the first 10,000-yard passer in major-college history. And when he went back outside an hour afterward, still in uniform so a friend could pose him in front of the Orange Bowl scoreboard, the evidence still glistened in the gloaming: Boston College 47, defending national champion Miami 45. Cast it in bronze and put it on the mantel.

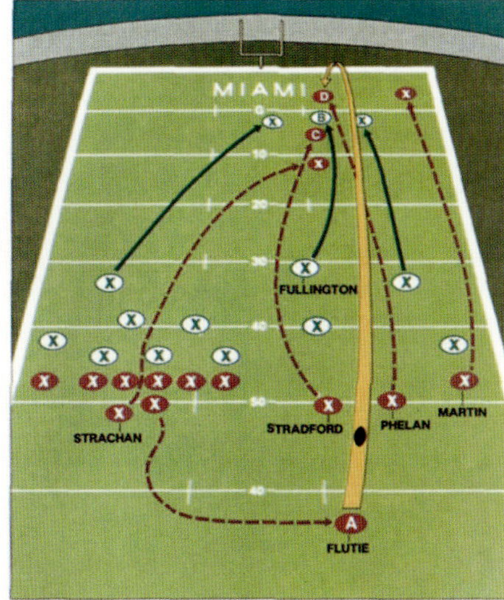

At 0:06, Flood Tip began with a Flutie (A) scramble. As he heaved the ball, four receivers zeroed in on the target point; Phelan (D) made the catch behind Fullington (B).

There were more than a few touches of improbability in this victory, however, just as Flutie's entire career has seemed so improbable. For in this game of breathtakingly proficient, precision passing—little Flutie and Miami's 6′ 5″ sophomore phenom Bernie Kosar put the ball up 84 times for 919 yards between them—it was that most imprecise of passes that did the dirty deed. The Hail Mary. The Everybody Go Long. The play you launch on a wing and a prayer when all time is gone and all else has failed. In the BC playbook, it's called Flood Tip, and it works (rarely) the way it sounds.

With six seconds on the clock and Miami ahead 45–41, three BC receivers were deployed far to the right side, with Phelan as the middle man. At the snap, they were to sprint downfield as fast and as far as they could, in hopes of arriving in the end zone together—flooding it—about the same time Flutie's pass got there. (Fullback Steve Strachan was supposed to block for Flutie, but he, too, ran deep downfield.) If any one was near the ball but couldn't catch it, his job was to tip it up in the air for somebody who could, somebody, the Eagles hoped, in the same color jersey. On the sideline as the play started, coach Jack Bicknell was "already forming in my mind what I would tell our kids after we lost." That's how much faith he had in Flood Tip.

continued

22 23

And So It Came to Pass

DOUG FLUTIE

Photograph by HEINZ KLUETMEIER, November 23, 1984

AS BOSTON COLLEGE LINED UP to attempt what everyone knew would be a last-second desperation pass against Miami, Heinz Kluetmeier, working the game solo, faced an essential dilemma: Where to set up? Rather than rush to the end zone and risk being obscured from a possible catch, he chose a position where he'd be guaranteed an unobstructed view of Doug Flutie throwing. After snapping Flutie, Kluetmeier followed the ball through the air but was blocked from a clear shot of Gerard Phelan's catch. Still, he had a perfect shot of what would turn out to be the most famous pass in college football, the ultimate Hail Mary. And, as the layout shows, he also captured the moment of celebration as the ref signaled touchdown.

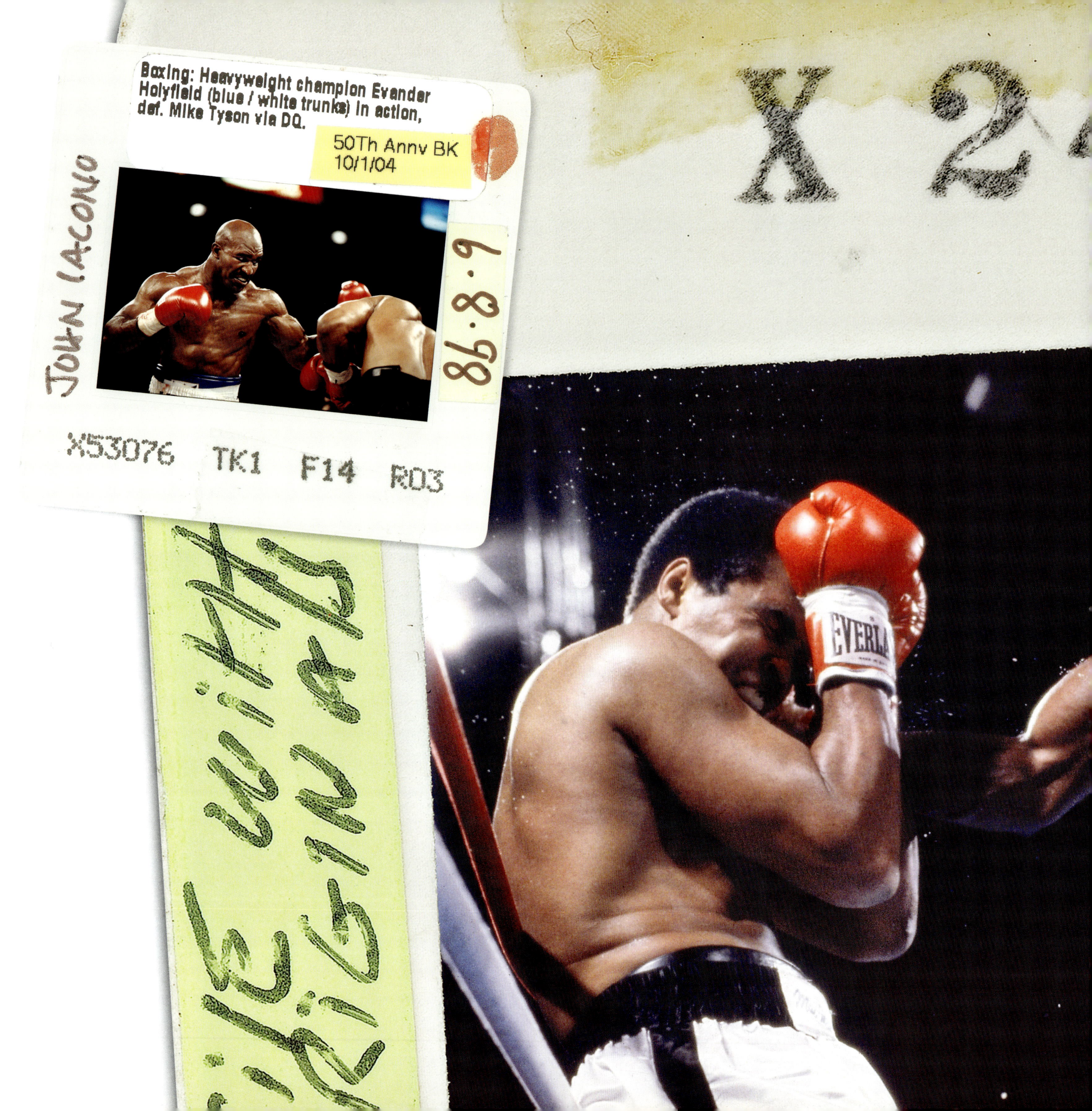

Boxing: Heavyweight champion Evander Holyfield (blue / white trunks) in action, def. Mike Tyson via DQ.
50Th Annv BK
10/1/04
JOHN IACONO
X53076 TK1 F14 R03
X 2
EVERLA

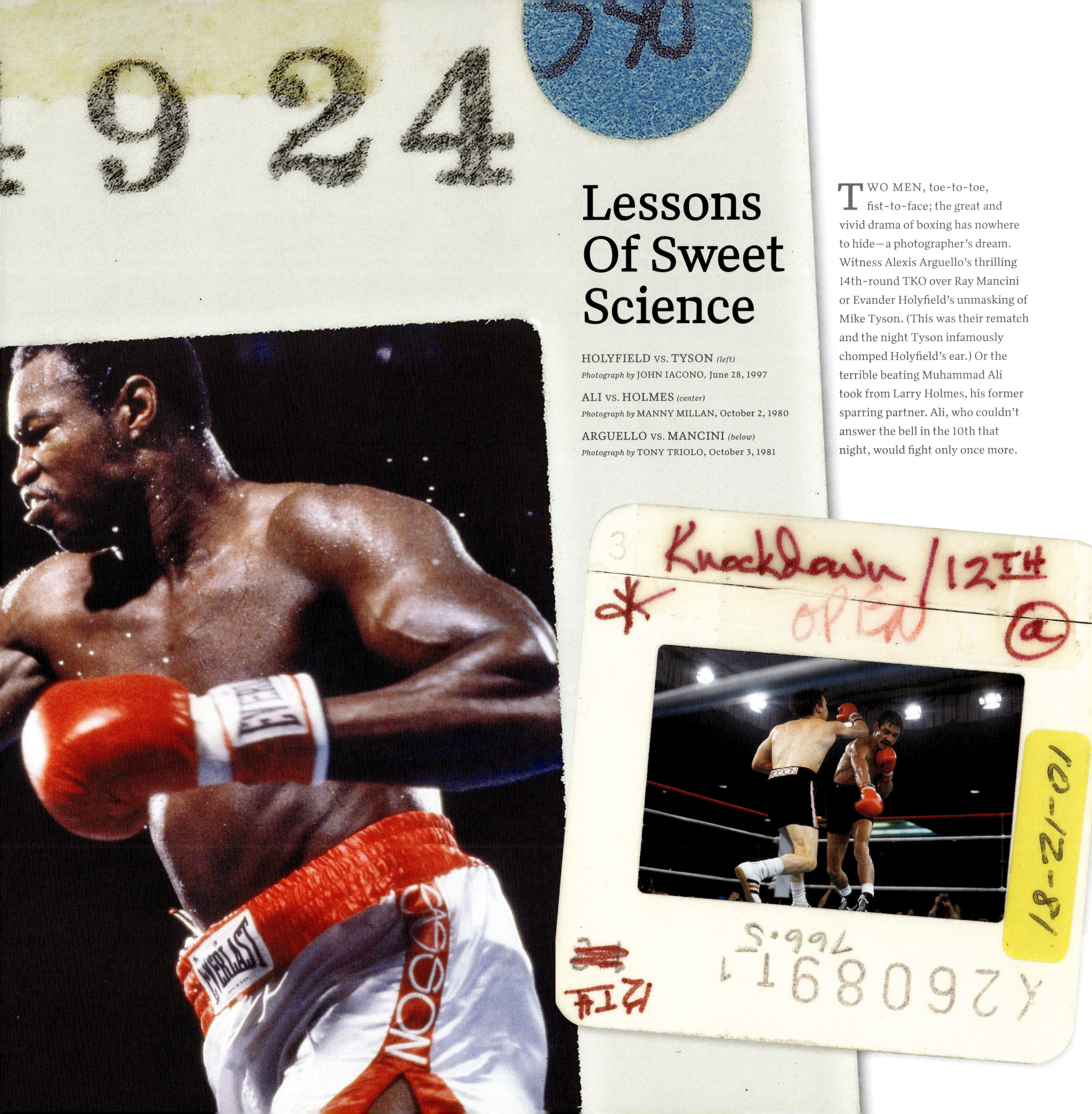

Lessons Of Sweet Science

HOLYFIELD vs. TYSON *(left)*
Photograph by JOHN IACONO, June 28, 1997

ALI vs. HOLMES *(center)*
Photograph by MANNY MILLAN, October 2, 1980

ARGUELLO vs. MANCINI *(below)*
Photograph by TONY TRIOLO, October 3, 1981

TWO MEN, toe-to-toe, fist-to-face; the great and vivid drama of boxing has nowhere to hide—a photographer's dream. Witness Alexis Arguello's thrilling 14th-round TKO over Ray Mancini or Evander Holyfield's unmasking of Mike Tyson. (This was their rematch and the night Tyson infamously chomped Holyfield's ear.) Or the terrible beating Muhammad Ali took from Larry Holmes, his former sparring partner. Ali, who couldn't answer the bell in the 10th that night, would fight only once more.

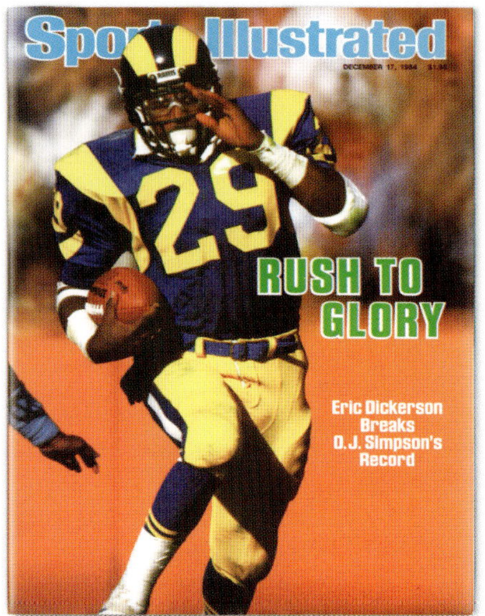

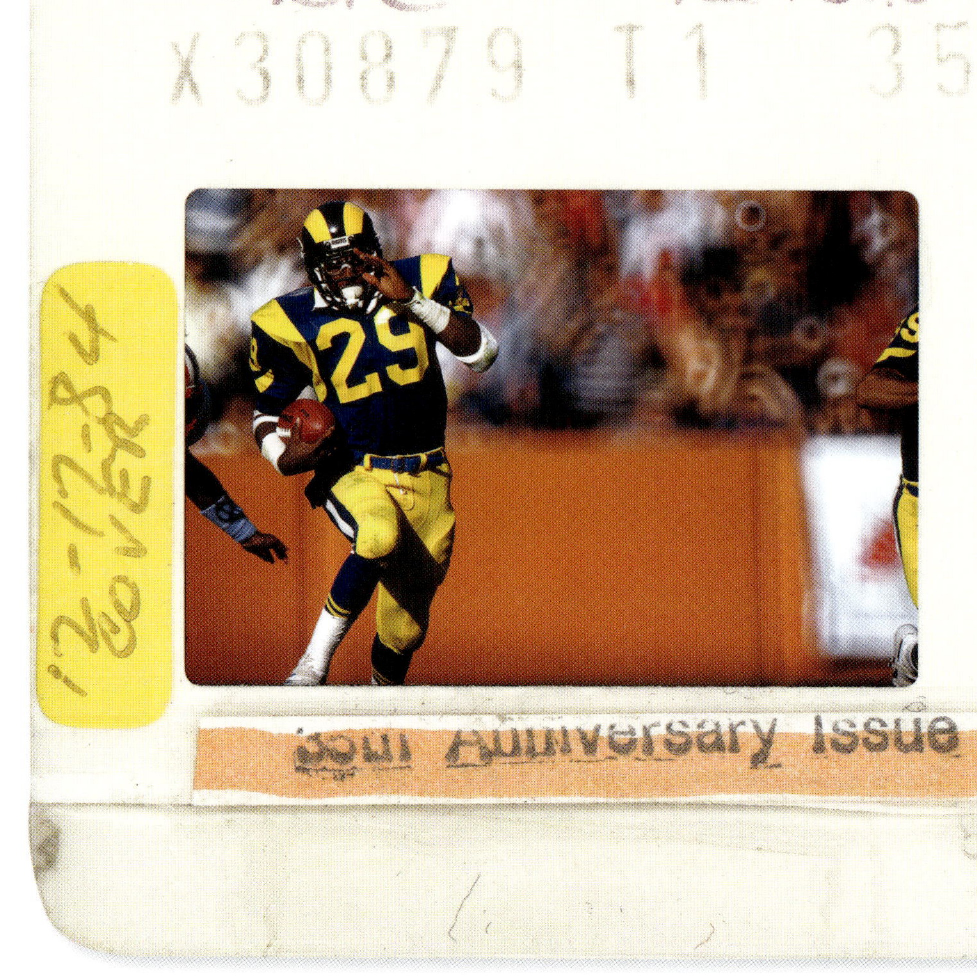

A Bumper Crop

ERIC DICKERSON

Photograph by PETER READ MILLER, December 9, 1984

SO, WHAT'S ON THE COVER? Choosing that subject, and then the right image, is often the most important decision a weekly magazine editor has to make. Finding the ideal cover photo is an art that requires looking at the world through a rectangular-shaped lens, sometimes seeing what might be hidden in plain sight. At first glance, for example, the above shot of Rams running back Eric Dickerson may appear to be fatally off-center. The frame of 49er Earl Cooper, while dramatic, might be overlooked as unfortunately horizontal. And in the third slide, Browns receiver Dave Logan looks to be lost in space. But by applying a mental scythe to each, and cropping accordingly, a powerful cover image takes shape.

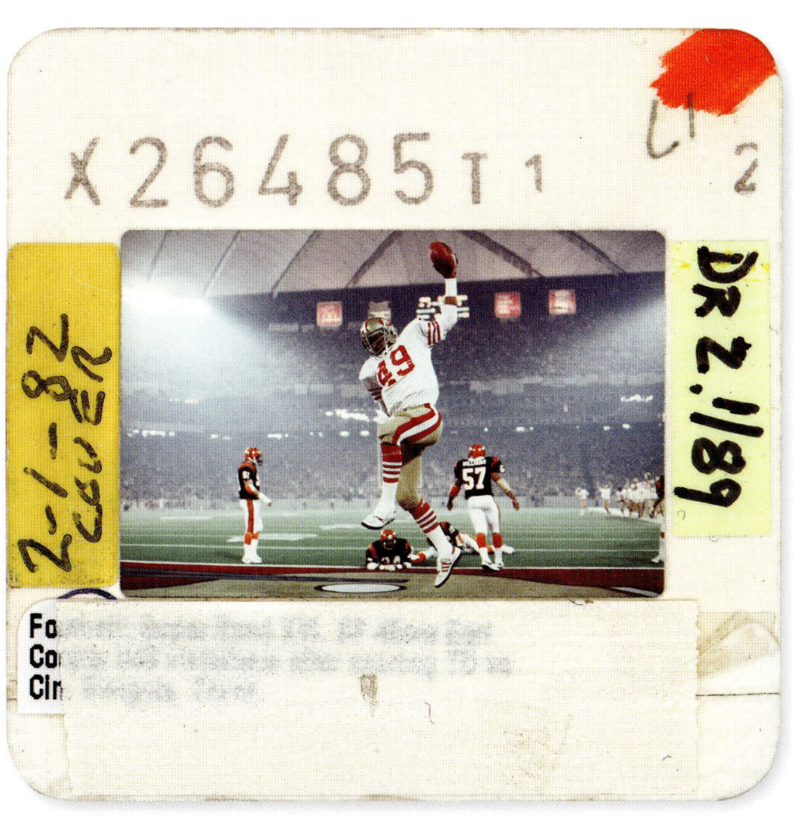

SUPER BOWL XVI

Photograph by ANDY HAYT, January 24, 1982

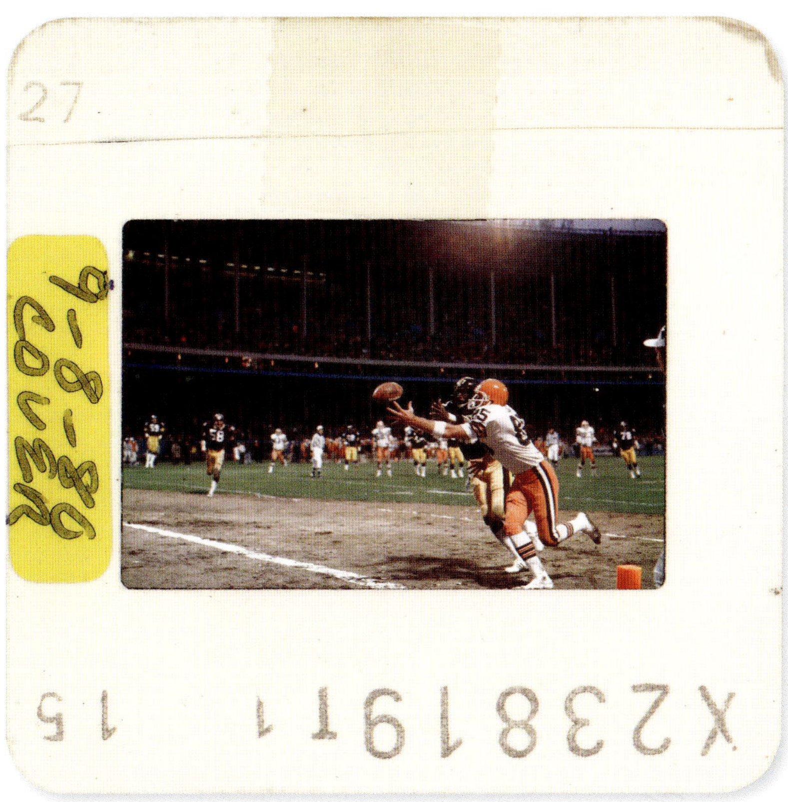

STEELERS vs. BROWNS

Photograph by WALTER IOOSS JR., October 7, 1979

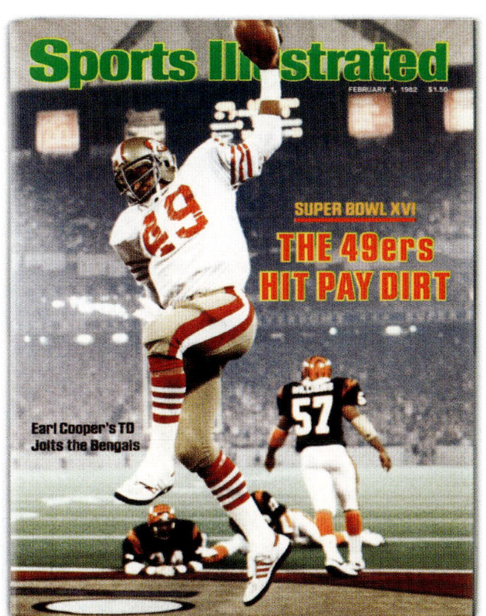

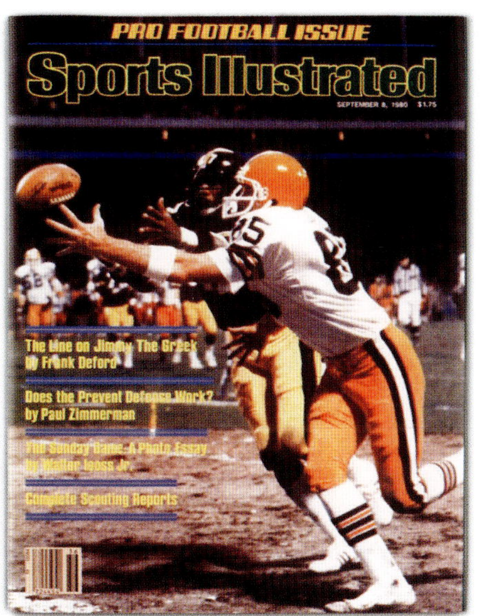

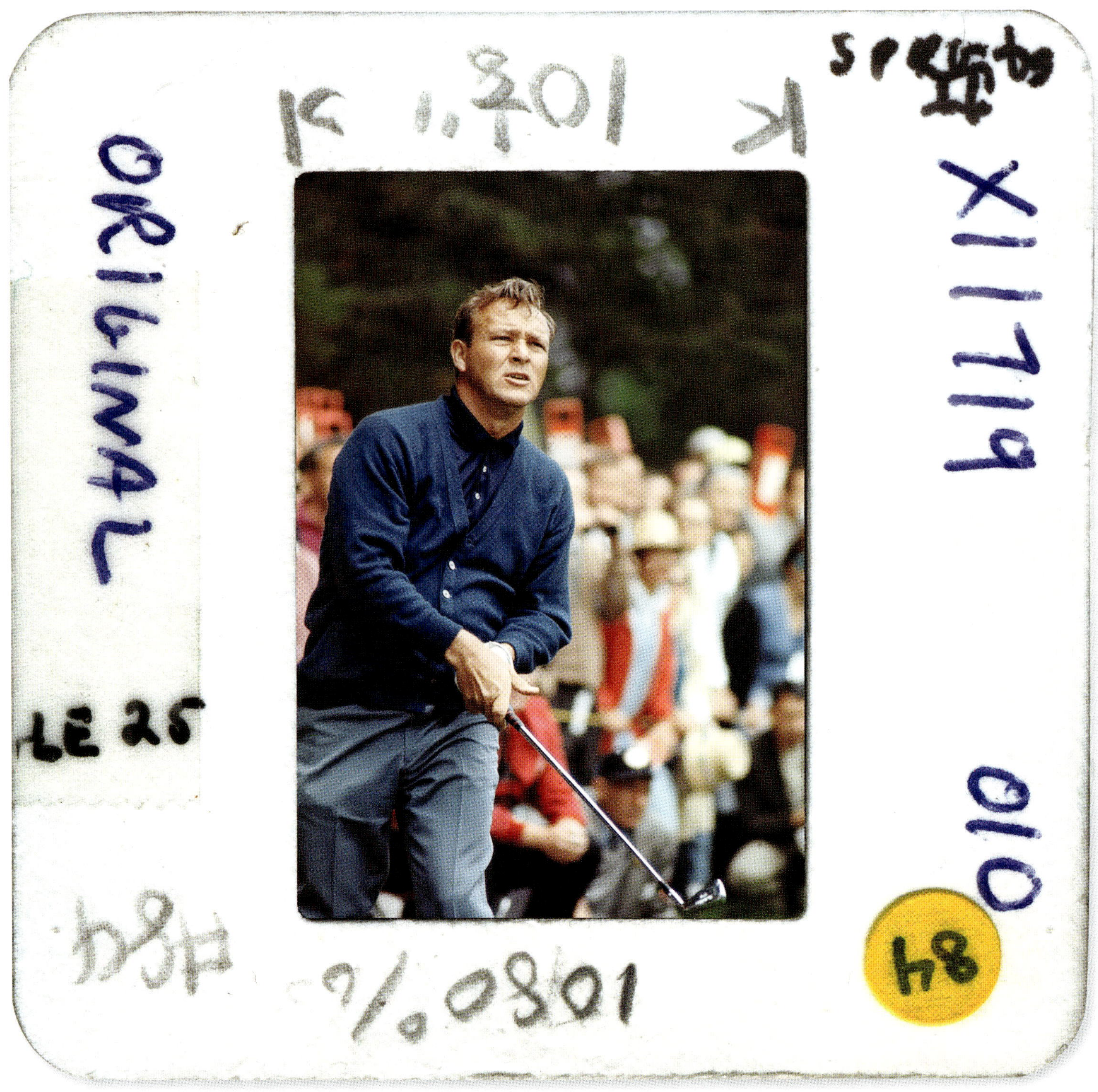

A King and a Giant

ARNOLD PALMER *(above). Photograph by* NEIL LEIFER, June 19, 1966 • Y.A. TITTLE *(opposite). Photograph by* NEIL LEIFER, October 1, 1961

SOME BACKGROUND INFO (LITERALLY): Leifer shot Y.A. Tittle with a then-new mirror lens, which is why the faces in the crowd are blurred. The gallery behind Arnie, his Army, had a singular focus—on their dashing, slashing hero.

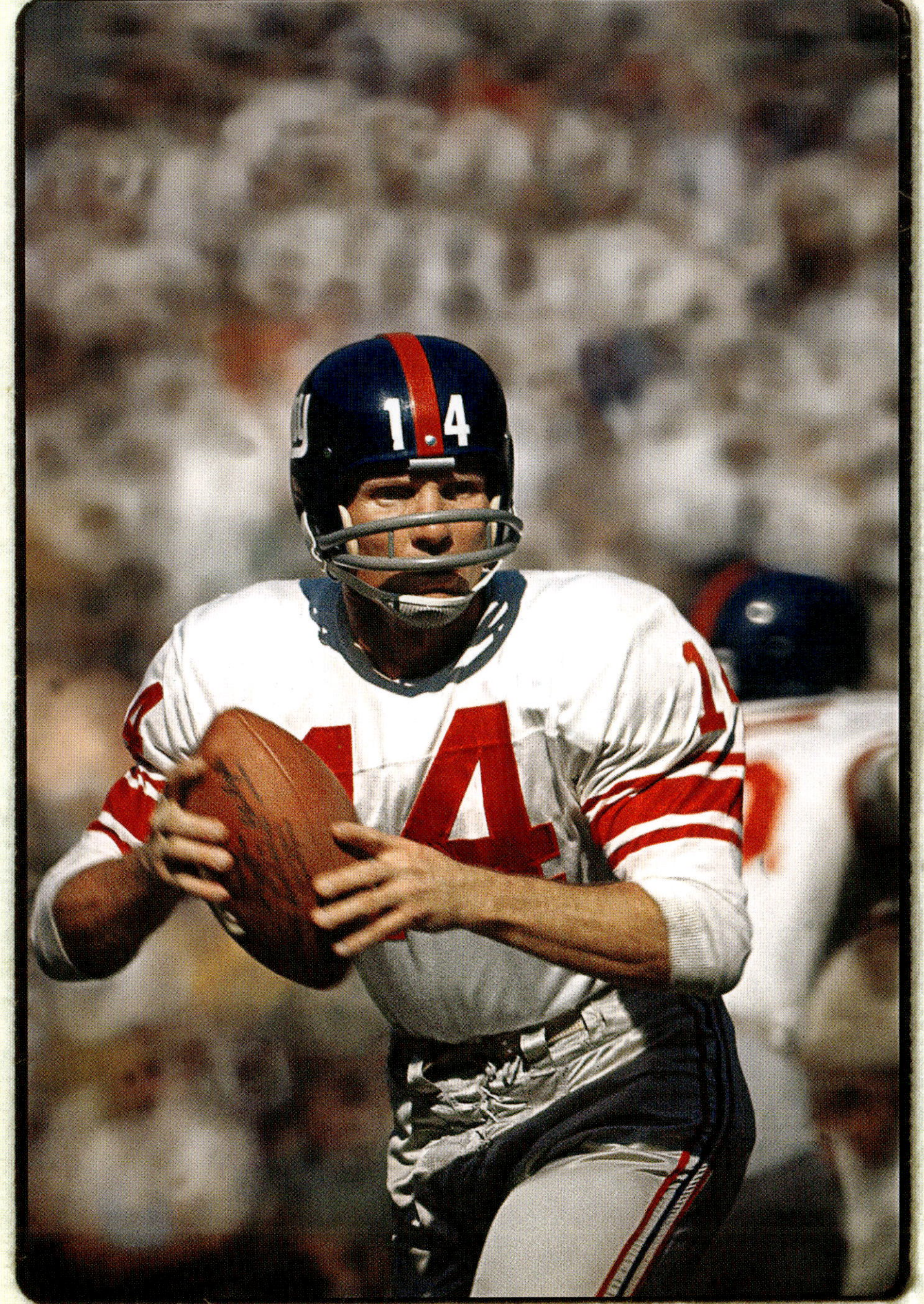
78
ORIGINAL
17975-99

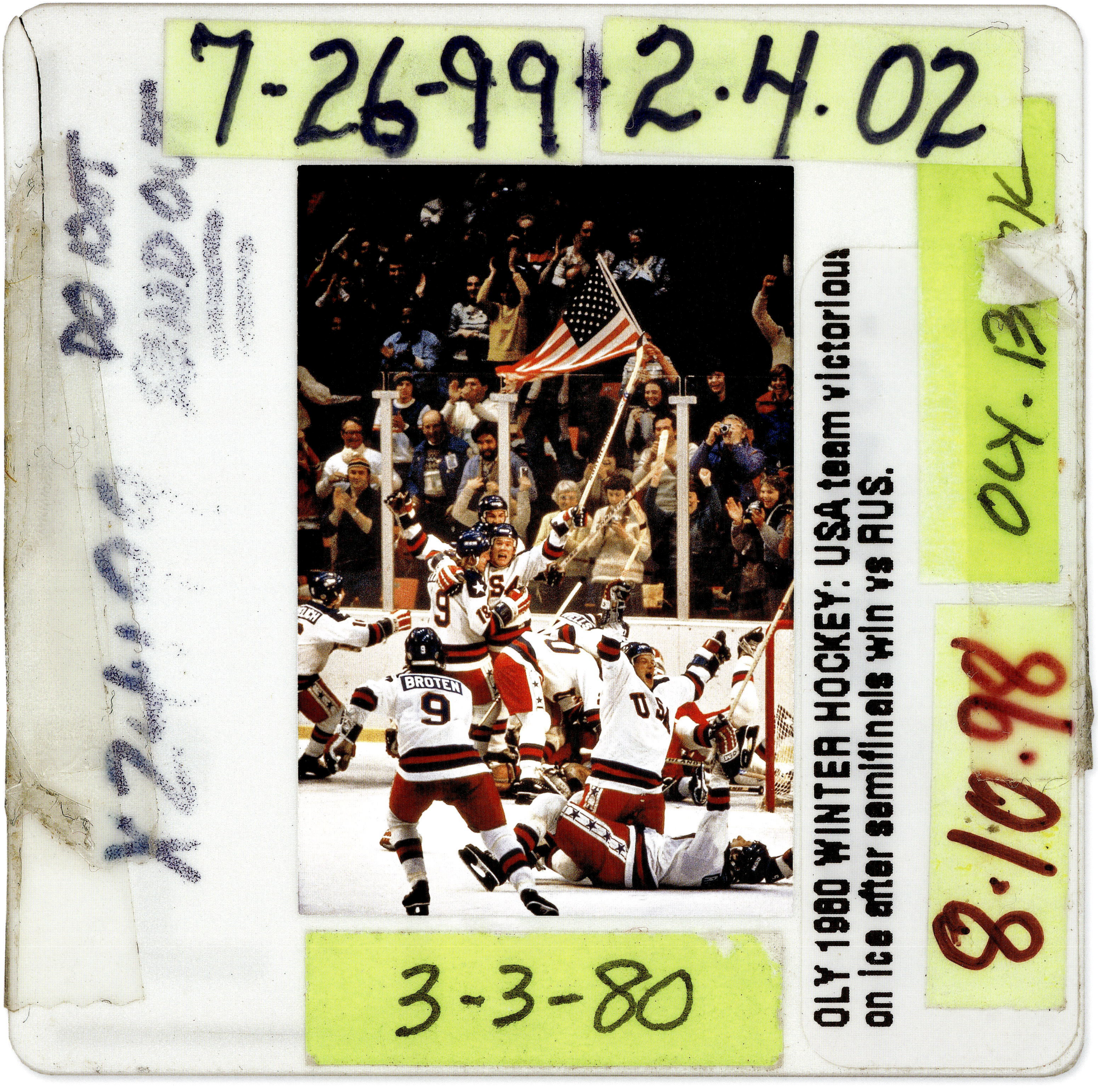

7-26-99 2.4.02

OLY 1980 WINTER HOCKEY: USA team victorious on ice after semifinals win vs RUS.

8.10.98

3-3-80

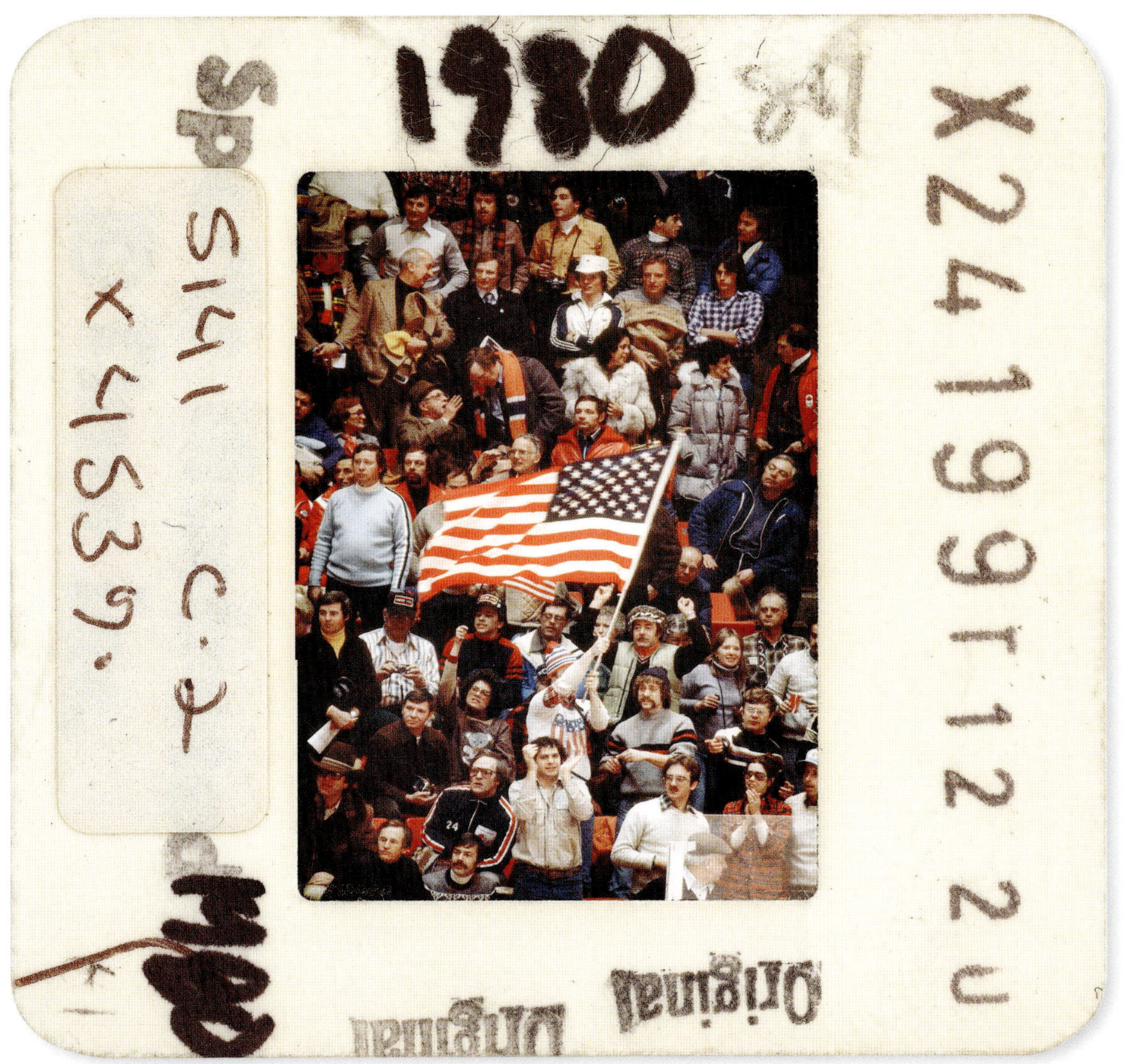

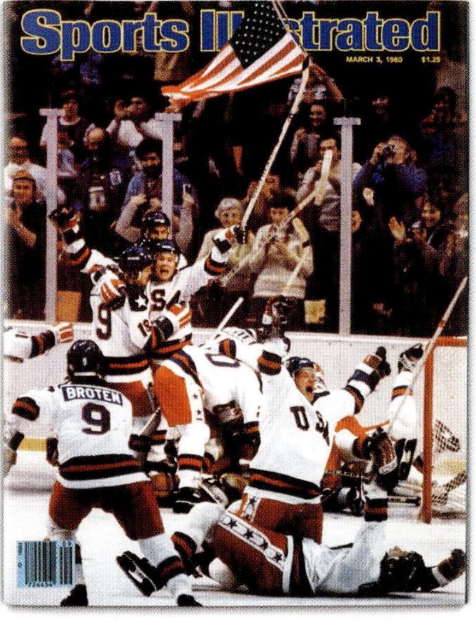

Ready for The Miracle

U.S. vs. RUSSIA

Photographs by HEINZ KLUETMEIER, February 22, 1980

AFTER A DISMAL DECADE defined by Vietnam, Watergate and a hostage crisis, Americans were in need of a success story. They found one in a group of underdog college kids challenging the mighty Russians in Olympic hockey. As Heinz Kluetmeier prepared to shoot the epic semifinal game in Lake Placid, he knew he wanted fan reaction as part of his pictures. He couldn't get both ice and crowd from the elevated photographer's area, so he went to a friend at ABC and got permission to set up on their low-angle TV platform. When the end-of-game celebration broke loose, he was able to capture, in one frame, players and fans celebrating the Miracle on Ice.

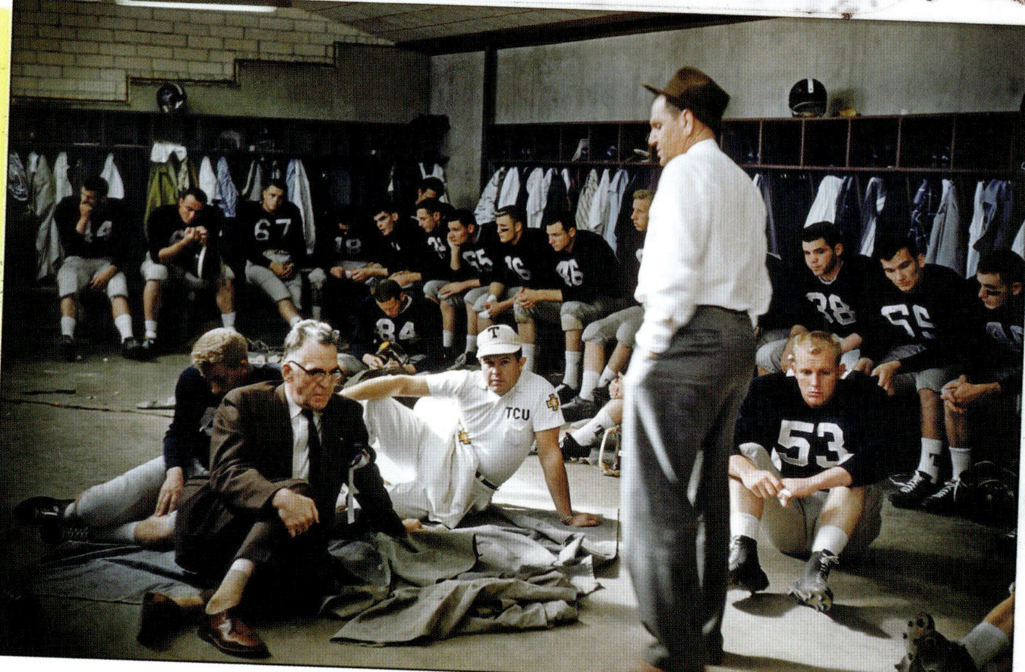

Before The Battle

COTTON BOWL
Photographs by MARVIN E. NEWMAN
January 1, 1957

FROM THE SINGLE photo, above, of TCU players in the locker room before taking on Jim Brown's Syracuse team, SI's Gary Smith extracted a 7,720-word story in 1999. The re-use of the photo explains the white slide mount; the film had to be cut from its original frame to be reprinted. (The final score? TCU 28, Syracuse 27.)

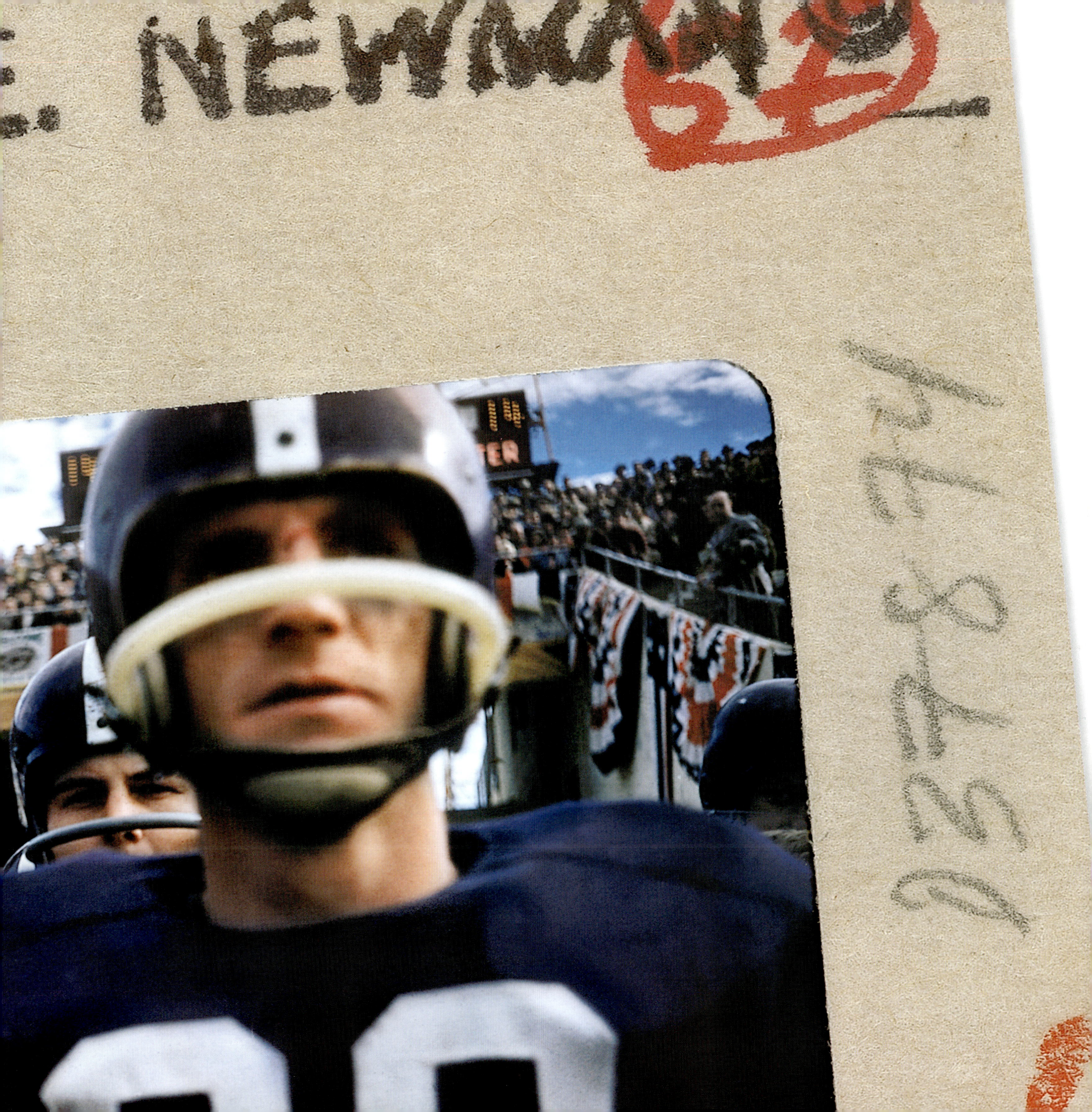
NEWMAN

A Hero Exhales

HANK AARON

Photograph by TONY TRIOLO, April 8, 1974

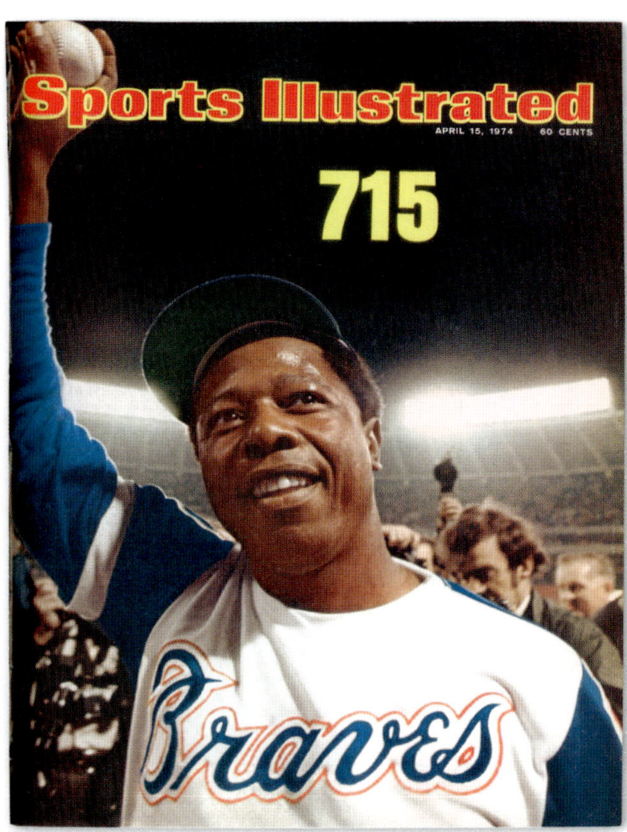

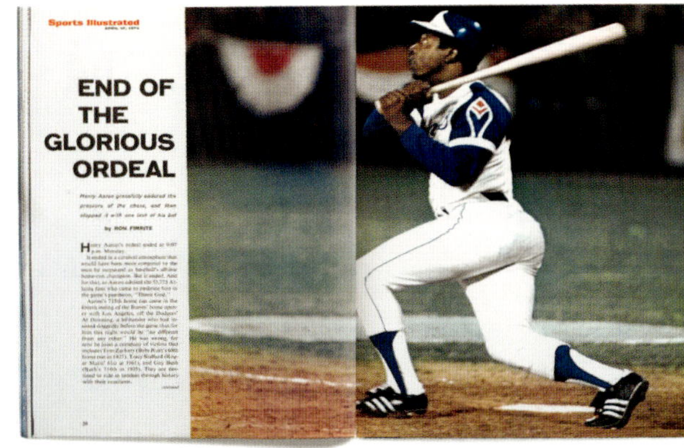
Sports Illustrated

END OF THE GLORIOUS ORDEAL

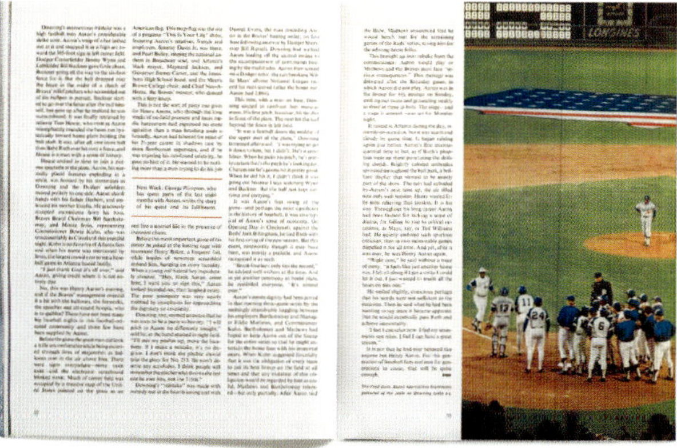

DESPITE HIS ACHIEVEMENTS as a slugger, Hank Aaron had appeared in the playoffs only three times. As he closed in on Babe Ruth's career home run record, he faced a spotlight more intrusive than anything he was used to. Even on the base paths: In Tony Triolo's shot of the record-breaker, in a tableau never seen today, two photographers join the throng at home plate. Neither of them was Neil Leifer, who got the cover shot during the on-field ceremony immediately afterward. It was only Aaron's third SI cover, a number that now seems strangely small, almost unfair. Ron Fimrite's account of that night explains the weary relief so evident in Aaron's face: "It ended in a carnival atmosphere that would have been more congenial to the man he surpassed. But it ended. And for that, as Aaron advised the 53,775 Atlanta fans who came to enshrine him in the game's pantheon, 'Thank God.' "

X18545

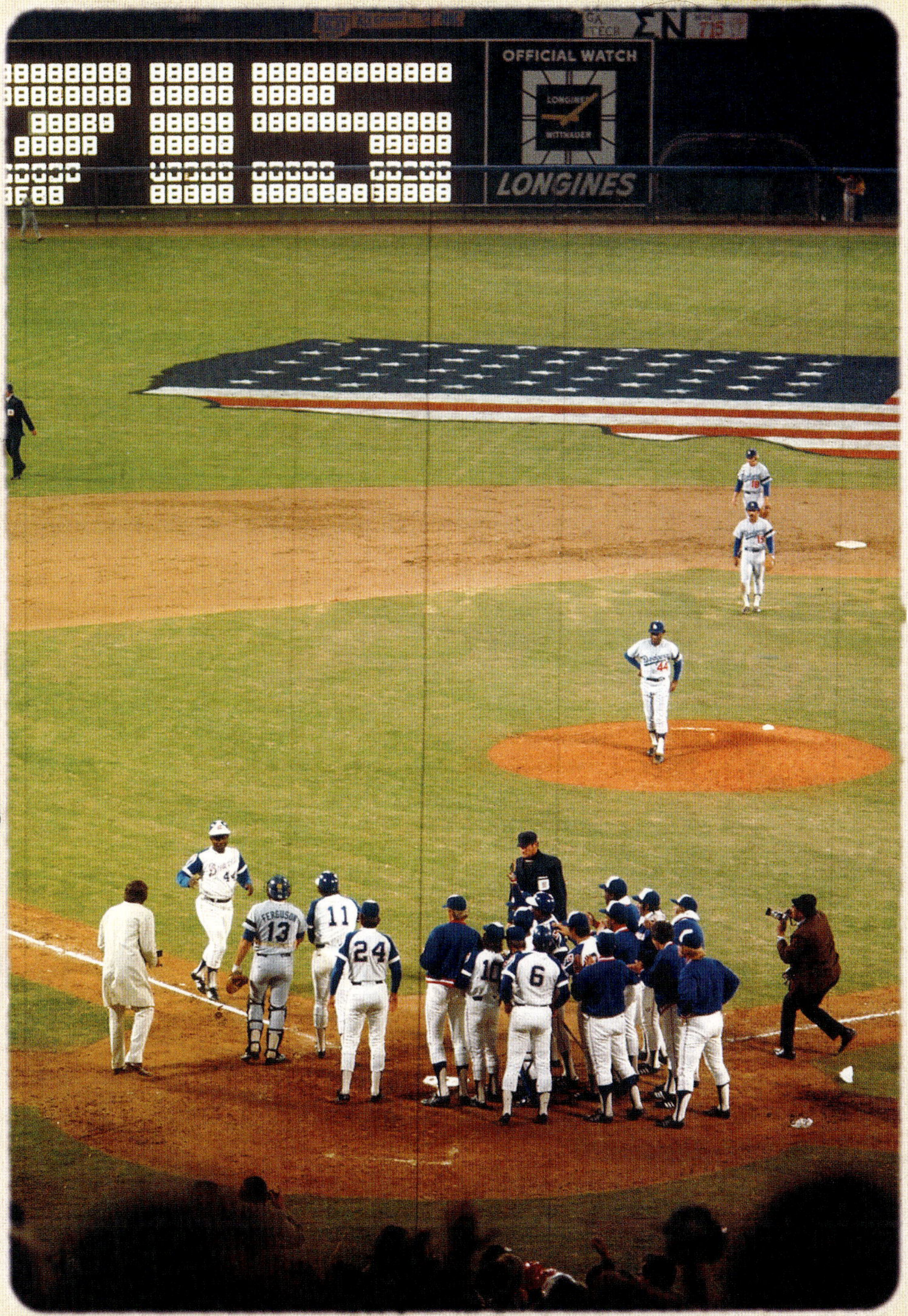

4-15-74

TRIOLO X18545

ROLL #1

FRAME #17

4-15-74

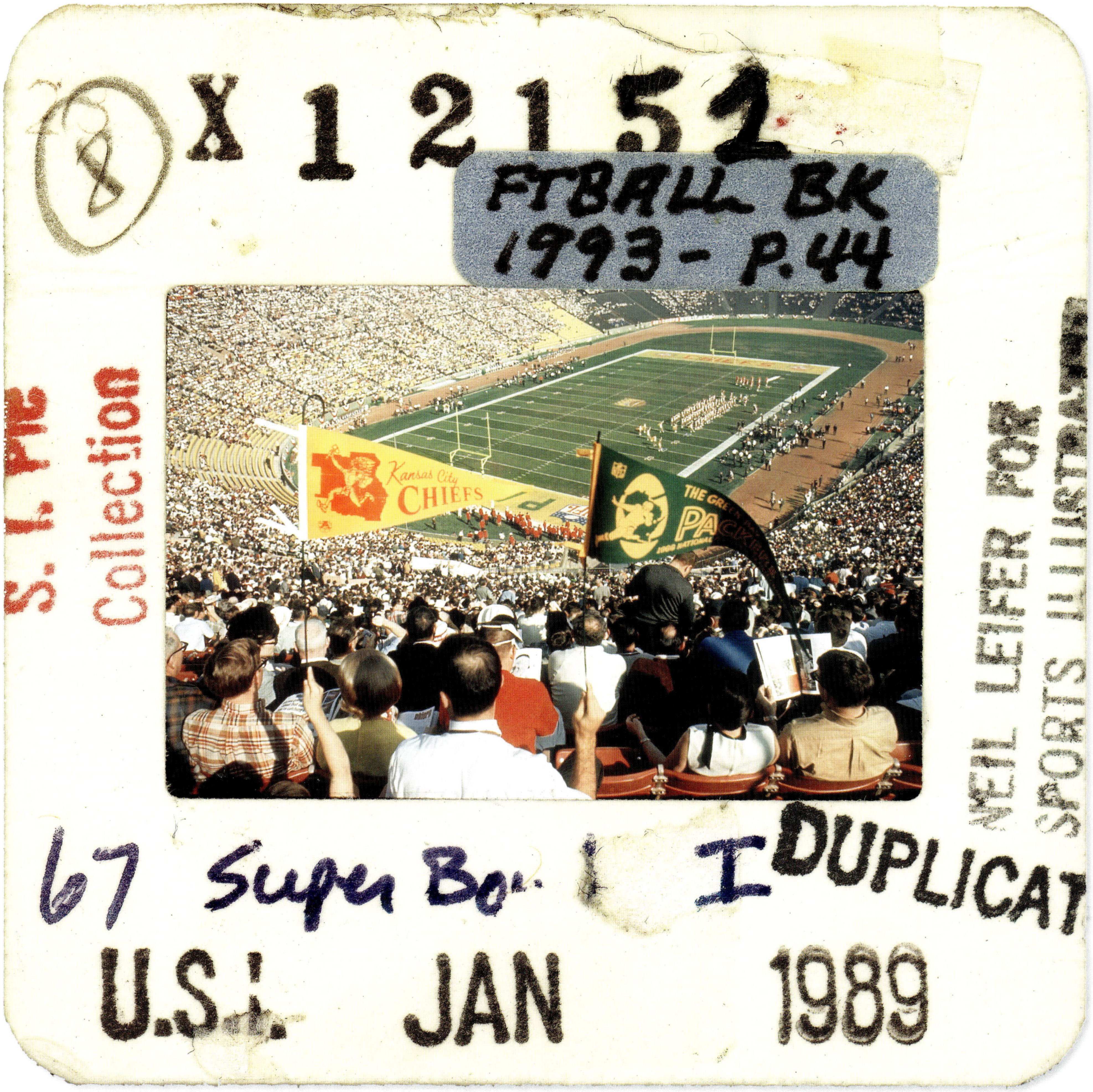

X12151

FTBALL BK
1993 - P.44

S. I. Pic
Collection

NEIL LEIFER FOR
SPORTS ILLUSTRATED

67 Super Bowl I

DUPLICAT

U.S.I. JAN 1989

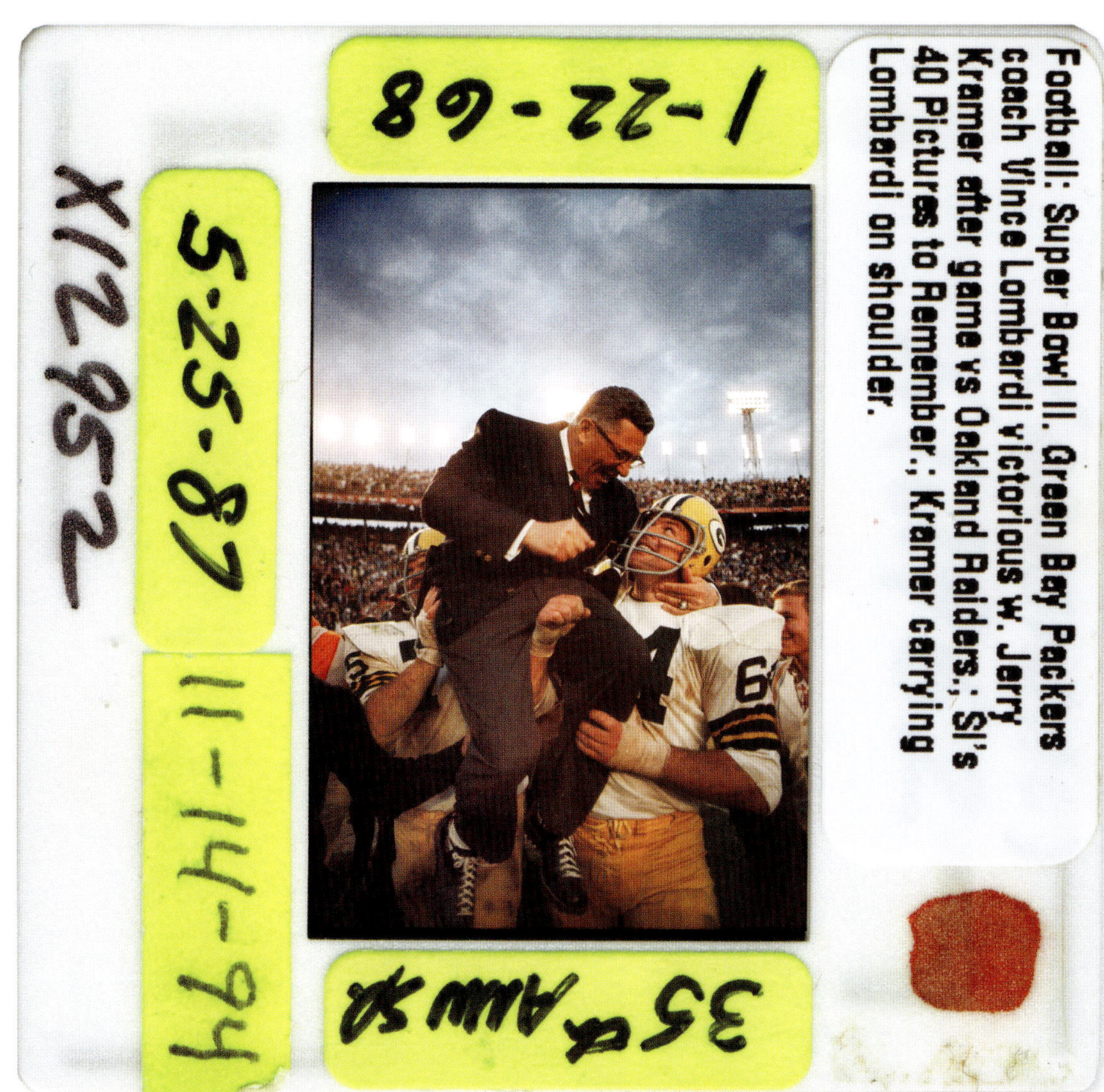

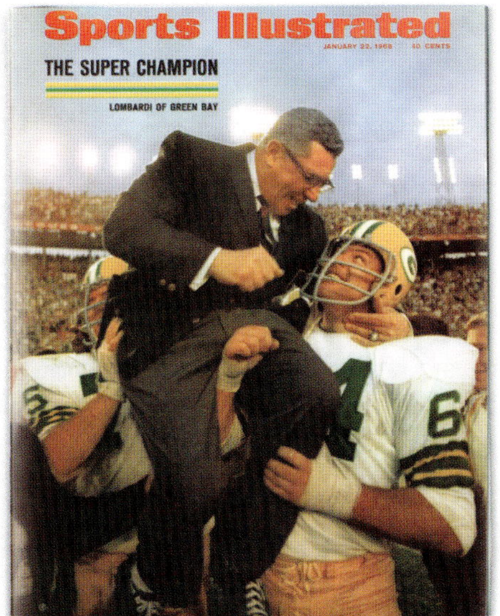

In the Beginning

SUPER BOWL I *(opposite)*
Photograph by NEIL LEIFER, January 15, 1967

SUPER BOWL II *(above)*
Photograph by NEIL LEIFER, January 14, 1968

AS SUPER BOWL II APPROACHED, the prevailing rumor was that Vince Lombardi, the coach who had won five old school NFL titles and the first Super Bowl, was about to retire. SI's editors asked Neil Leifer to go after a potential cover shot of Lombardi, and Leifer was worried. A couple weeks earlier, he had angered Lombardi by edging onto the field to snap pictures with about 40 seconds left in a blowout, and the coach had him thrown off the field. In the Super Bowl, Green Bay was again well ahead, and this time Leifer showed just enough restraint: He waited until there were 20 seconds left to break loose from the sideline and get his cover shot.

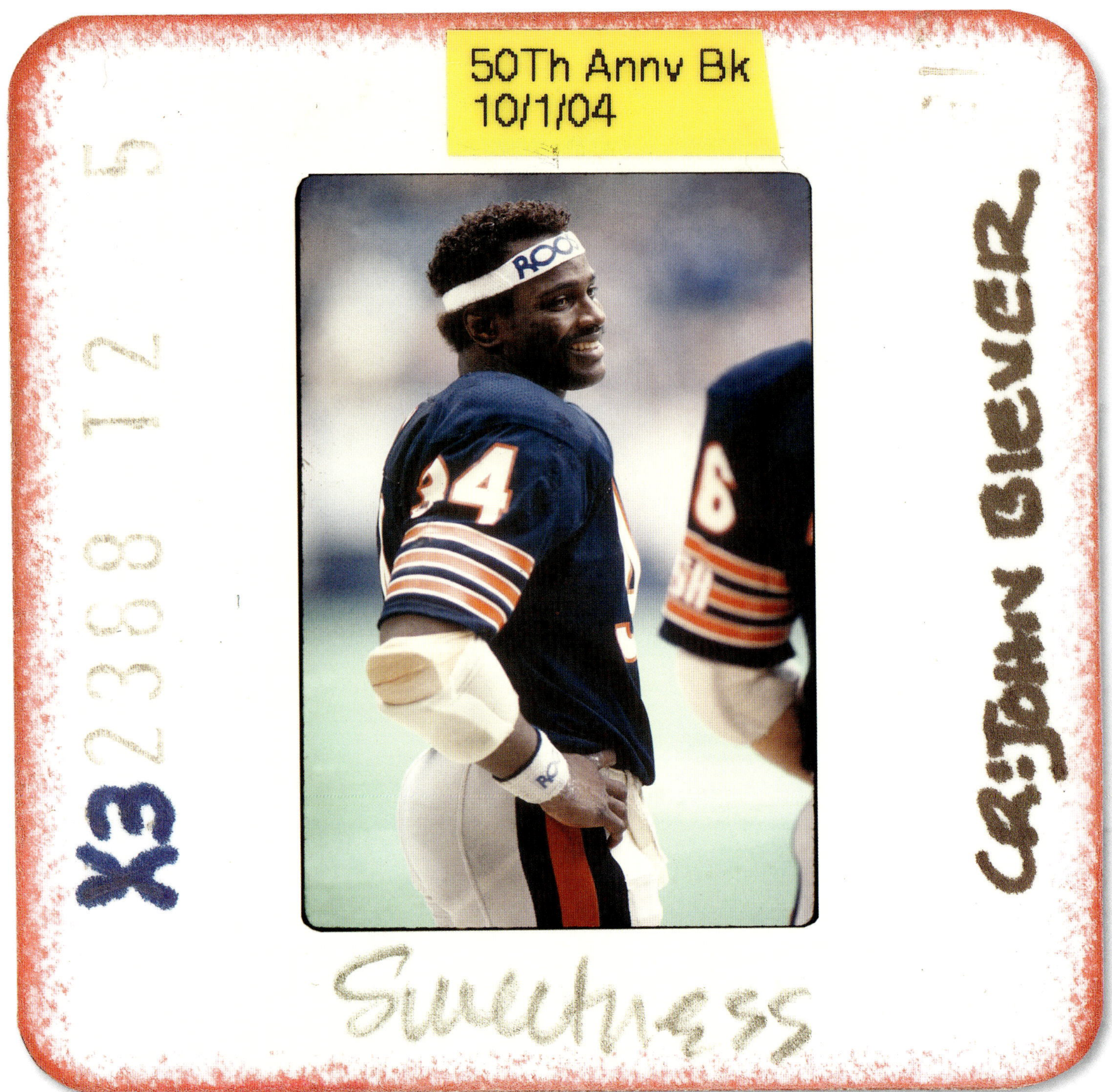

Men at Their Best

WALTER PAYTON *(above). Photograph by* JOHN BIEVER, November 17, 1985 • NOLAN RYAN *(opposite). Photograph by* JOHN G. ZIMMERMAN, June 1, 1975

SWEETNESS, AS THEY CALLED HIM, took a breather during his Super Bowl season; Nolan Ryan had his own sweet stuff in the fourth of his seven no-hitters. Why is the slide of Payton etched in red? It was just one photo editor's way of marking a favorite.

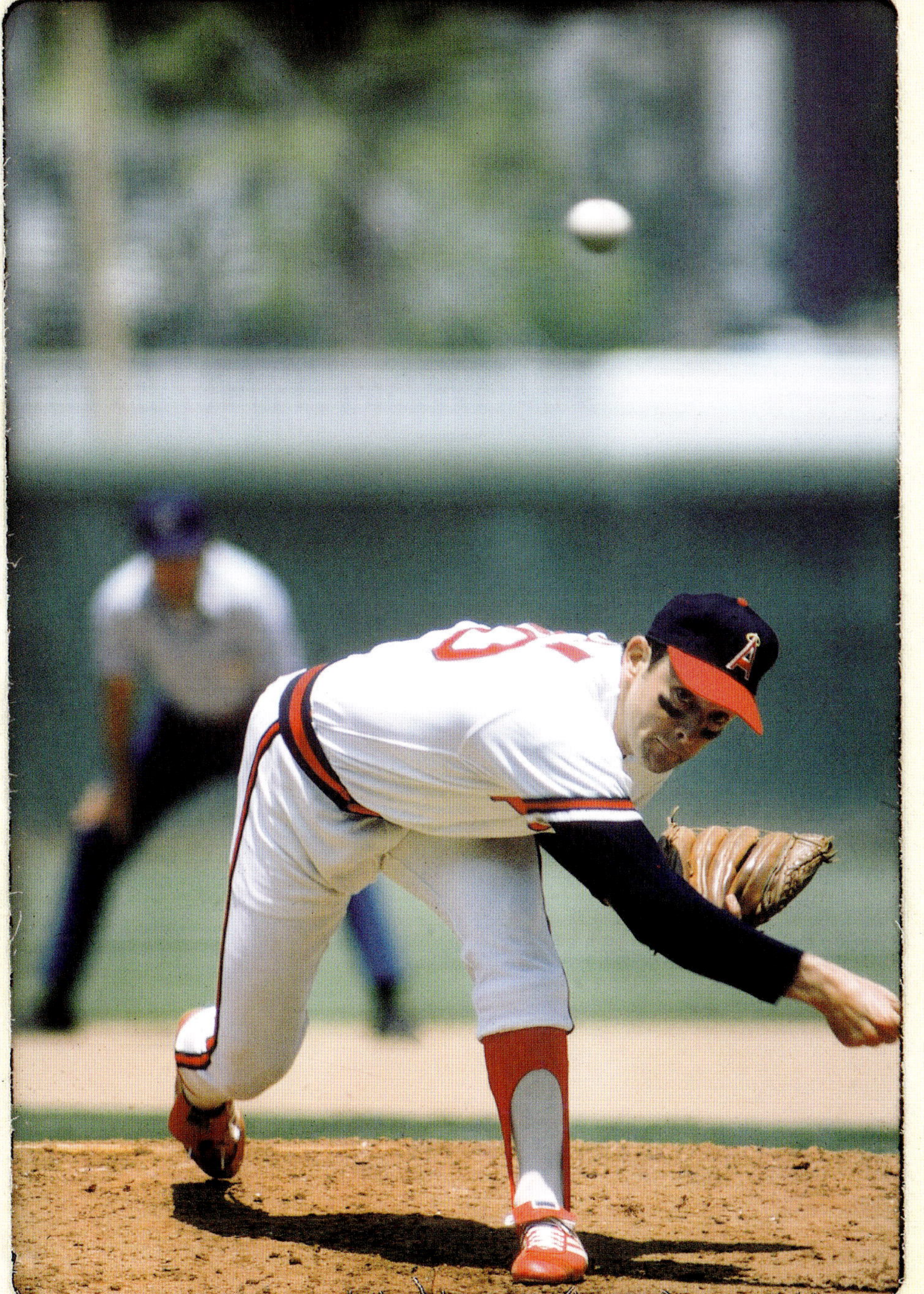
X19599 original
John Zimmerman
S. I. Pic Collection
RYAN
90A

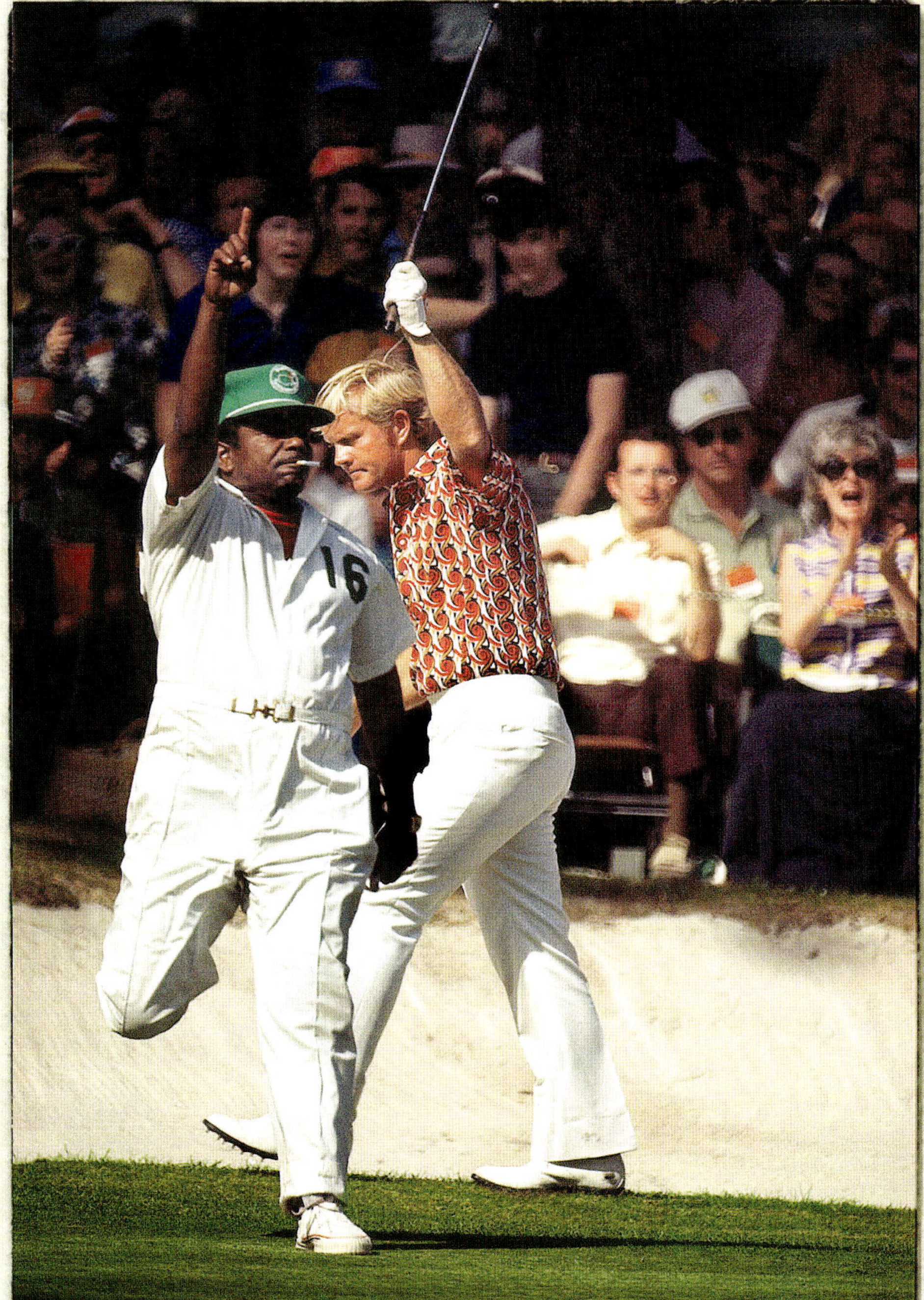

NL
021787
106
0-38166
ORIGINAL
X16702
Neil Leifer sports
16

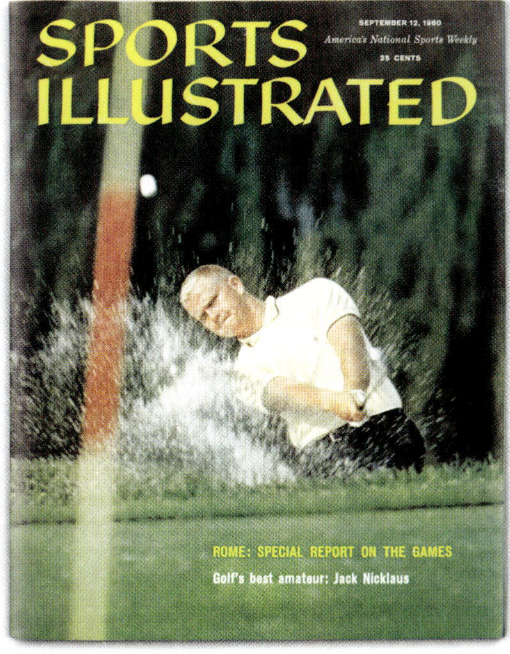

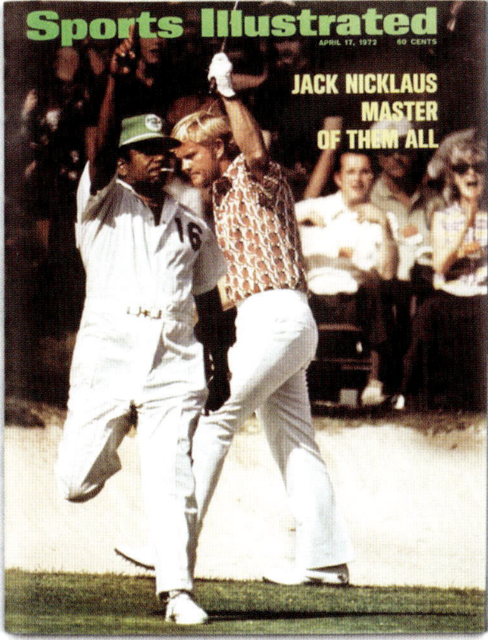

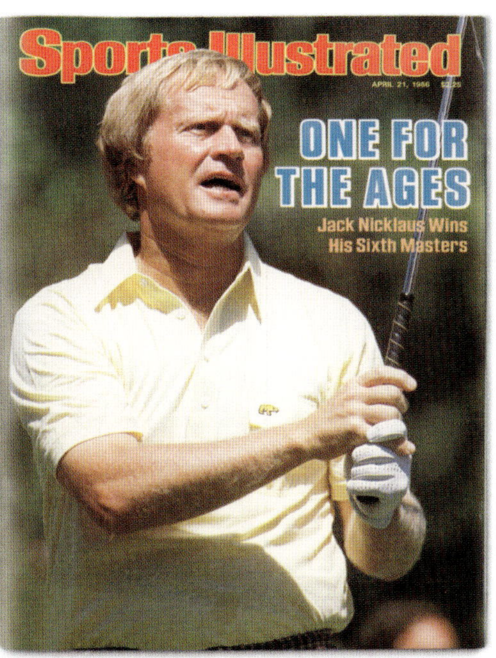

The Golden Years

JACK NICKLAUS
Photograph by NEIL LEIFER, April 9, 1972

JACK NICKLAUS has been featured on the cover of SPORTS ILLUSTRATED 22 times: That's what he gets for being so good for so long. He made his first cover, on the left, as an amateur; in that issue Nicklaus told writer Ray Cave that the tournament he most wanted to win was the Masters. (Cave, tweaking the young golfer for his chubbiness, as many did back then, wrote, "Tell the tailor to have plenty of green cloth ready.") Nicklaus would do more than win at Augusta National; he took ownership of the place. The middle cover shows Nicklaus, svelte and in his prime, on the way to his fourth Masters title (though his caddie, Willie Peterson, got better exposure). The cover on the right—his last for SI—is from 1986, when, at the improbable age of 46, the Golden Bear got his sixth green jacket and final PGA Tour win.

X38243T6

03

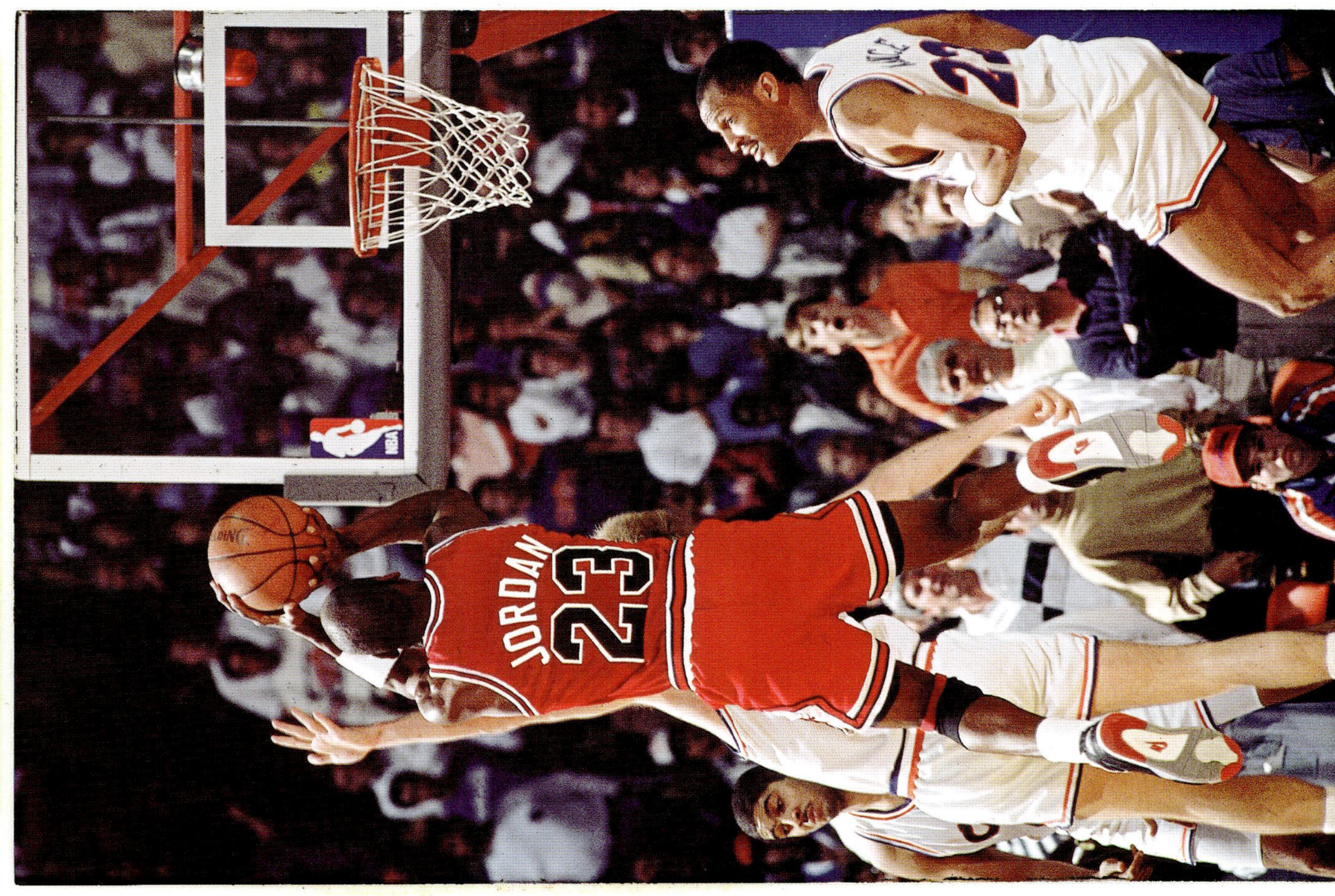

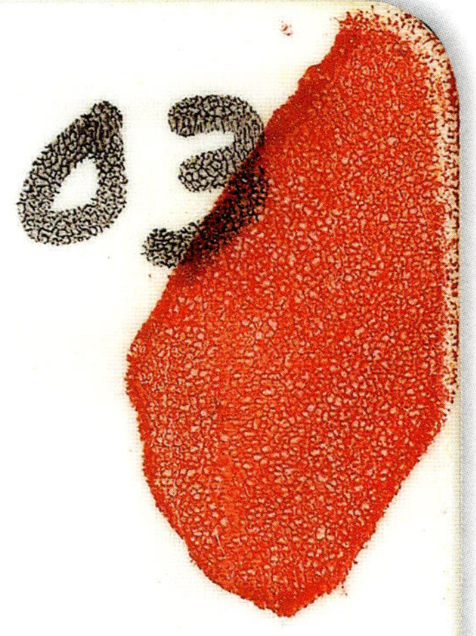

5-15-89

SI Bulls 96

Basketball: NBA playoffs. Rear view of Chicago Bulls Michael Jordan #23 in action, shooting

Rarefied Air

MICHAEL JORDAN *(opposite)*
Photograph by MANNY MILLAN, May 7, 1989

MICHAEL JORDAN *(below)*
Photograph by WALTER IOOSS JR., March 5, 1987

WHEN MICHAEL JORDAN flew, shutters clicked. Of course, some shots (his, not the photographers') were bigger than others, like the one that sank the Cavaliers in the '89 playoffs. (As any Cleveland fan can tell you, that's Craig Ehlo, obscured by Jordan, flailing eternally in vain.) And some shots (the photographer's, not Jordan's) are more spectacular than others, such as when Walter Iooss Jr. painted a parking lot blue and shot Jordan from a cherry-picker. Leaving nothing to chance, Iooss had painted another section red, in case Jordan showed up in home whites.

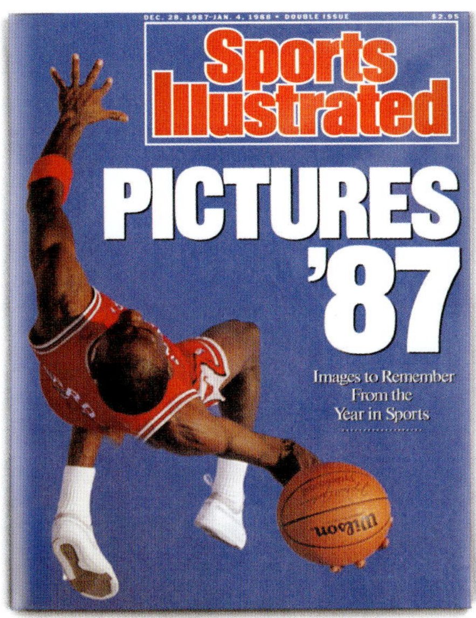

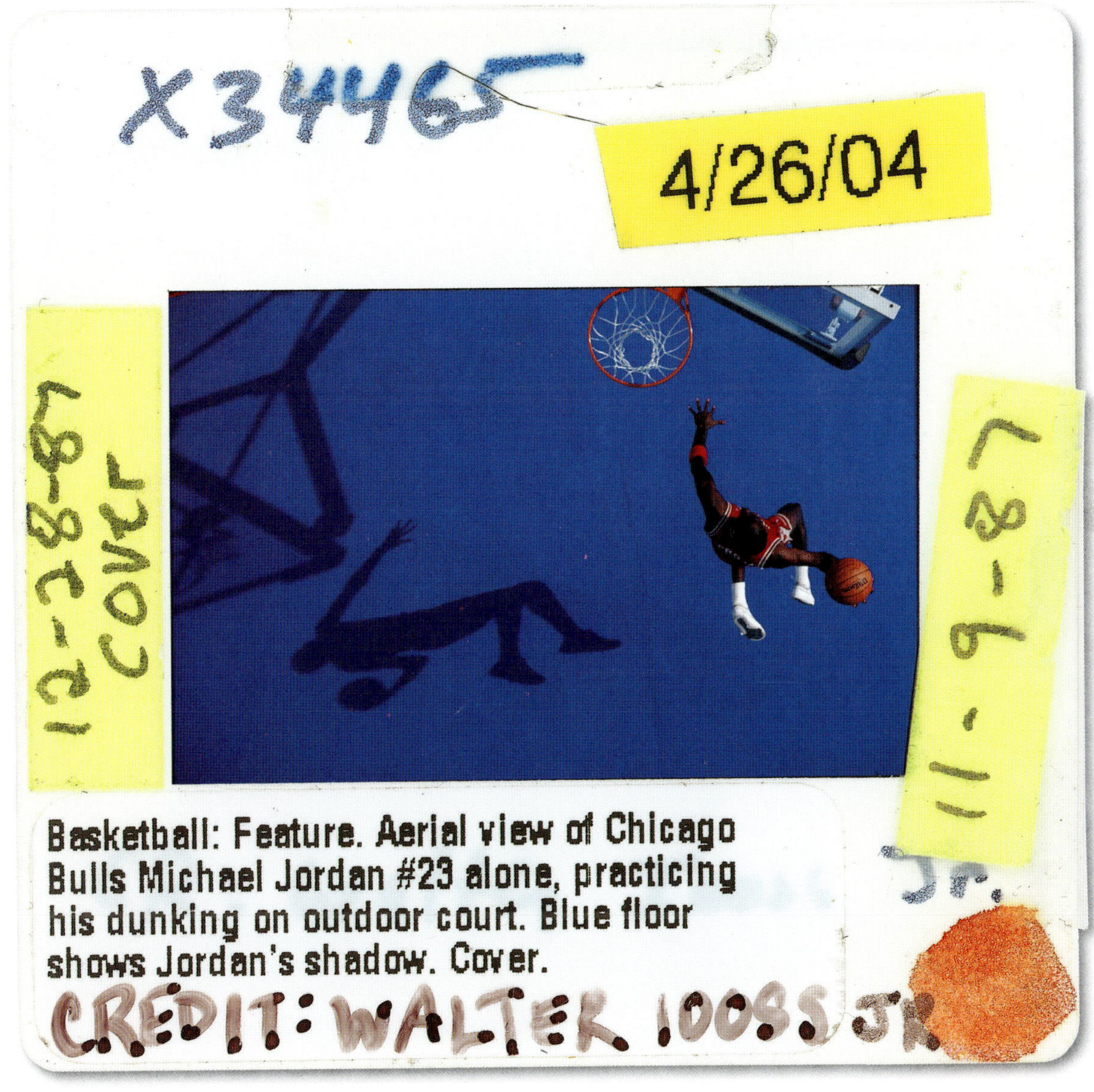

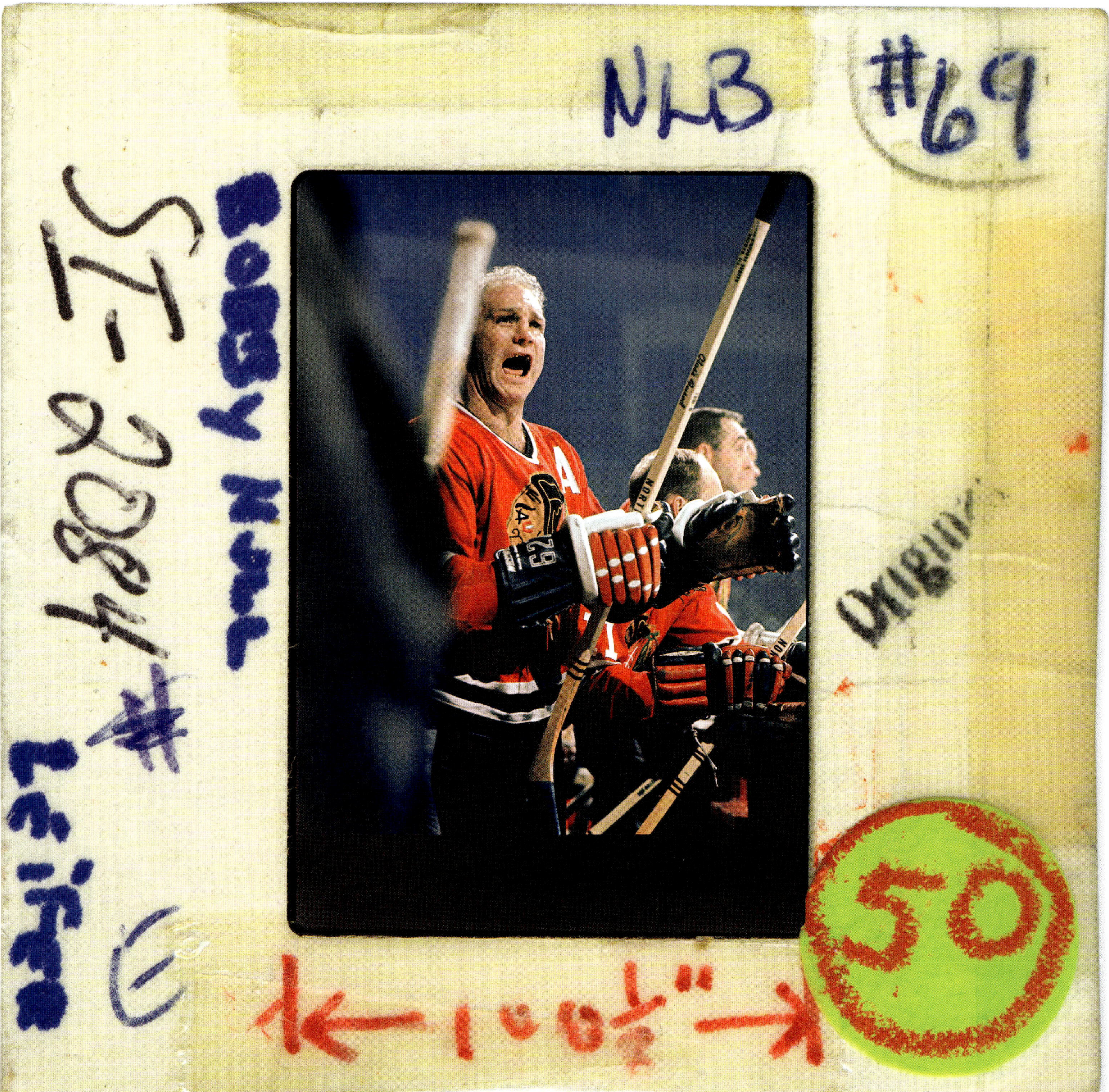
NLB
#69
Bobby Hull
ST-2084#
Leifer
100½"
50
Original

In Hockey, A Jump Shot

BOBBY HULL

Photograph by NEIL LEIFER, February 1967

EVEN THE GREATS ON THE BENCH can get worked up sometimes—which is how Neil Leifer ended up with an unplanned cover shot of Bobby Hull. Leifer went to Chicago in 1968 to shoot a story on the Blackhawks' "Scooter Line" of Stan Mikita, Ken Wharram and Doug Mohns, the three gentlemen seen on the cover on the right. Leifer was clicking away on the bench when Hull, reacting to a play on the ice, jumped up and into the frame. The watchful faces of the Scooter Line made the cover the following month, but, says Leifer, "My shots of those guys weren't a tenth as good as the one of Hull." But Hull was not lost: The following season SI did a story on Hull, and Leifer had his second cover from the same shoot. On the Hull cover you can see the Scooter Line in the background.

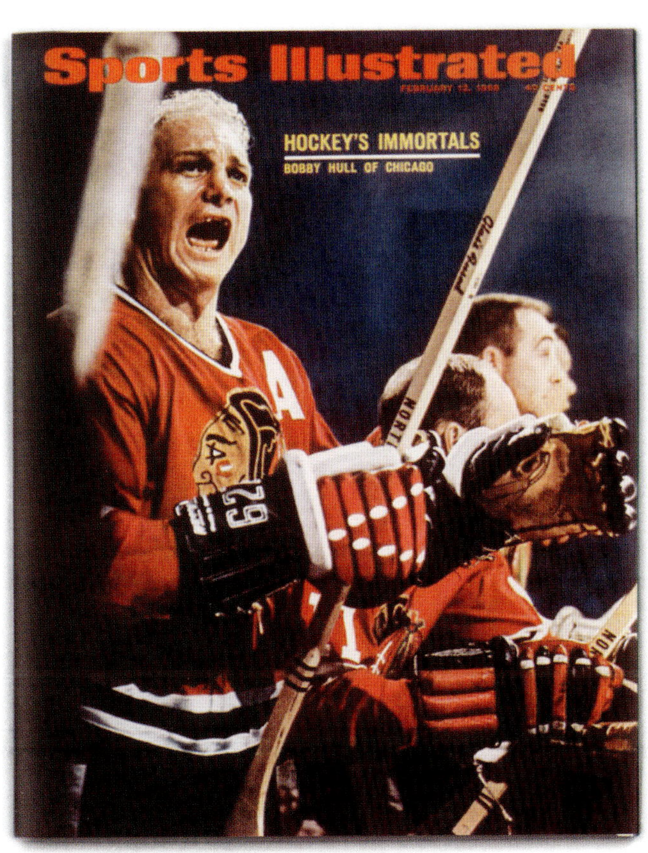

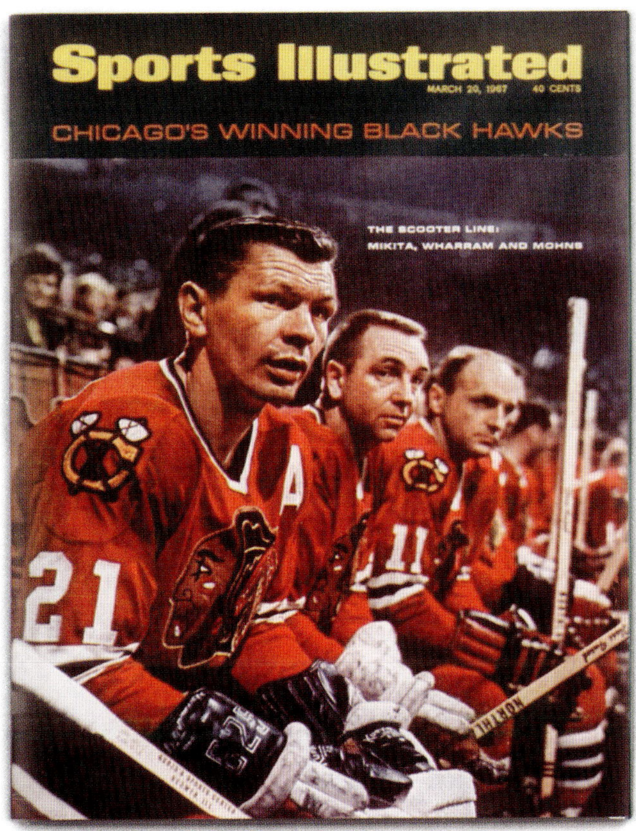

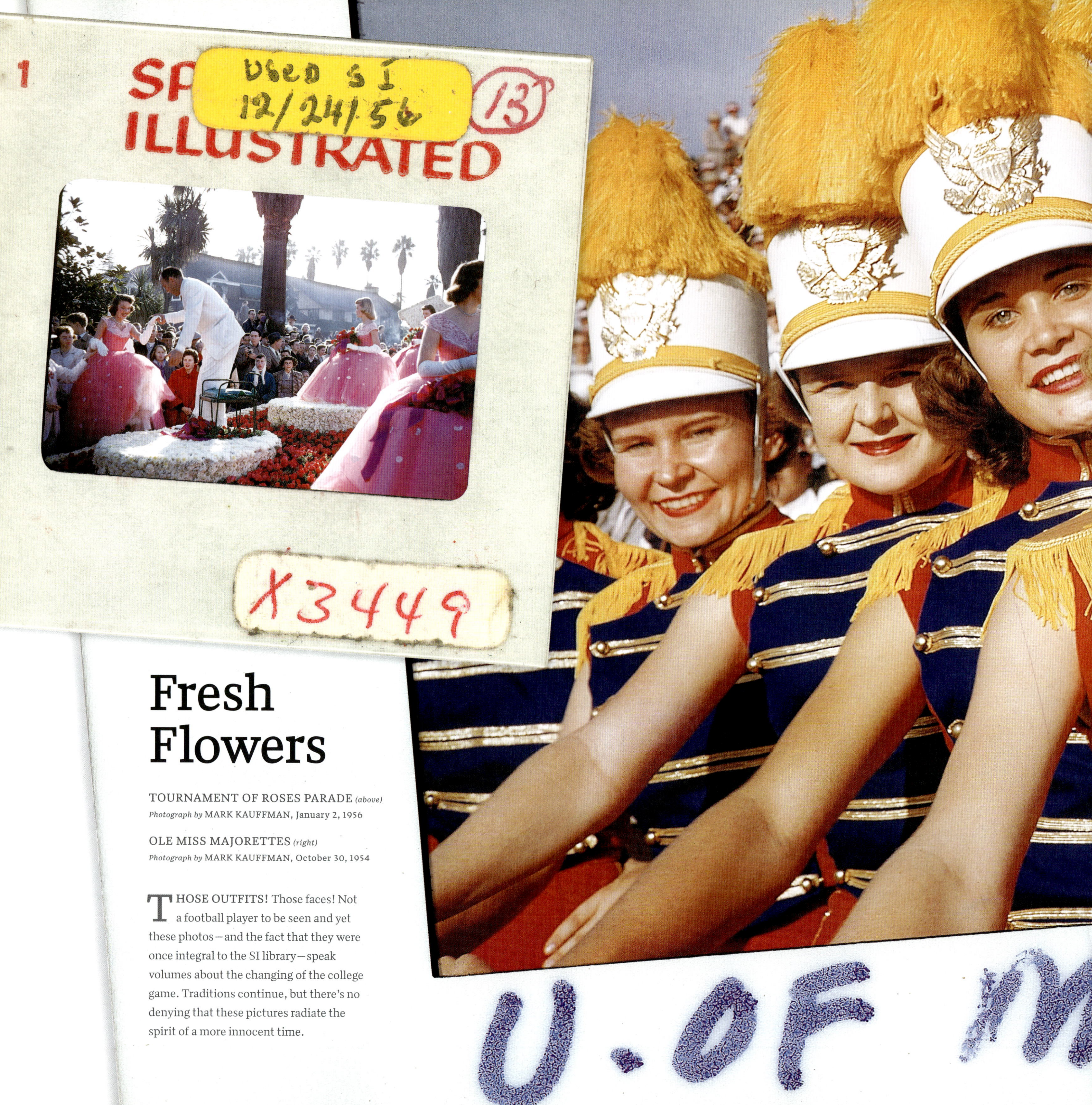

Fresh Flowers

TOURNAMENT OF ROSES PARADE *(above)*
Photograph by MARK KAUFFMAN, January 2, 1956

OLE MISS MAJORETTES *(right)*
Photograph by MARK KAUFFMAN, October 30, 1954

THOSE OUTFITS! Those faces! Not a football player to be seen and yet these photos—and the fact that they were once integral to the SI library—speak volumes about the changing of the college game. Traditions continue, but there's no denying that these pictures radiate the spirit of a more innocent time.

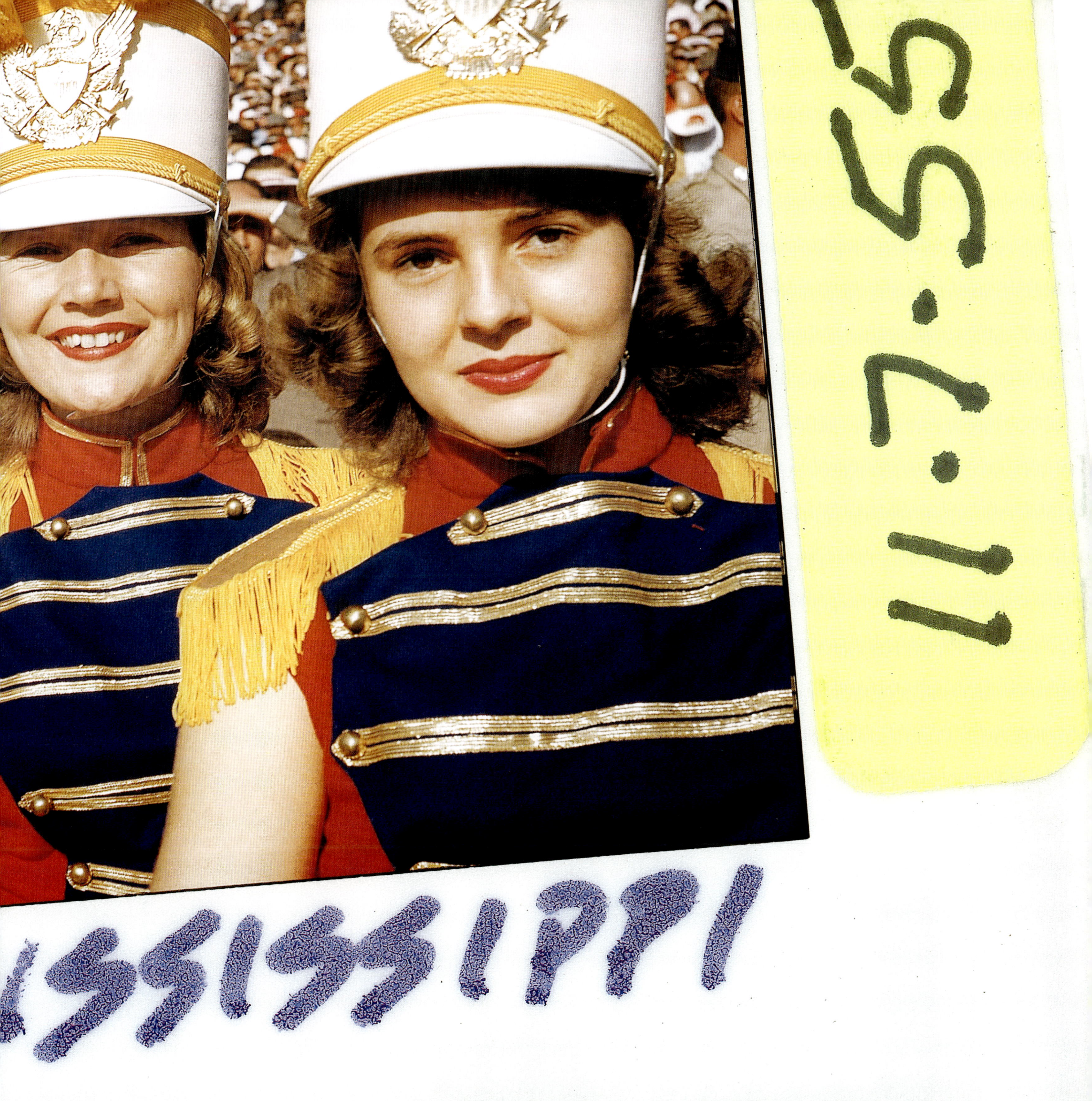

ISSISSIPPI
11.7.55

Alan

4/27/92

S.I. PIC Collection

(2)

X33828 T39

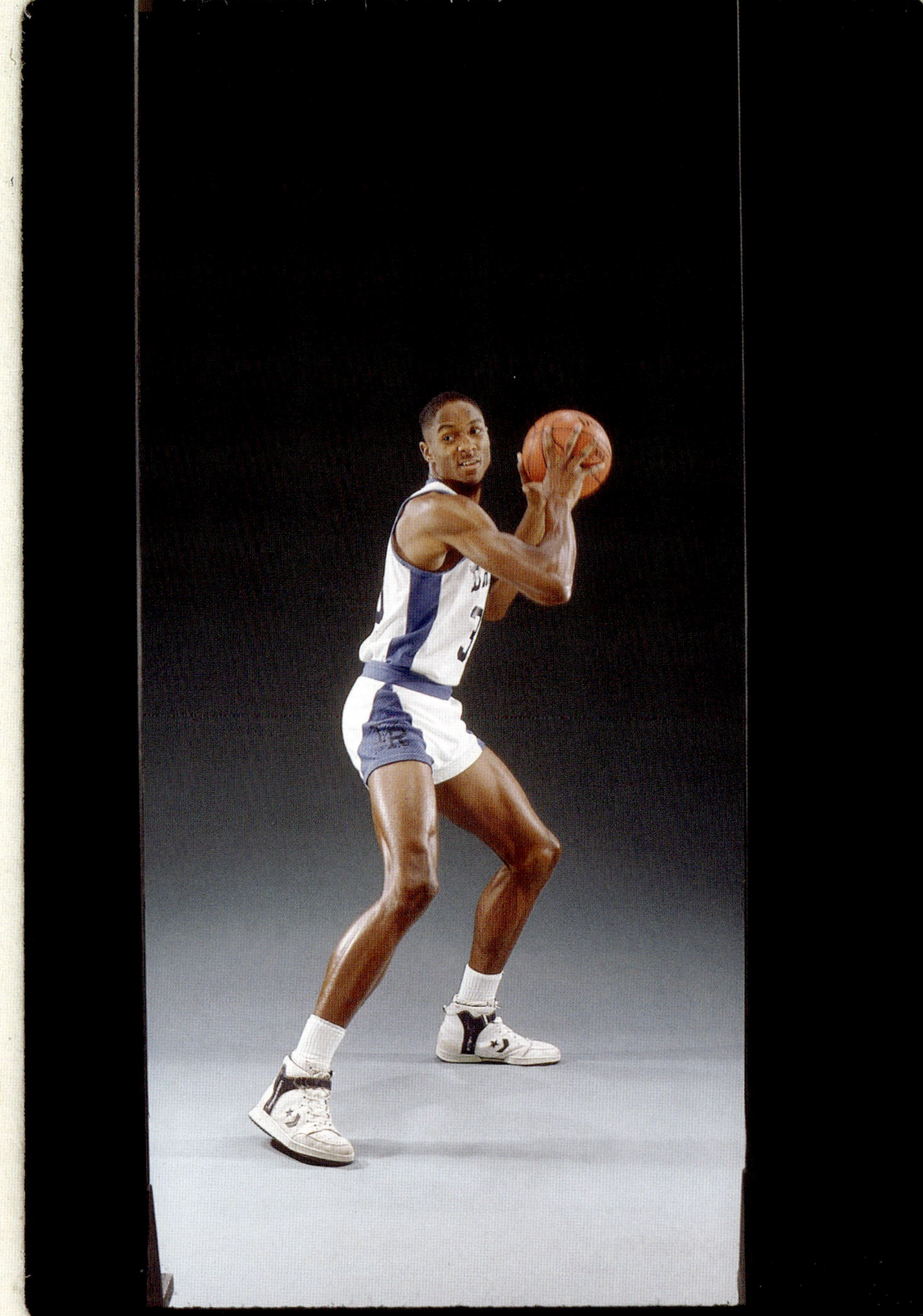

HS Basketball: Portrait of 11th grader Alonzo Mourning of Indian River HS, alone w.

11-19-86
BKB.

Playing Crystal Ball

ALONZO MOURNING *(left)*
KENNY ANDERSON *(right)*
Photographs by GEORGE TIEDEMANN/GT IMAGES, October 10, 1986

AS PART OF A 1986 FEATURE on college recruiting, SPORTS ILLUSTRATED polled college coaches and scouting gurus on the best basketball prospects in grades six through 12 at that time. The experts did well, up to a point: Their choices for the best 12th-grader (Marcus Liberty), 11th-grader (Alonzo Mourning), 10th-grader (Kenny Anderson) and ninth-grader (Damon Bailey) all made it to the NBA; none of the younger players did. On two occasions we followed up with this group: first in 1992, and again in 2004, after starting SI's annual WHERE ARE THEY NOW? issues. (The slides only bear added stickers from the '92 issue; in 2004 we showed the original magazine spread but not the individual photos.) In '04 we learned that sixth-grade pick Michael Irvin was running an AAU program, seventh-grader Brian Crow was a marketing coordinator, and 8th-grader Barnabas James was in the construction business.

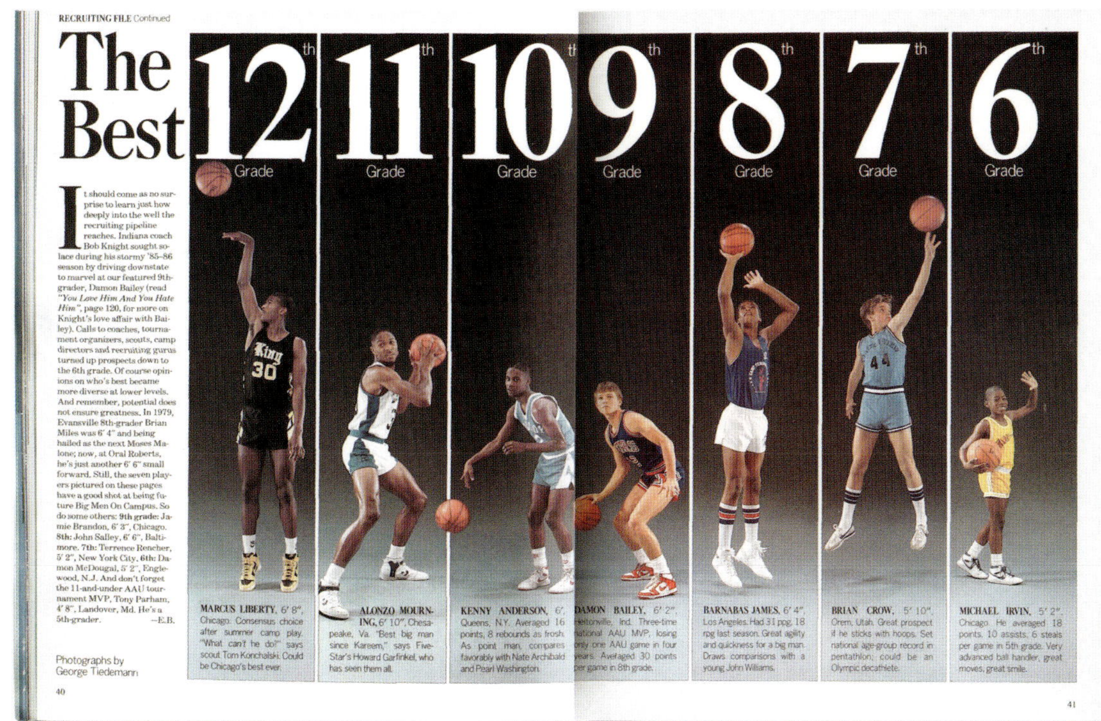
RECRUITING FILE Continued

The Best

12th Grade 11th Grade 10th Grade 9th Grade 8th Grade 7th Grade 6th Grade

It should come as no surprise to learn just how deeply into the well the recruiting pipeline reaches. Indiana coach Bob Knight sought solace during his stormy '85-86 season by driving downstate to marvel at our featured 9th-grader, Damon Bailey (read *"You Love Him And You Hate Him"*, page 120, for more on Knight's love affair with Bailey). Calls to coaches, tournament organizers, scouts, camp directors and recruiting gurus turned up prospects down to the 6th grade. Of course opinions on who's best became more diverse at lower levels. And remember, potential does not ensure greatness. In 1979, Evansville 8th-grader Brian Miles was 6' 4" and being hailed as the next Moses Malone; now, at Oral Roberts, he's just another 6' 6" small forward. Still, the seven players pictured on these pages have a good shot at being future Big Men On Campus. So do some others: **9th grade:** Jamie Brandon, 6' 3", Chicago. **8th:** John Salley, 6' 6", Baltimore. **7th:** Terrence Rencher, 5' 2", New York City. **6th:** Damon McDougal, 5' 2", Englewood, N.J. And don't forget the 11-and-under AAU tournament MVP, Tony Parham, 4' 8", Landover, Md. He's a 5th-grader. —E.B.

Photographs by George Tiedemann

MARCUS LIBERTY, 6' 8", Chicago. Consensus choice after summer camp play. "What can't he do?" says scout Tom Konchalski. Could be Chicago's best ever.

ALONZO MOURNING, 6' 10", Chesapeake, Va. "Best big man since Kareem," says Five-Star's Howard Garfinkel, who has seen them all.

KENNY ANDERSON, 6', Queens, N.Y. Averaged 16 points, 8 rebounds as frosh. As point man, compares favorably with Nate Archibald and Pearl Washington.

DAMON BAILEY, 6' 2", tonville, Ind. Three-time national AAU MVP, losing only one AAU game in four years. Averaged 30 points per game in 8th grade.

BARNABAS JAMES, 6' 4", Los Angeles. Had 31 ppg, 18 rpg last season. Great agility and quickness for a big man. Draws comparisons with a young John Williams.

BRIAN CROW, 5' 10", Orem, Utah. Great prospect if he sticks with hoops. Set national age-group record in pentathlon; could be an Olympic decathlete.

MICHAEL IRVIN, 5' 2", Chicago. He averaged 18 points, 10 assists, 6 steals per game in 5th grade. Very advanced ball handler, great moves, great smile.

40 41

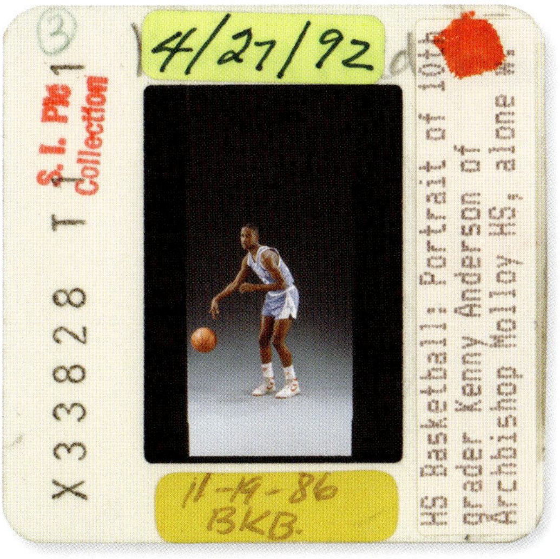

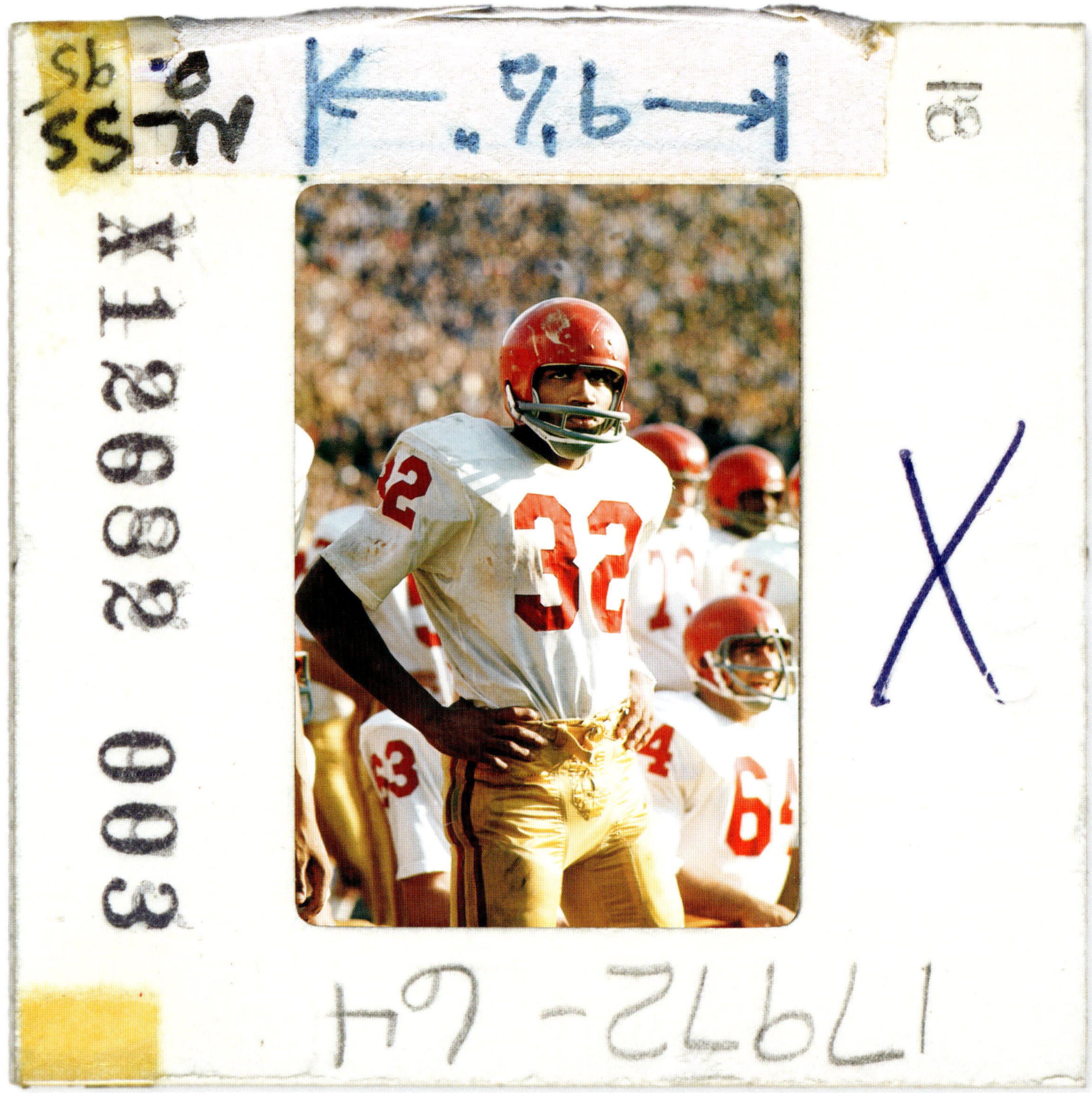

Take Another Look

O.J. SIMPSON *(above). Photograph by* NEIL LEIFER, October 14, 1967 • ROGER MARIS *(opposite). Photograph by* NEIL LEIFER, June 1960

SOME PHOTOS gain unexpected impact with the passage of time. It is rare to see Maris this young and in color; most shots of him then were taken by newspapers, all in black and white. As for that young Trojans tailback . . . well, let's leave it at that.

17972-137 C5-9

MADE IN U.S.A.
P.701

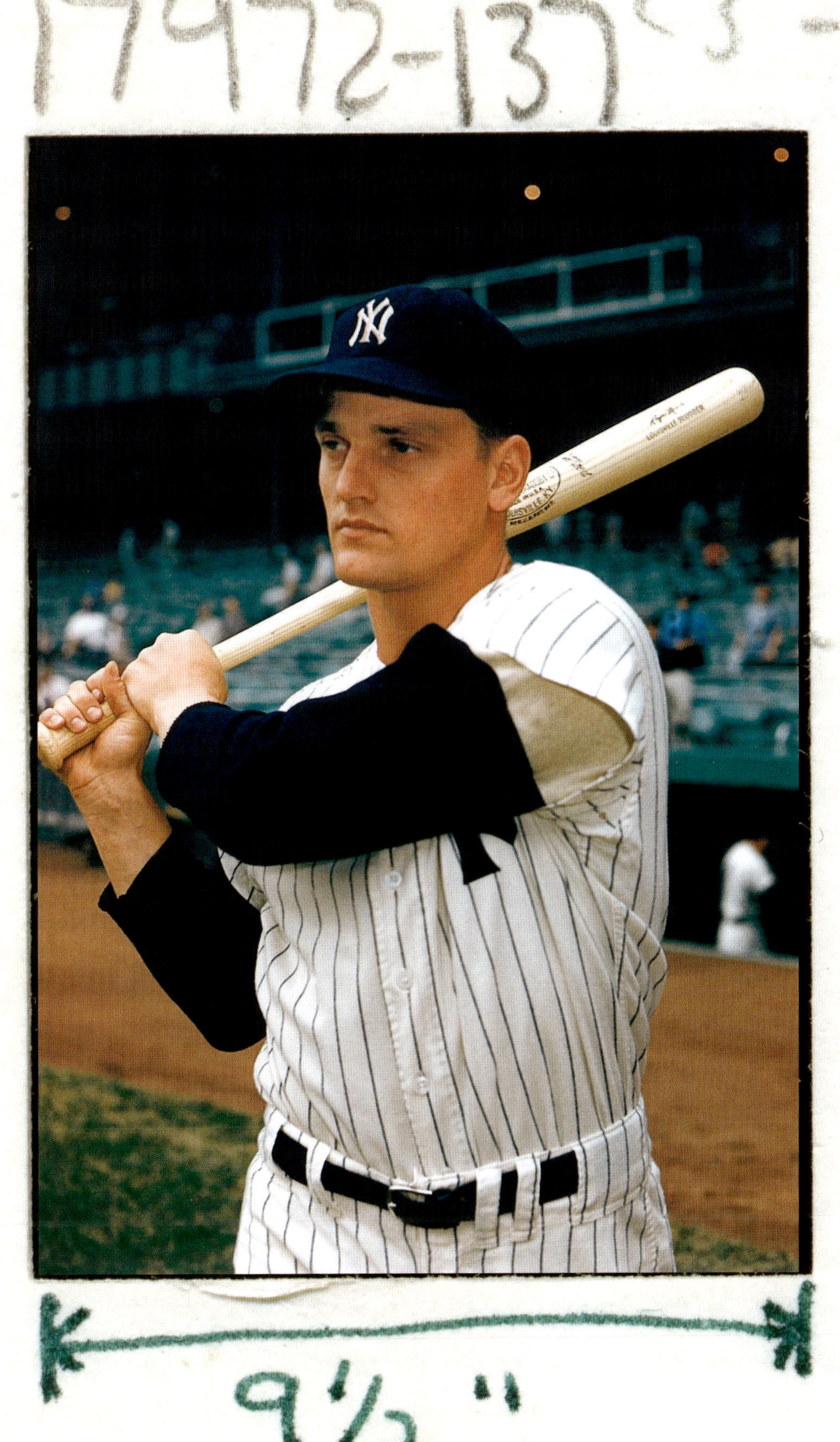

...TO BY
NEIL LEIFER

NL SS
3
p113

9½"

Tire Tracks

KEN SCHRADER *(right)*
Photograph by BILL EPPRIDGE, August 14, 1988

DALE EARNHARDT *(below)*
Photograph by HEINZ KLUETMEIER, July 4, 1980

THE NOTES on a slide can reveal details great and small; a scribble on the shot of Ken Schrader at Watkins Glen drolly points out, “wheel off ground.” On the Dale Earnhardt slide, the sticker from a 2001 commemorative is a reminder of the crash that took his life.

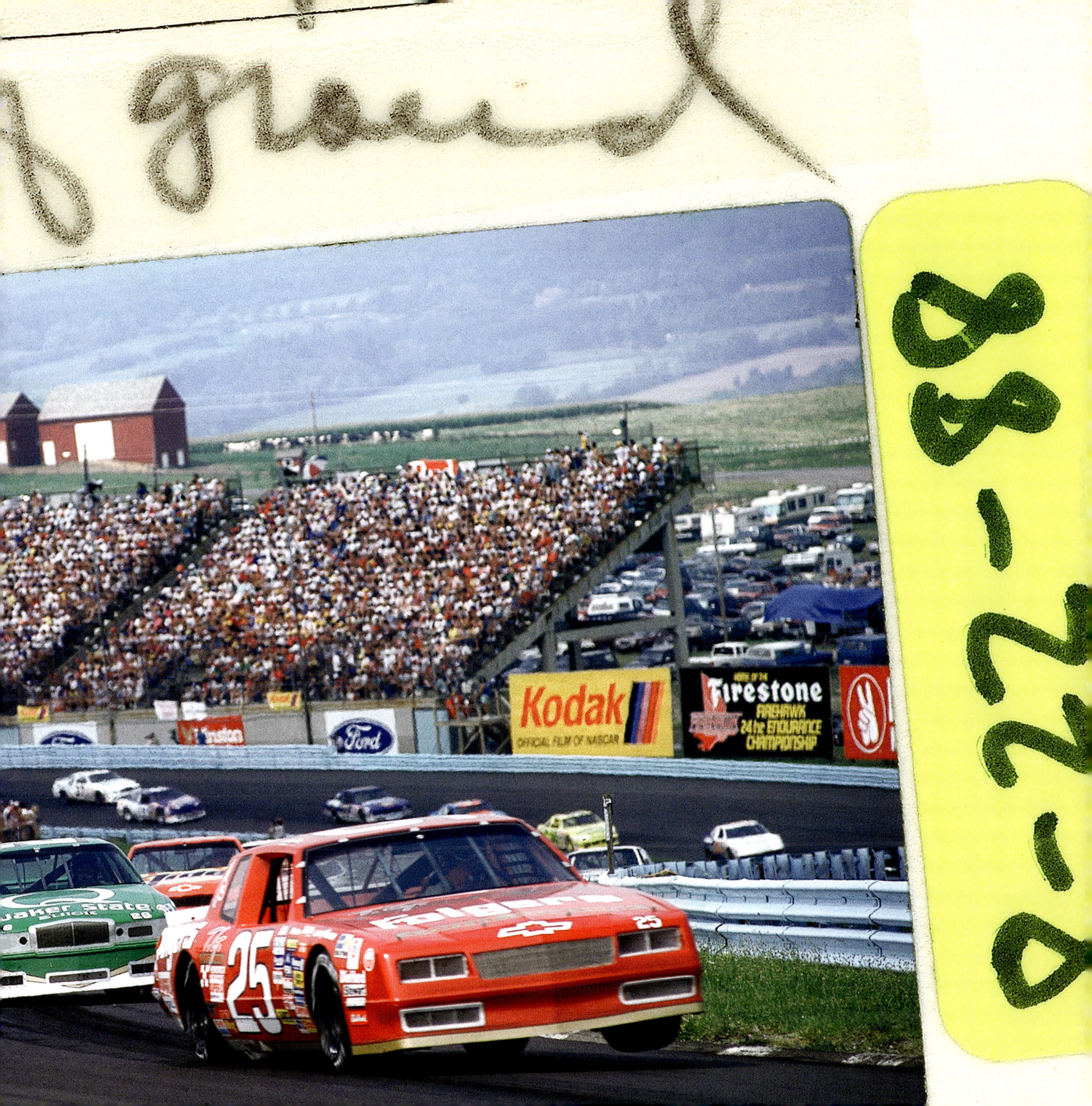
Kodak
OFFICIAL FILM OF NASCAR
Firestone
FIREHAWK 24 hr ENDURANCE CHAMPIONSHIP
Ford
Folgers
25

10·4·99

50Th Anny BK
10/1/04

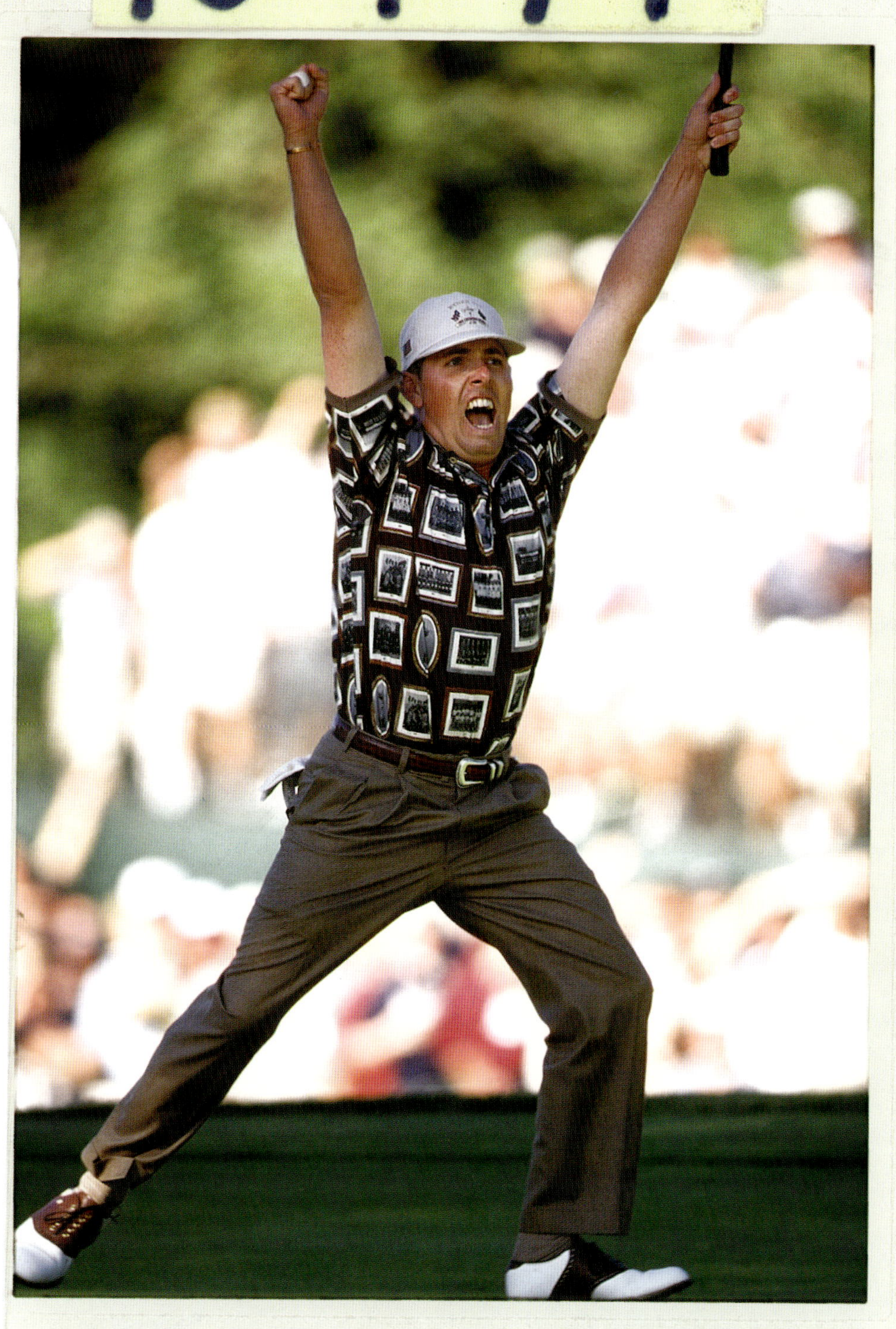

Golf: Ryder Cup. USA Justin Leonard victorious after making a birdie putt on the 17th green to win tournament. Cover

001076355

SI: SIMON BRUTY

X55764 TK3 F06 R15

Gentlemen Gone Wild

JUSTIN LEONARD

Photograph by SIMON BRUTY, September 26, 1999

THIS IS GOLF? Why are these professionals racing across the putting surface with no regard for course decorum? Rewind: The Americans began this last day of the 1999 Ryder Cup down to Europe by a margin greater than any team had ever overcome. The U.S. squad, so tight earlier, loosened up; players began making shots. The final blow was dealt by Justin Leonard, who, a few holes earlier, down in his match, had been in tears. When Leonard drained his 45-foot shocker on the 17th green, mayhem ensued (and led to some angry finger-wagging by the Euros). That putt, wrote Rick Reilly, "sent the Yanks into a fit of boorish, shameful and ridiculously emotional behavior. Wasn't it great?" The cover shot only heightened another controversy: Who was responsible for those shirts?

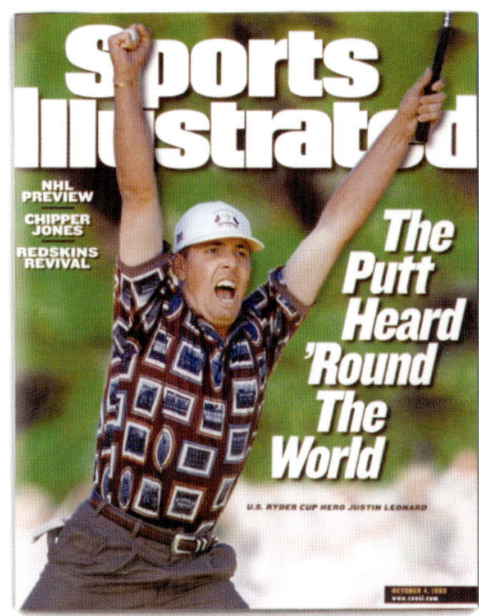
Sports Illustrated

NHL PREVIEW

CHIPPER JONES

REDSKINS REVIVAL

The Putt Heard 'Round The World

U.S. RYDER CUP HERO JUSTIN LEONARD

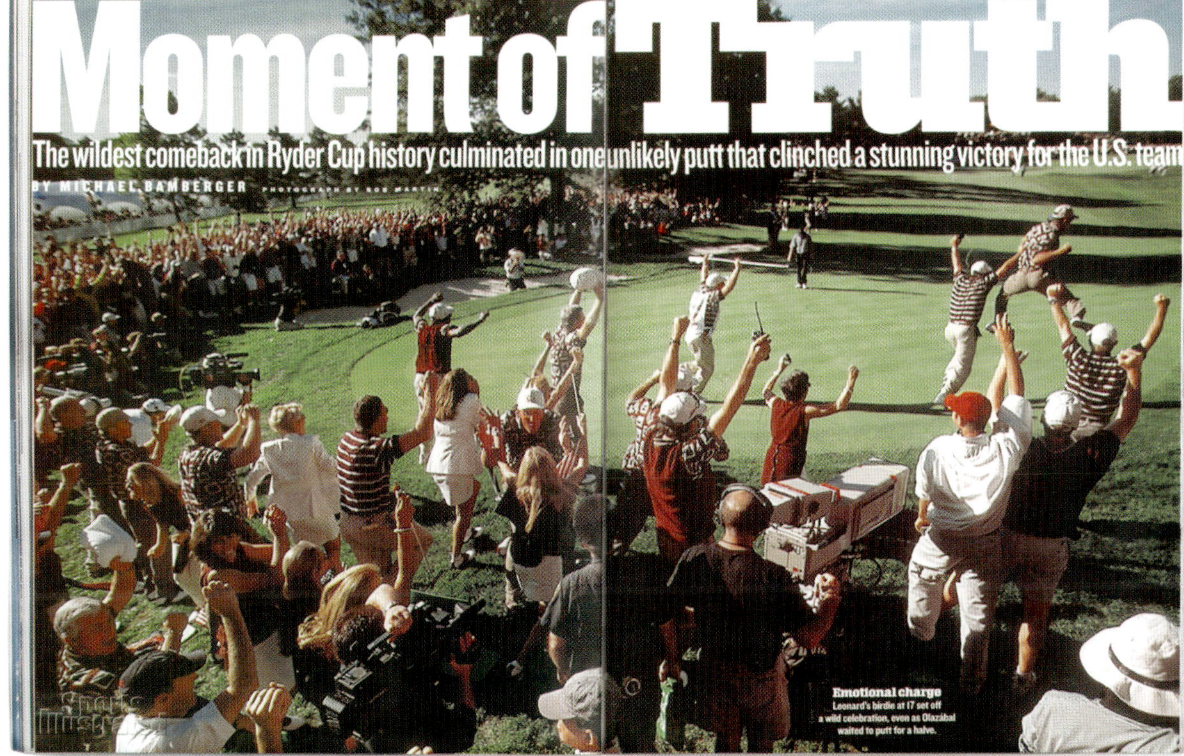
Moment of Truth

The wildest comeback in Ryder Cup history culminated in one unlikely putt that clinched a stunning victory for the U.S. team

BY MICHAEL BAMBERGER

Emotional charge
Leonard's birdie at 17 set off a wild celebration, even as Olazábal waited to putt for a halve.

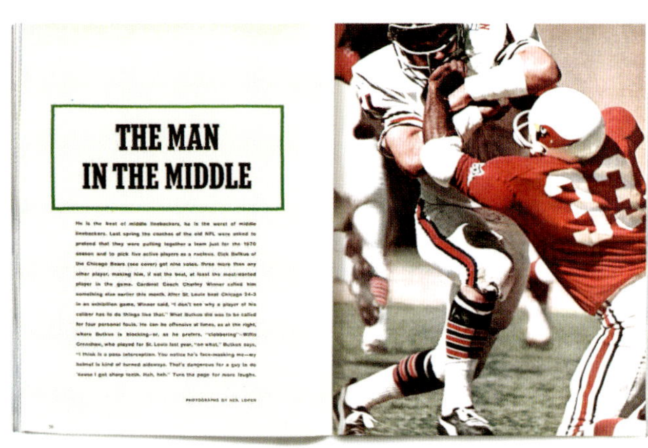
THE MAN IN THE MIDDLE

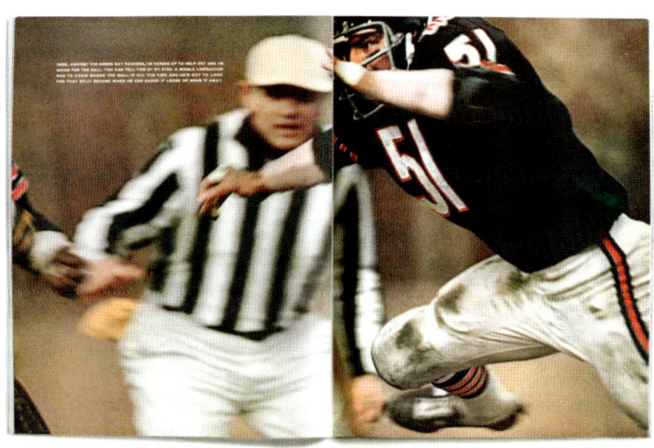

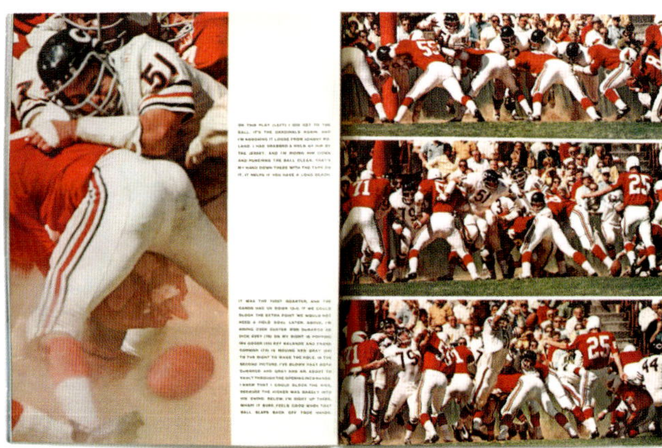

Monster in Motion

DICK BUTKUS

Photograph by NEIL LEIFER, December 14, 1969

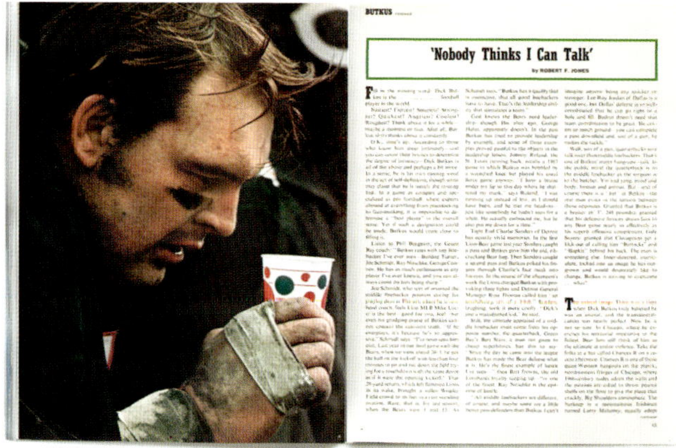
'Nobody Thinks I Can Talk'

FOR FOUR GAMES Neil Leifer shadowed Dick Butkus, following him through the lens on every snap, and came away with a new appreciation of the Bears' middle linebacker. The best defenders will get run out of the play every now and then, but "even when Butkus was blocked, he ended up around the ball," Leifer says. Green Bay quarterback Bart Starr had his own view of Butkus over the years, and gave his assessment to writer Robert F. Jones: "He's the finest example of hustle I've seen." The one misfire on this slide is its label: As the bit of yellow jersey suggests, this game is against the Packers, not the Cardinals.

Football: Chicago Bears Dick Butkus in action vs St. Louis Cardinals.

SI/CHICAGO

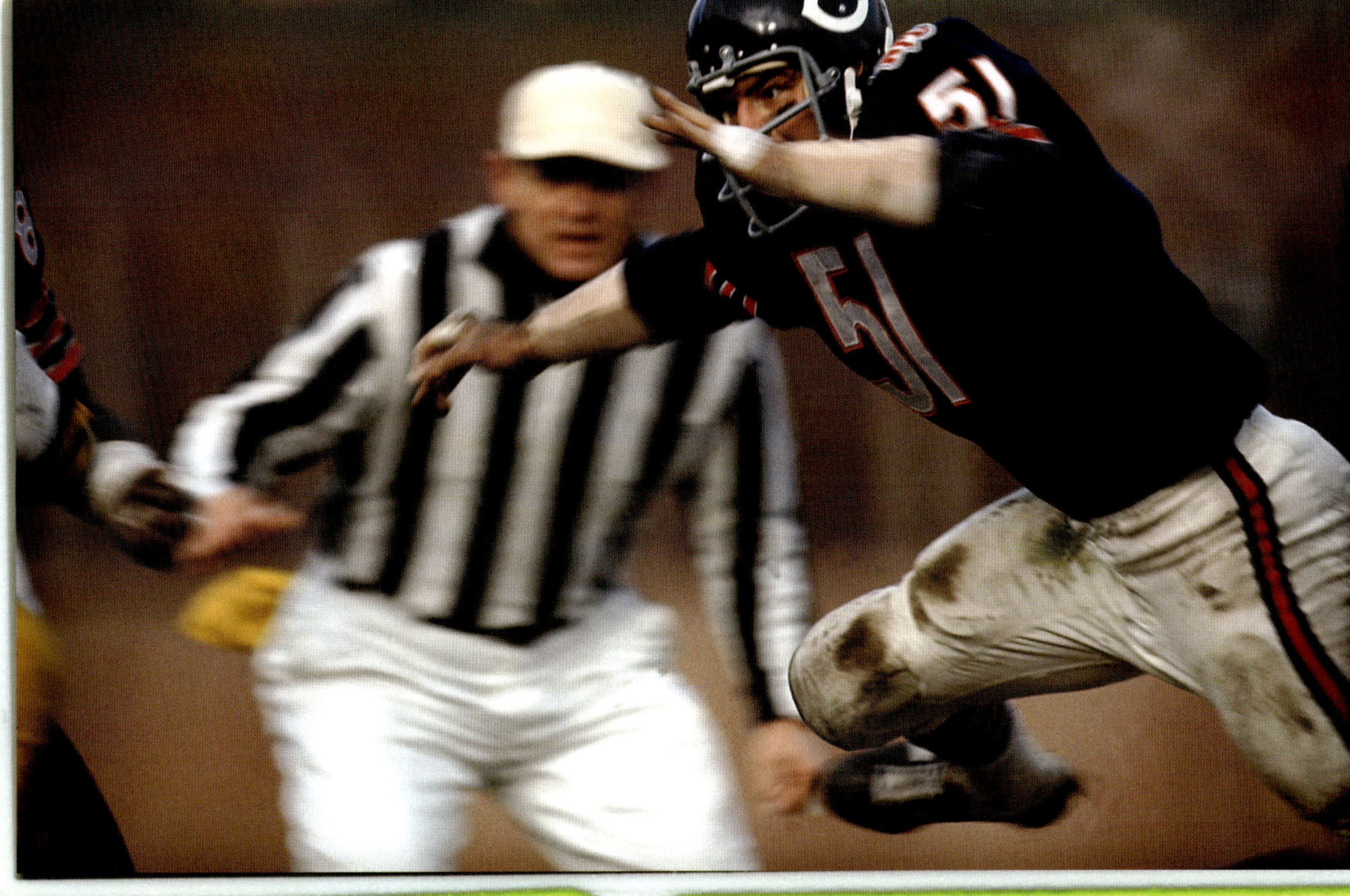

X14397

12-23-74

9-21-70

9-6-93

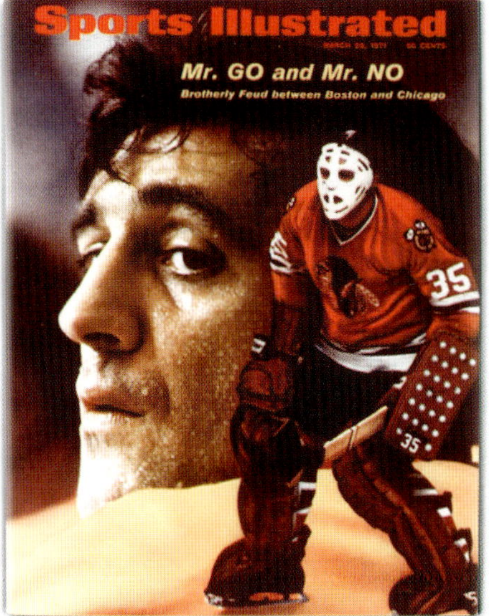

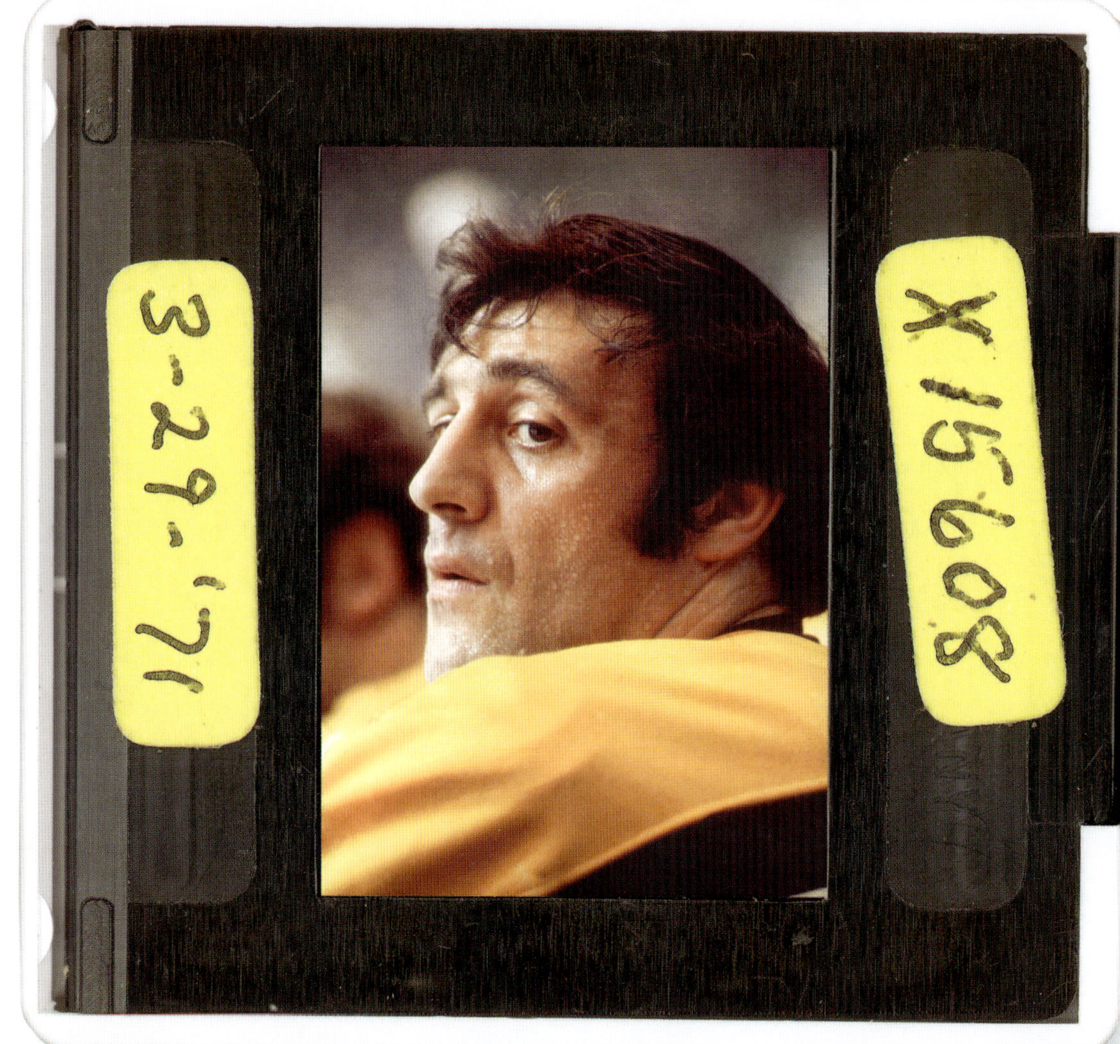

Deep Background

PHIL ESPOSITO

Photograph by TONY TRIOLO, February 19, 1971

TODAY YOU CAN CUT and paste a photo with a few computer clicks, but creating covers like these was once a labor-intensive process. First a person known as a "color separator" would convert a photo into four films, in the basic colors used in printing: cyan, magenta, yellow and black. Then another craftsman, a "stripper," would cut a mask of the main image (say, a goalie or a car or Don Drysdale), and use that mask to make plates of the image in each of the four colors. The process took up to eight hours. Strippers were rendered obsolete by computers in the mid-1980s. Color separators started to disappear in the late '90s with the rise of digital photography—not unlike slides themselves.

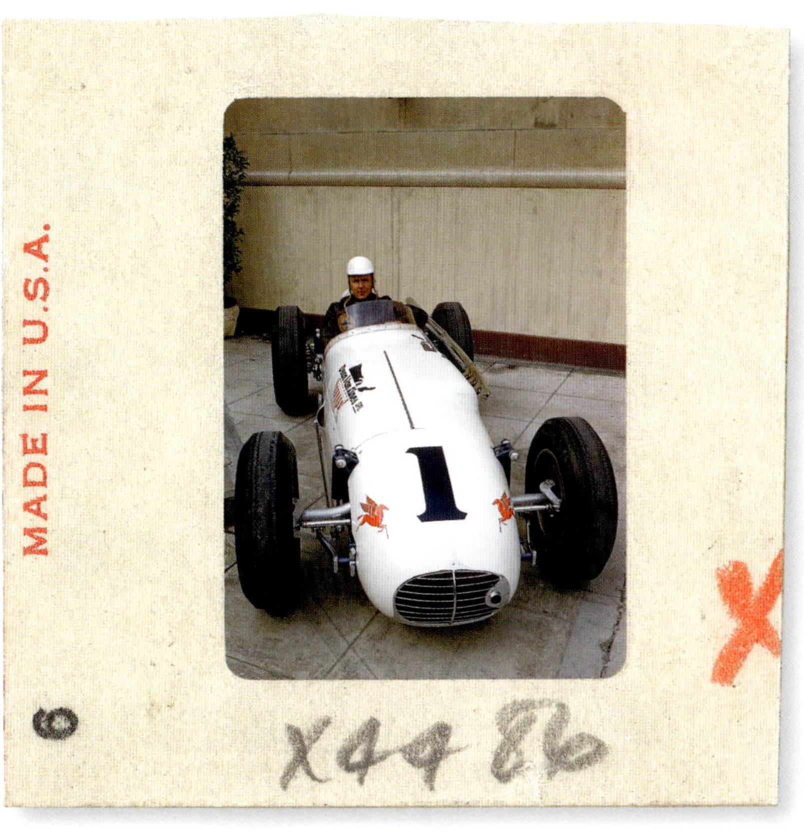

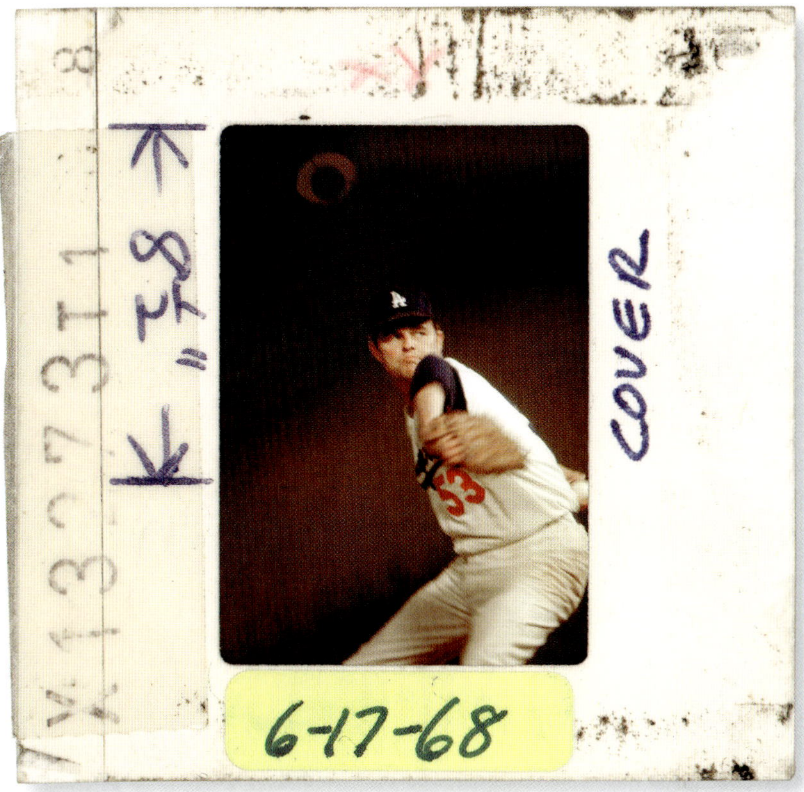

JIMMY BRYAN
Photograph by PHIL BATH, April 11, 1957

DON DRYSDALE
Photograph by SHEEDY & LONG, June 4, 1968

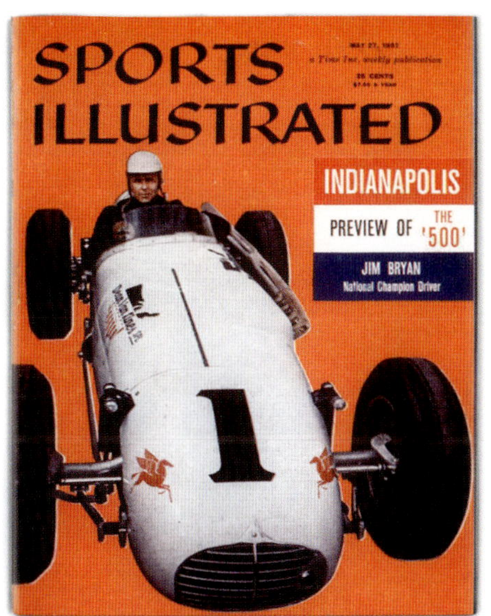

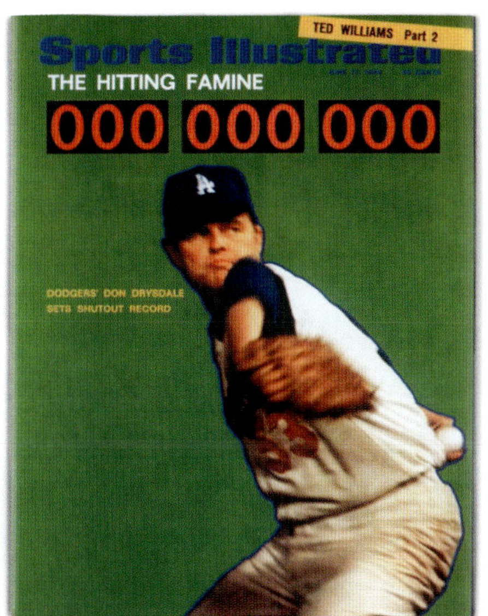

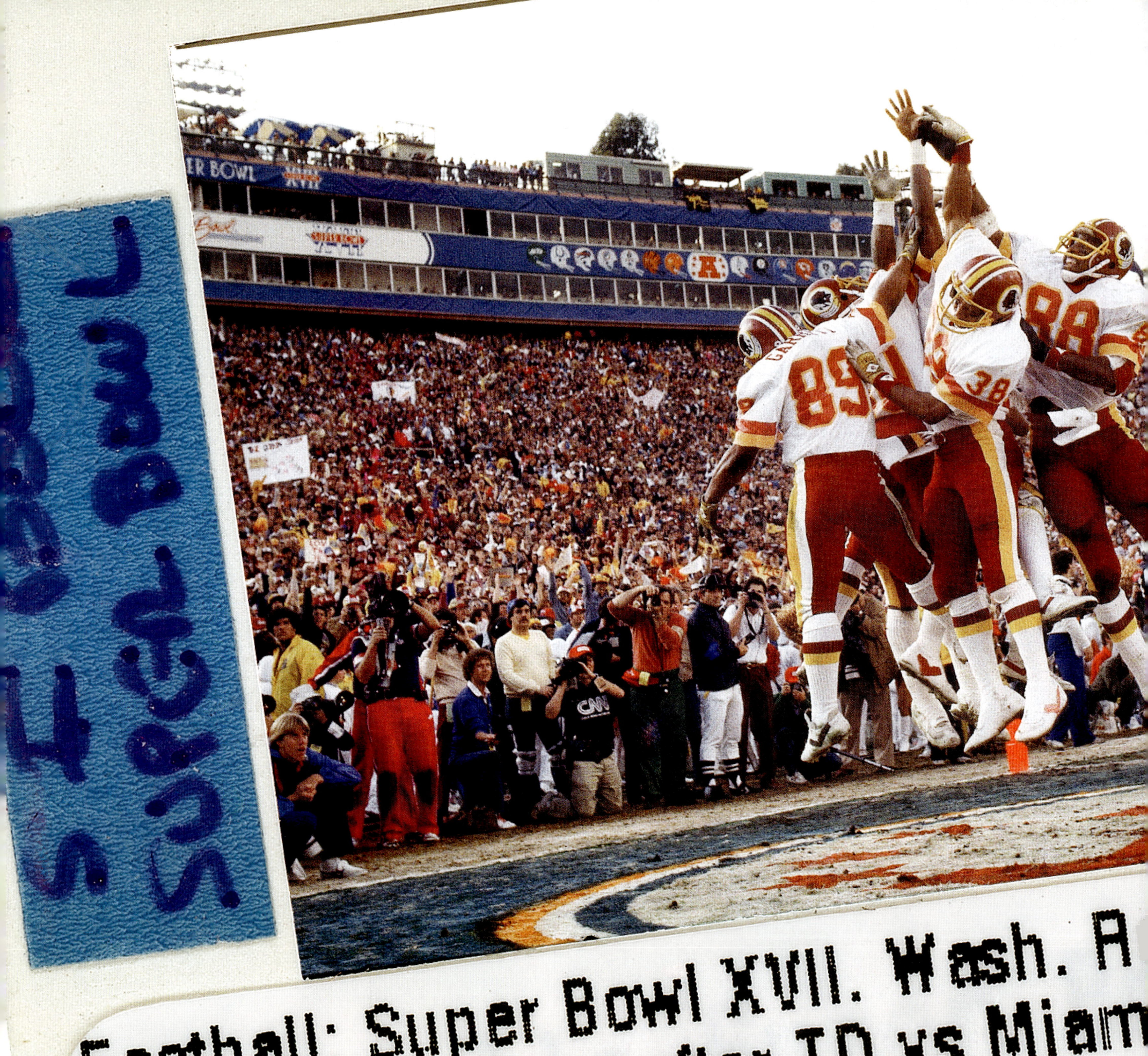

Football: Super Bowl XVII. Wash. R
players victorious after TD vs Miam
Redskins playe

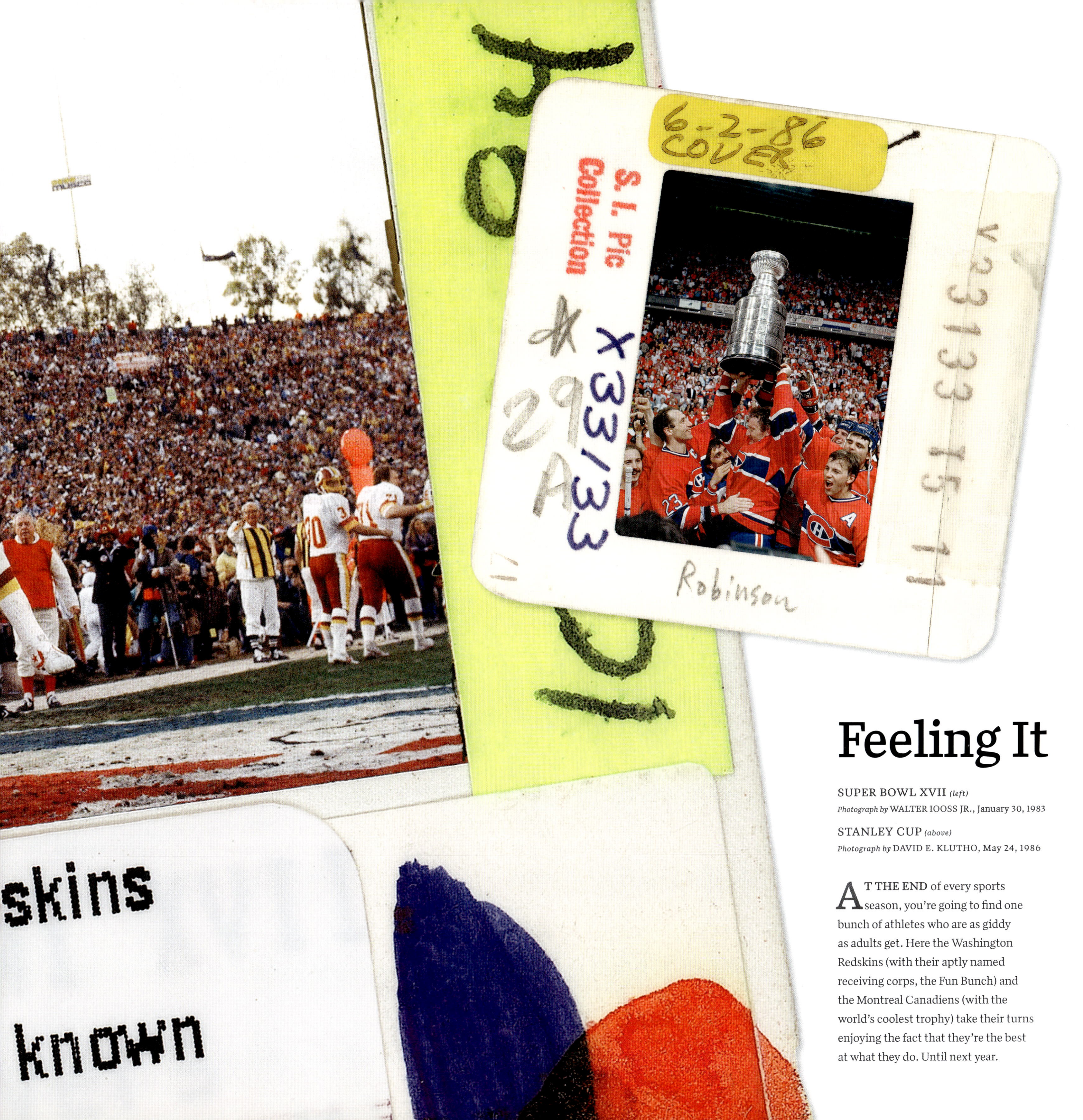

Feeling It

SUPER BOWL XVII *(left)*
Photograph by WALTER IOOSS JR., January 30, 1983

STANLEY CUP *(above)*
Photograph by DAVID E. KLUTHO, May 24, 1986

AT THE END of every sports season, you're going to find one bunch of athletes who are as giddy as adults get. Here the Washington Redskins (with their aptly named receiving corps, the Fun Bunch) and the Montreal Canadiens (with the world's coolest trophy) take their turns enjoying the fact that they're the best at what they do. Until next year.

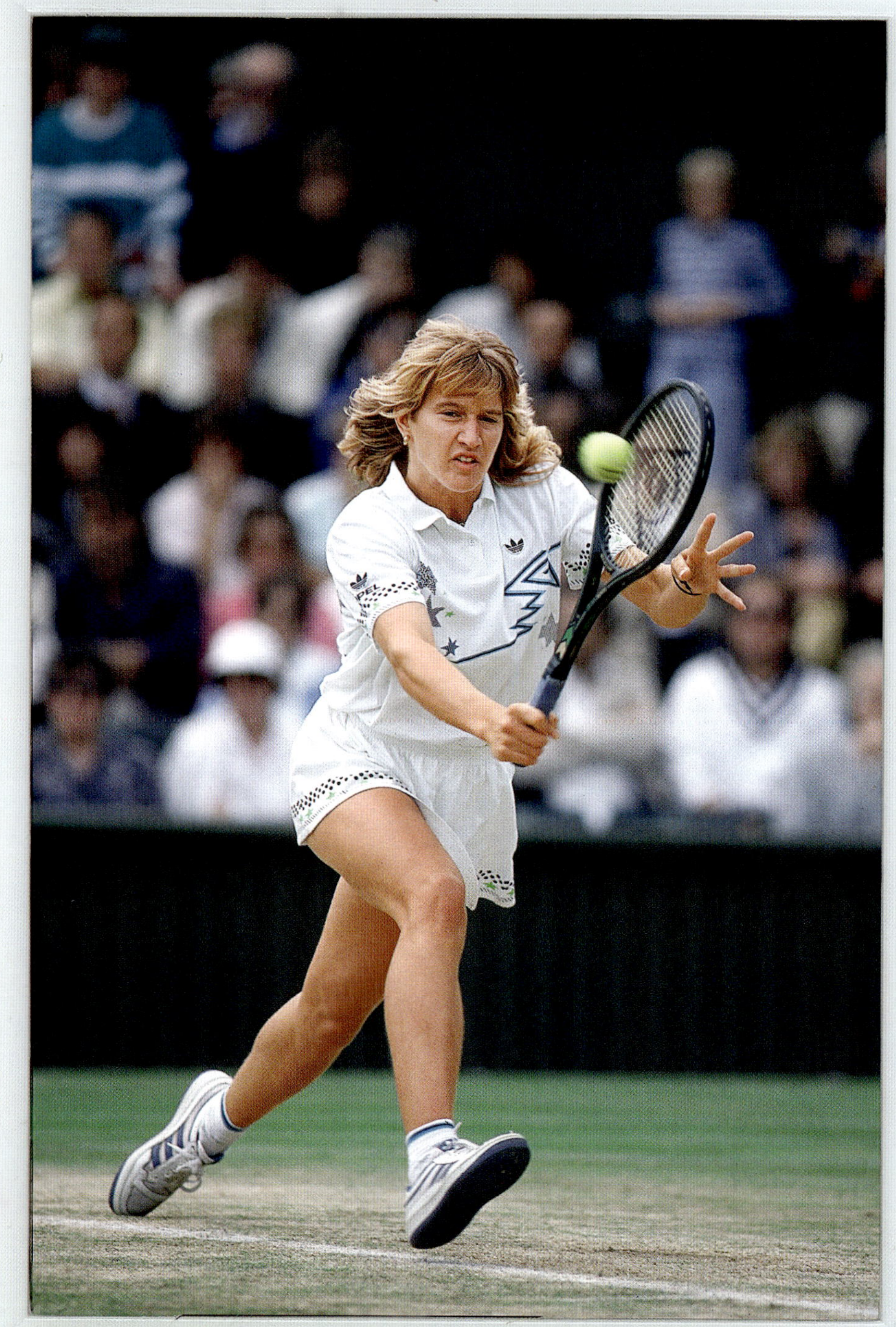
CUT II
TENNIS 128 A
20
X36806
TAKE 5 ROLL 4
8-29-88
FINAL VS. G. NAV.

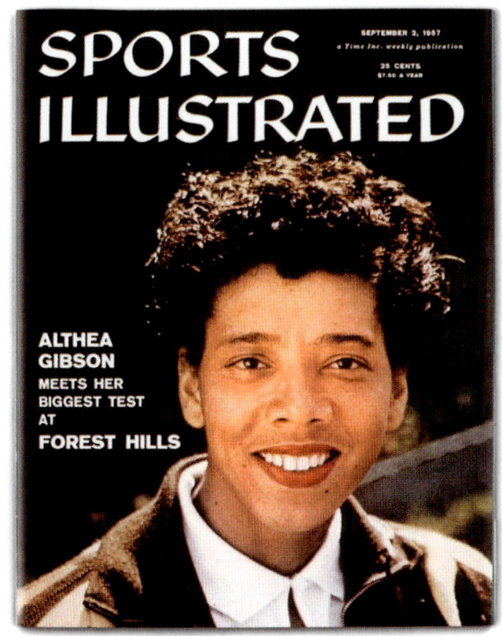

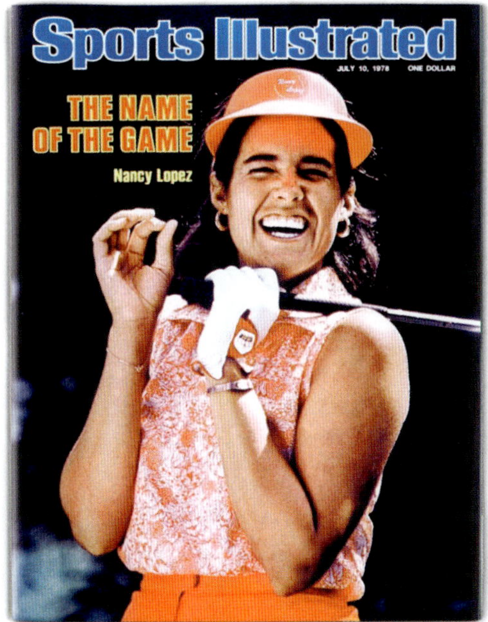

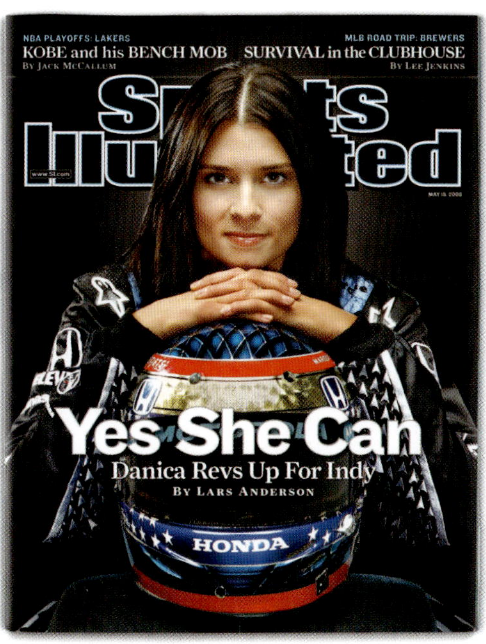

Front Page News

STEFFI GRAF

Photograph by STEVE POWELL, July 2, 1988

THE SPORT OF TENNIS has produced the most appearances by women on the SI cover—including this one of the great Althea Gibson in 1957 *(above left)*, the first African-American to win Wimbledon, the French Open and also the U.S. Open. Steffi Graf, shown here defeating Martina Navratilova (or NAV in slide shorthand) for the first of her seven Wimbledon championships, made her first cover later that year, after taking the U.S. Open to complete the '88 Grand Slam. (She would have two more covers after that.) But other sports, too, have contributed cover girls. Golf gave us the dominant Nancy Lopez, who won 48 LPGA tour events. And racing delivered Danica Patrick to a 2008 cover, a month after she became the first woman to win an IndyCar race.

The Greatest Fight of All

ALI vs. FOREMAN

Photograph by TONY TRIOLO, October 30, 1974

FOR THEIR RUMBLE IN THE JUNGLE in Zaire, it was expected that Muhammad Ali would bob about the ring against the frightening and favored George Foreman. Instead, Ali famously went to the "rope-a-dope," as he would dub it, first inviting Foreman to flail himself into exhaustion and then unleashing his fists in the eighth round. "In the sad business of dispatching a hulk," George Plimpton wrote, "he did it quickly and crisply." Decades later that hulk would make an unlikely return, as would this photo (see yellow stickers), when Foreman fought Evander Holyfield in 1991 and beat Michael Moorer in '94.

Sports Illustrated
NOVEMBER 11, 1974

BREAKING A DATE FOR THE DANCE

All through his training Ali had promised the fancy footwork that would elude Foreman's power, but he had a secret plan that stunned them all—and especially the champion

by GEORGE PLIMPTON

It is hard to imagine what the extraordinary events in the predawn hours under a pale African moon in Zaïre are going to do to the future of boxing. Kids who for years in the backlots of the world have emulated the flamboyant and graceful style of their idol, Muhammad Ali, the butterfly who floats and stings like a bee, will now imagine themselves coming off their stools and standing stolidly and flat-footed in the corner of the ring, or, more extreme, lolling back against the ropes, their upper torsos out over the press-row typewriters at the angle of someone looking out his window to see if there's a cat on his roof. For such were the Ali tactics that surprised everyone—including the men in his own corner and proved insoluble to George Foreman, the heavily favored heavyweight champion, leading him to destruction as surely as the big cartoon wolf, licking his chops, is tricked into some extravagantly ghastly trap laid by a sly mouse.

The witnesses to all this, those lucky enough to see what will surely be considered one of the greatest fights in boxing history, began to fill the 60,000-capacity stadium at nightfall, hours before the main event scheduled for 4 a.m. They had come from all parts of a country that had thought of little else for a month. Both fighters had their strong partisans in Zaïre, and many among the crowd were *féticheurs*, the witch doctors of Kinshasa who often turn up at sporting events on behalf of clients, handsomely paid to try to influence the outcome. Indeed, among many Zaïrians the rumor was that Muhammad Ali himself had gone to one of the best *féticheurs* in town, perhaps even the Pygmy reputedly used by President Mobutu, and had paid a considerable sum for a spell to be cast against George Foreman. The odds were almost 3 to 1 against Ali and it seemed the sensible thing to do. The spell was supposed to manifest itself in the form of a beautiful girl "with slightly trembling hands" who would clasp Foreman's hand in some chance meeting—like Blind Pew passing the Black Spot—and the strength would slowly drain from him.

The *féticheurs* (often with their clients packed around them in adjacent seats) occasionally raise their voices in a loud, humming incantation. They wear a

continued

Saying "Now it's my turn," Ali flashed a series of quick blows that sent Foreman tumbling.

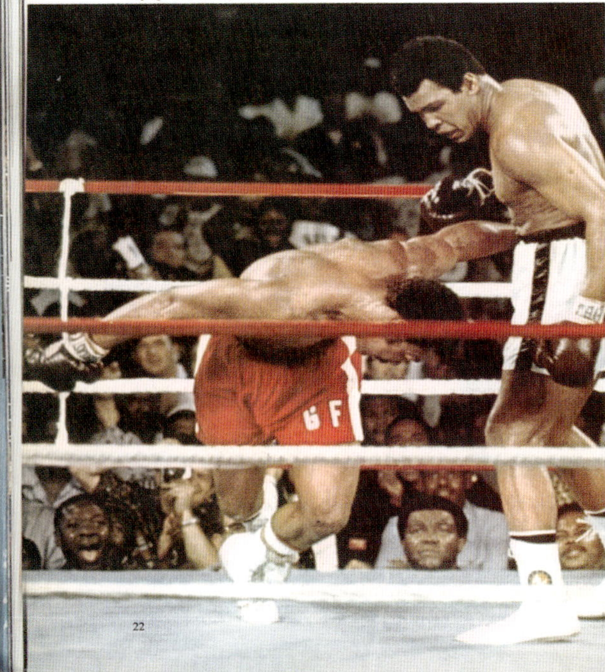

Still dazed and desperately tired, Foreman started a ponderous attempt to roll over and get up as Referee Zack Clayton tolled the count.

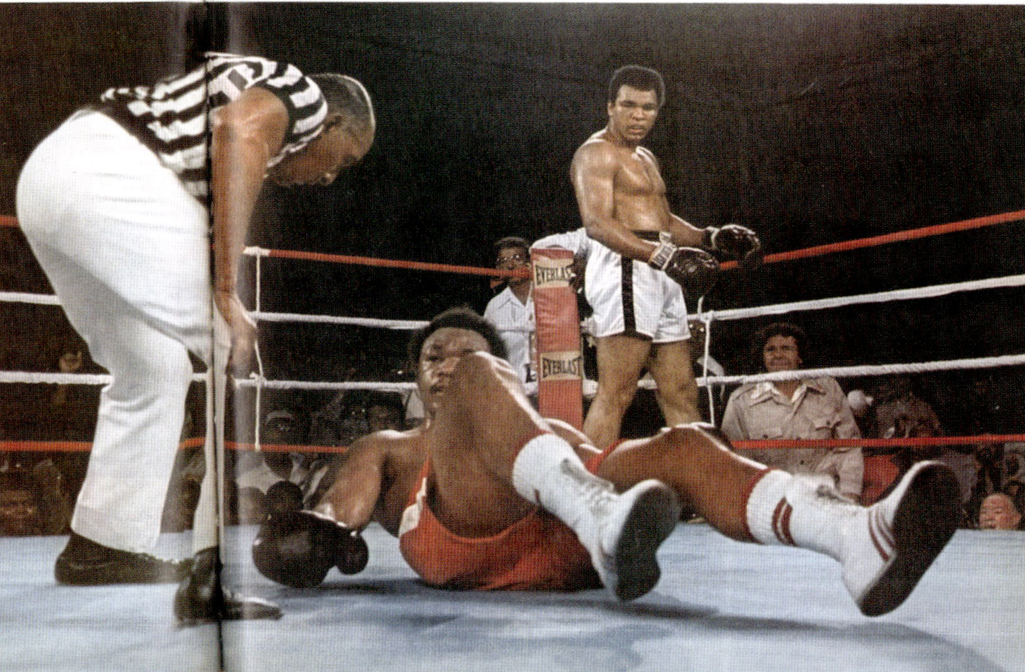

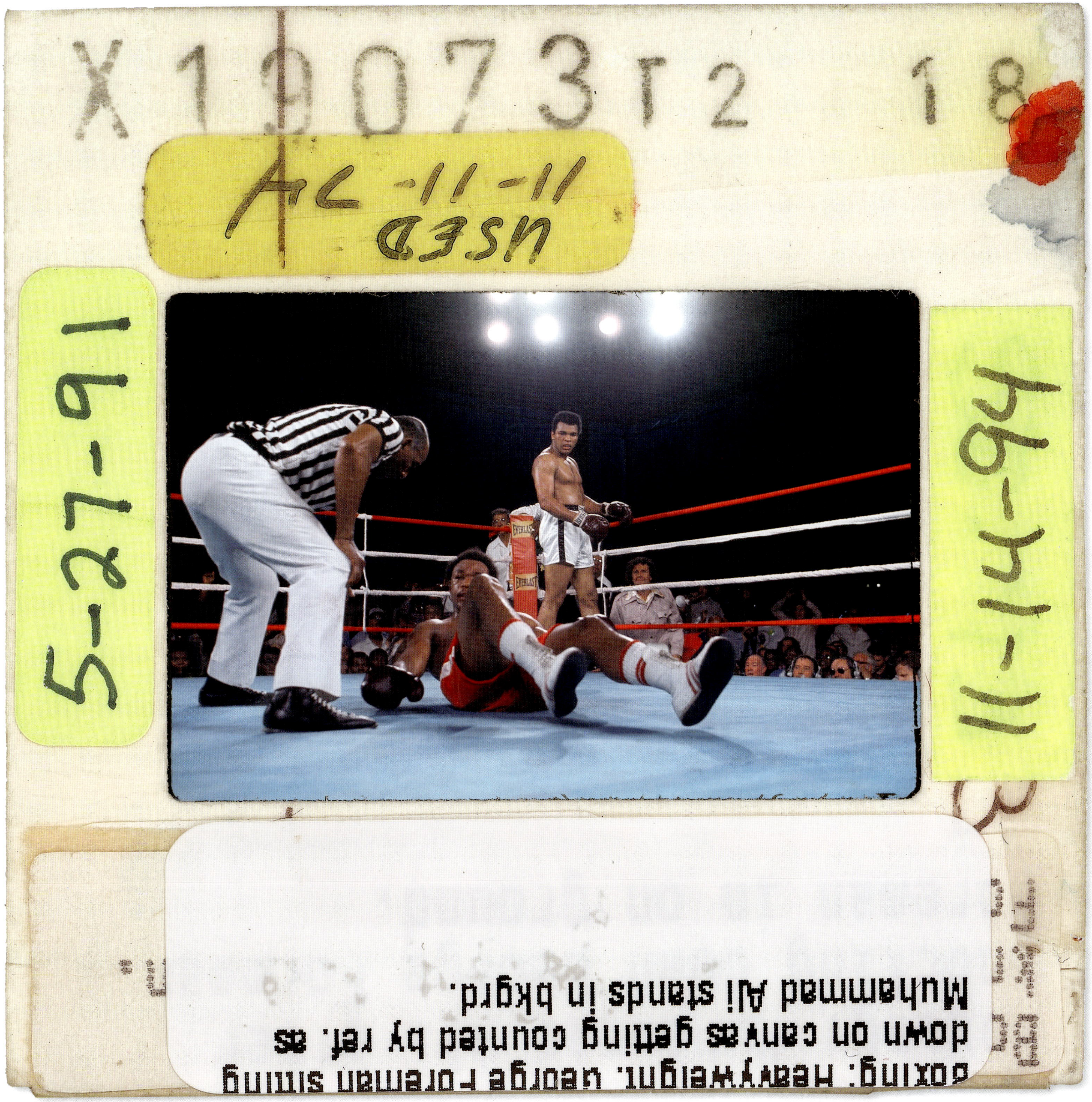

X19073 T2 18

AL-11-11
USED

5-27-91

11-14-94

Boxing: Heavyweight. George Foreman sitting down on canvas getting counted by ref. as Muhammad Ali stands in bkgrd.

27 TEXAS FAN

Original +

8

X21888T2

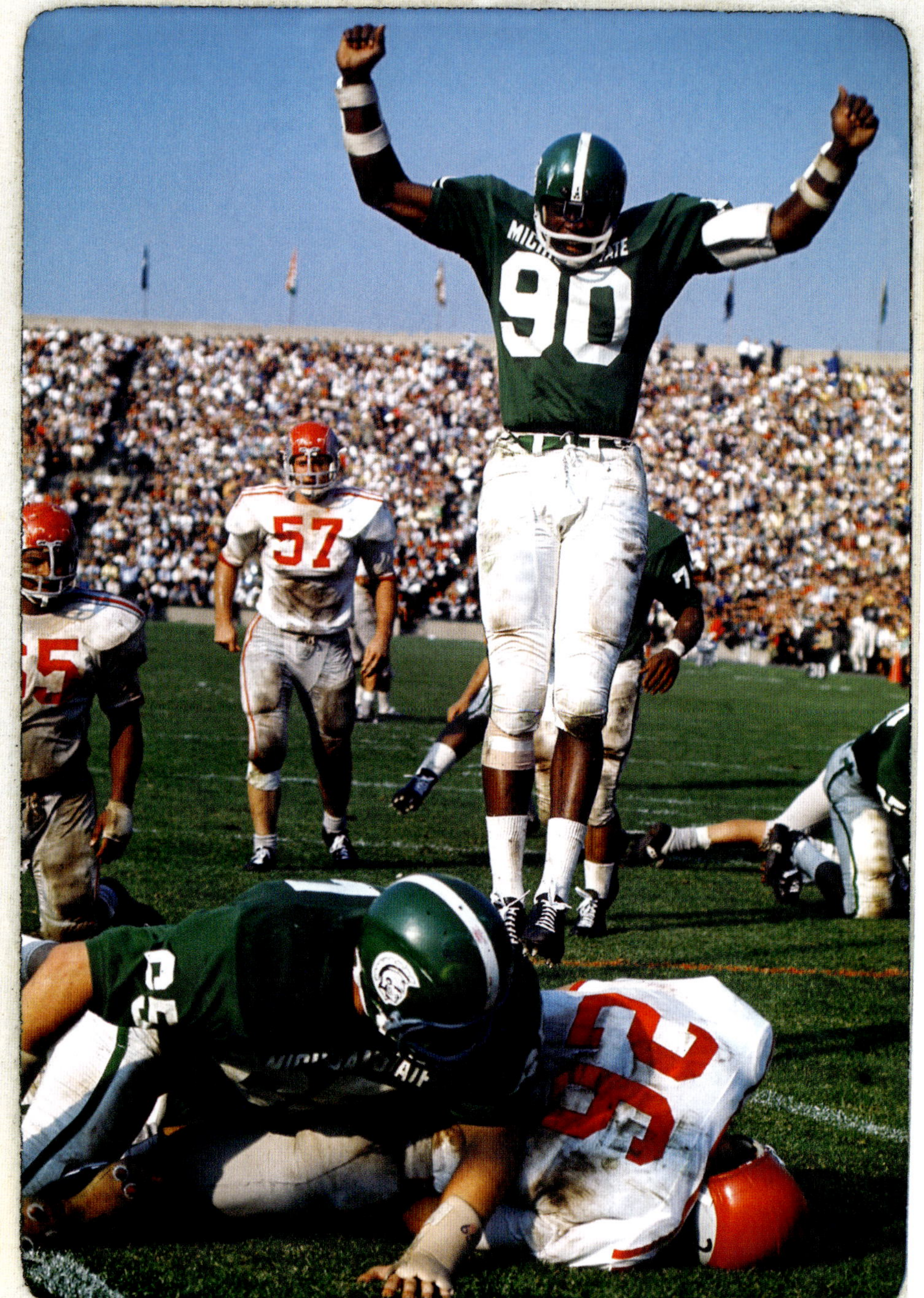

SPORTS ILLUSTRATED
017078754

2 WALTER IOOSS JR.

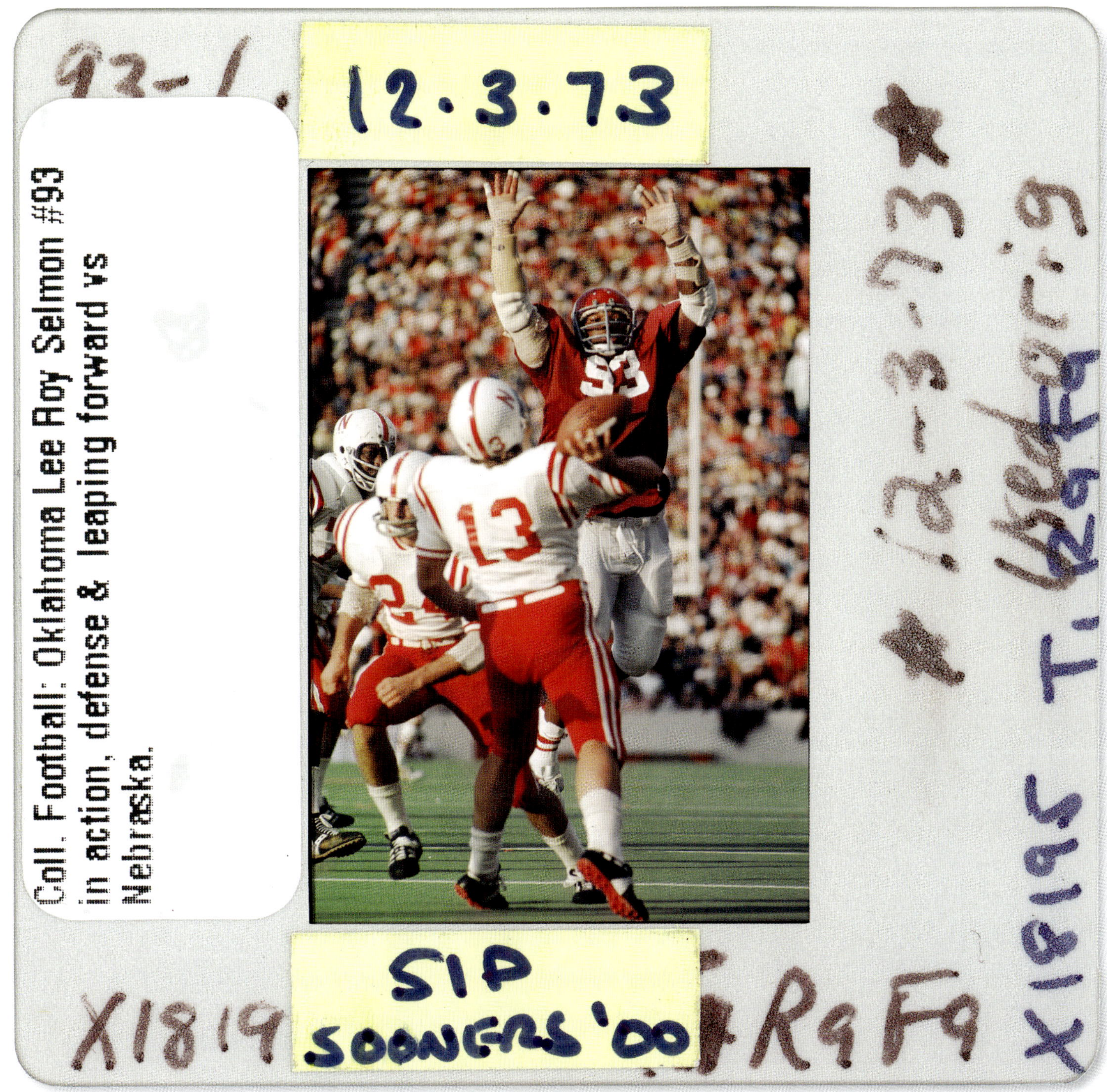

Jumping to Conclusions

GEORGE WEBSTER *(opposite). Photograph by* WALTER IOOSS JR., October 16, 1965 • LEE ROY SELMON *(above). Photograph by* RICH CLARKSON, November 23, 1973

THE SHOT of Lee Roy Selmon is, at least, properly identified and captioned. But what happened with the slide of this other All-America defensive player, Michigan State's George Webster? Best guess: The film was cut from its mount to be computer scanned, then mistakenly placed in another mount that originally housed a "Texas fan" photo also shot by Walter Iooss Jr.

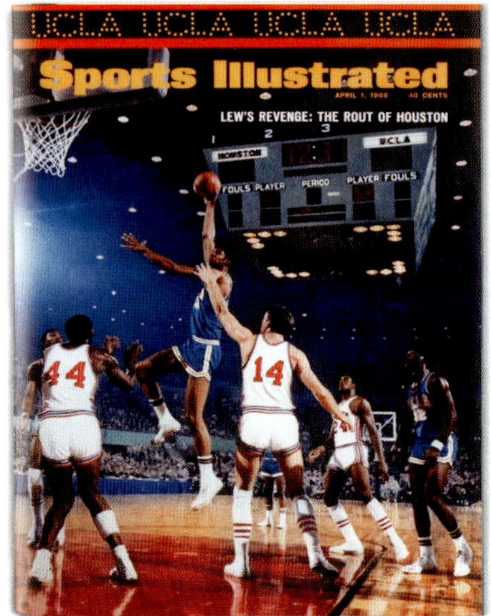

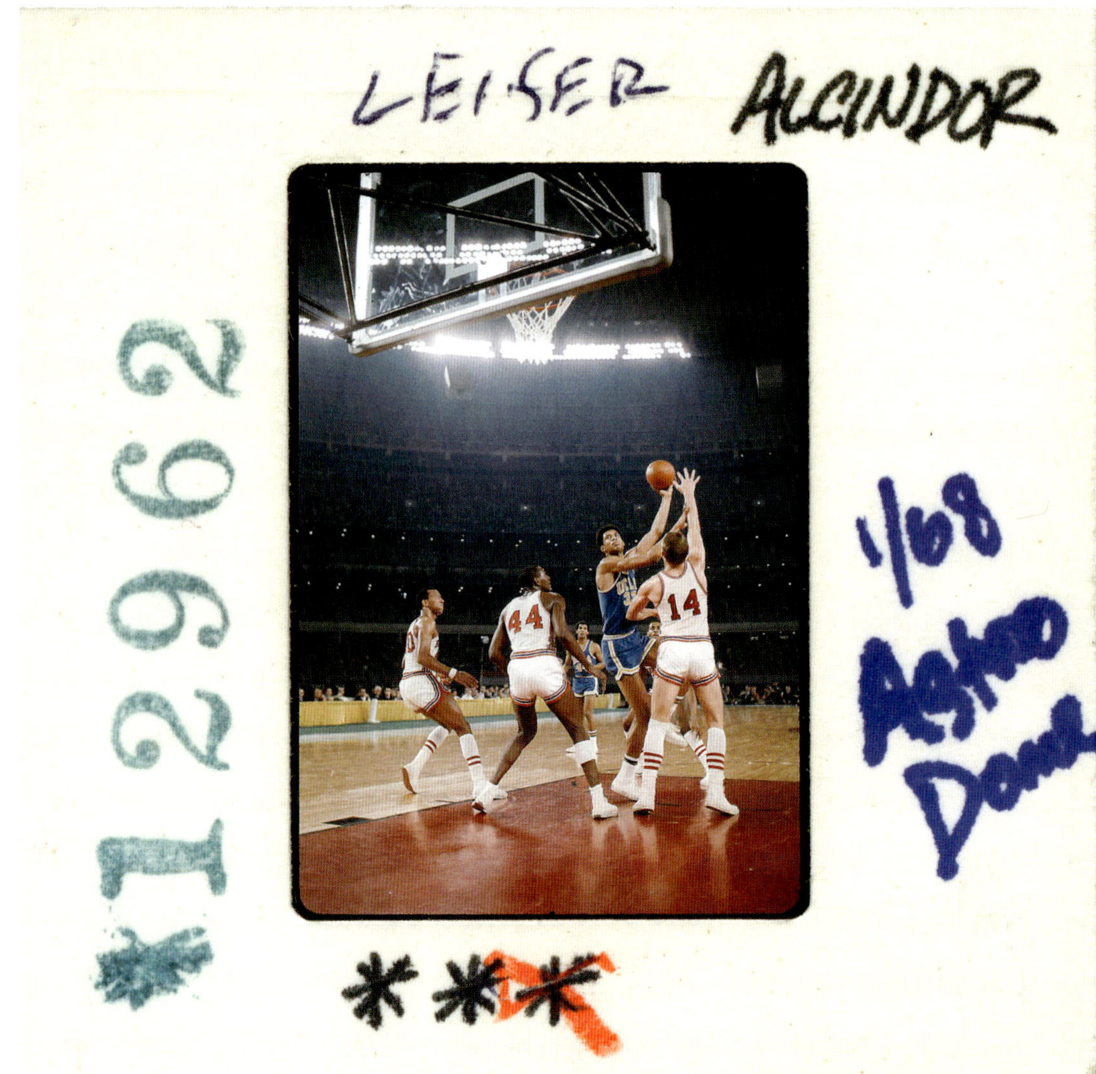

Play It Again, Lew

UCLA vs. HOUSTON
Photographs by NEIL LEIFER, January 20, 1968

THE FIRST NATIONAL TELECAST of a regular-season college basketball game showcased No. 1 UCLA and No. 2 Houston, teams that had met in the previous year's NCAA Final Four and for whom little had changed. (Note how the players and positioning are nearly identical in the above game photo and in the adjacent cover shot of UCLA's 1967 semifinal.) The game took place at the Astrodome, enabling Neil Leifer to shoot with a remote camera above midcourt. Houston won the rematch, but Lew Alcindor's UCLA team still took the '68 NCAA title. After coach John Wooden left in '75, the Bruins would not win it all again until '95, when this bird's-eye view ran in a commemorative issue.

Coll. Basketball: Aerial view of UCLA's Lew Alcindor in action, jump ball, vs Houston's

UCLA '95

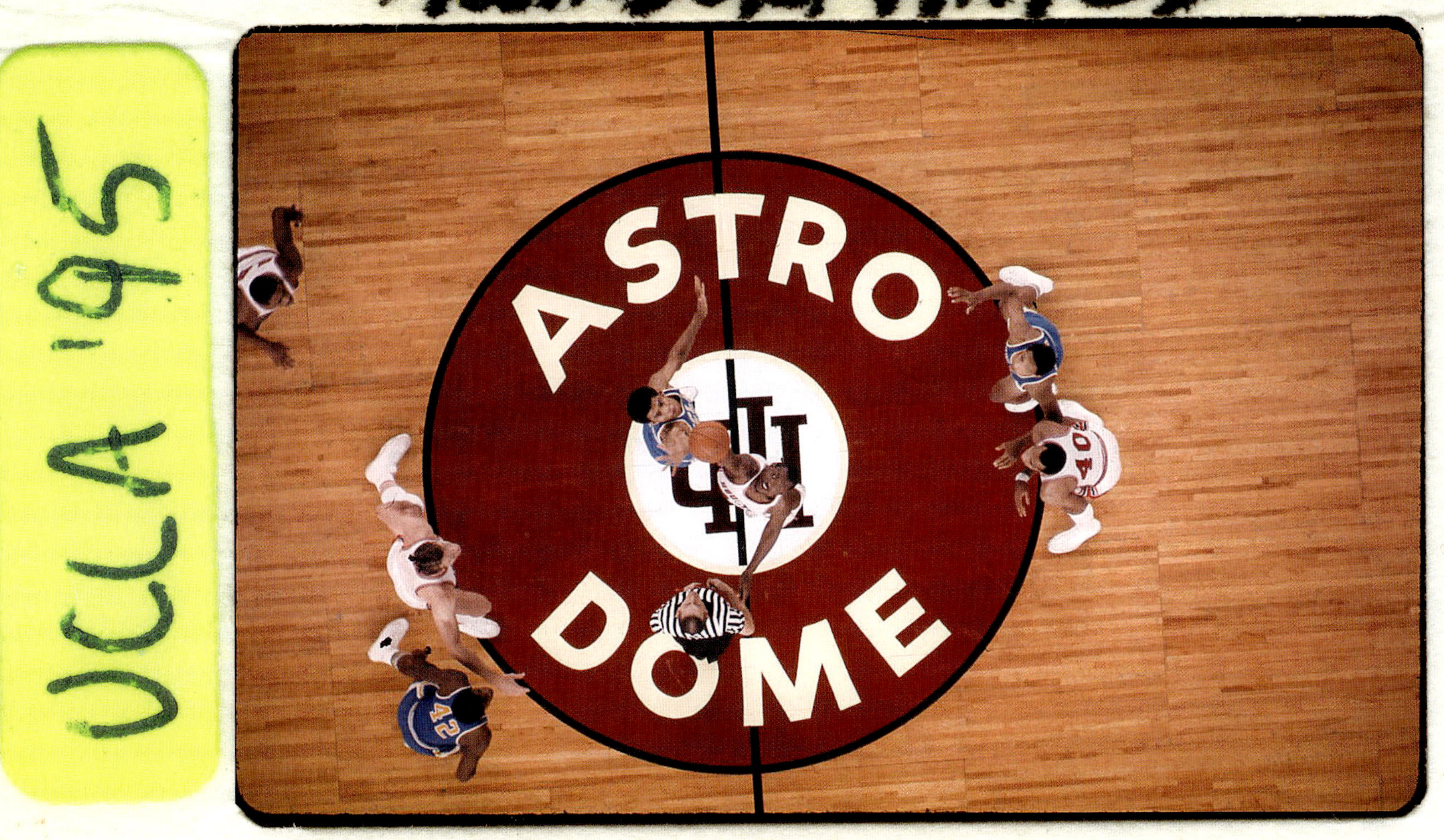

***

1/68

129 62

D88768

4-22-96

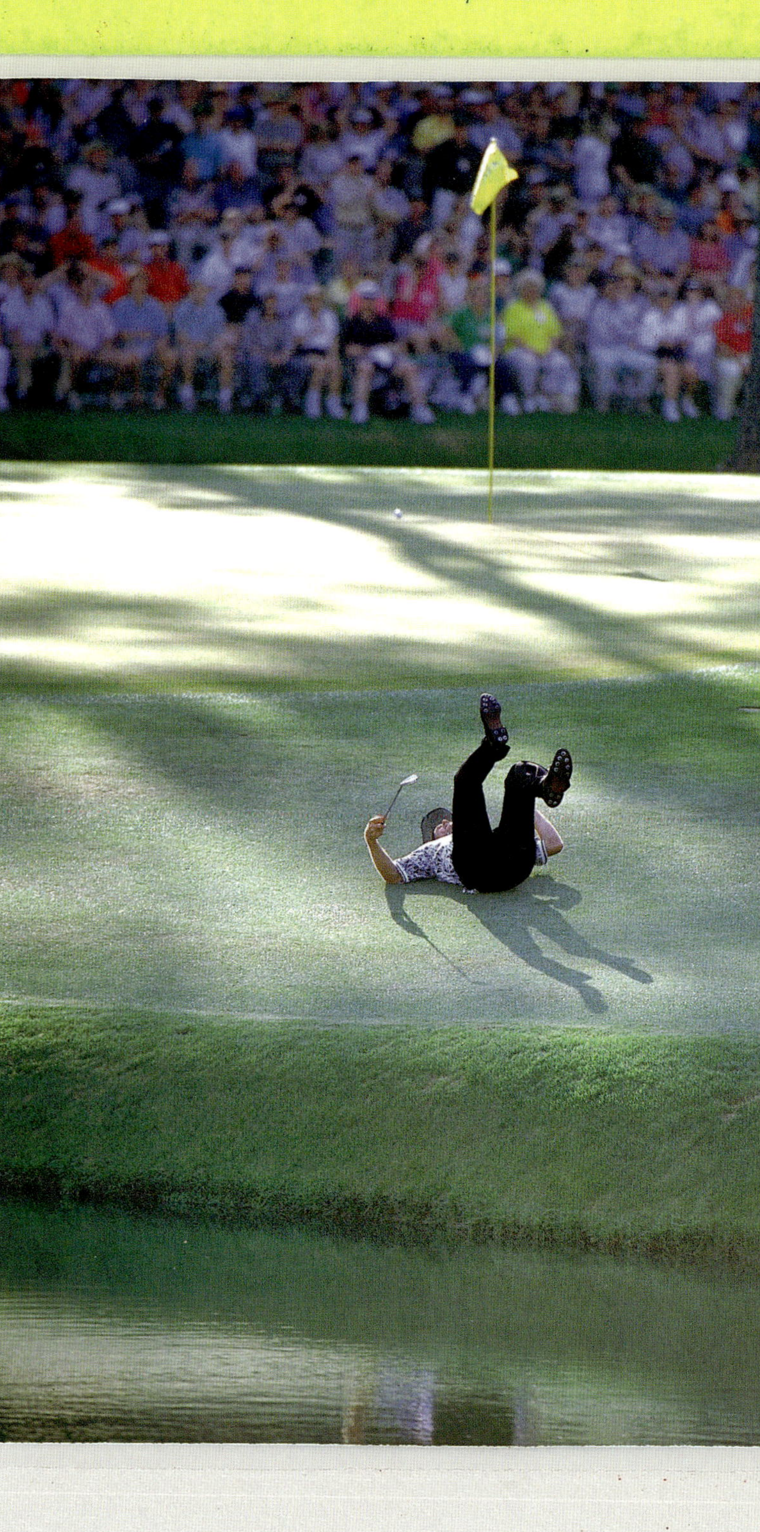

Golf: The Masters. Greg Norman alone, upset, collapses on back after missing chip for eagle;

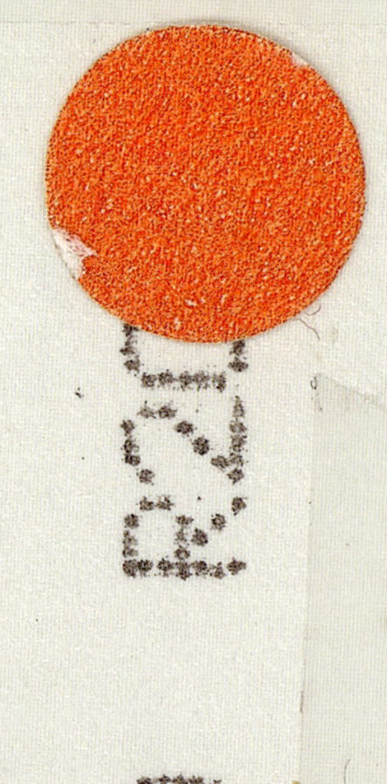

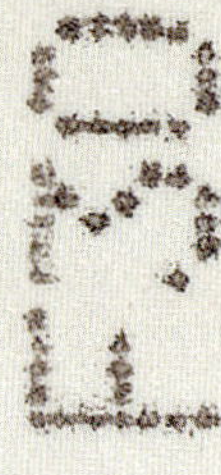

X50551 TK6 F30 R2

Human Error

GREG NORMAN *(opposite)*
Photograph by JACQUELINE DUVOISIN, April 14, 1996

GREG NORMAN AND NICK FALDO *(right)*
Photograph by JOHN BIEVER, April 14, 1996

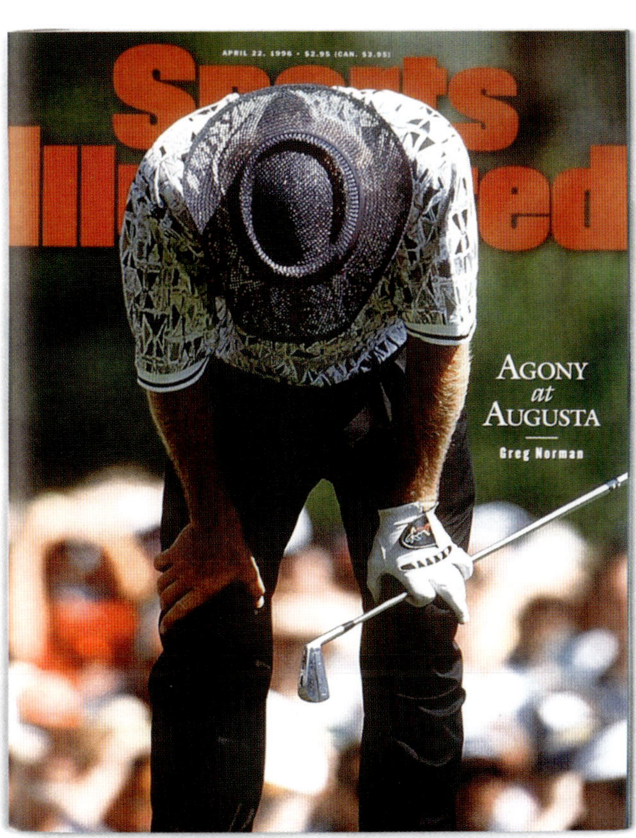

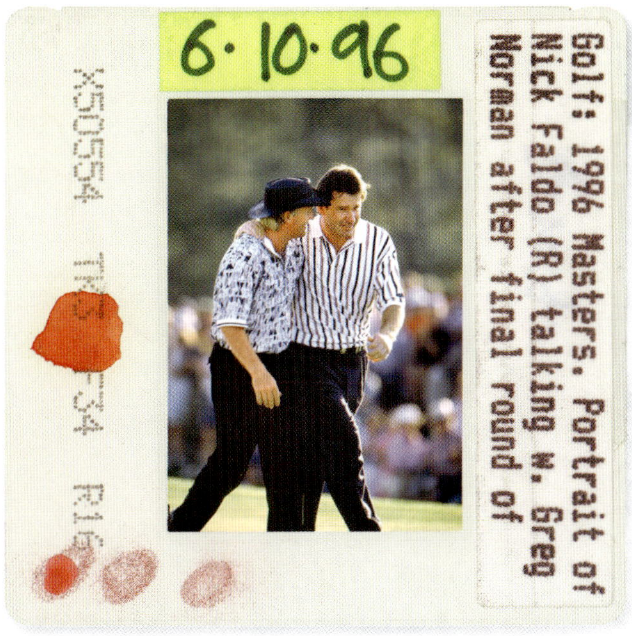

THE COVER is usually the province of winners, but sometimes the real story is the guy who didn't get it done. Of all the collapses in sports history, Greg Norman's at the 1996 Masters may have been the most painful to watch. "Spectators actually looked down, hoping not to make eye contact, as Norman passed among them on his way to the 18th tee," wrote Rick Reilly. Even before this tournament Norman had a star-crossed history in the Masters' final round, but past shortcomings paled when he blew a six-shot lead on Sunday, losing by five to Nick Faldo—a generally aloof player who couldn't help but give the Shark a consoling hug. Perhaps you are asking why we aren't showing here the slide of John Biever's cover shot. Because, with all our systems of archiving and making duplicates, we somehow lost it—soon after the photo appeared on the cover. So on the subject of fallability, let's just say we sympathize.

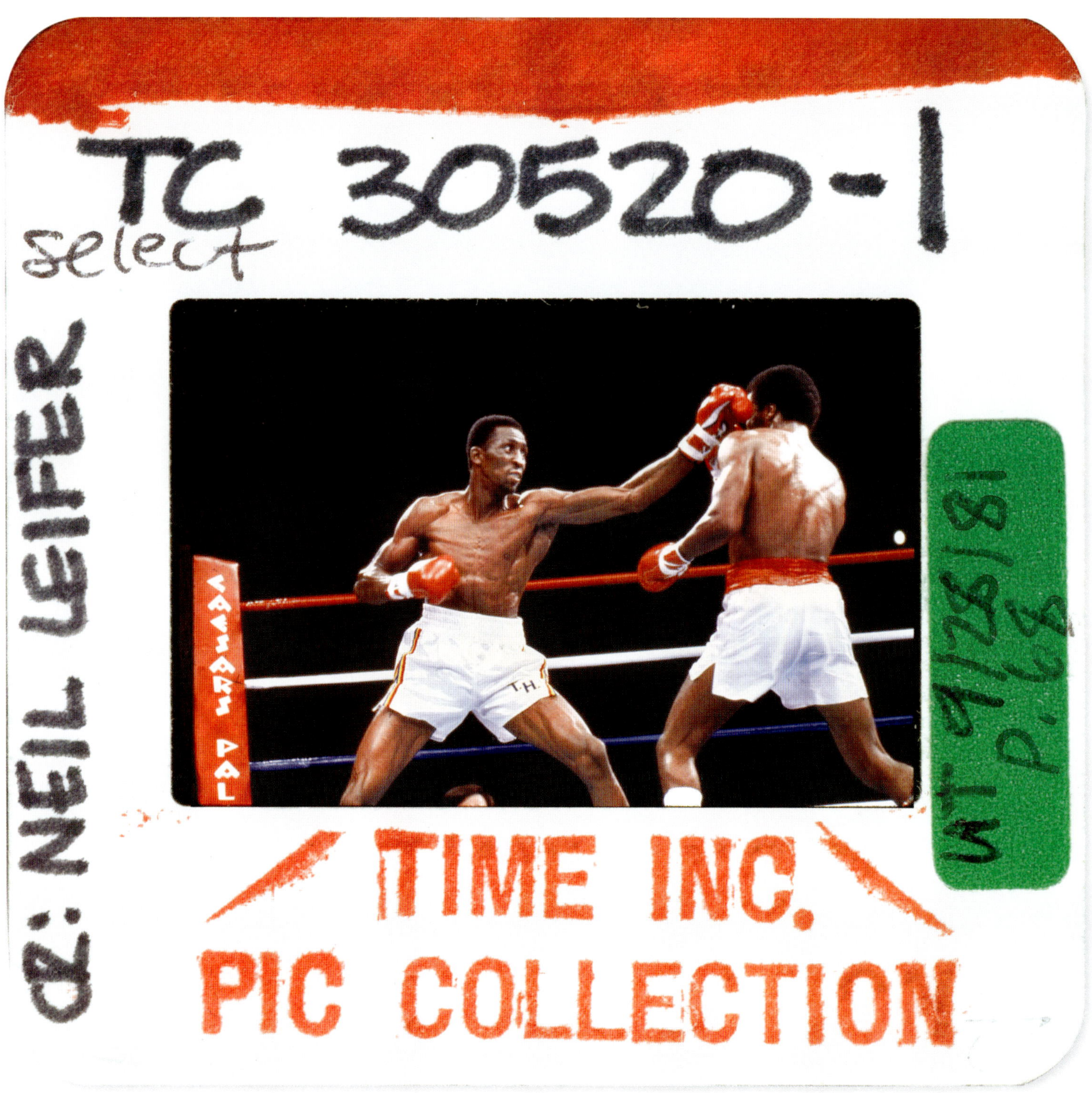

His Sweetest Years

LEONARD VS. HEARNS *(above). Photograph by* NEIL LEIFER, September 16, 1981 • LEONARD VS. DURAN *(opposite). Photograph by* NEIL LEIFER, November 25, 1980

THE EARLY 1980s were electric for boxing and for ringside dwellers like Leifer, and especially for Sugar Ray Leonard. Included in his greatest hits: getting Roberto Durán to lay down his gloves (*"No más!"*) and rallying for a 14th-round TKO of Thomas Hearns.

SI 35th Anniversary Issue

TIME INC PIC COLLECTION

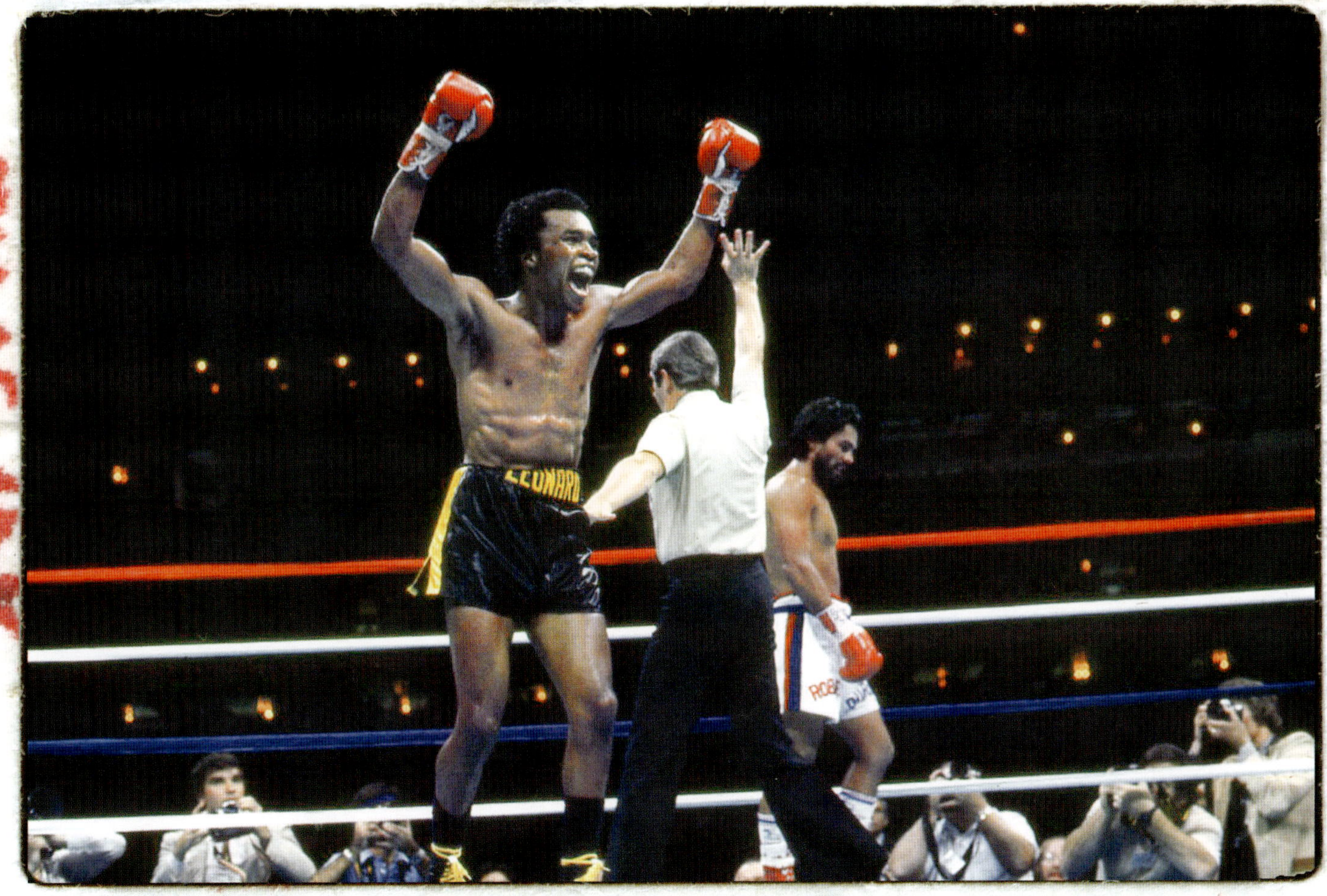

Football: AFC playoffs. Denver Broncos QB John Elway #7 in action, passing for TD vs Cleveland Browns. "The Drive".

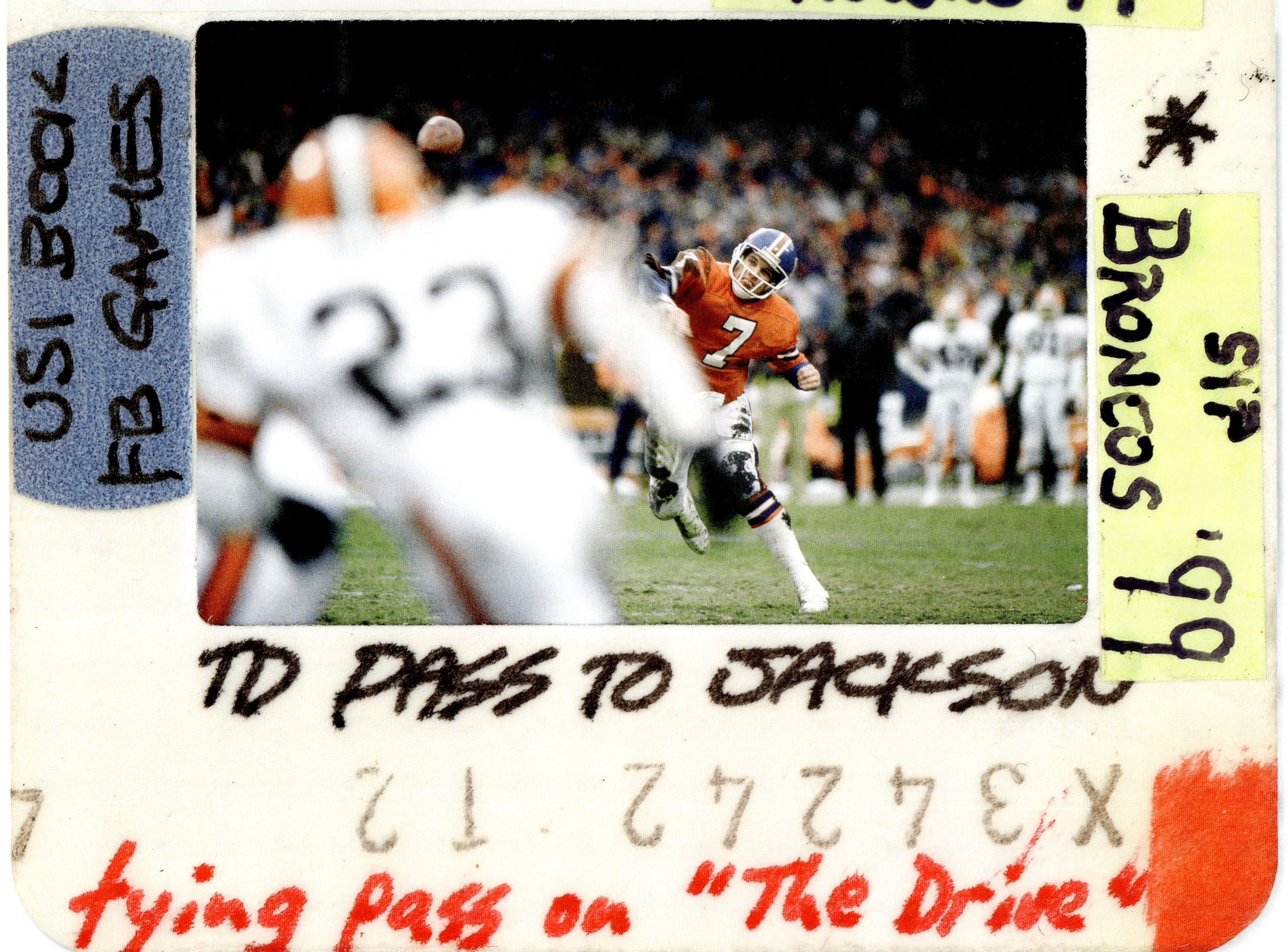

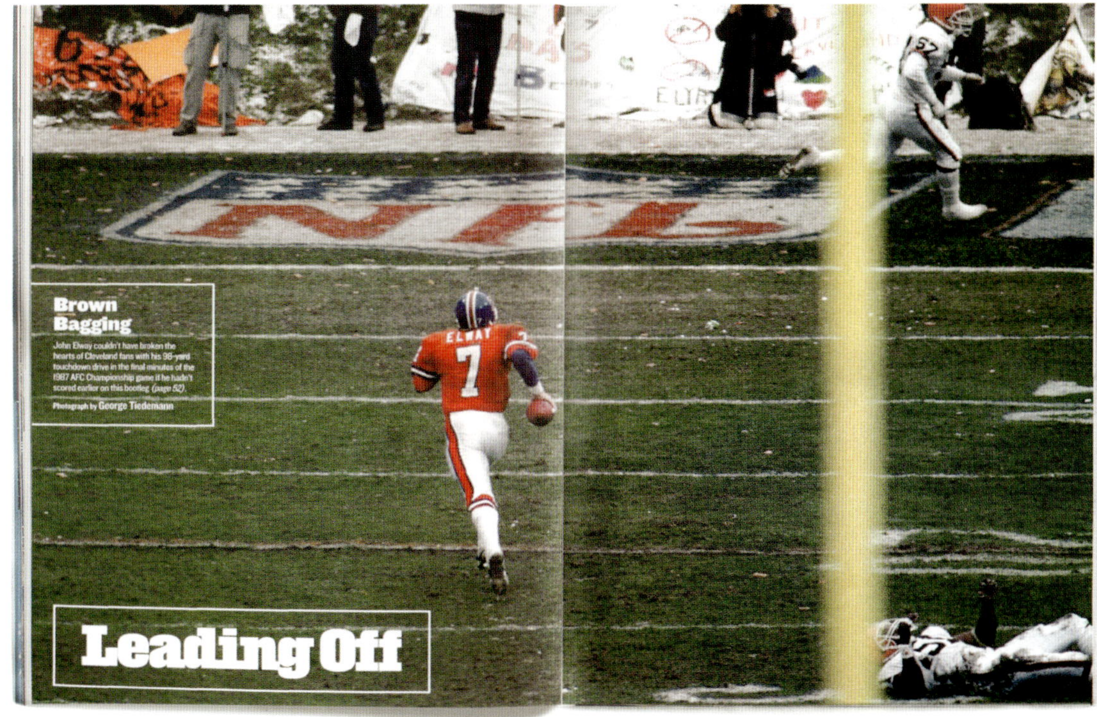

Brown Bagging

John Elway couldn't have broken the hearts of Cleveland fans with his 98-yard touchdown drive in the final minutes of the 1987 AFC Championship game if he hadn't scored earlier on this bootleg *(page 52)*.

Photograph by George Tiedemann

Leading Off

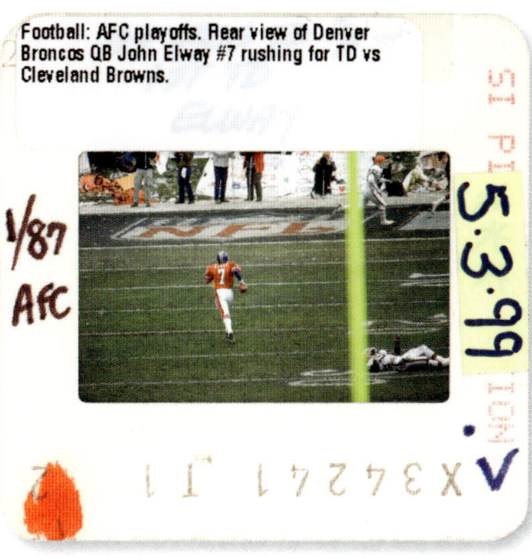

Along for The Ride

JOHN ELWAY *(opposite)*
Photograph by JOHN BIEVER, January 11, 1987

JOHN ELWAY *(above)*
Photograph by GEORGE TIEDEMANN/GT IMAGES, January 11, 1987

WHEN A TEAM marches down the field late in the fourth quarter, a herd of photographers generally goes with it. John Biever's memory of shooting The Drive (as it was christened for posterity) in the 1987 AFC Championship Game is of hustling downfield with five cameras and assorted lenses and jostling for a new spot with every advance of the ball. He reached the end zone in time to snap the Elway TD pass that sent the game to overtime. Soon the Browns fans would be heartbroken. "I felt sorry for them," Biever says, "but that's football." The shot of an Elway scramble from that game ran when the QB retired in '99. The photo of his TD pass was used that year in two SI commemoratives—one celebrating Denver's Super Bowl win, the other welcoming the Browns back to Cleveland after a sad three-year absence.

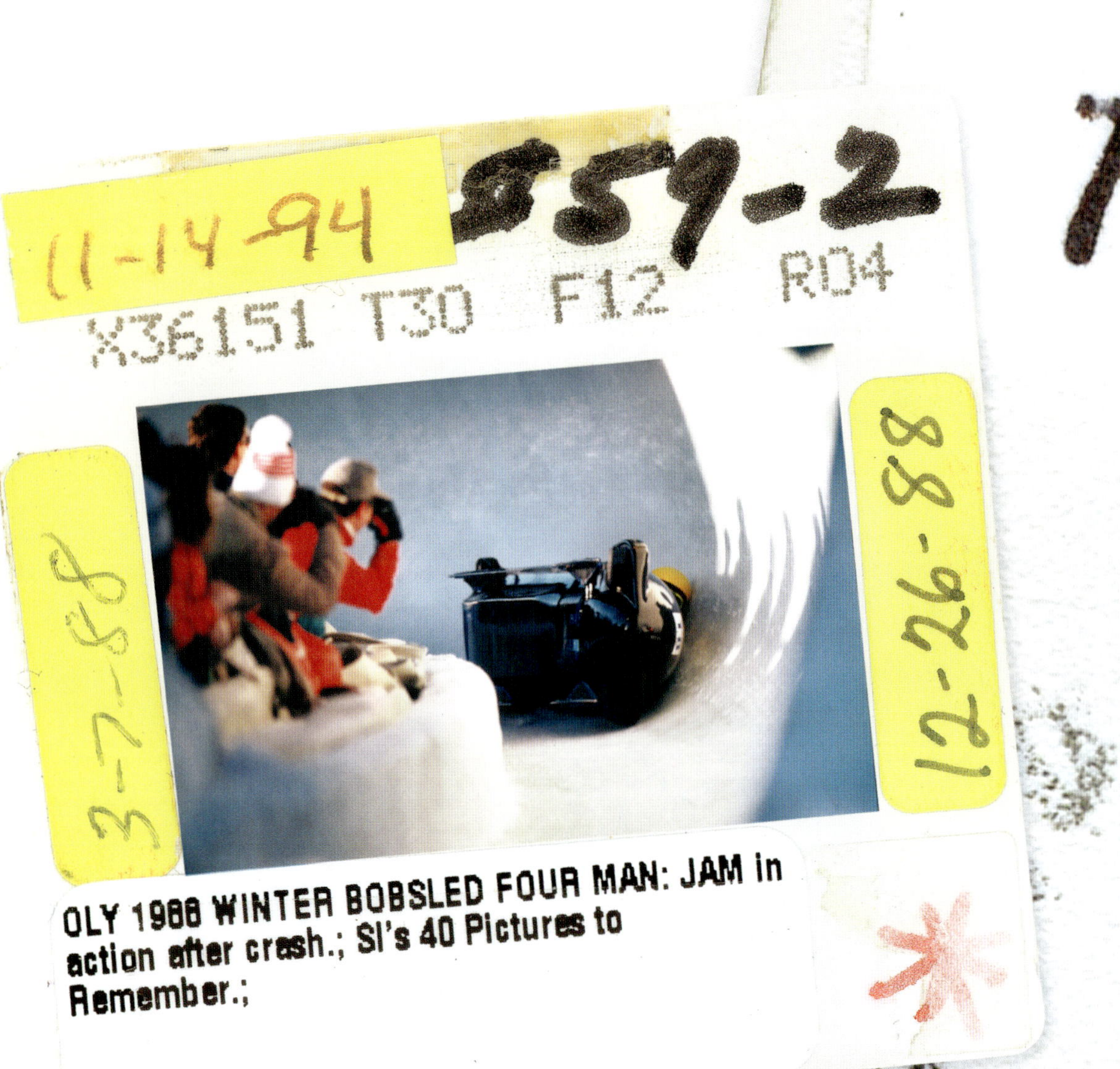

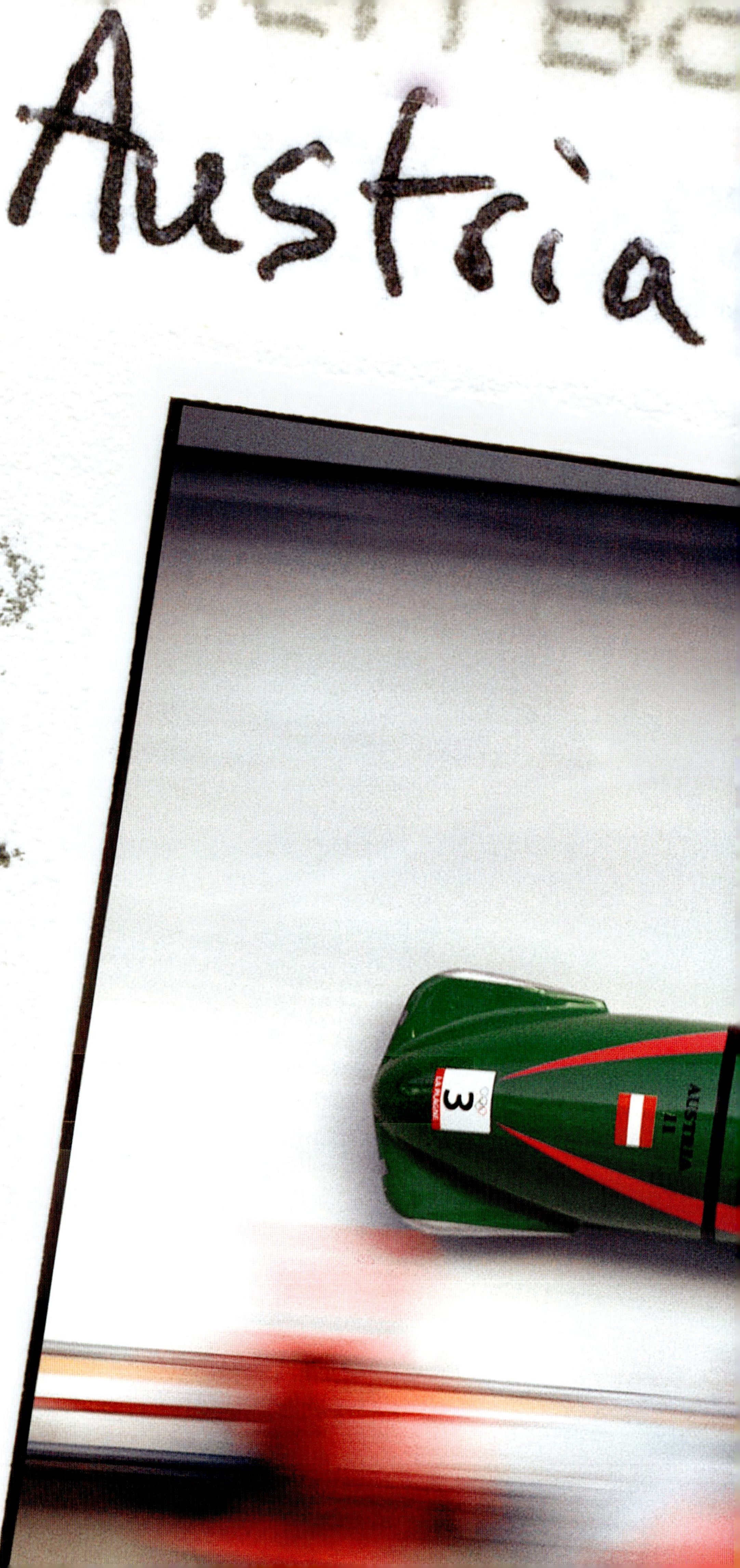

Evidence Of Cool

AUSTRIAN BOBSLED TEAM *(right)*
Photograph by NEIL LEIFER, February 22, 1992

JAMAICAN BOBSLED TEAM *(above)*
Photograph by BILL EPPRIDGE, February 28, 1988

THE AUSTRIANS won Olympic gold in 1992, but the photo of a crash-prone Jamaican team has collected more gold stickers, signifying re-use in the magazine. After all, medals are won in every Olympics, but the tropical island's first foray into bobsledding became a rare pop-culture phenomenon.

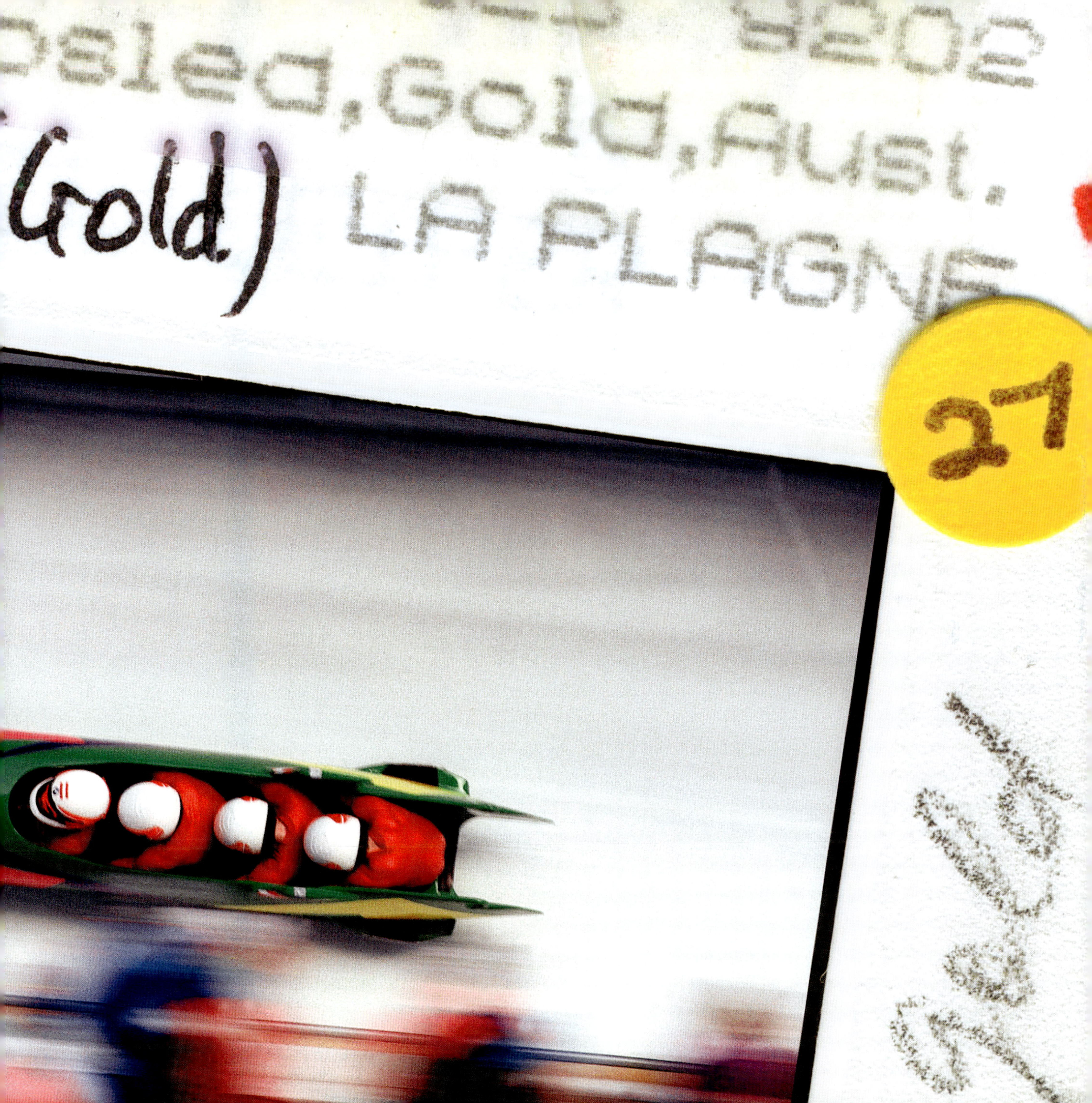

sled,Gold,Aust.
(Gold) LA PLAGNE
27
Gold

Baseball Book

9-13

X39011 T

Sip '01 Com
RIPKEN Jr.

TIME INC. PICTURE COLLECTION

35th Anniv
9/11/89

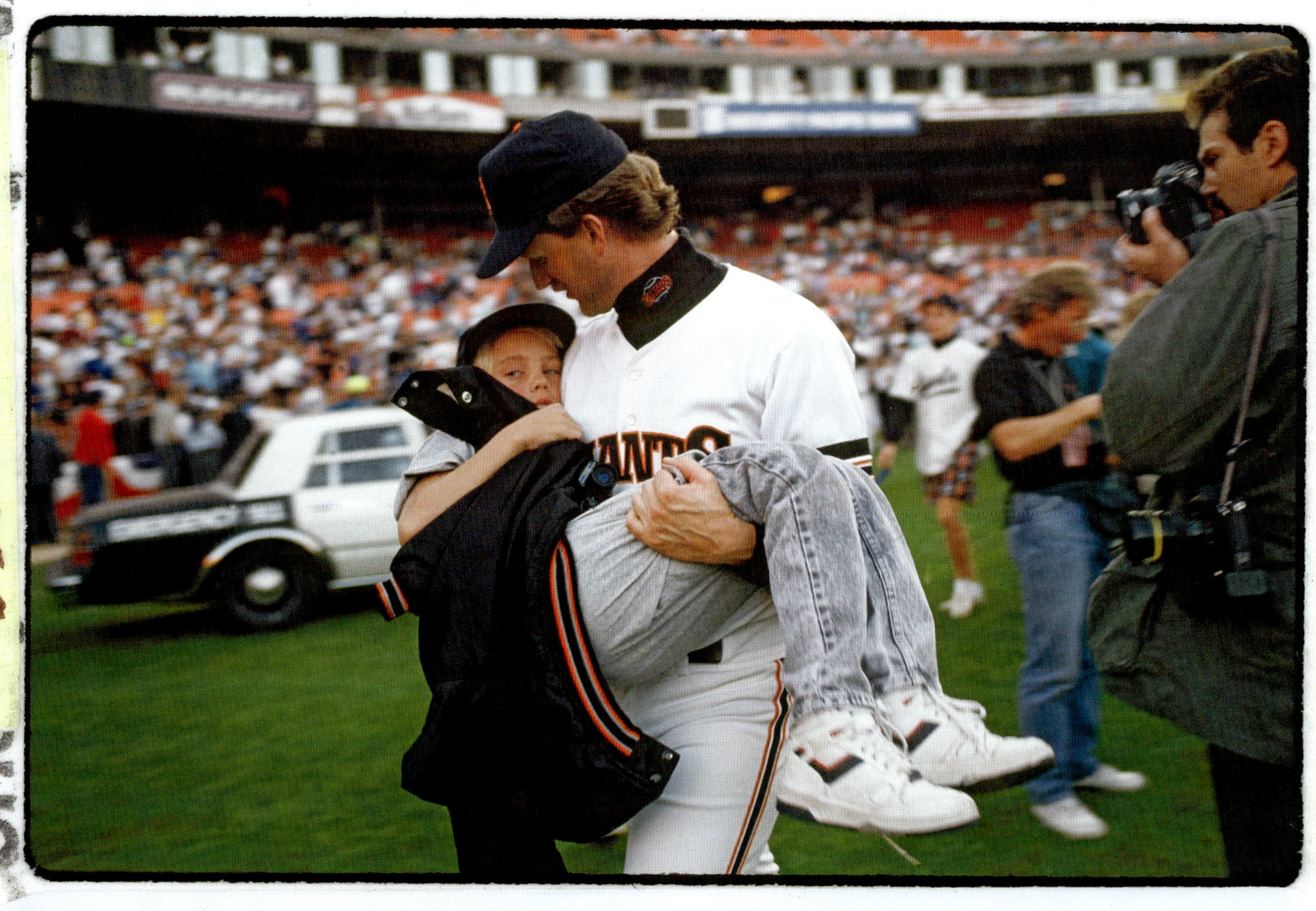

10-30-89
COVER

Baseball: World Series. SF Giants Kelly Downs carrying frightended child fan Billy Kehl after earthquake before start of game vs Oakland A's. Cover.

After the Darkest Days

WORLD SERIES

Photograph by JOHN IACONO, October 17, 1989

AT THE 1989 WORLD SERIES between Oakland and San Francisco, an earthquake struck just before Game 3, putting play on hold for 10 days. John Iacono's photo shows the Giants' Kelly Downs carrying his 11-year-old nephew to safety. (Why the "Ripken Jr." sticker? The photo was used in SI's Cal Ripken Jr. commemorative, in a timeline of historical events during his consecutive-games streak.) The Sept. 11, 2001, terror attacks brought to a halt sporting events around the country; the murder of 11 Israeli athletes at the 1972 Munich Olympics drew outrage from around the world. Yet one of these tragedies was never an SI cover. While TIME had Munich as its cover, SI covered instead with Dallas Cowboys fullback Walt Garrison, a bizarre reflection of managing editor Andre Laguerre's disdain for the Olympics and his distaste for covering them.

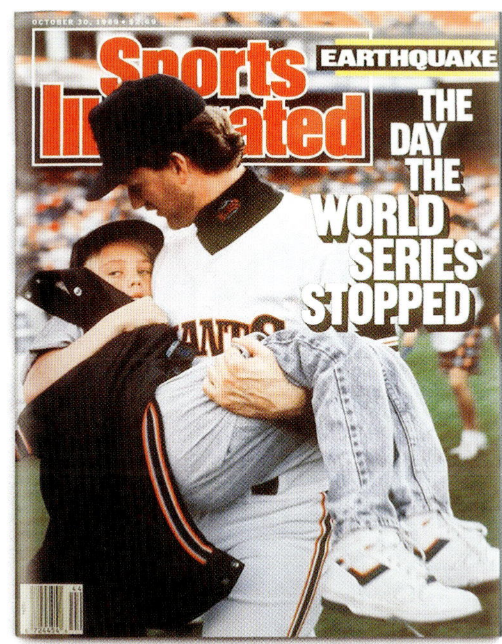

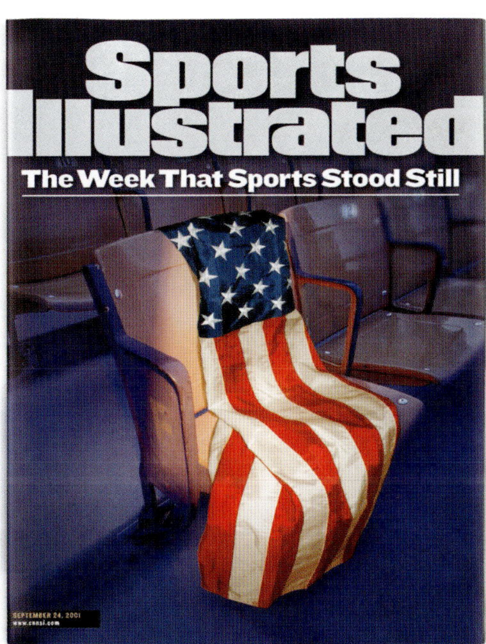

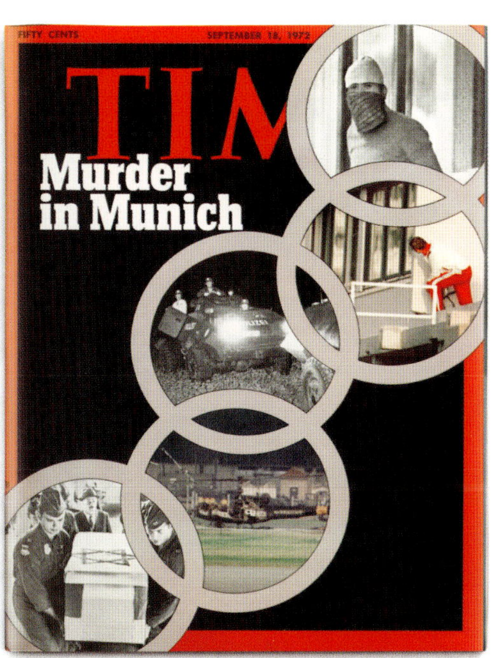

Original
Clemente

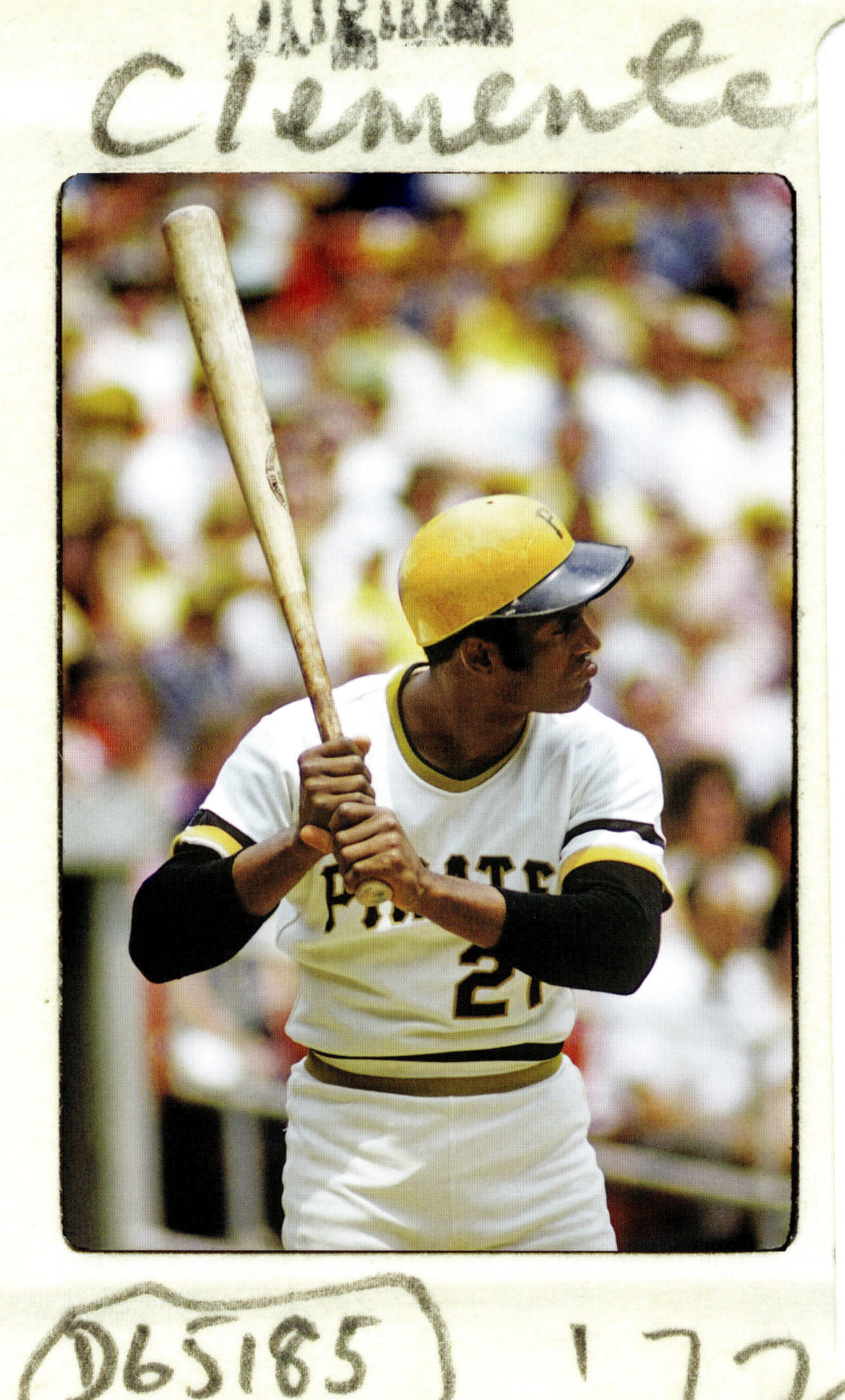

X 16990

D65185 '72

Seeing Heroes

ROBERTO CLEMENTE *(opposite)*
Photograph by NEIL LEIFER, June 1972

HANK AARON *(right)*
Photograph by NEIL LEIFER, April 1964

WHENEVER HE WENT TO THE BALLPARK Neil Leifer followed this self-directive: Look for the "poster shot." He always had an eye out for the timeless image of a great player at work, even if it didn't necessarily tell the story of that day. Both photos of these two Hall of Famers have an epic quality. If you were going to commission a sculpture of Clemente, this slide would serve beautifully as reference material. Amazingly, this classic photo of Aaron, lean and ready, did not appear in print for more than 40 years, when, in 2007, SI ran an appreciation of the great hitter, adorning the cover just before steroid-tainted Barry Bonds supplanted Aaron as the alltime home run leader—at least in the record books. As Reggie Jackson told writer Tom Verducci in that issue, "I guess you can call [Aaron] the people's home run king." For baseball fans, he's still the guy in the poster.

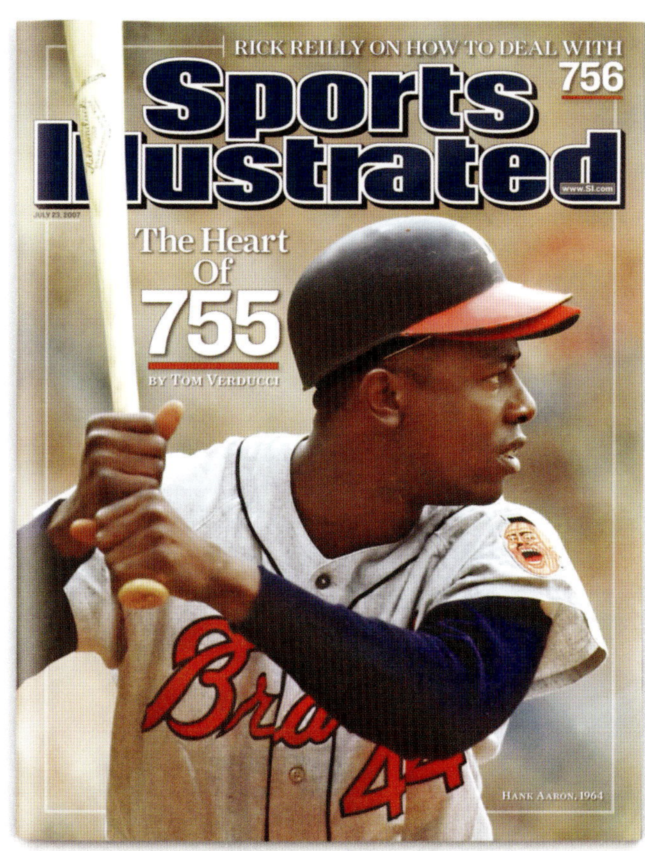

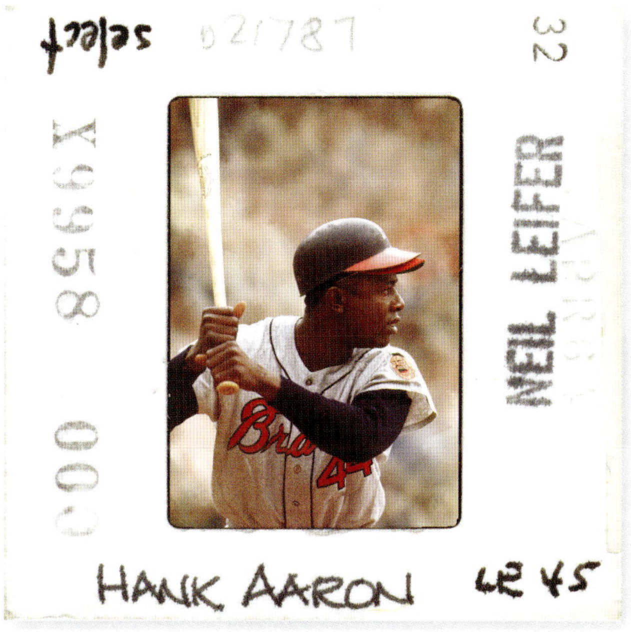

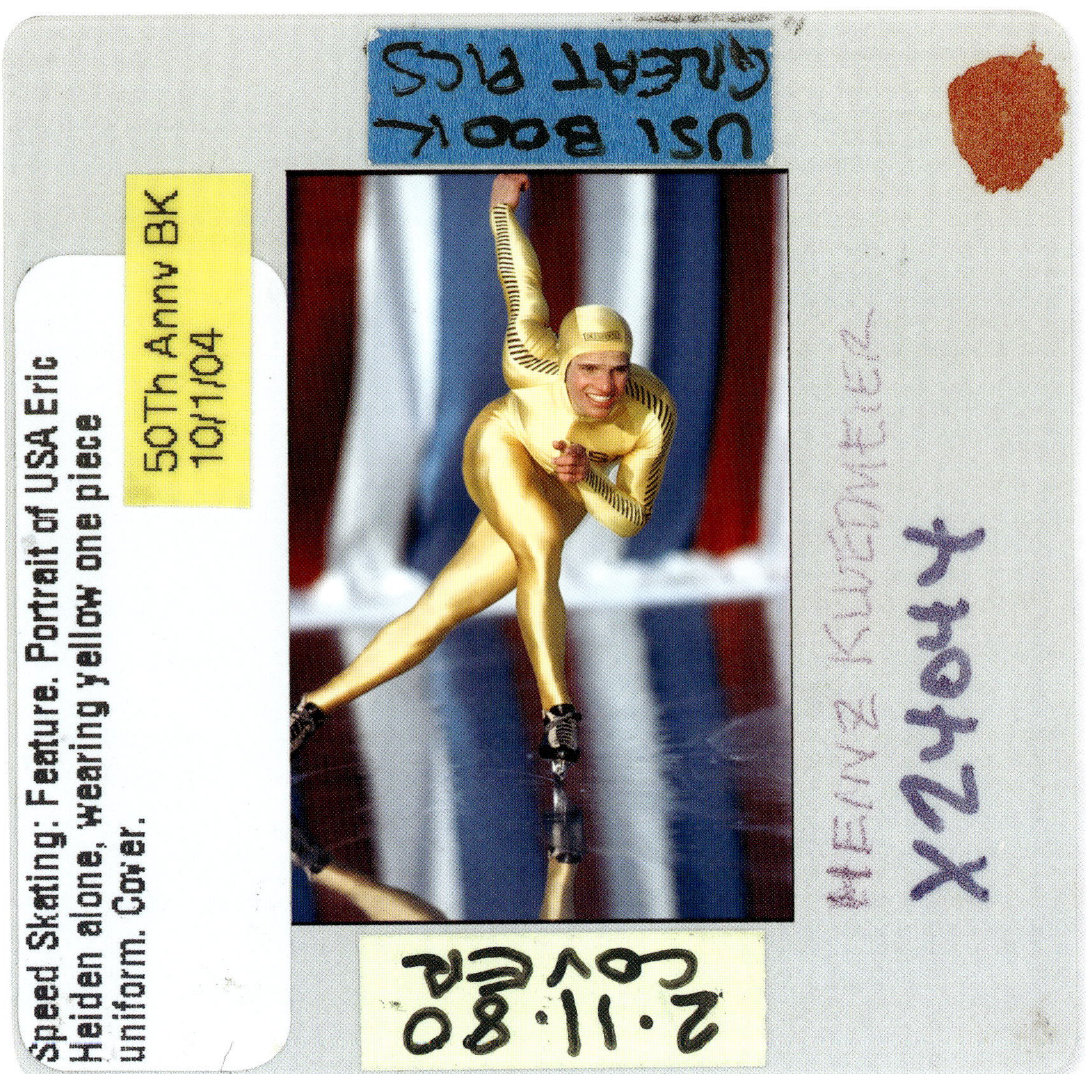

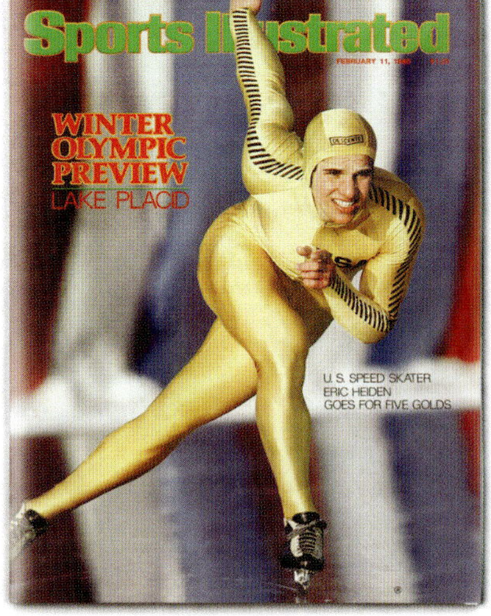

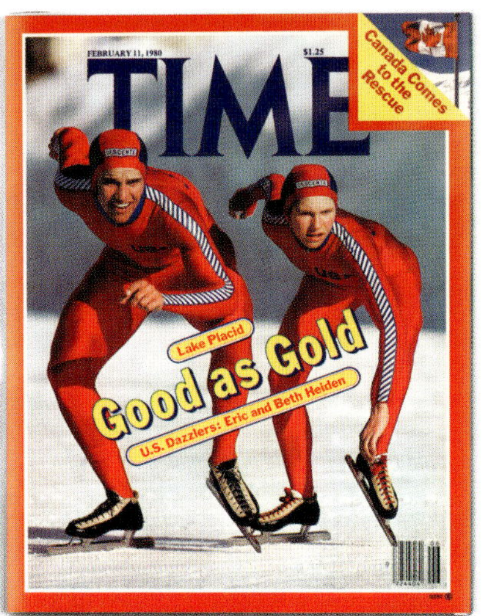

Give Him A Medal

ERIC HEIDEN *(above)*
Photograph by HEINZ KLUETMEIER, December 17, 1979

ERIC AND BETH HEIDEN *(opposite)*
Photograph by NEIL LEIFER, January 1980

IF ATHLETES ARE COMPETITIVE by nature, so are photographers. When Heinz Kluetmeier requested a chance to shoot Eric Heiden for the cover of SI's Olympics preview, an agent for speedskating siblings Eric and Beth denied him, saying the pair would be shot exclusively for the cover of TIME. So Kluetmeier simply showed up without an appointment at Heiden's Wisconsin practice facility. The skater agreed to pose right then, and Kluetmeier was ready not only with a gold suit for Heiden to wear, but also with a Zamboni driver. After each pass Heiden took around the track, Kluetmeier had the Zamboni driver smooth the ice for a pristine reflection in every take.

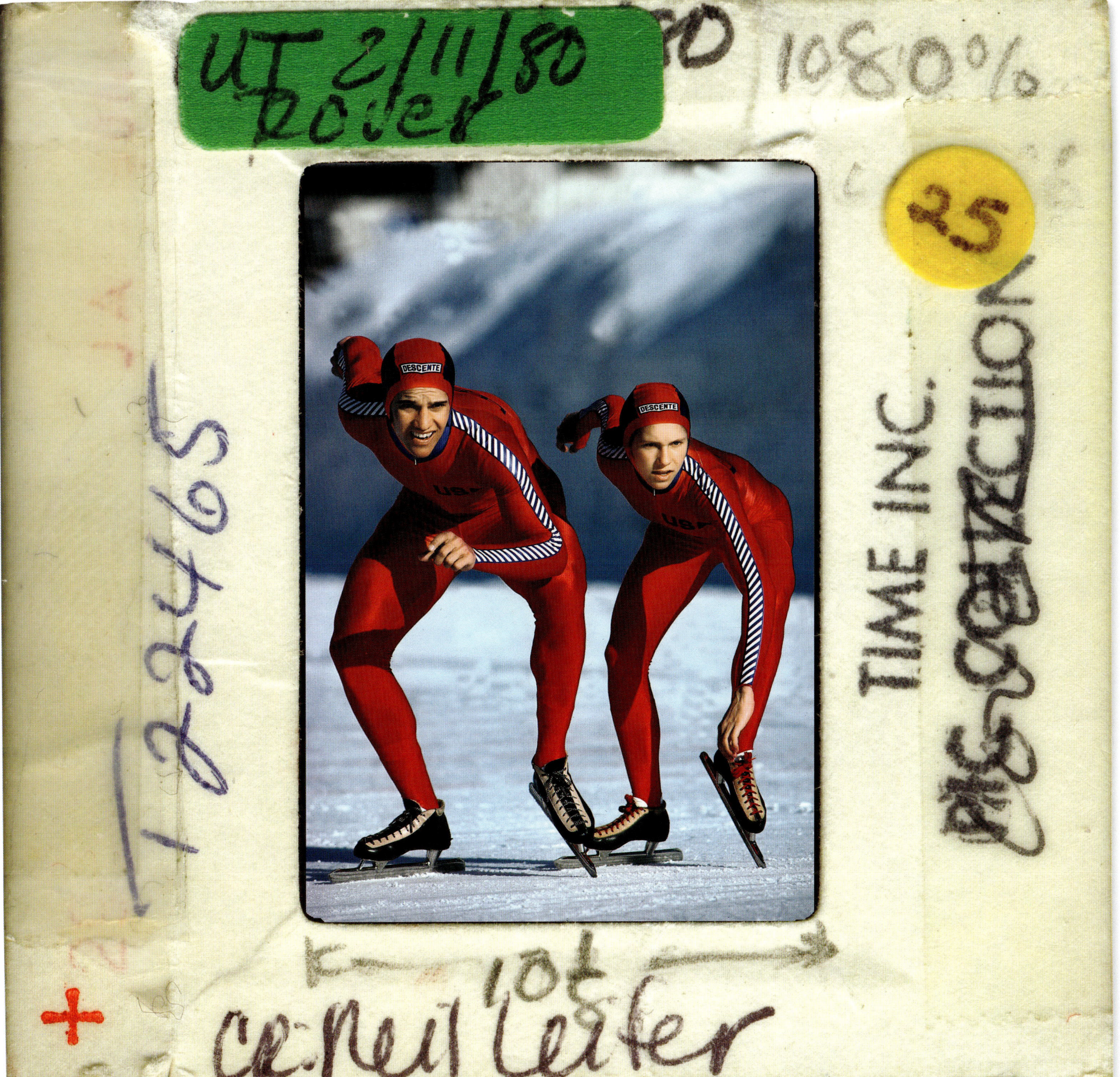

DESCENTE
DESCENTE
USA
USA
TIME INC.
1080%
25
cr: Neil Leifer

Basketball: Boston Celtics Bob Cousy #14 in action vs Fort Wayne Pistons.

12-2-91

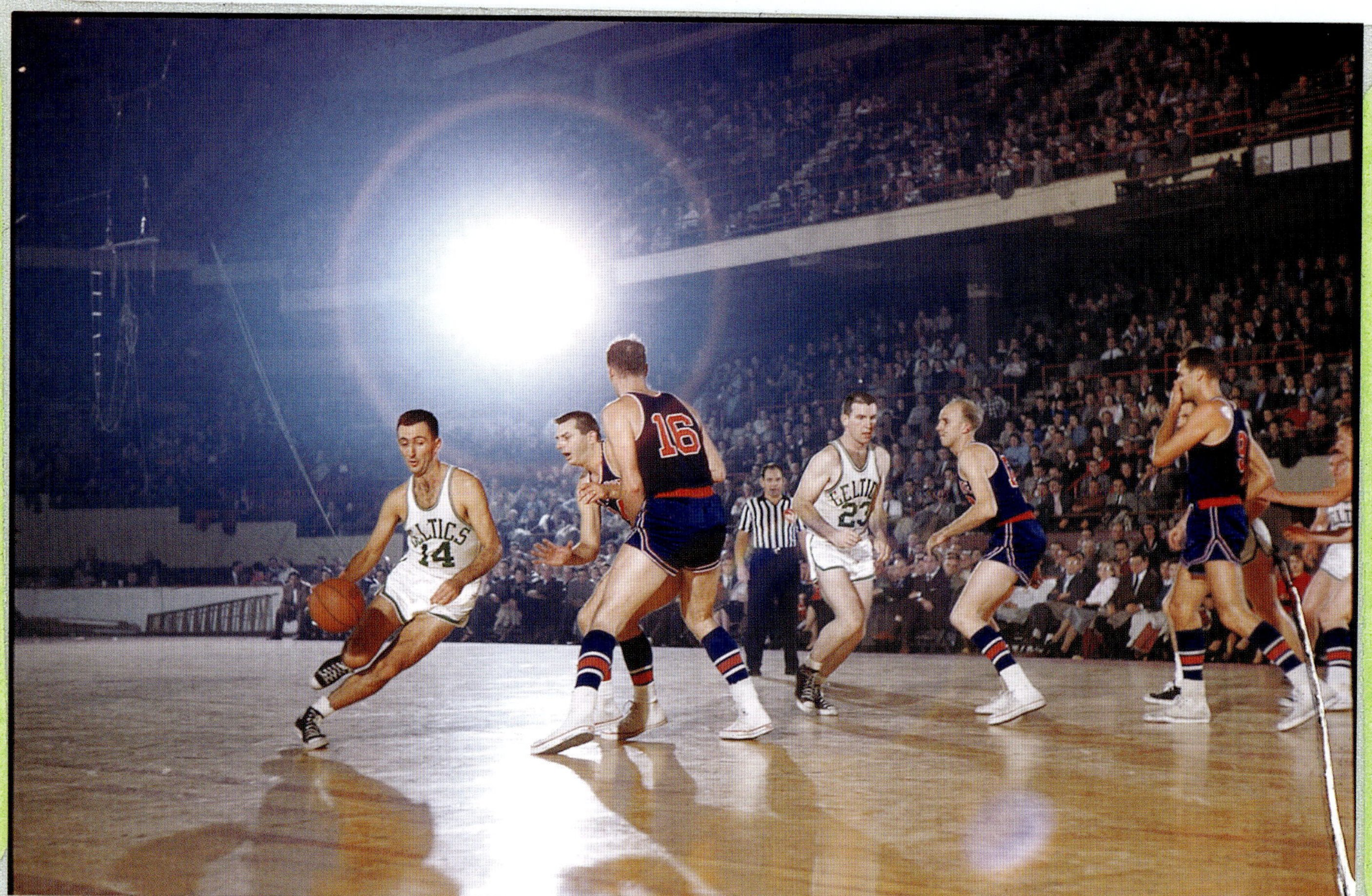

1-9-56

Hy Peskin

X3304

50Th Anny BK
10/1/04

Original Magic

BOB COUSY

Photograph by HY PESKIN, November 19, 1955

MANY TIMES the cropping of a photo for use as a cover shot does the original a favor, eliminating dead space and bringing the main image to the fore. In the case of Hy Peskin's picture of Cousy turning the corner, though, one look at this slide tells you that this photo is best seen in full. A look back at the accompanying story provides another kind of revelation. Many of today's fans think of the Celtics' Cousy as the classic old school point guard, but in his day he was seen as newfangled razzle-dazzle. (A behind-the-back dribble in a game? Get me a pen-and-ink diagram of that!) In his story, Herbert Warren Wind correctly prophesied that this new style, flash with purpose, was the future of the NBA: "Bob Cousy has been called a once-in-a-lifetime player. He may prove to be. But from now on the new stars that arise will play like Cousy."

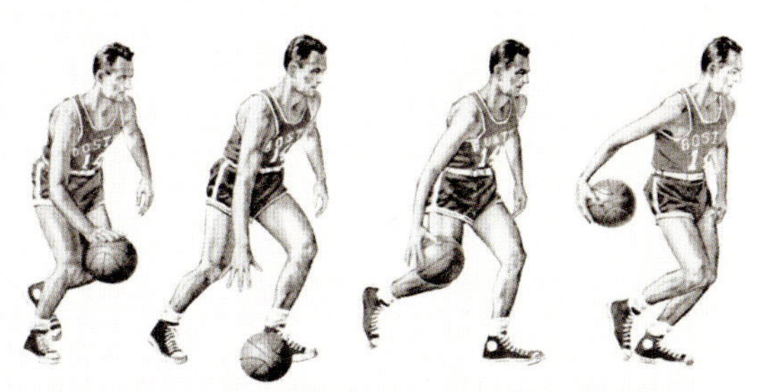

IF COUSY HAS A TRADEMARK, IT IS HIS FAMOUS BEHIND-THE-BACK DRIBBLE AT FULL TILT

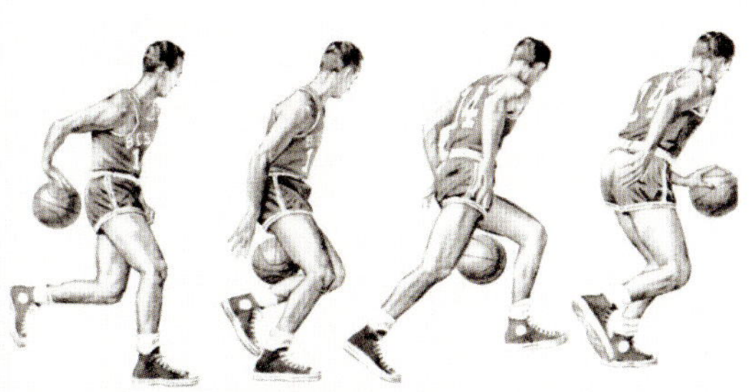

AS THIS ACTION SEQUENCE SHOWS, IT ENABLES HIM TO CHANGE HIS DIRECTION ABRUPTLY

PART I

BOB COUSY: BASKETBALL'S CREATIVE GENIUS

All imagination and agility, the great Celtic star is leading the youngest of the major games out of one of its periodic wildernesses

by HERBERT WARREN WIND

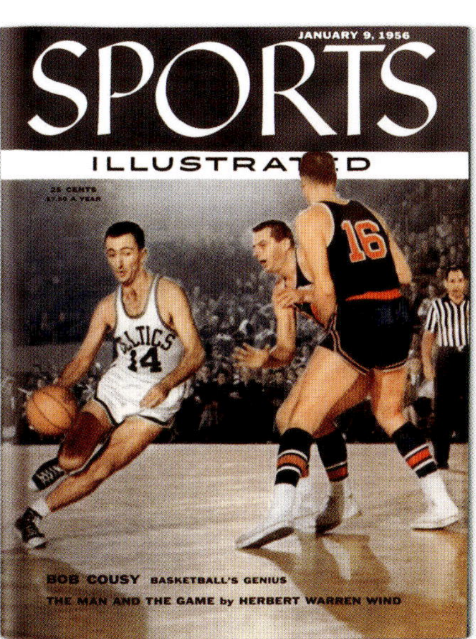

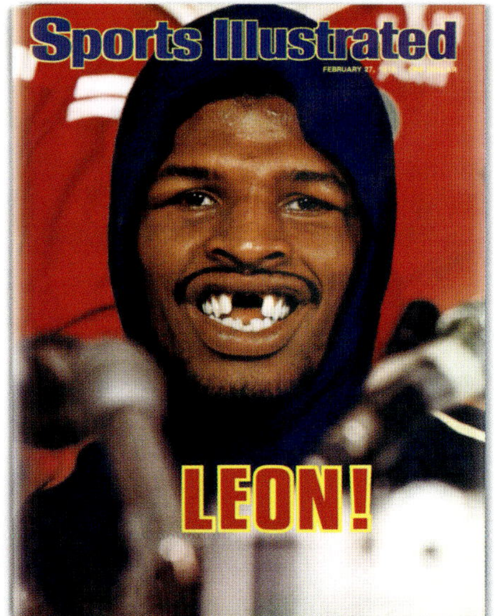

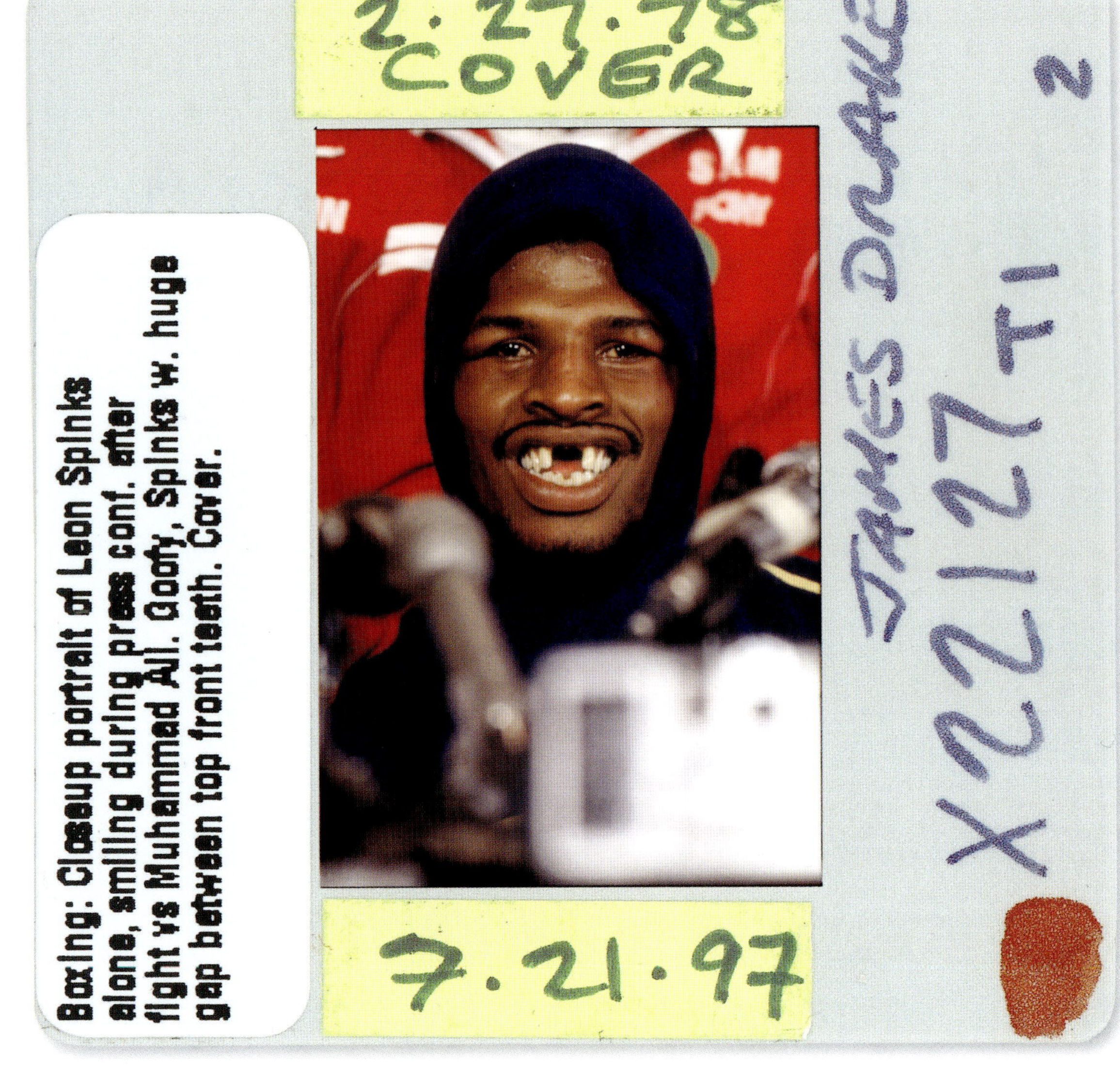

Smile!

LEON SPINKS *(above)*
Photograph by JAMES DRAKE, February 15, 1978

TERRY BRADSHAW *(opposite)*
Photograph by NEIL LEIFER, November 1971

SOME MIGHT SAY there are gaps in the SI photo collection, and Leon Spinks and Terry Bradshaw can confirm it. Bradshaw, one of sports' irrepressible characters, flashed this good ol' grin during the losing season of 1971, before the quarterback led the Steelers to their run of four Super Bowl wins between '74 and '79. Spinks's photo was taken when the boxer was at the top of his game—defying all expectations, he had just defeated Muhammad Ali for the heavyweight title. (He would lose it back to Ali later that year.) Spinks's happy mug was later included in the magazine's '97 cover story, *A Gallery of Unforgettable Portraits*. Those teeth were still missing.

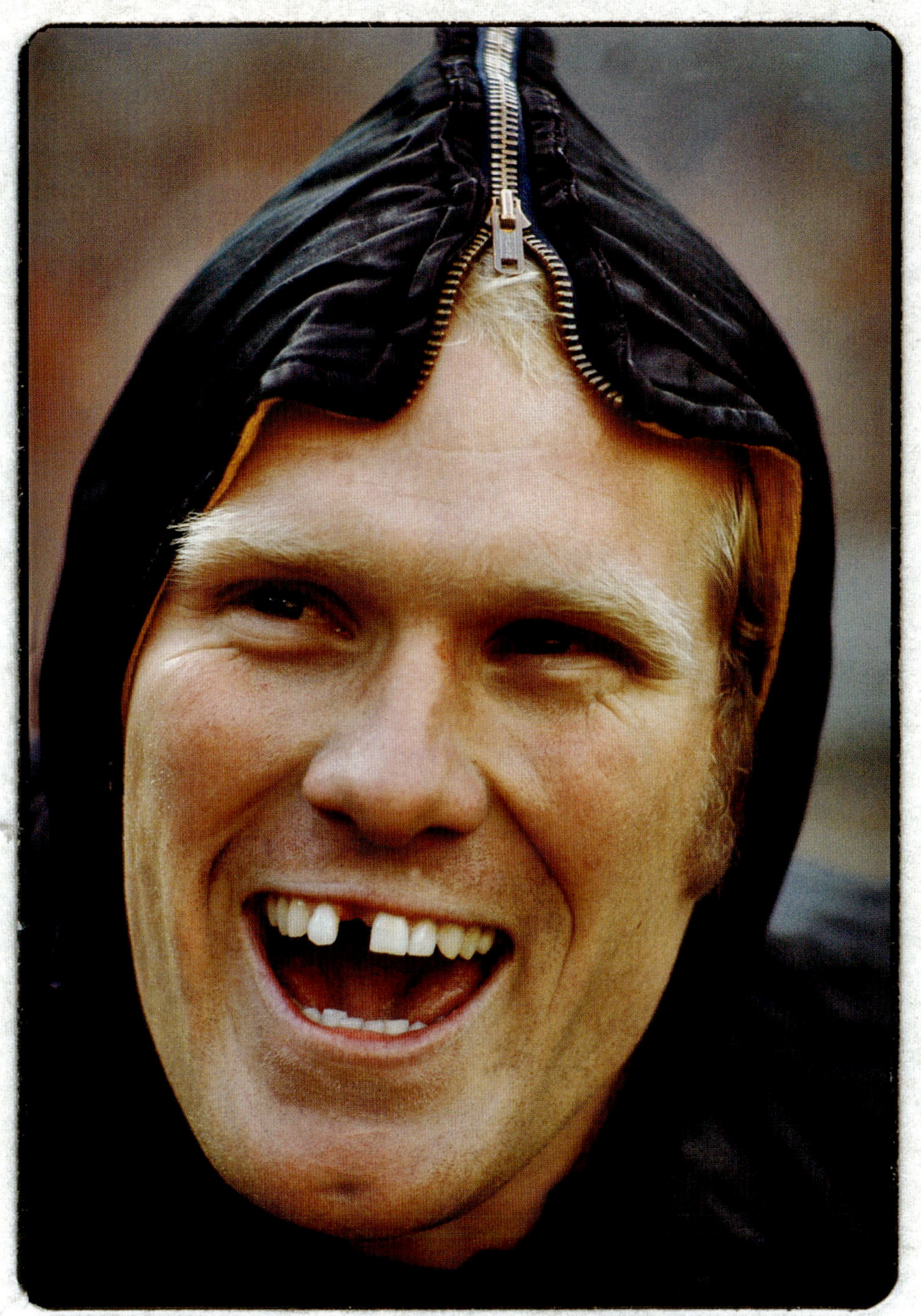

Select
NEIL LEIFER
33
BRADSHAW

Life of The Party

JOE NAMATH

Photograph by WALTER IOOSS JR., January 10, 1969

WHEN HE WAS ASSIGNED to follow the Jets as his designated team for Super Bowl III, Walter Iooss Jr. was disappointed—he was sure his pictures were destined for the scrap pile after an easy win by the heavily favored Colts. That smiling fellow in the lounge chair, though, would make this picture famous. Besides capturing Namath's easy charm, the photo is also a document of the Super Bowl as it once was. Back then Namath could drop by the team's hotel pool and banter with a few curious guests and a handful of attendant reporters (that's Brent Musburger, far left, and, behind, in dark coat and glasses, Paul Zimmerman—SI's illustrious football writer, Dr. Z). Asks Iooss, "Can you imagine what would happen if Tom Brady tried to do this today?"

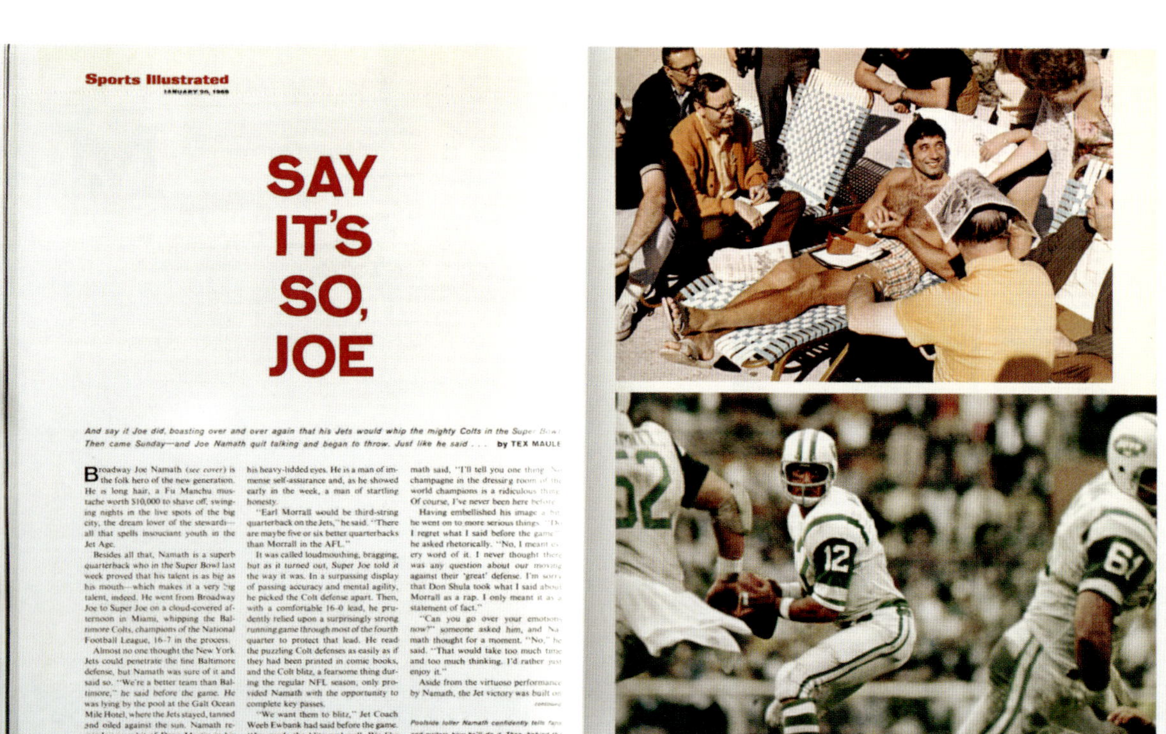

Sports Illustrated

SAY IT'S SO, JOE

And say it Joe did, boasting over and over again that his Jets would whip the mighty Colts in the Super Bowl. Then came Sunday—and Joe Namath quit talking and began to throw. Just like he said . . . **by TEX MAULE**

Broadway Joe Namath (*see cover*) is the folk hero of the new generation. He is long hair, a Fu Manchu mustache worth $10,000 to shave off, swinging nights in the live spots of the big city, the dream lover of the stewardi—all that spells insouciant youth in the Jet Age.

Besides all that, Namath is a superb quarterback who in the Super Bowl last week proved that his talent is as big as his mouth—which makes it a very big talent, indeed. He went from Broadway Joe to Super Joe on a cloud-covered afternoon in Miami, whipping the Baltimore Colts, champions of the National Football League, 16–7 in the process.

Almost no one thought the New York Jets could penetrate the fine Baltimore defense, but Namath was sure of it and said so. "We're a better team than Baltimore," he said before the game. He was lying by the pool at the Galt Ocean Mile Hotel, where the Jets stayed, tanned and oiled against the sun. Namath reminds you a bit of Dean Martin in his relaxed confidence and in the droop of his heavy-lidded eyes. He is a man of immense self-assurance and, as he showed early in the week, a man of startling honesty.

"Earl Morrall would be third-string quarterback on the Jets," he said. "There are maybe five or six better quarterbacks than Morrall in the AFL."

It was called loudmouthing, bragging, but as it turned out, Super Joe told it the way it was. In a surpassing display of passing accuracy and mental agility, he picked the Colt defense apart. Then, with a comfortable 16–0 lead, he prudently relied upon a surprisingly strong running game through most of the fourth quarter to protect that lead. He read the puzzling Colt defenses as easily as if they had been printed in comic books, and the Colt blitz, a fearsome thing during the regular NFL season, only provided Namath with the opportunity to complete key passes.

"We want them to blitz," Jet Coach Weeb Ewbank had said before the game. "Joe reads the blitz real well. We like blitzing teams." When it was over, Namath said, "I'll tell you one thing. No champagne in the dressing room of the world champions is a ridiculous thing. Of course, I've never been here before."

Having embellished his image a bit, he went on to more serious things. "Do I regret what I said before the game?" he asked rhetorically. "No, I meant every word of it. I never thought there was any question about our moving against their 'great' defense. I'm sorry that Don Shula took what I said about Morrall as a rap. I only meant it as a statement of fact."

"Can you go over your emotions now?" someone asked him, and Namath thought for a moment. "No," he said. "That would take too much time and too much thinking. I'd rather just enjoy it."

Aside from the virtuoso performance by Namath, the Jet victory was built on

continued

Poolside loller Namath confidently tells fans and writers how he'll do it. Then, behind the solid protection he had all day, he does it

10

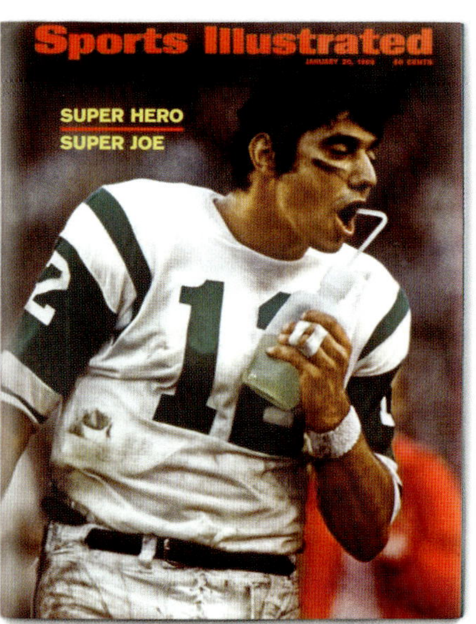

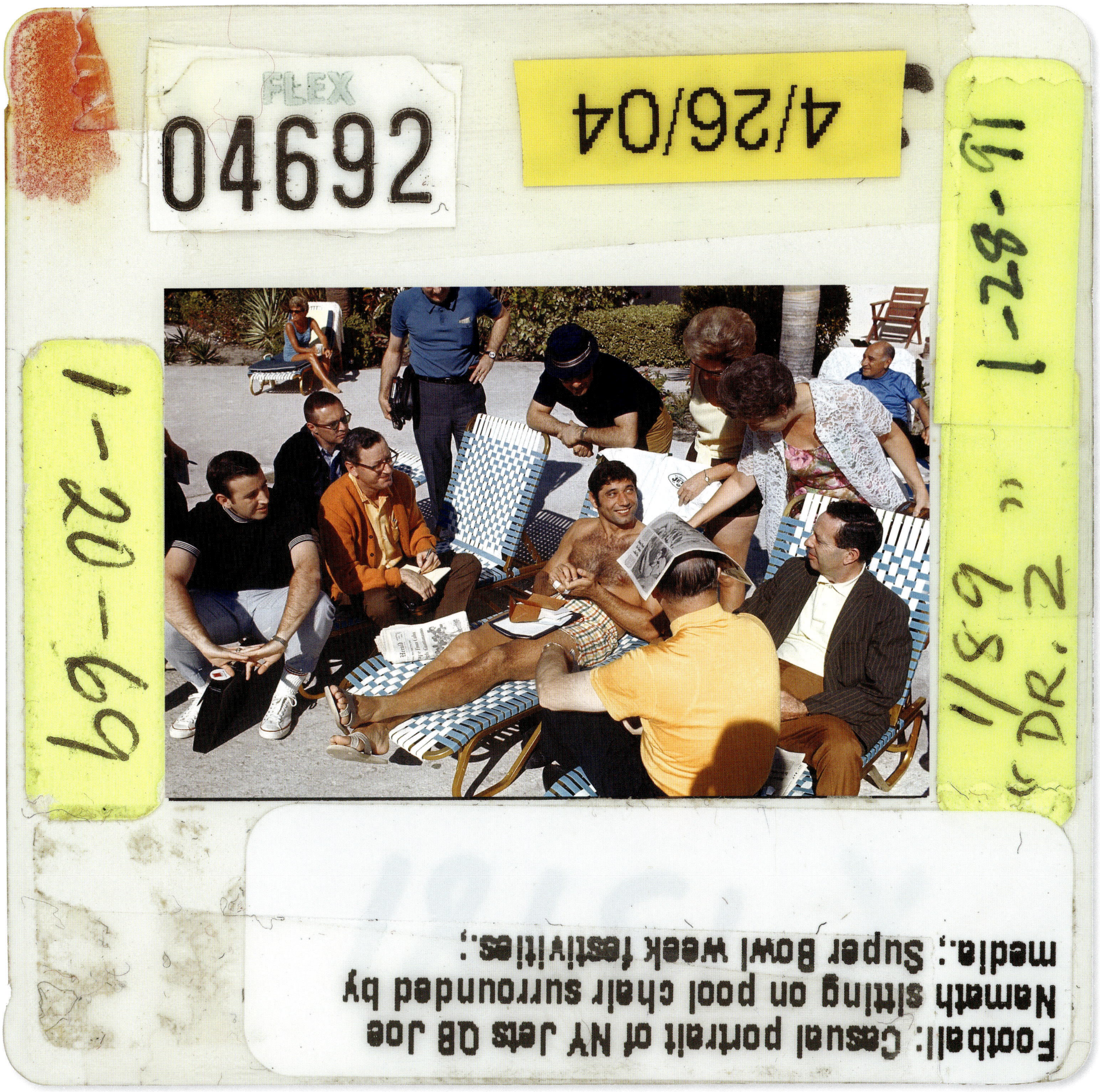

Football: Casual portrait of NY Jets QB Joe Namath sitting on pool chair surrounded by media.; Super Bowl week festivities.;

1-20-69

1/8 9 "DR. 2"

1-28-91

4/26/04

04692

FLEX

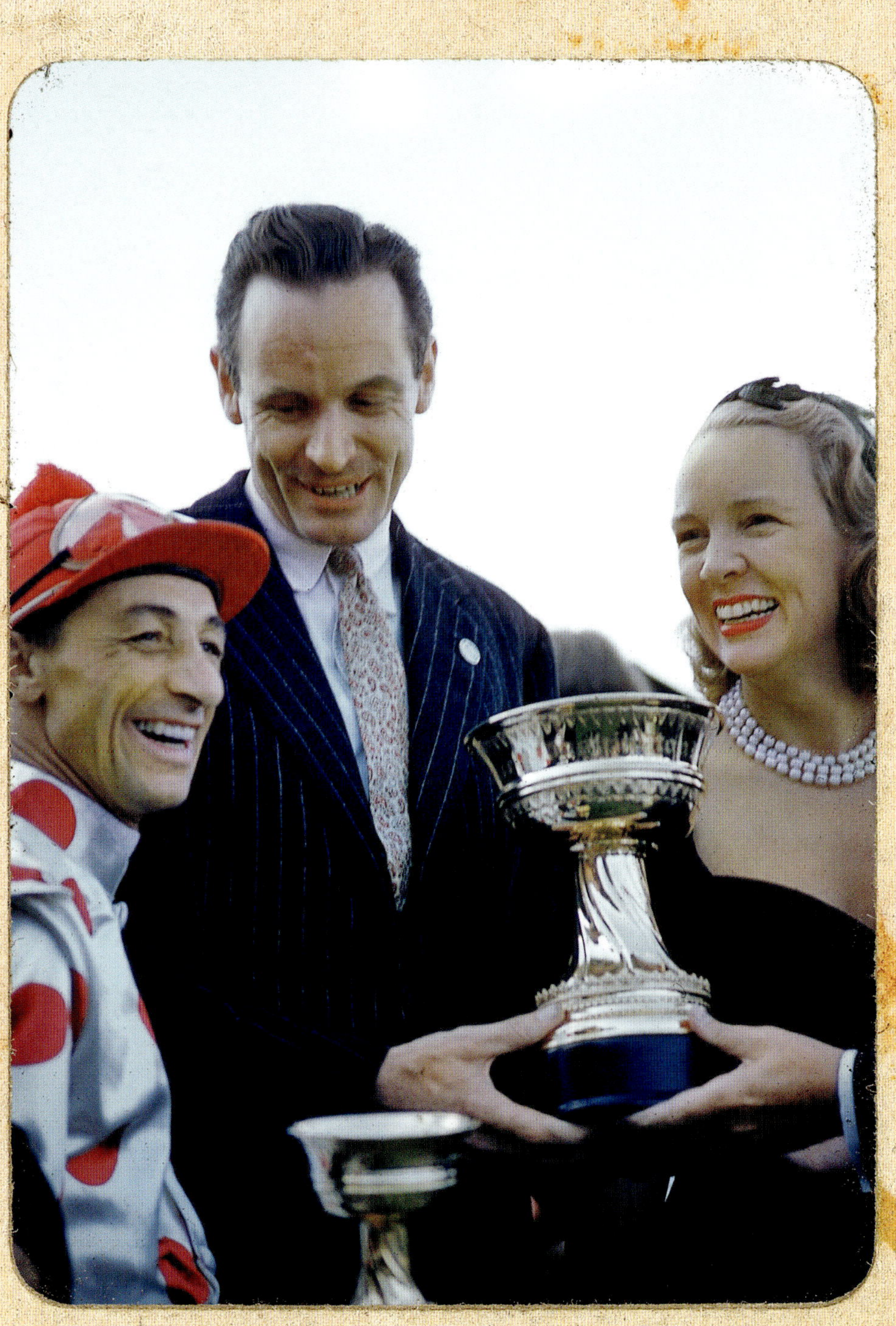
535615
KODAK READY-MOUNT

The Lost Sportsman

BILL WOODWARD JR. *(opposite)*
Photograph by MARK KAUFFMAN, September 1, 1955

JOHNNY PODRES *(below)*
Photograph by RICHARD MEEK, November 1955

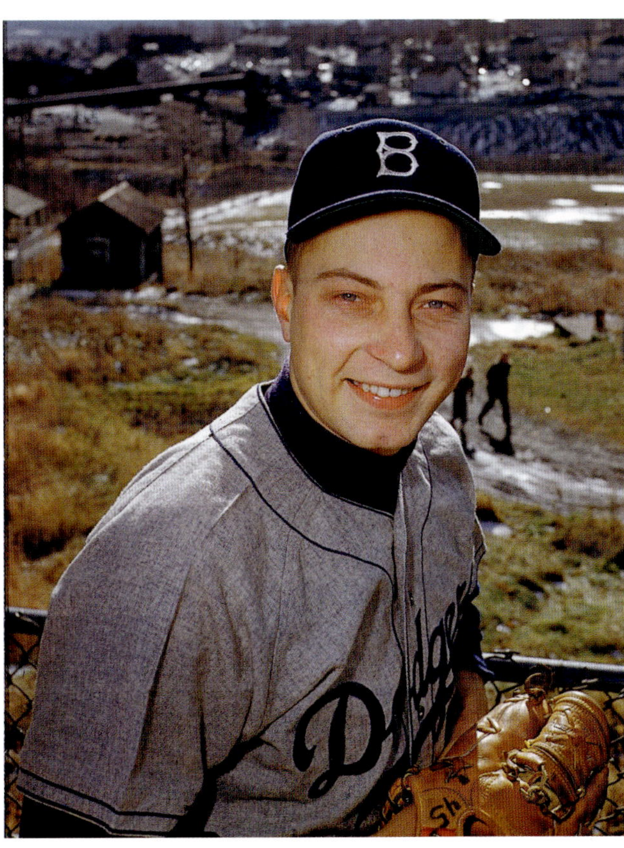

IT LOOKS LIKE A HAPPY SCENE of trophy and triumph, but the absence of any date-of-usage sticker on this slide hints at what is in fact a tragic tale. The tall gentleman is Bill Woodward Jr., owner of the racehorse Nashua, winner of the Preakness and the Belmont. Woodward had been selected to be SI's 1955 Sportsman of the Year, but as the story was being prepared for print, news came that Woodward had been shot and killed by his wife, Ann (she can be seen in the photo, along with Nashua's jockey Eddie Arcaro), in what police would rule an accident. Managing editor Sid James scrambled for an alternative Sportsman and came up with Johnny Podres, a borderline candidate at best; the Brooklyn Dodgers pitcher had won Game 7 of the World Series that year but had a losing record in the regular season. There was no time to arrange a shoot, so this rather ordinary photo—the only color portrait of Podres on hand—became the cover.

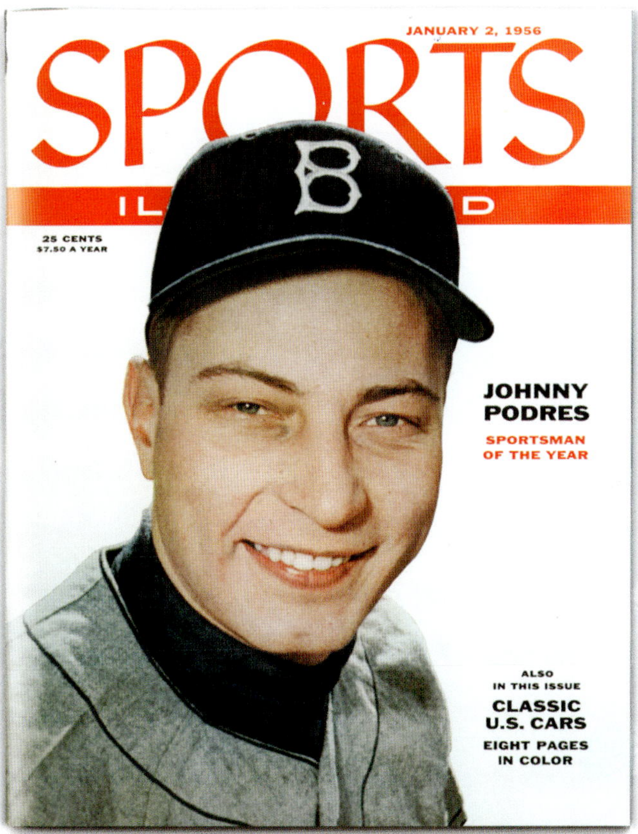

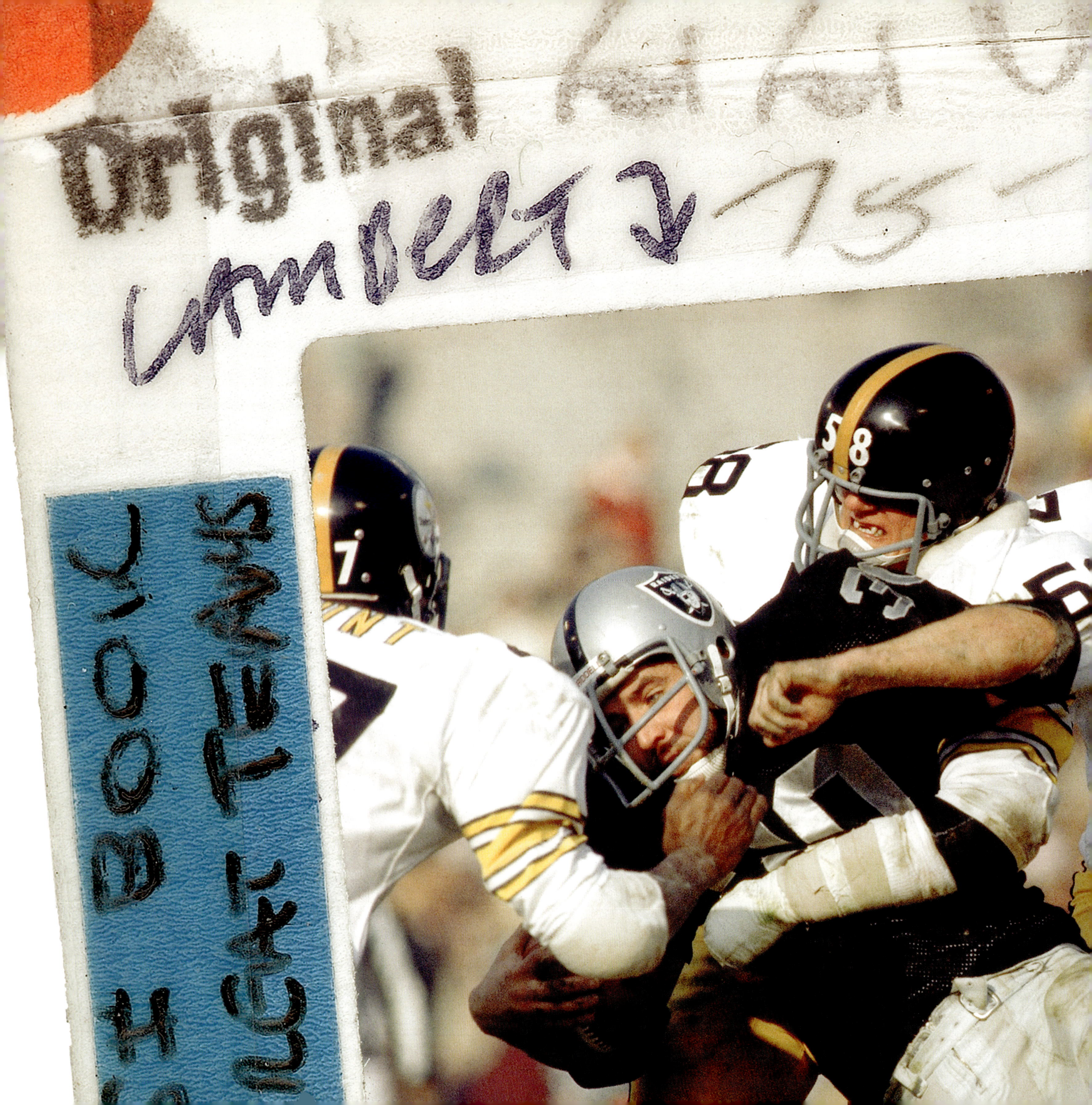

Original

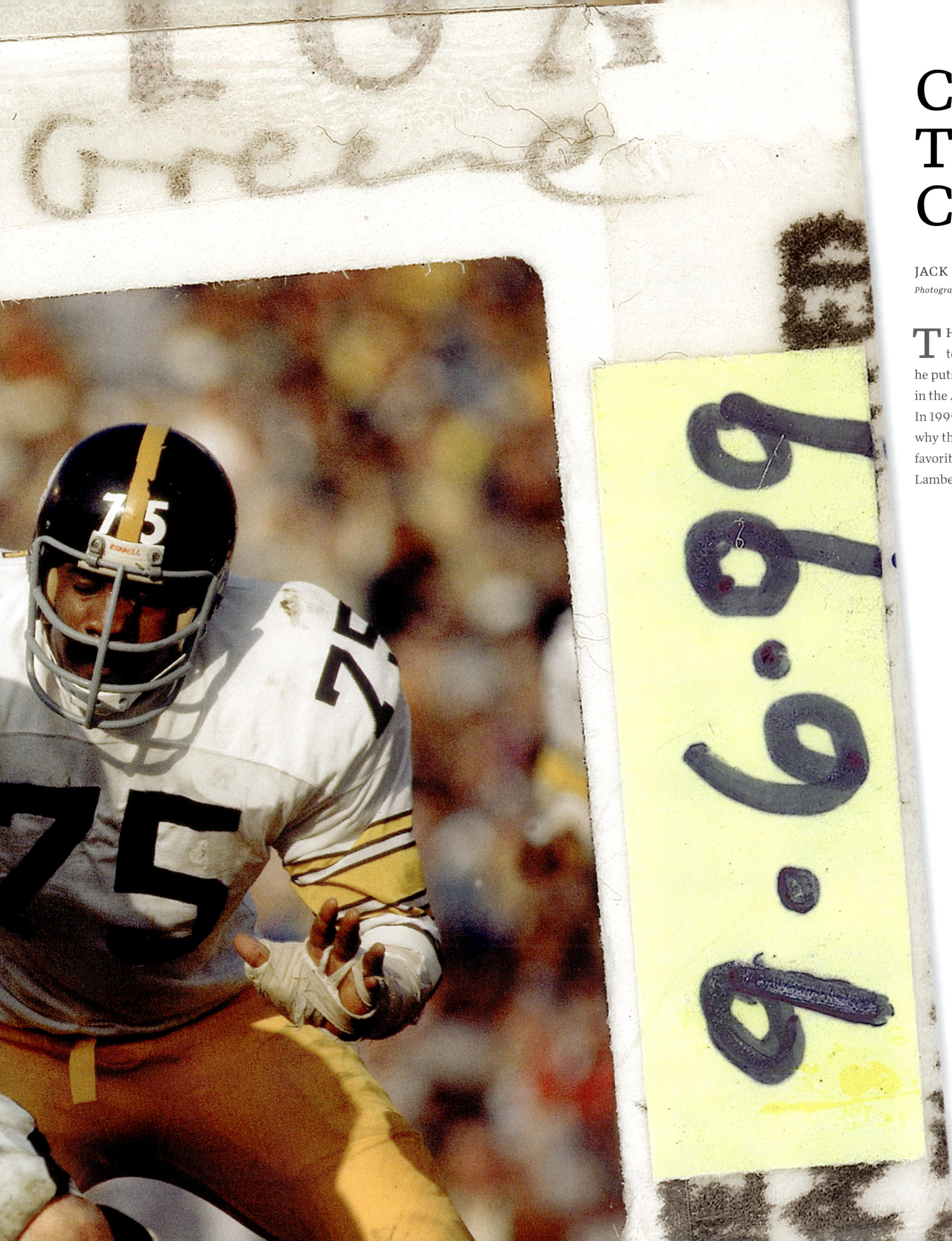

Closing The Steel Curtain

JACK LAMBERT

Photograph by NEIL LEIFER, December 26, 1976

THE ARROW on the slide points to Pittsburgh's Jack Lambert as he puts a nasty hit on Mark van Eeghen in the AFC title game against Oakland. In 1999 SI used the shot again to show why the Steelers belonged on our list of favorite sports teams. (It also shows why Lambert is missing a few teeth.)

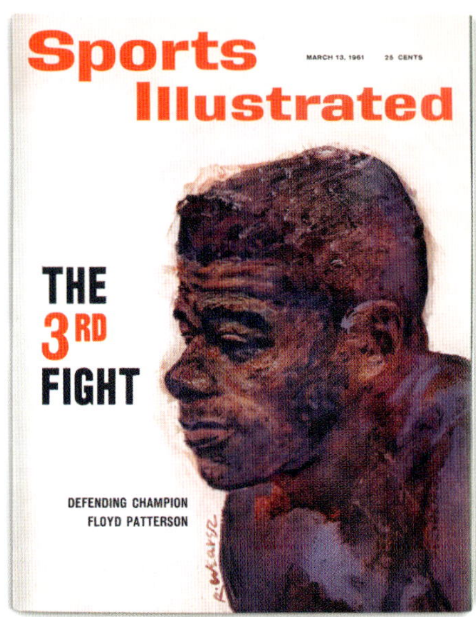

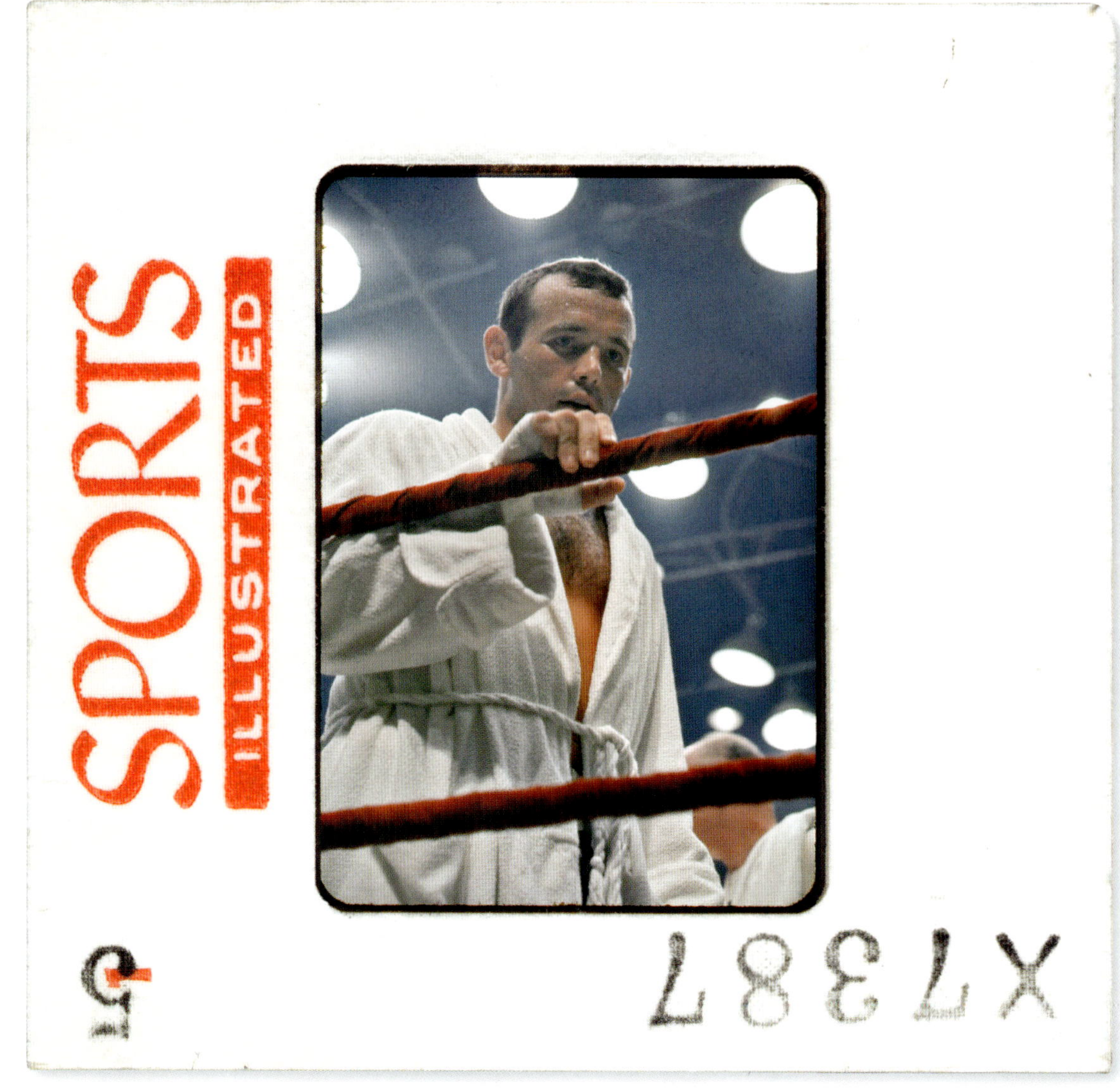

Three's A Charm

INGEMAR JOHANSSON *(above)*
Photograph by NEIL LEIFER, March 13, 1961

FLOYD PATTERSON *(opposite)*
Photograph by NEIL LEIFER, March 13, 1961

THESE TWO SHOTS come from the third heavyweight title fight between Ingemar Johansson and Floyd Patterson. (Patterson would win this rubber match and retain his crown.) Curiously, these slide mounts carry different versions of SI's logo—and neither matches SI's cover logo at the time of the fight. The logo on the Johansson slide was the original logo, used from 1954 (SI's debut year) until August '56. The slide with Patterson has the logo used until October '60, when SI switched to a custom typeface (seen on this cover) that the magazine has used, with modification, ever since. As with Johansson and Patterson, the third try settled it.

14 **SPORTS ILLUSTRATED** 36

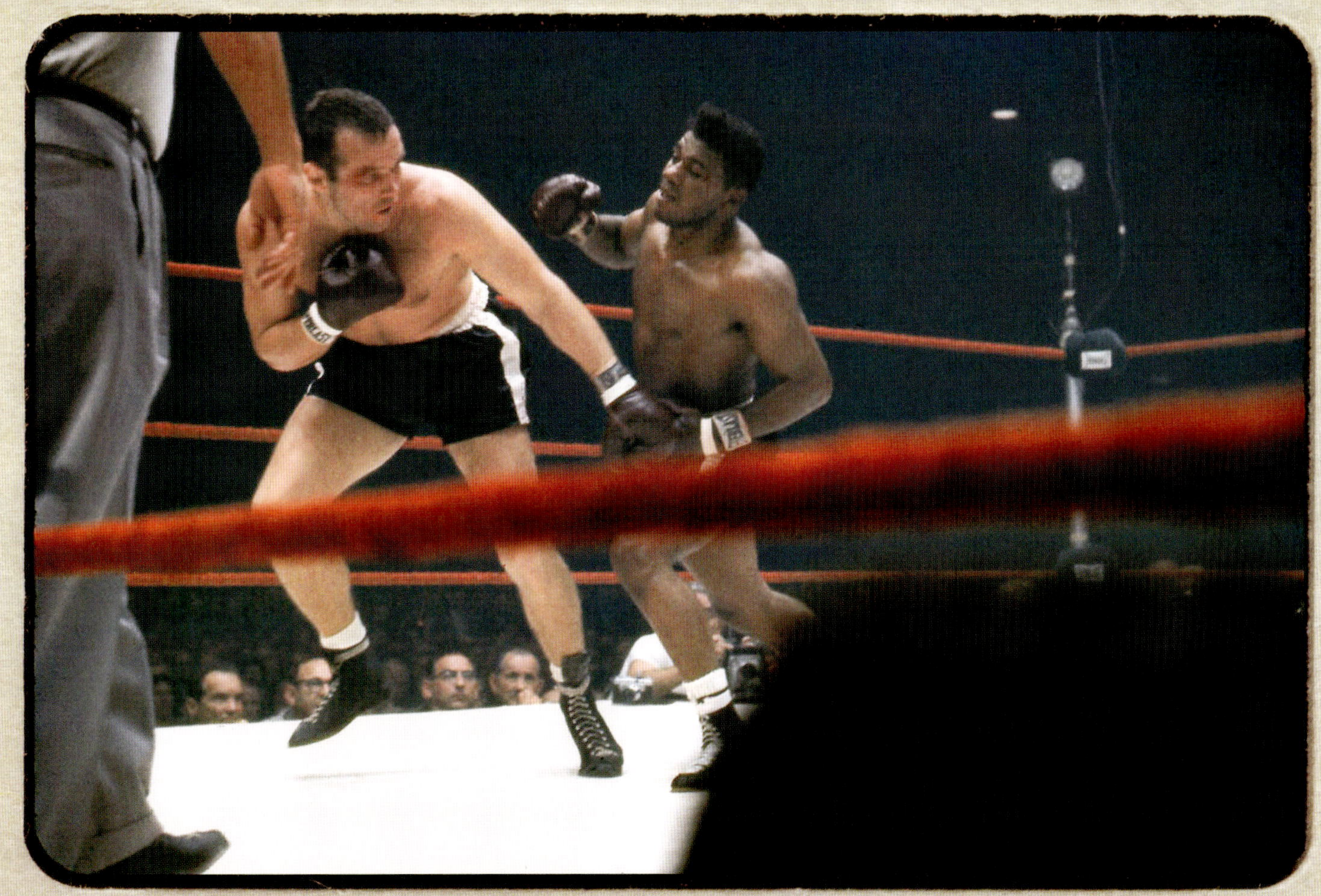

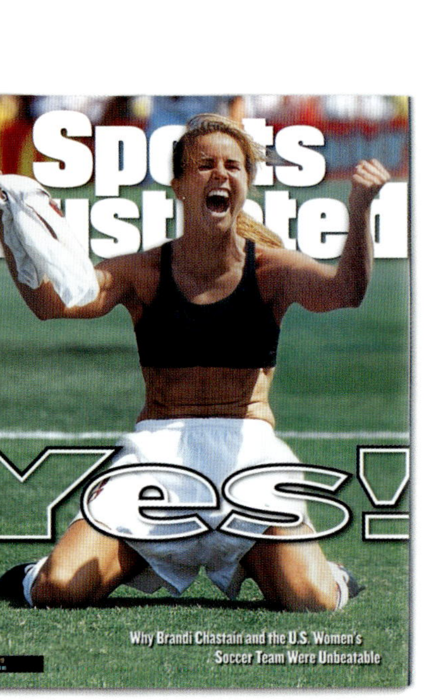

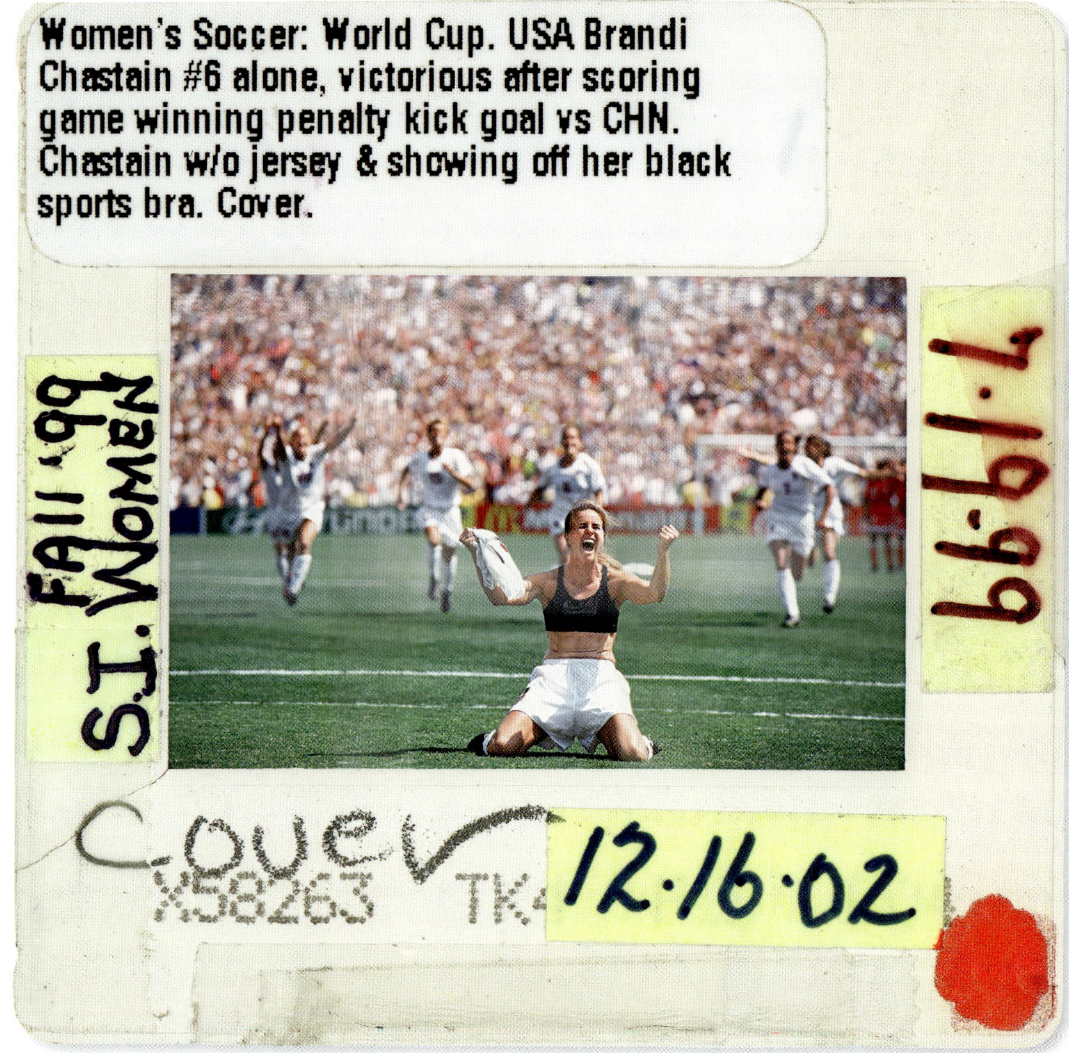

A Bra for The Ages

BRANDI CHASTAIN *(above)*
Photograph by ROBERT BECK, July 10, 1999

GAO HONG *(opposite)*
Photograph by PETER READ MILLER, July 10, 1999

ROBERT BECK spent the first half of the U.S.–China World Cup final penned up by President Clinton's security detail and the rest shooting from high in the stadium. But when the game went to penalty shots, he slipped down to set up directly behind the goal—a place he wasn't supposed to be. (Peter Read Miller had a "legal" position to the side, but did he get the ultimate shot? "No!") Security asked Beck to move, but he argued that it would distract the players. Thus did he snap the picture that launched Brandi Chastain to fame. "Yes!" When she and Beck met for the first time, seven years later at a basketball game, "she jumped into my arms and hugged me and wouldn't let go," Beck says. "Everyone was like, Wow, what went on with those two?"

Women's Soccer: World Cup. CHN goalie Gao Hong #18 in action, yielding ~~game winning~~ penalty kick goal vs USA ?

Lilly pen. goal

7·19·99

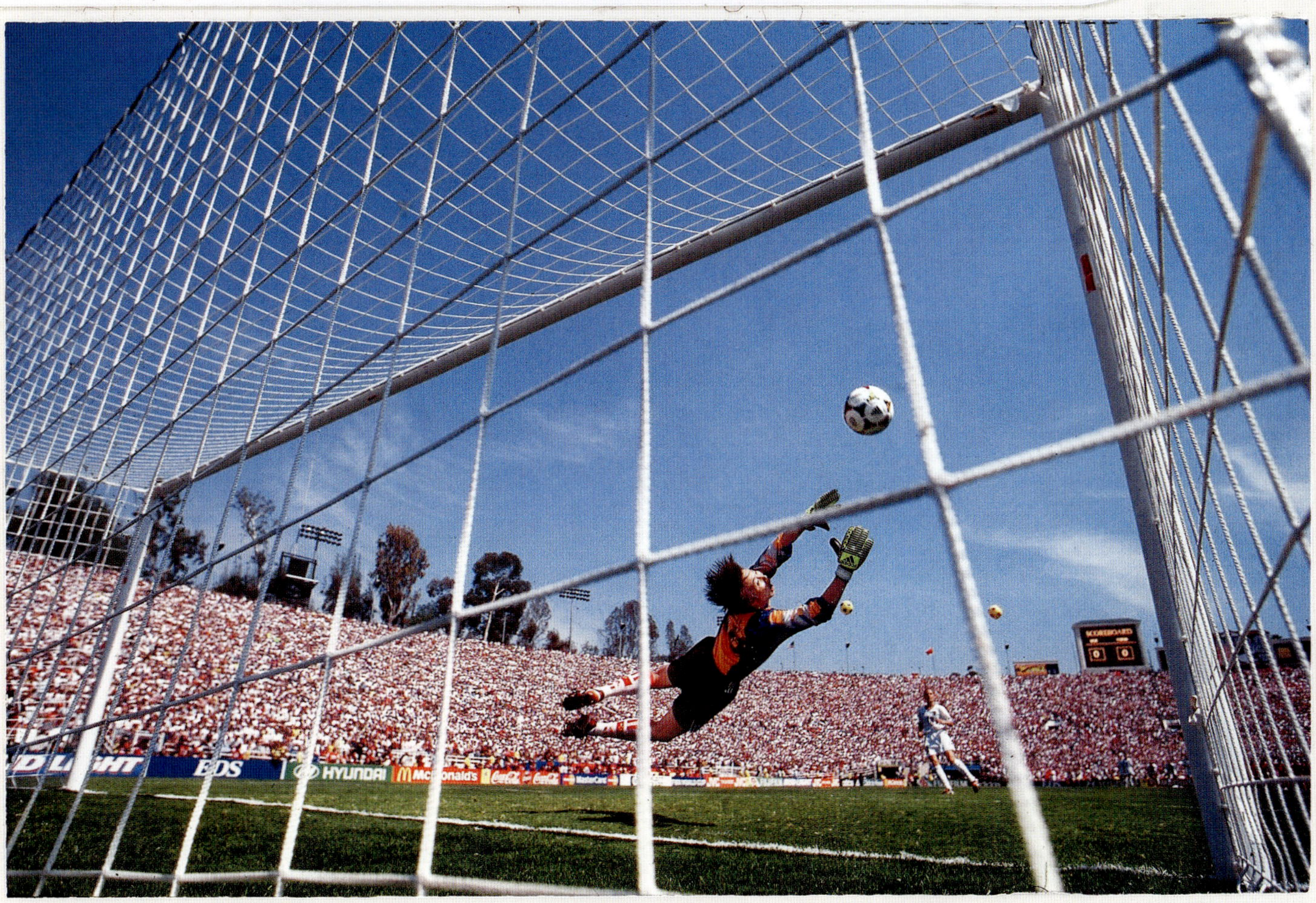

X56265 TK3 F13 R11

game winner ?? No!! 2

Karen Loucks
Sports Illustrated

Klammer
NLB #15

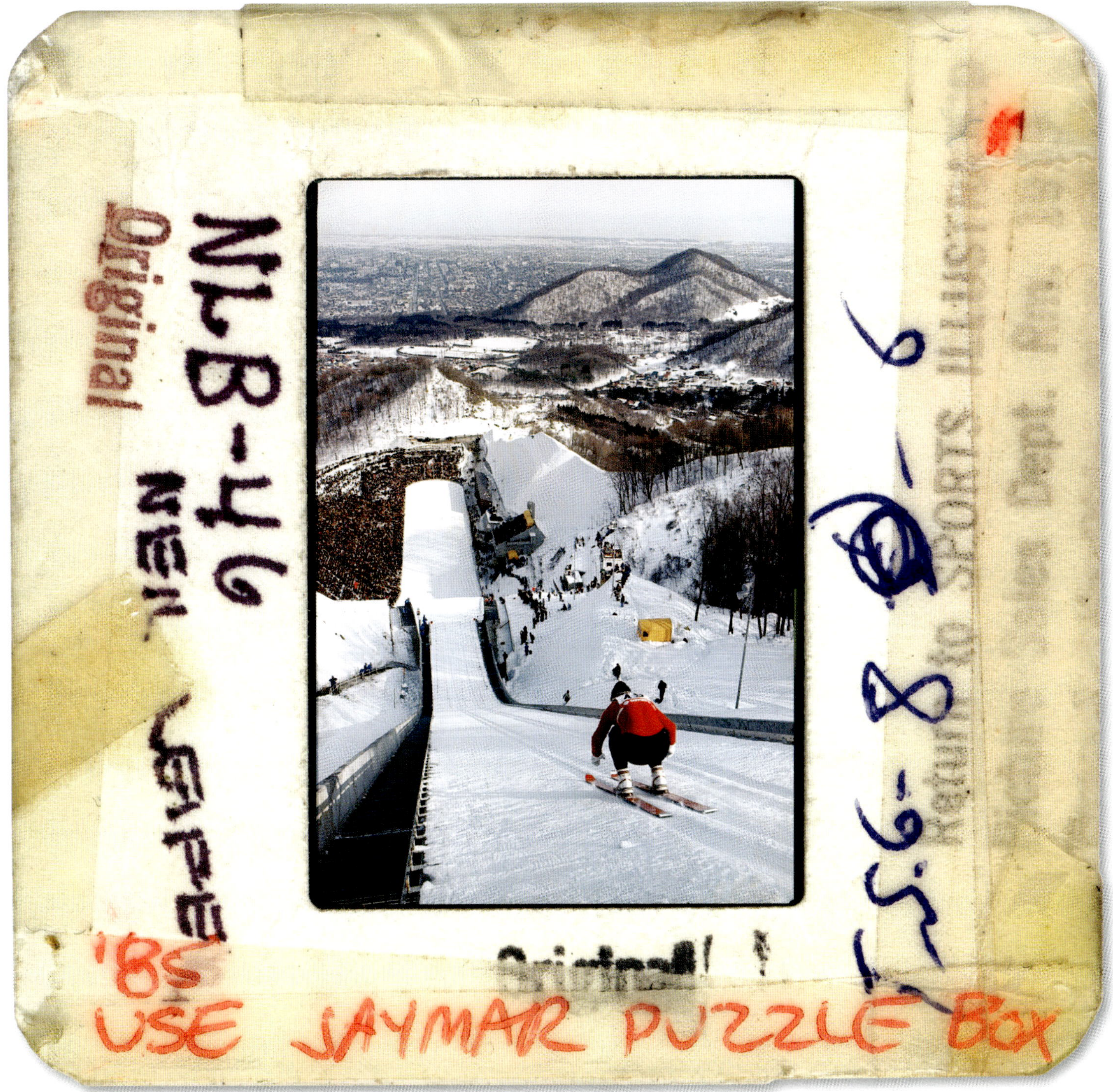

Comin' Down the Mountain

FRANZ KLAMMER *(opposite). Photograph by* NEIL LEIFER, February 5, 1976 • SKI JUMP *(above). Photograph by* NEIL LEIFER, February 1971

WHEN SHOOTING SKIING, Neil Leifer would set up at the start, knowing he would get a clean shot of every racer. This guaranteed him a picture of the winner—here, at the 1976 Olympics in Innsbruck, Austria's Franz Klammer. At the site of the '72 Olympics in Sapporo, Leifer saw that the real winner was the view from atop the ski jump. The shot (note red script on slide) was made into a jigsaw puzzle.

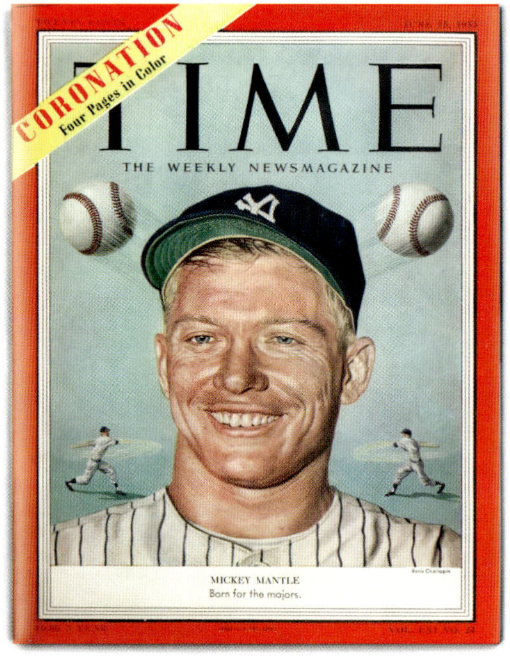

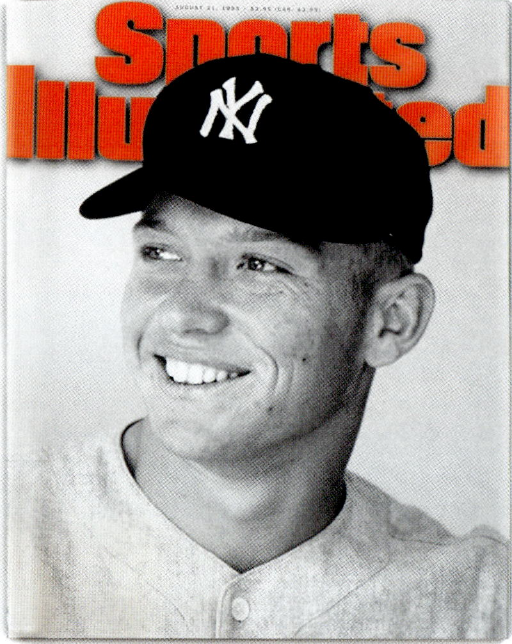

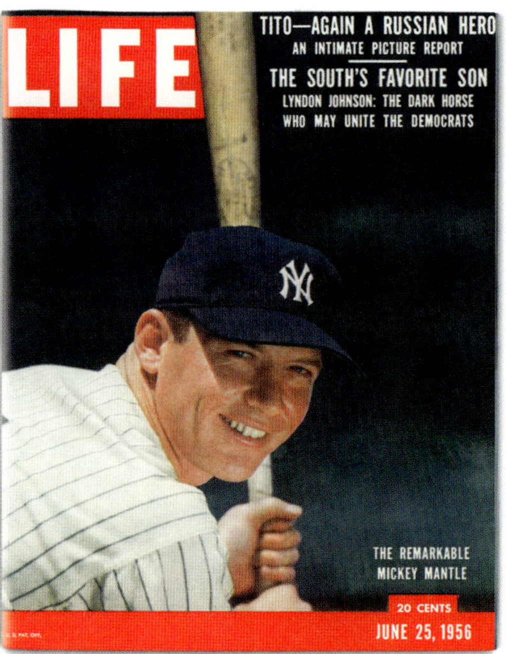

Simply Seven

MICKEY MANTLE
Photograph by NEIL LEIFER, circa 1960

AS THE UNMARKED mount suggests, this photo never ran in the magazine, perhaps because the face can't really be seen. Yet the swing and the 7 make it unmistakably The Mick. He belonged to the larger culture—not only to SI, but also to LIFE and to TIME. The above SI cover ran in 1995, when Mantle died at age 63. It, too, was unmarked, one of the very few SI covers without any type—the famous face spoke for itself. In that issue Richard Hoffer wrote, "For generations of men, he's the guy, has been the guy, will be the guy. What does that mean? A woman beseeches Mantle, who survived beyond his baseball career as a kind of corporate greeter, to make an appearance, to surprise her husband. Mantle materializes at some cocktail party, introductions are made, and the husband weeps in the presence of fantasy made flesh. That's what it means."

2 SPORTS ILLUSTRATED D24652

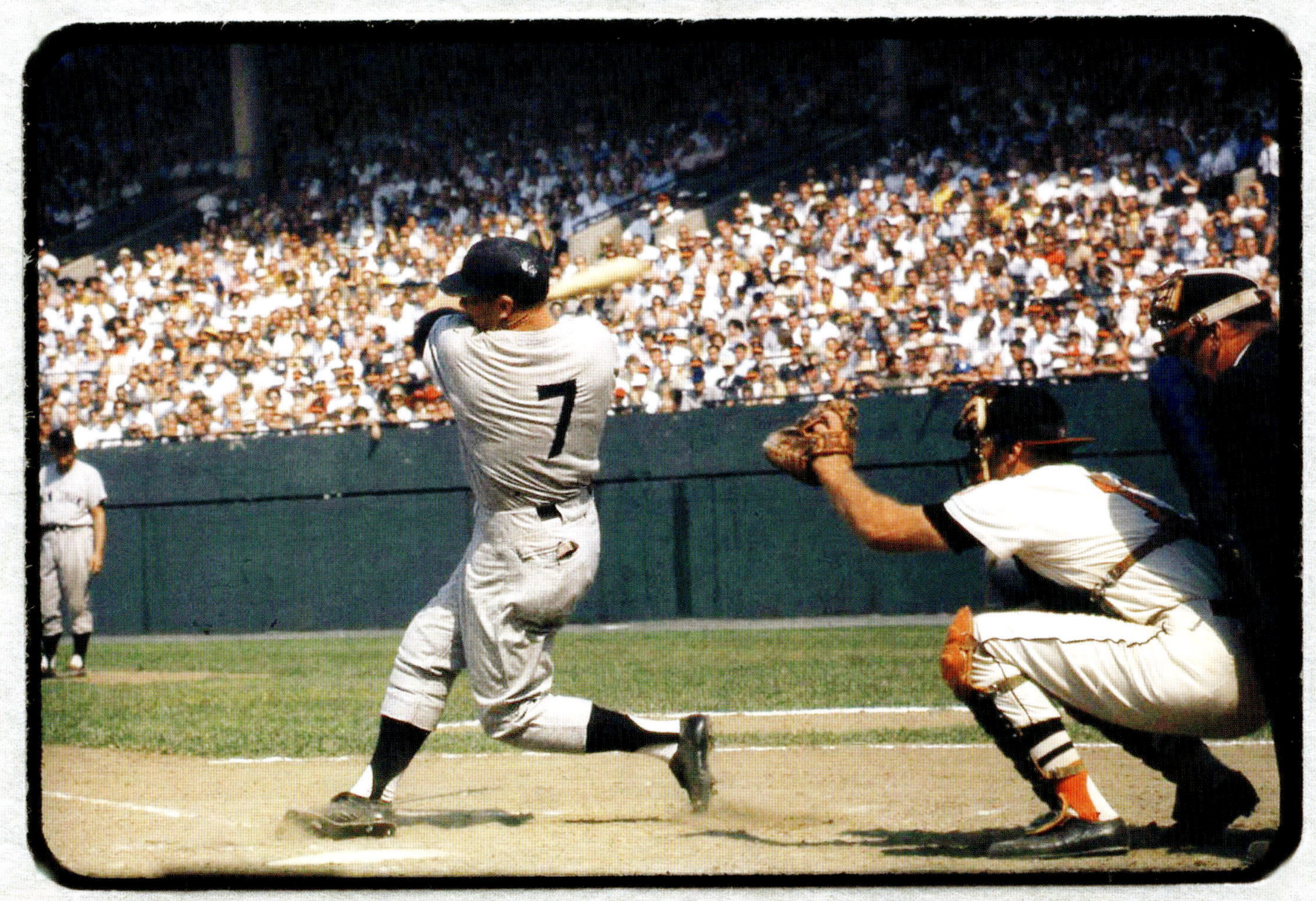

O BY NEIL LEIFER

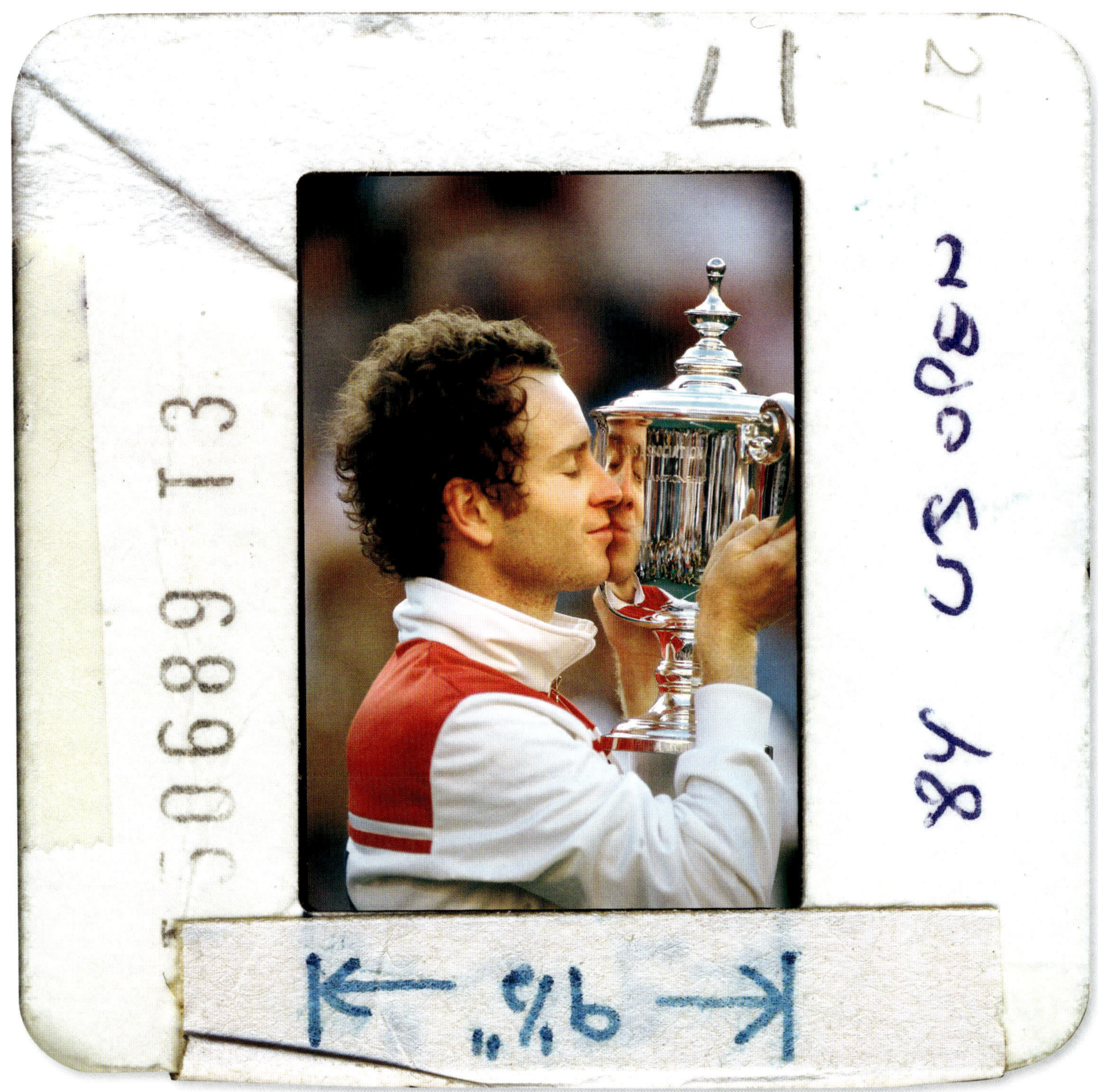

Ecstasy, Agony

JOHN McENROE *(above). Photograph by* NEIL LEIFER, September 9, 1984 • PAYNE STEWART *(opposite). Photograph by* JOHN IACONO, April 13, 1986

THE GAMES GIVETH, and they taketh away. The visage of the usually irascible McEnroe was a reflection of quiet bliss after he won the U.S. Open. The look on the face of Stewart at the Masters (and the scribble on the slide) tells you he missed the putt.

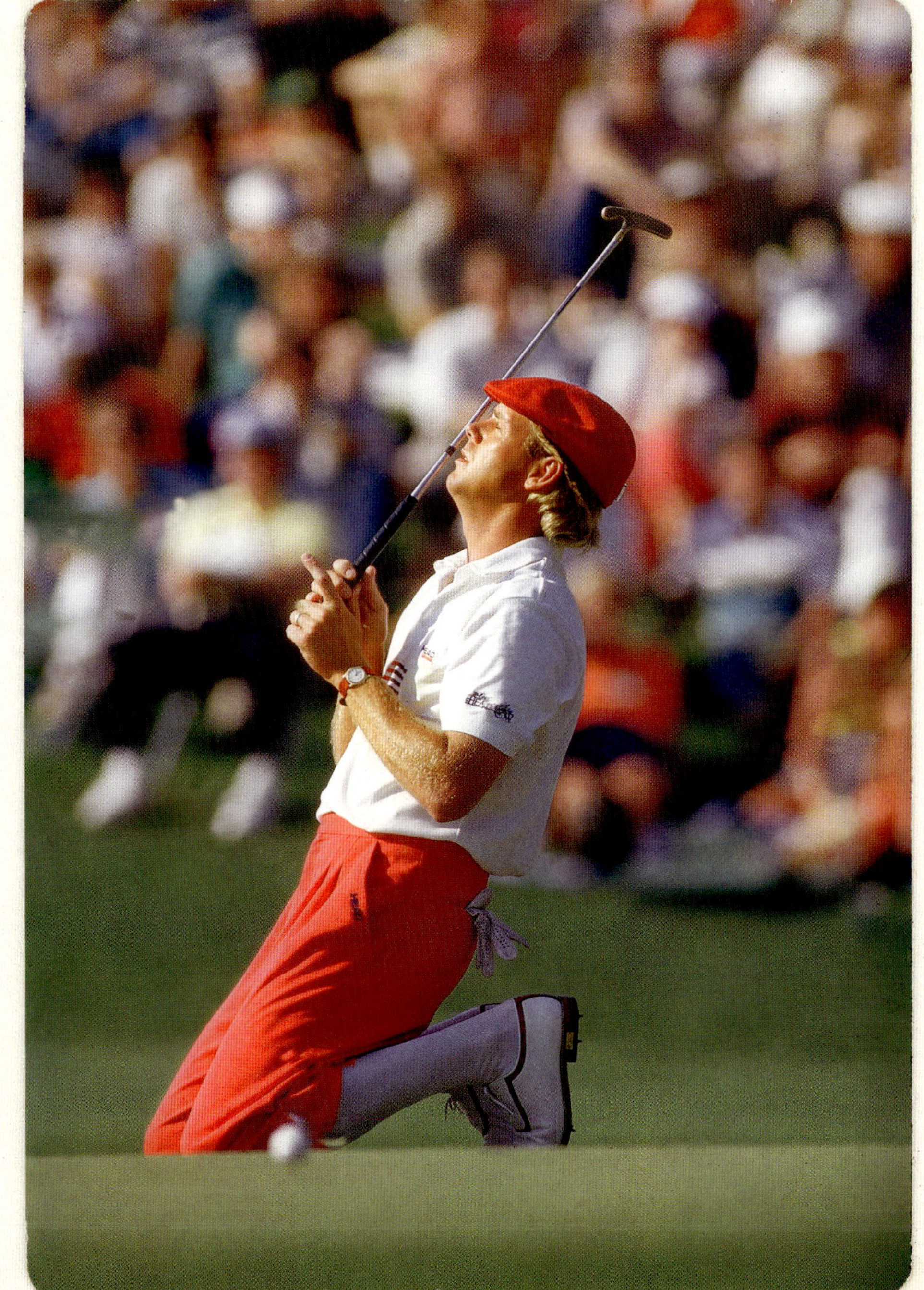

X32934 T4

972

5-18-87

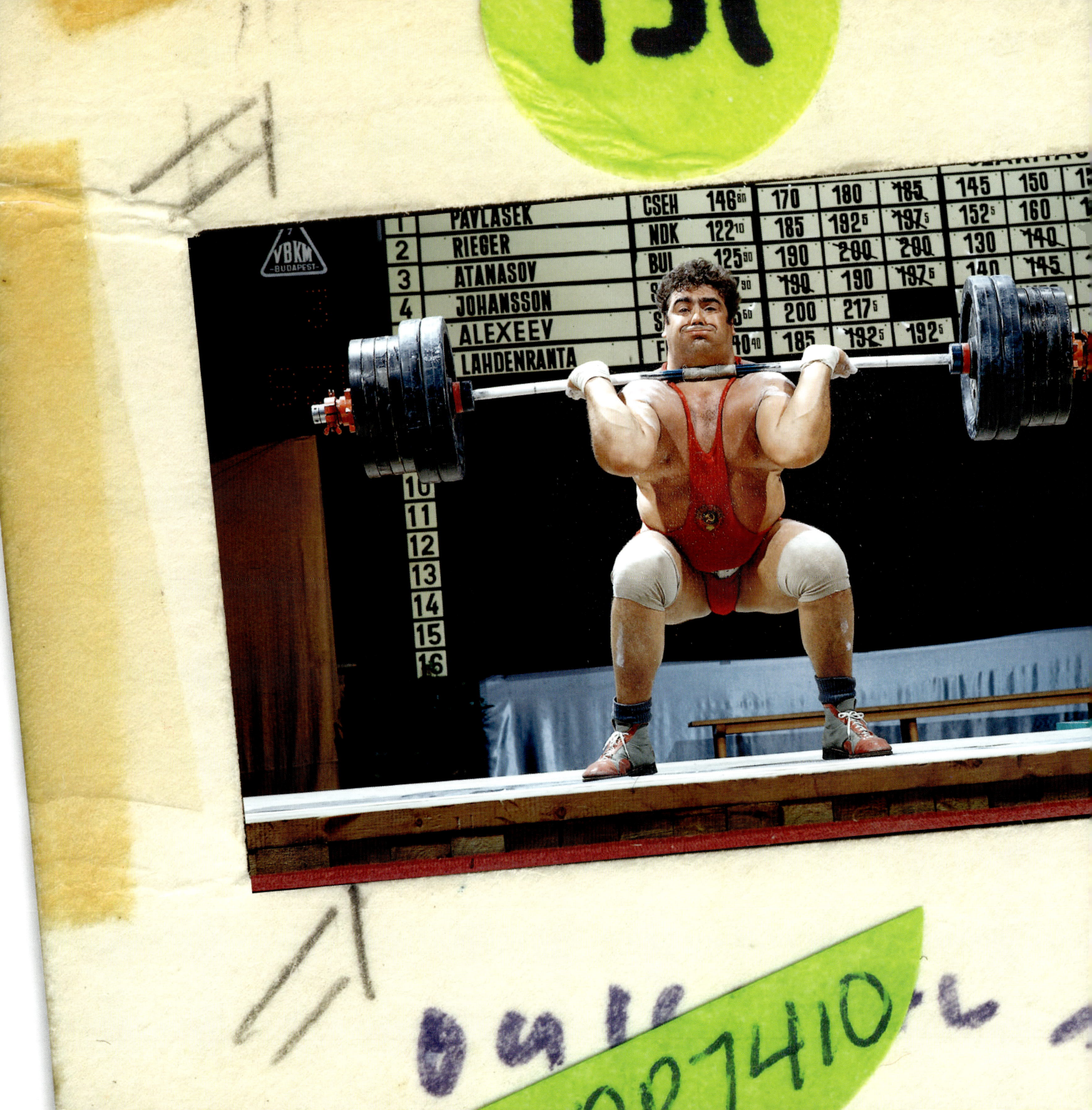
VBKM
BUDAPEST
PAVLASEK
RIEGER
ATANASOV
JOHANSSON
ALEXEEV
LAHDENRANTA
CSEH
NDK
BUL
087410

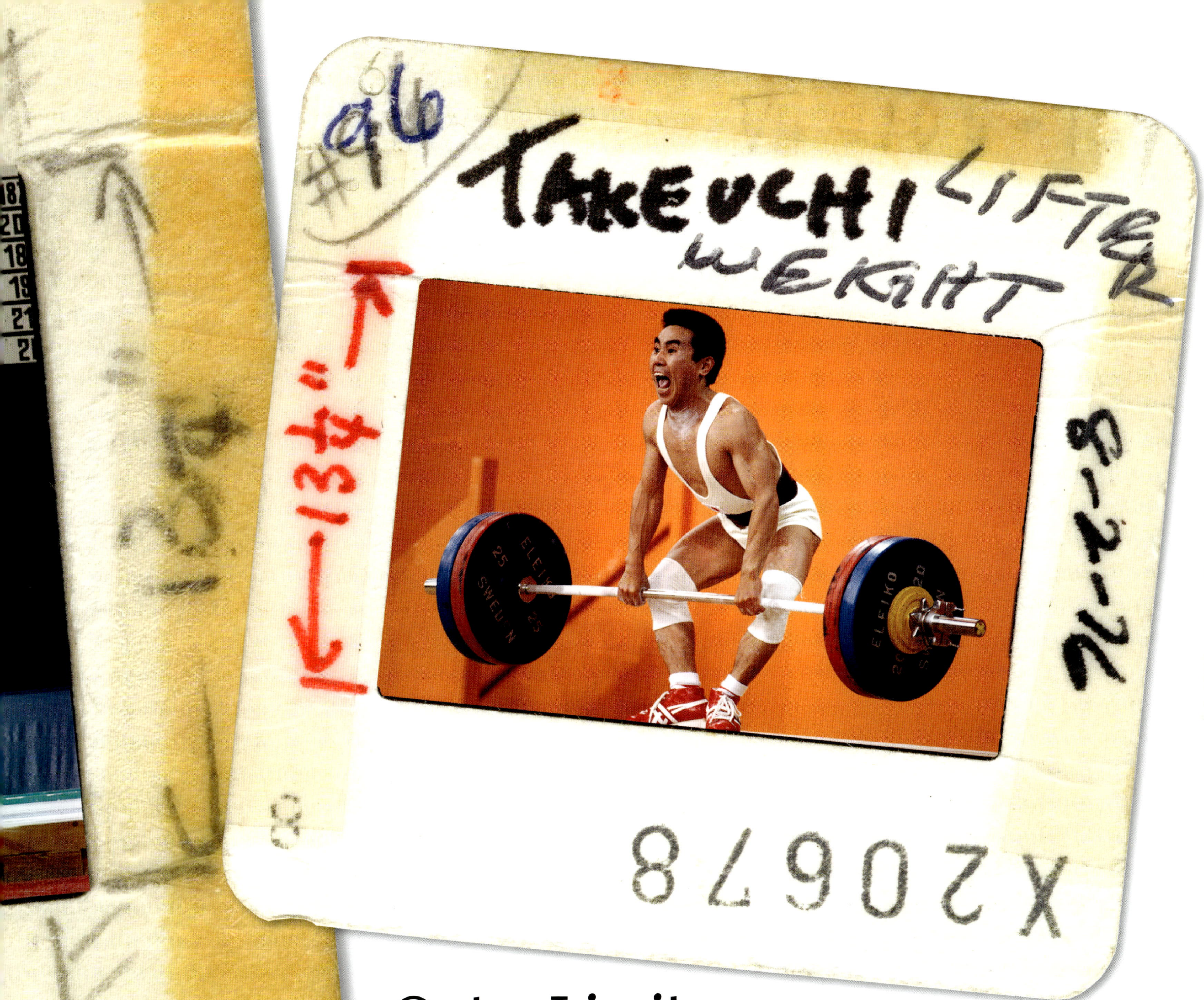

Outer Limits

VASILY ALEXEYEV *(opposite). Photograph by* NEIL LEIFER, June 1970 • MASATOMO TAKEUCHI *(above). Photograph by* NEIL LEIFER, JULY 18, 1976

WHEN TRYING TO LIFT a weight that could crush him, a man isn't concerned about the faces he makes (see the howl of Japanese flyweight Masatomo Takeuchi), which is why the sport is one of Leifer's favorites. For the Alexeyev photo, Leifer set up at the front edge of the stage, putting himself at risk from falling dumbbells.

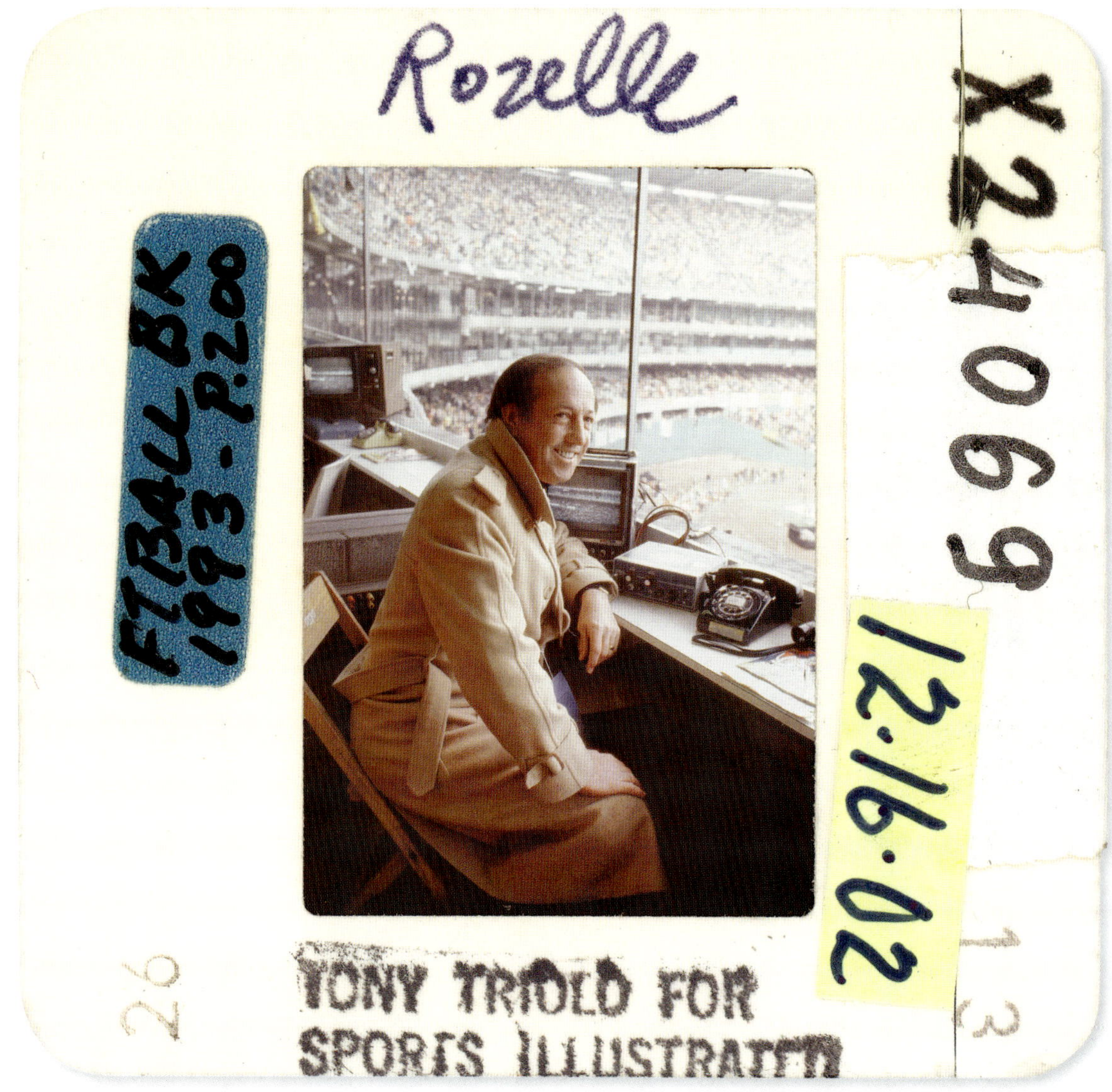

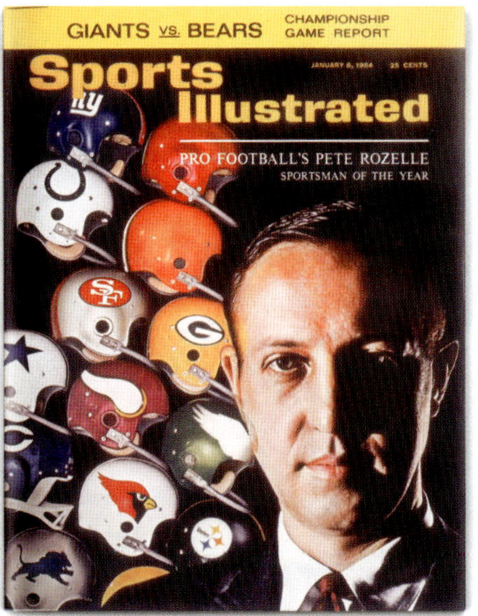

The Night Shift

PETE ROZELLE *(above)*
Photograph by TONY TRIOLO, December 30, 1979

HOWARD COSELL *(opposite)*
Photograph by LANE STEWART, July 1983

FAR FROM THE FIELD OF PLAY, Pete Rozelle and Howard Cosell helped change forever how—and when—we watch sports. Rozelle, together with ABC's Roone Arledge, launched *Monday Night Football* in 1970, with Cosell as the show's opinionated, abrasive announcer. By its second season the show was drawing 30 million viewers a week. In the 1994 story in which the Cosell photo ran, Steve Rushin wrote that the success of *Monday Night Football* soon led the World Series and the Super Bowl to abandon their afternoon time slots. As Arledge told Rushin, executives realized that "the way to get more money is to play your games in prime time."

Media: Portrait of ABC's Howard Cosell alone during taping of "Speaking of Everything" radio

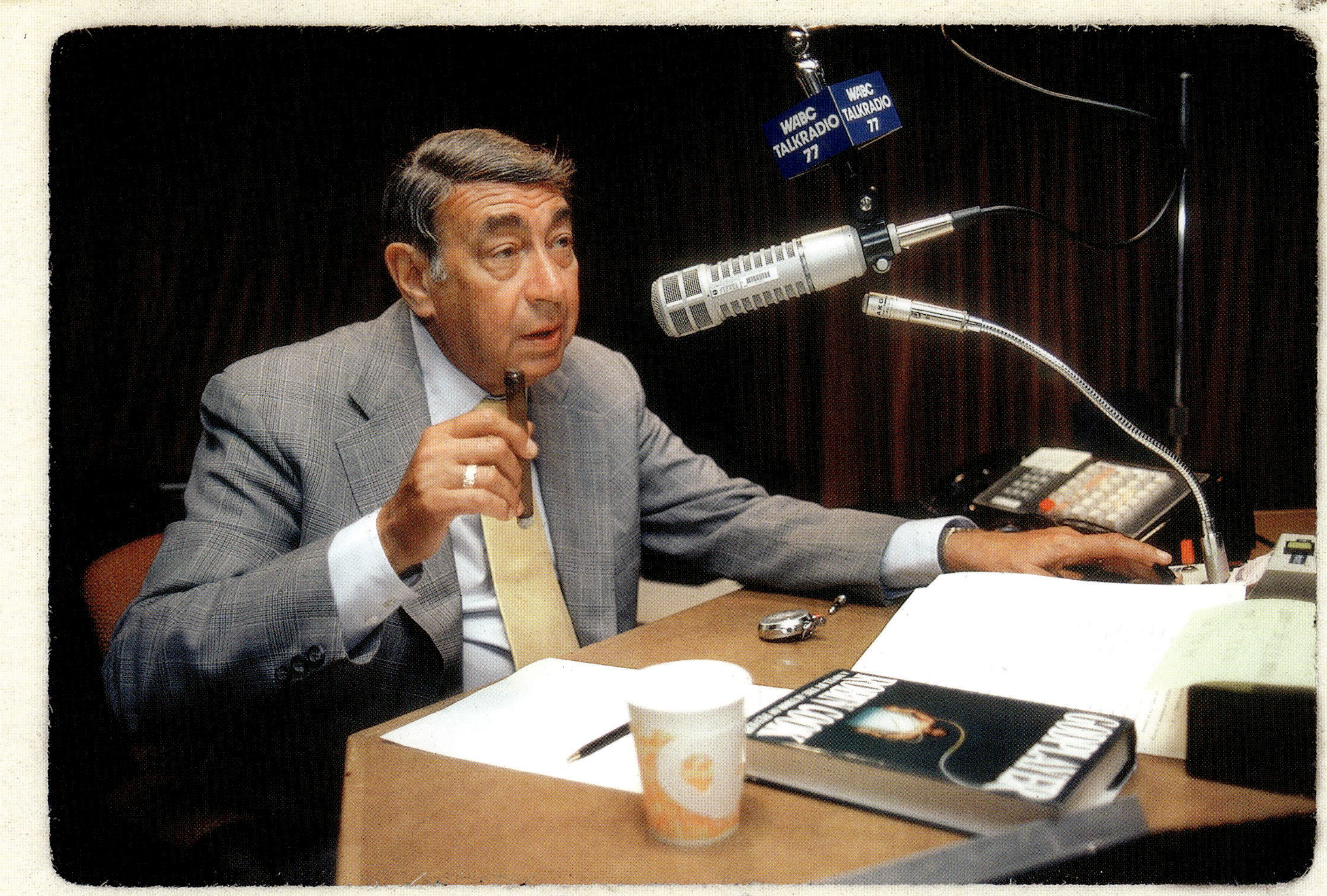

1983 Original

LANE STEWART FOR SPORTS ILLUSTRATED

"Speaking of Everything" Radio show

LANE STEWART FOR SPORTS ILLUSTRATED

8/15/94

6

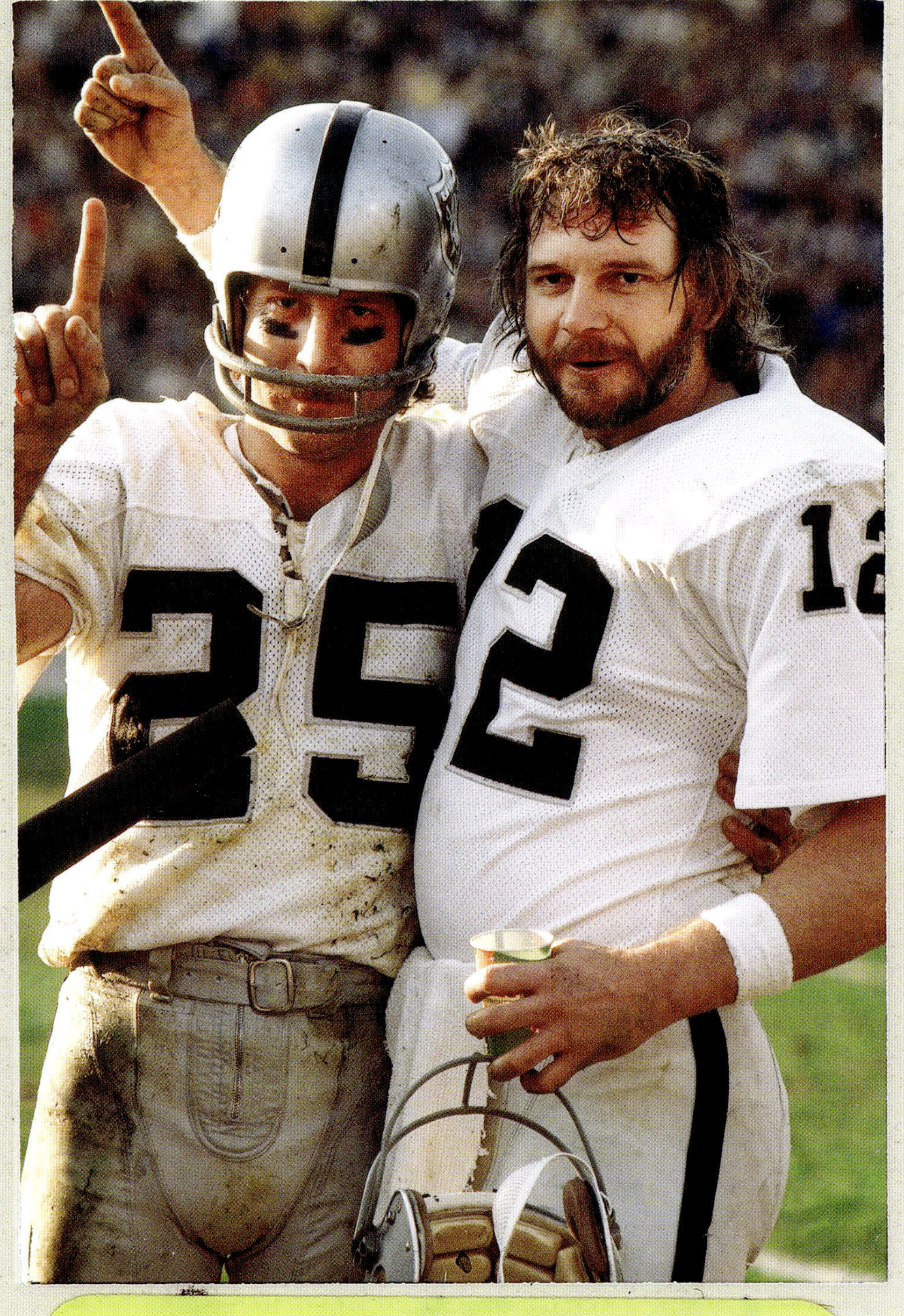
16 x 20
S. I. Pic Collection
25
12
12-11-89

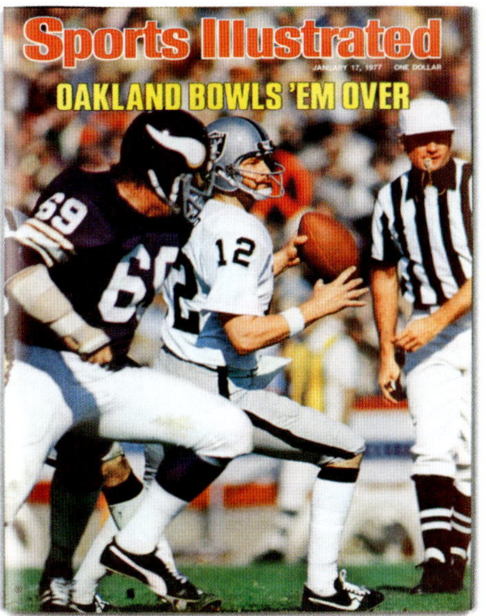

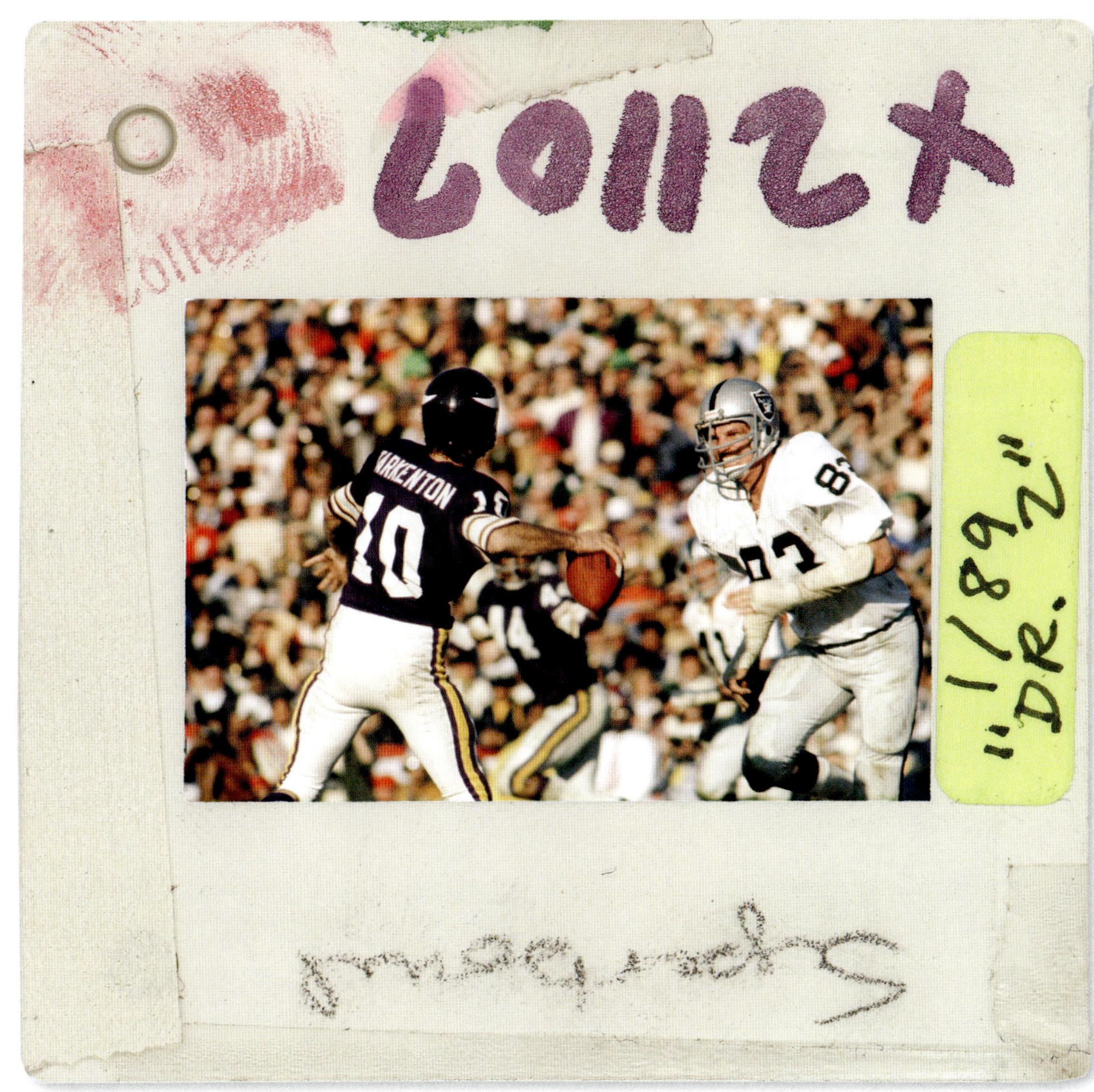

Purple Prose

SUPER BOWL XI

Photographs by WALTER IOOSS JR., January 9, 1977

IT MAY BE MORE THAN COINCIDENCE, perhaps some photo editor's cruel joke, that these slides were inscribed with a violet marker, color-coordinated to the Vikings' uniforms. The tale they tell is of Minnesota's losing to the Raiders and falling to an ignominious 0 for 4 in Super Bowls. Neither of these photos actually ran with SI's Super Bowl XI game story; both only made it into print, somewhat randomly, in 1989. The above shot of Ted Hendricks bearing down on Fran Tarkenton ran in a special issue of Paul Zimmerman's Super Bowl memories; the photo of Ken Stabler with receiver Fred Biletnikoff illustrated a feature that year on Raiders owner Al Davis.

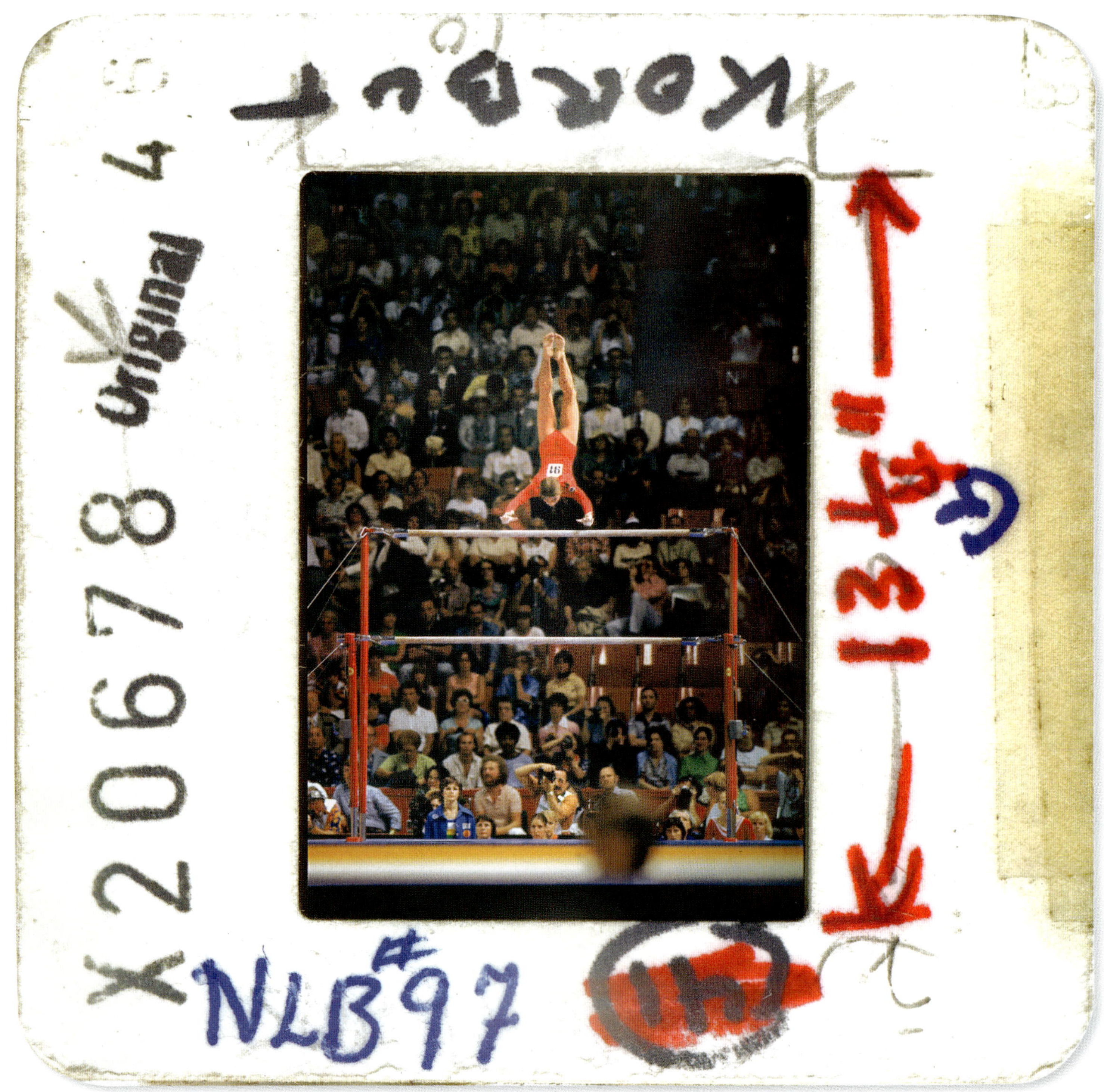

Small Wonder

OLGA KORBUT *(above). Photograph by* NEIL LEIFER, July 1976 • NADIA COMANECI *(right). Photograph by* NEIL LEIFER, July 1976

THE BIGGEST CLASH of the 1976 Olympics was between two tiny women. Nadia Comaneci scored the Games' first perfect 10s and won three golds to Olga Korbut's one. The tape on the slides is from the mounts being cut open to remove the film for scanning.

20678

35th Anniversary Issue

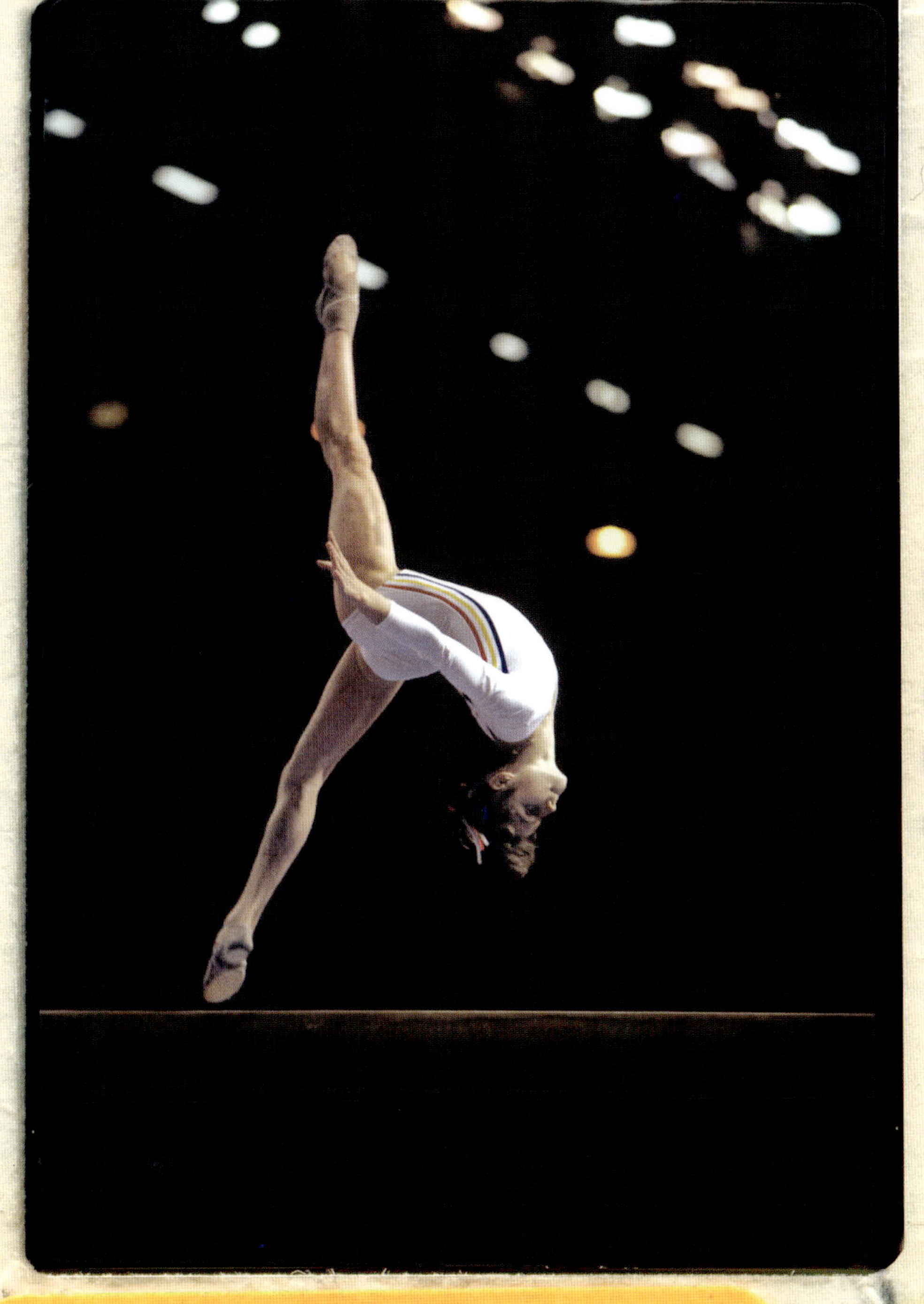

ORIGINAL

Board Meeting

NBA FINALS

Photograph by MANNY MILLAN, May 11, 1980

WHY POSE PLAYERS when you get organic choreography like this? Here the players have thoughtfully arranged themselves in a ring (with the NBA's alltime leading scorer, Kareem Abdul-Jabbar, and its most acrobatic player, Julius Erving, locked in the middle—nice touch!). Manny Millan recalls having to argue for this photo to run. An editor had initially discarded the image because it was missing one thing: the ball.

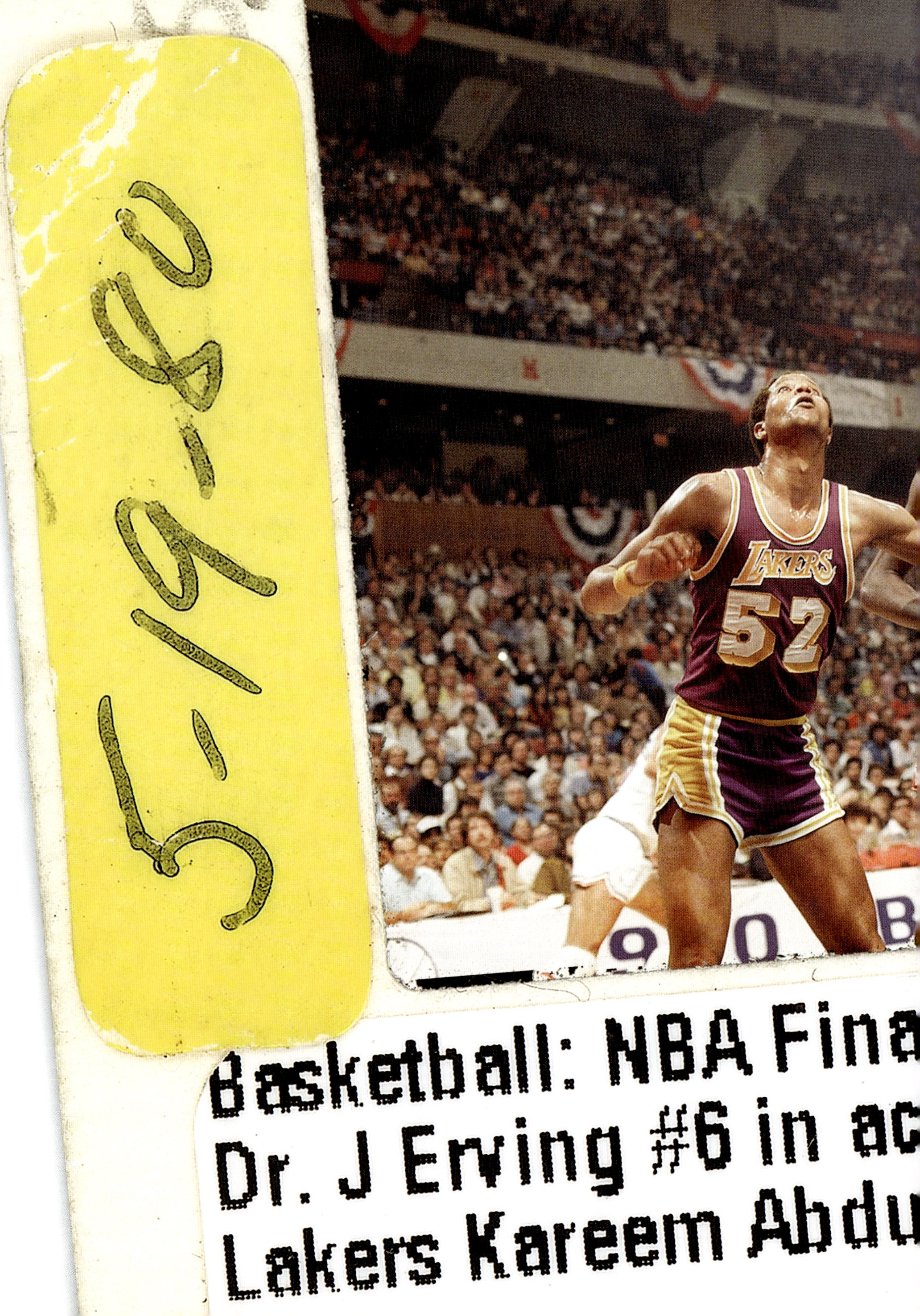

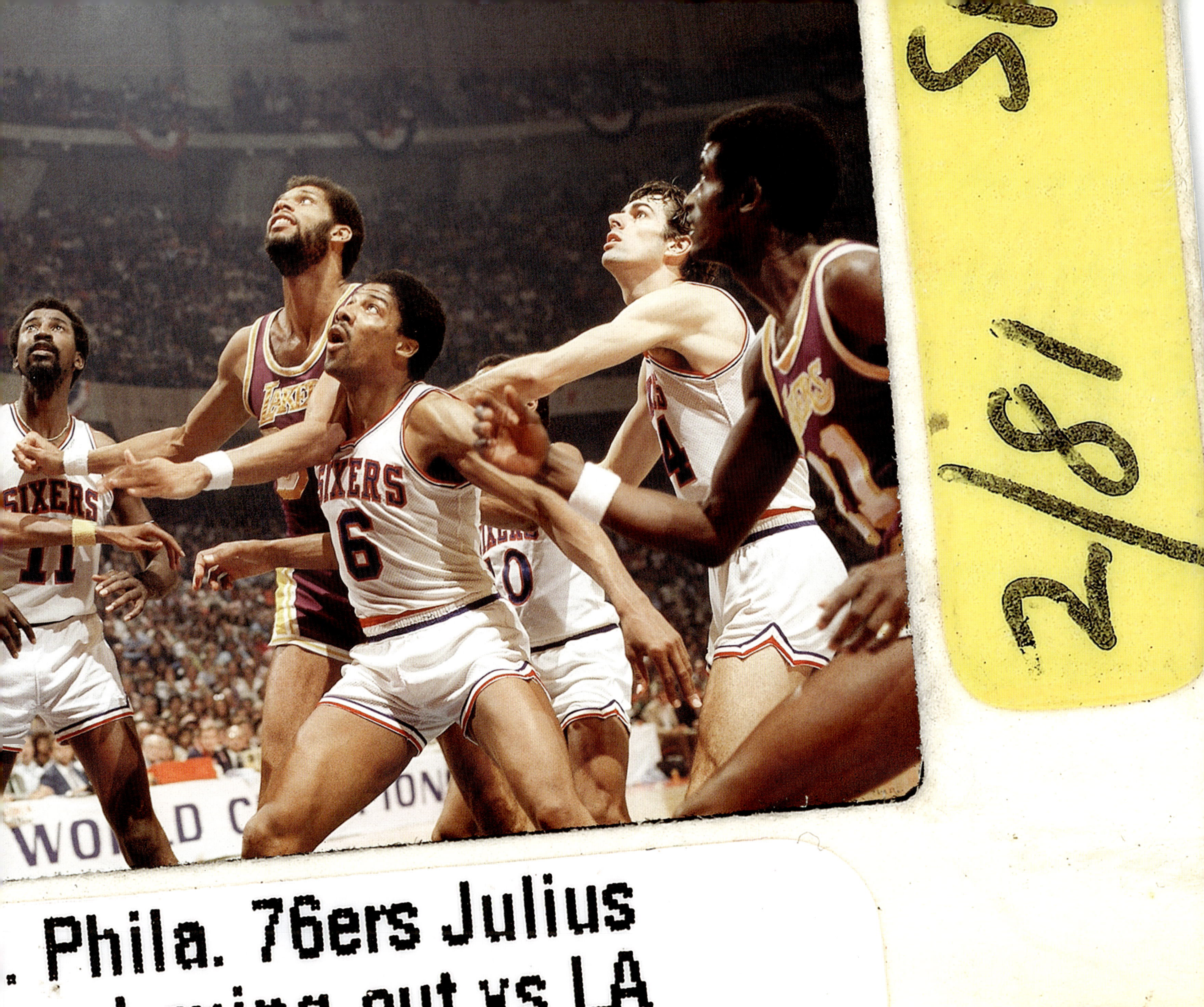

. Phila. 76ers Julius
on, boxing out vs LA
Jabbar #33.

The Catch (Not the Throw)

NFC CHAMPIONSHIP GAME *(near right)*
Photograph by CARL IWASAKI, January 10, 1982

NFC CHAMPIONSHIP GAME *(opposite)*
Photograph by WALTER IOOSS JR., January 10, 1982

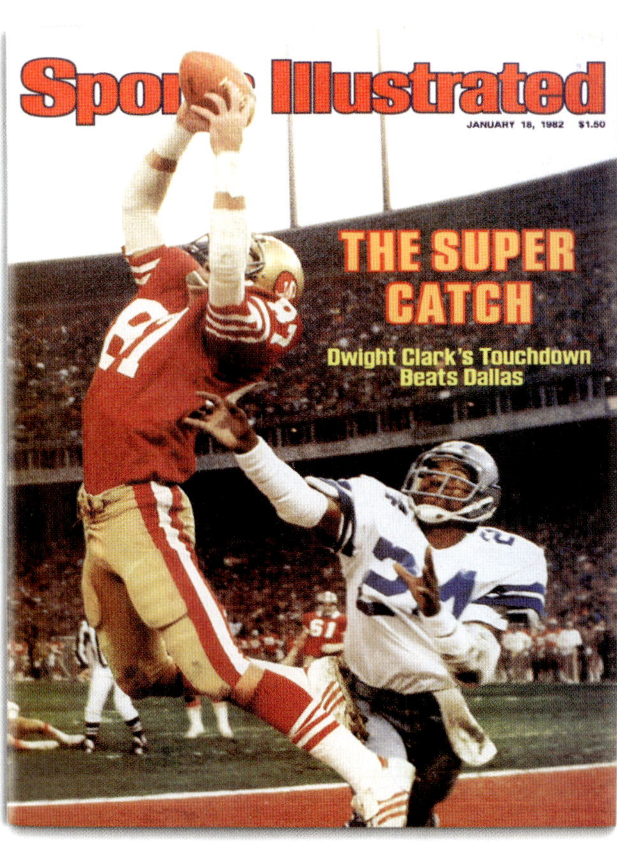

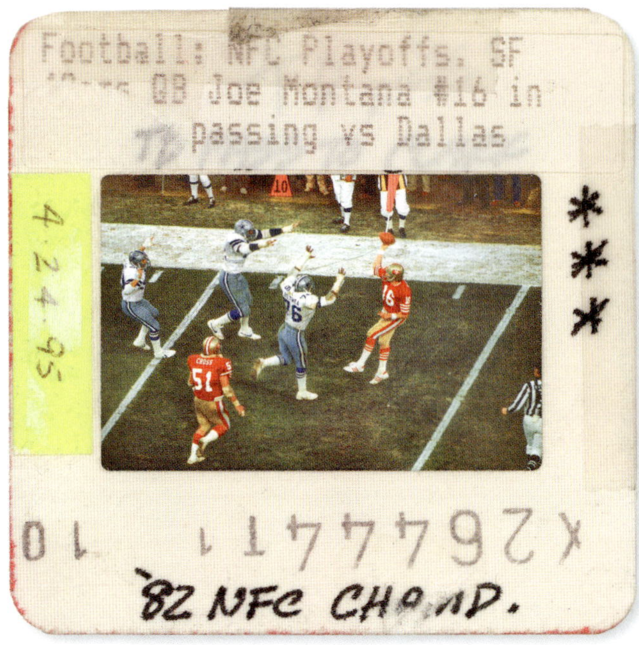

RIGHT PLACE, RIGHT TIME. Any sports photographer will tell you that's half the battle. Carl Iwasaki's picture of Joe Montana's game-winning throw didn't even merit inclusion in the game story. (It ran only when Montana retired in 1995.) Meanwhile, Walter Iooss Jr. had set up in the end zone and snapped a soaring Dwight Clark in what has become one of the magazine's enduring images (as the abundant gold stickers on the slide attest). Iooss's picture, though, was the result of more than positioning. He'd been shooting the beginning of this play with a telephoto lens, but as he saw the action coming his way he quickly switched to a camera around his neck with a 50-millimeter lens, better suited to close-up action. He framed the moment perfectly. Clark and Montana weren't the only ones to come through in the clutch that day.

Football: NFC playoffs. SF 49ers Dwight Clark #87 in action, scoring TD vs Dallas Cowboys. The Catch.

7·26·99

12·28·98

SIP HITS 97

8-13-90

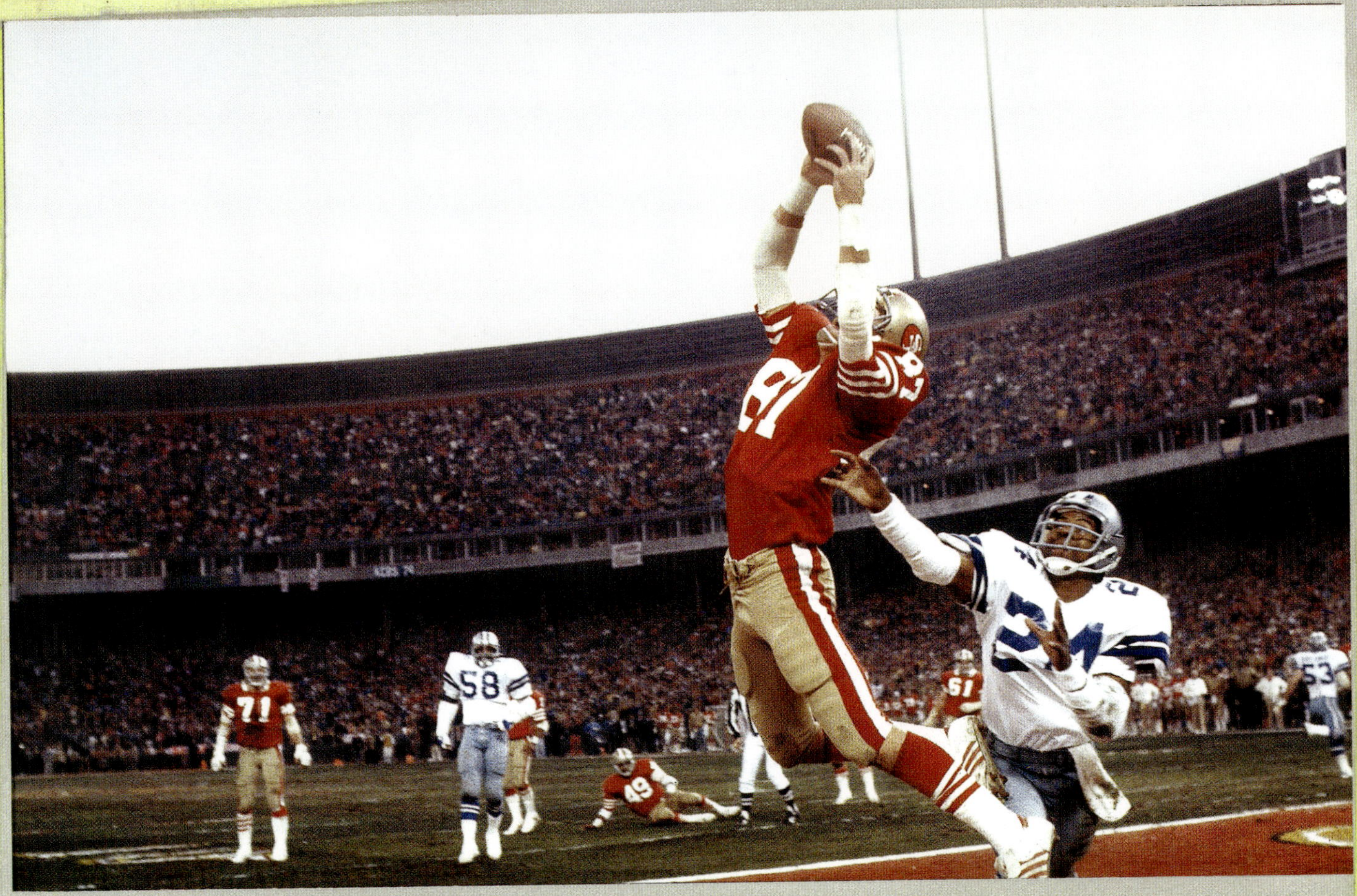

DALLAS SP.

11-14-94

9-7-92

X26442

1-18-82

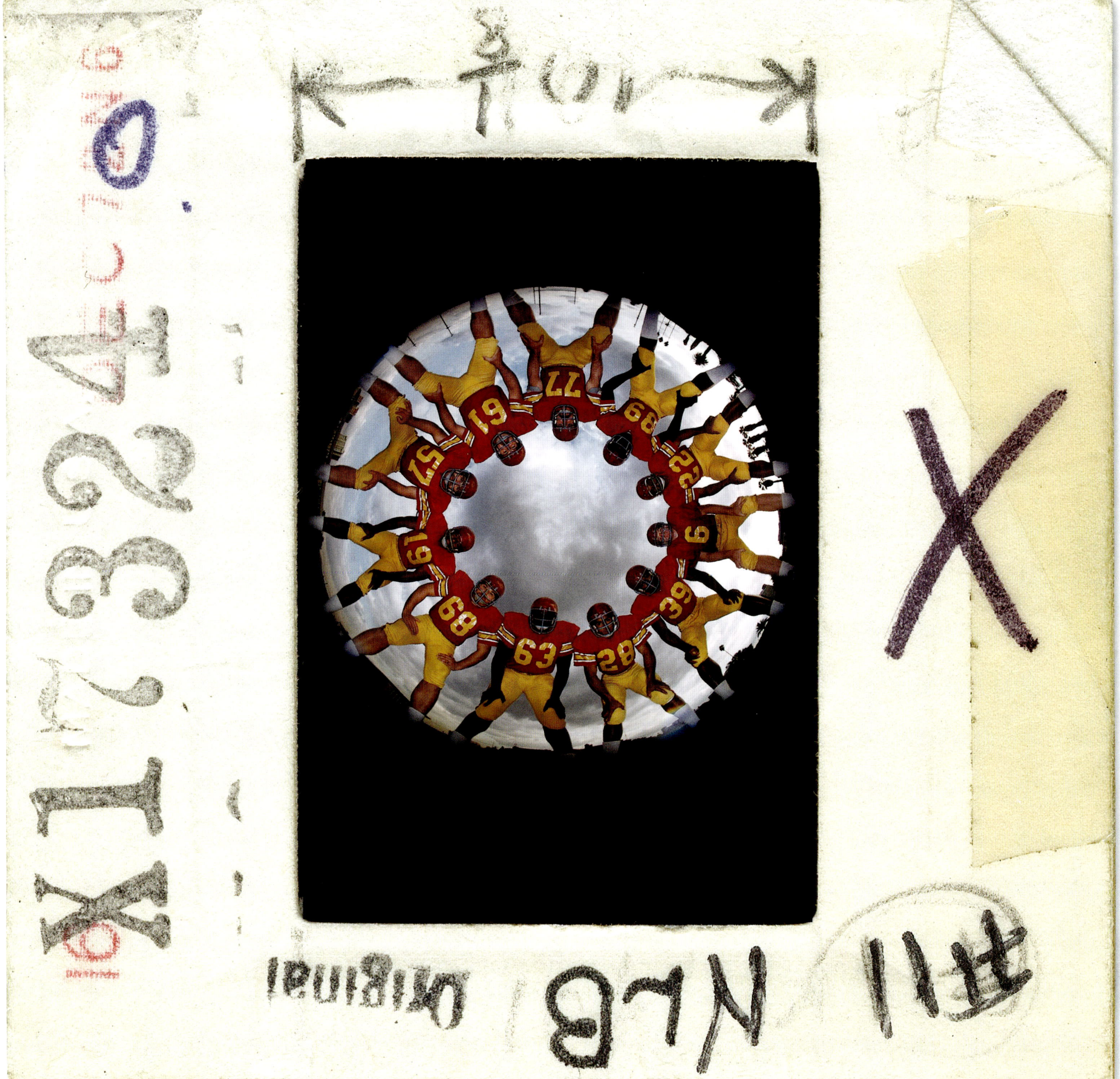

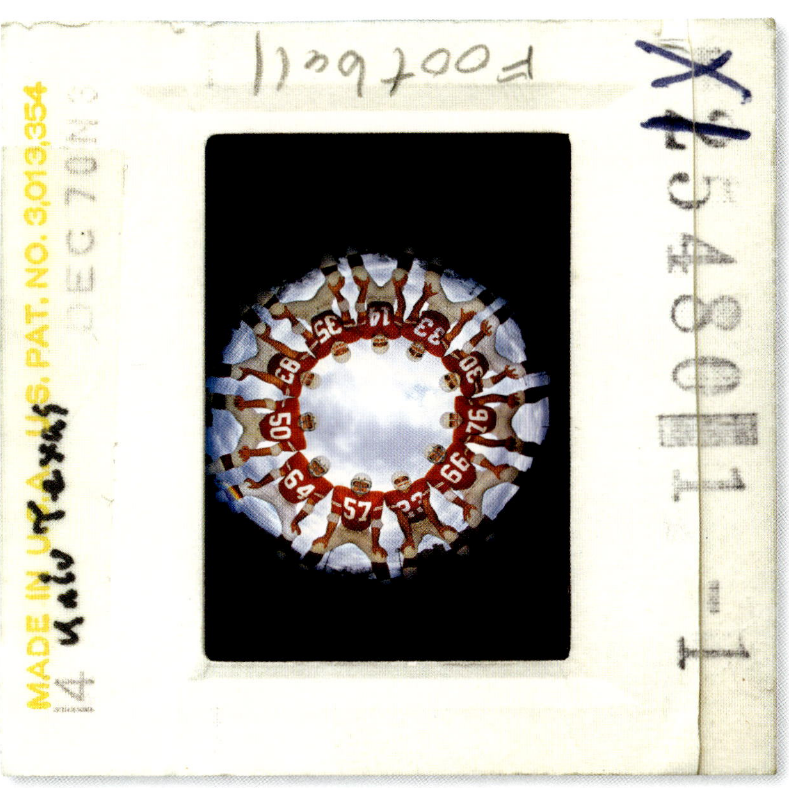

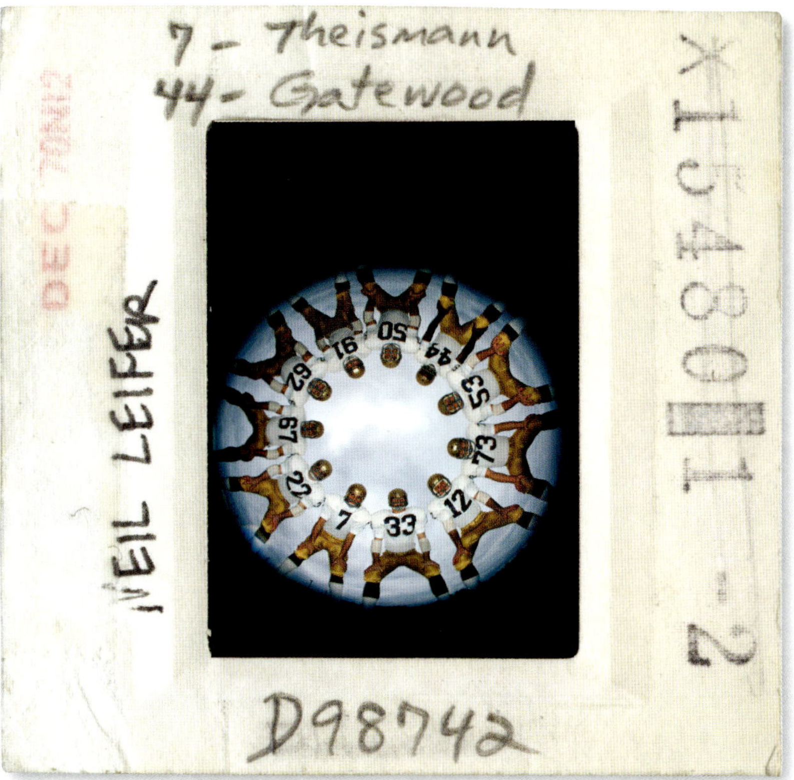

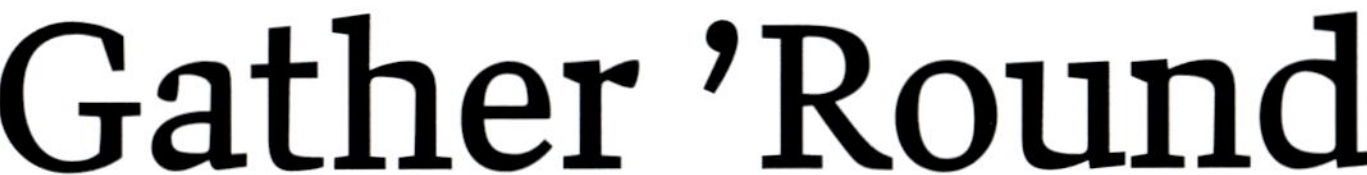

Gather ’Round

USC *(opposite)*
Photograph by NEIL LEIFER, December 1972

TEXAS *(above)*
Photograph by NEIL LEIFER, December 1970

NOTRE DAME *(above right)*
Photograph by NEIL LEIFER, December 1970

A HUDDLE IS USUALLY not nearly so orderly, but these players were happy to encircle Neil Leifer’s fisheye lens, which was fired by remote. The photos all show teams with national title aspirations. In 1970, Texas won the final coaches’ poll (which took place before bowl games were played), despite going on to lose in the Cotton Bowl to a Notre Dame team featuring, as noted on the mount, the passing combo of Joe Theismann to Tom Gatewood. In ’72 USC (that’s Lynn Swann, number 22) won the prebowl coaches’ poll, then the AP national title after defeating Ohio State in the Rose Bowl.

X37089 T026

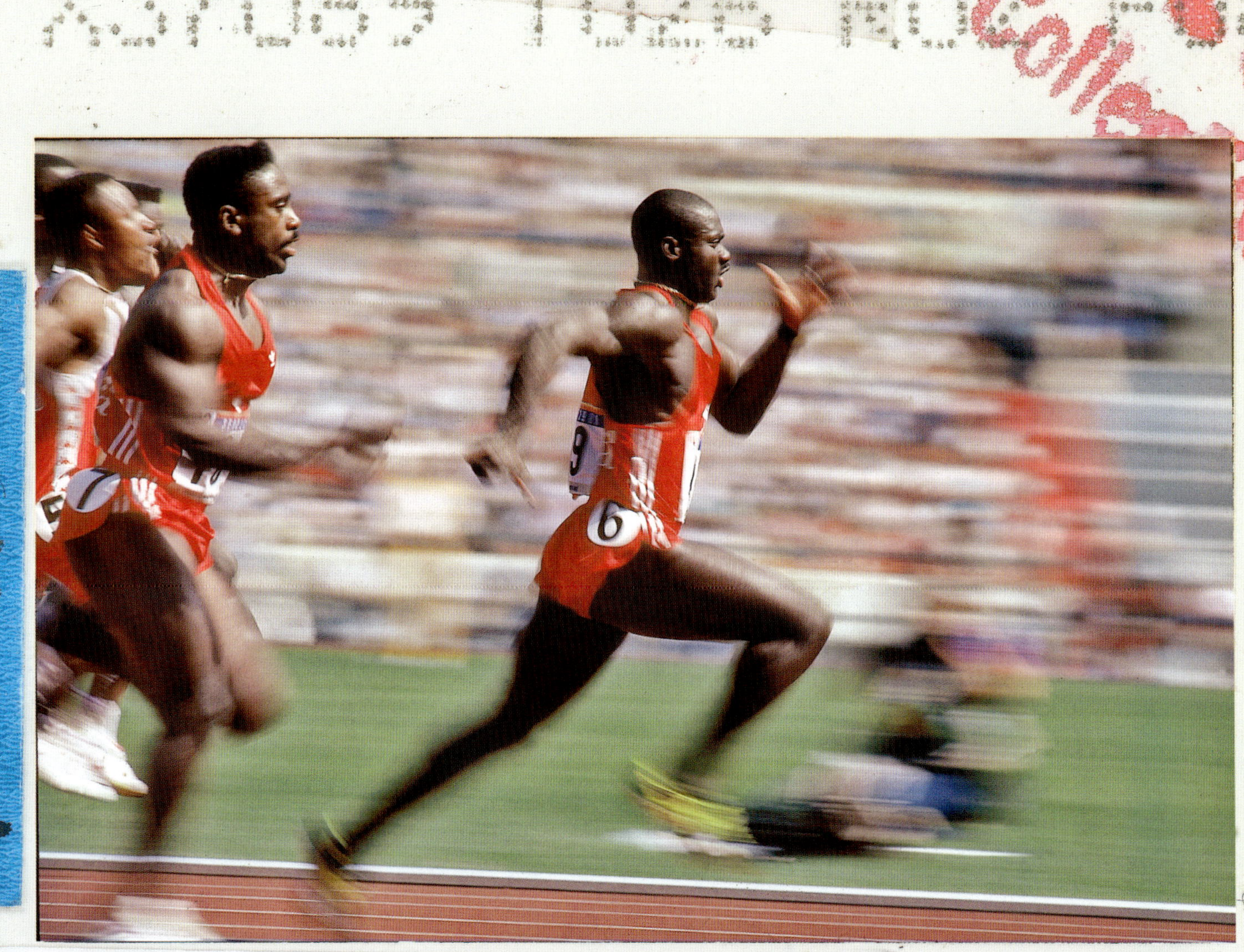

OLY 1988 SUMMER MEN'S TRACK & FIELD 100M FINALS. CAN Ben Johnson in action, leading during race. Cover.

10-3-88 Cover

How Fast It Changes

BEN JOHNSON

Photograph by RONALD C. MODRA, September 24, 1988

THIS COVER on Ben Johnson's record-setting, Olympic gold-medal performance in the 100 meters was originally captioned "WHOOOOOSH!" But at 4 p.m. on the afternoon the issue was closing, managing editor Mark Mulvoy received a call from Cliff Fletcher, G.M. of the Calgary Flames, tipping him off that Johnson, a Canadian, had failed a doping test. (Canada's Olympic team had offices in Calgary's Saddledome, home of the Flames.) Mulvoy called his writers at the Olympic site in Seoul, where it was 6 a.m., roused them from bed and within hours they had cobbled together a remarkably detailed exposé of Johnson's steroid usage for that issue. The cover photo stayed the same, but, as you can see, the line was changed.

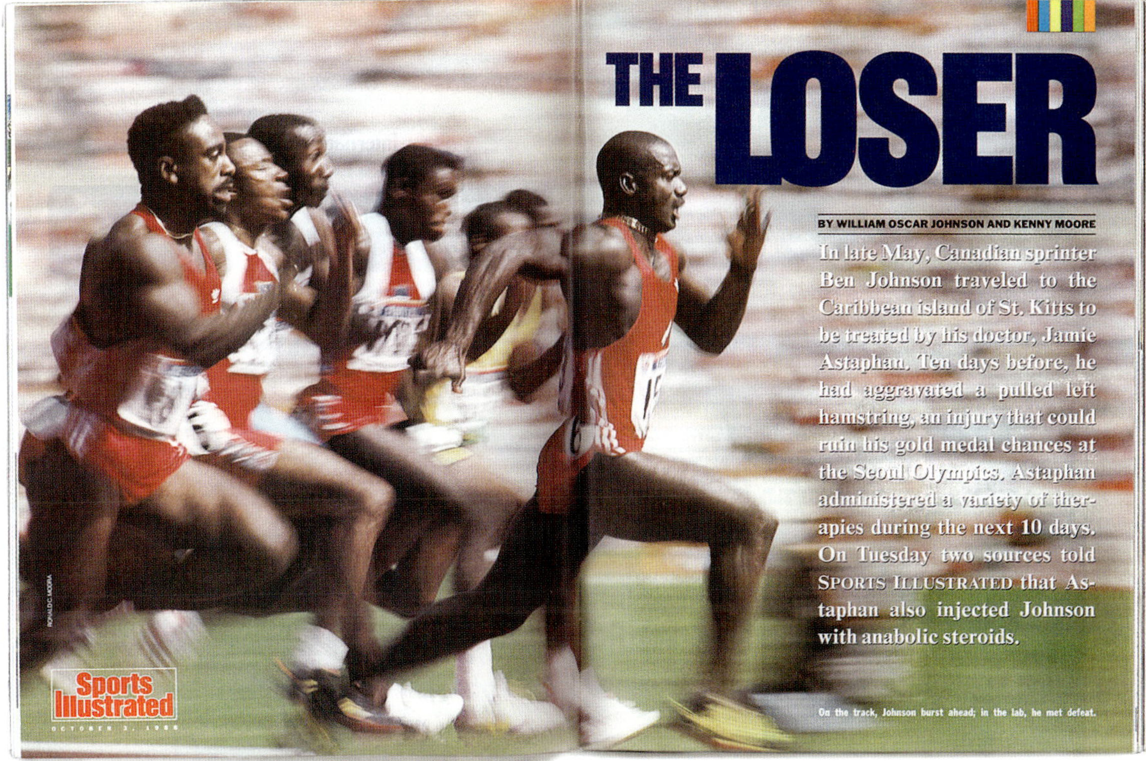

THE LOSER

BY WILLIAM OSCAR JOHNSON AND KENNY MOORE

In late May, Canadian sprinter Ben Johnson traveled to the Caribbean island of St. Kitts to be treated by his doctor, Jamie Astaphan. Ten days before, he had aggravated a pulled left hamstring, an injury that could ruin his gold medal chances at the Seoul Olympics. Astaphan administered a variety of therapies during the next 10 days. On Tuesday two sources told SPORTS ILLUSTRATED that Astaphan also injected Johnson with anabolic steroids.

On the track, Johnson burst ahead; in the lab, he met defeat.

Sports Illustrated

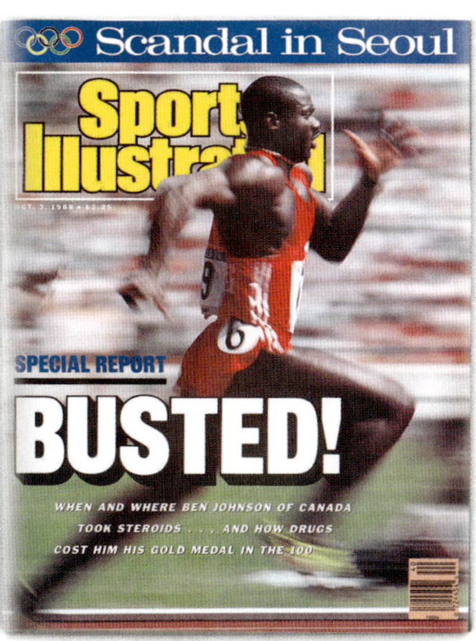

Dressed to The Nines

BETTY JAMESON

Photograph by HY PESKIN, February 9, 1956

THEY WERE PIONEERS of their game, and they came sporting a multitude of fashions, variety from head to toe. In this 1956 story, writer Betty Hicks looked at the progress made by the LPGA, then just six years into its existence, and happily declared, "Everything in women's golf is getting bigger. The tournaments are more frequent, the purses plumper and the field larger." Betty Jameson—whose photo ran on an earlier spread in the story—was a founding member of the LPGA and one of the game's powerhouses. When this story ran, she had already won every LPGA major championship.

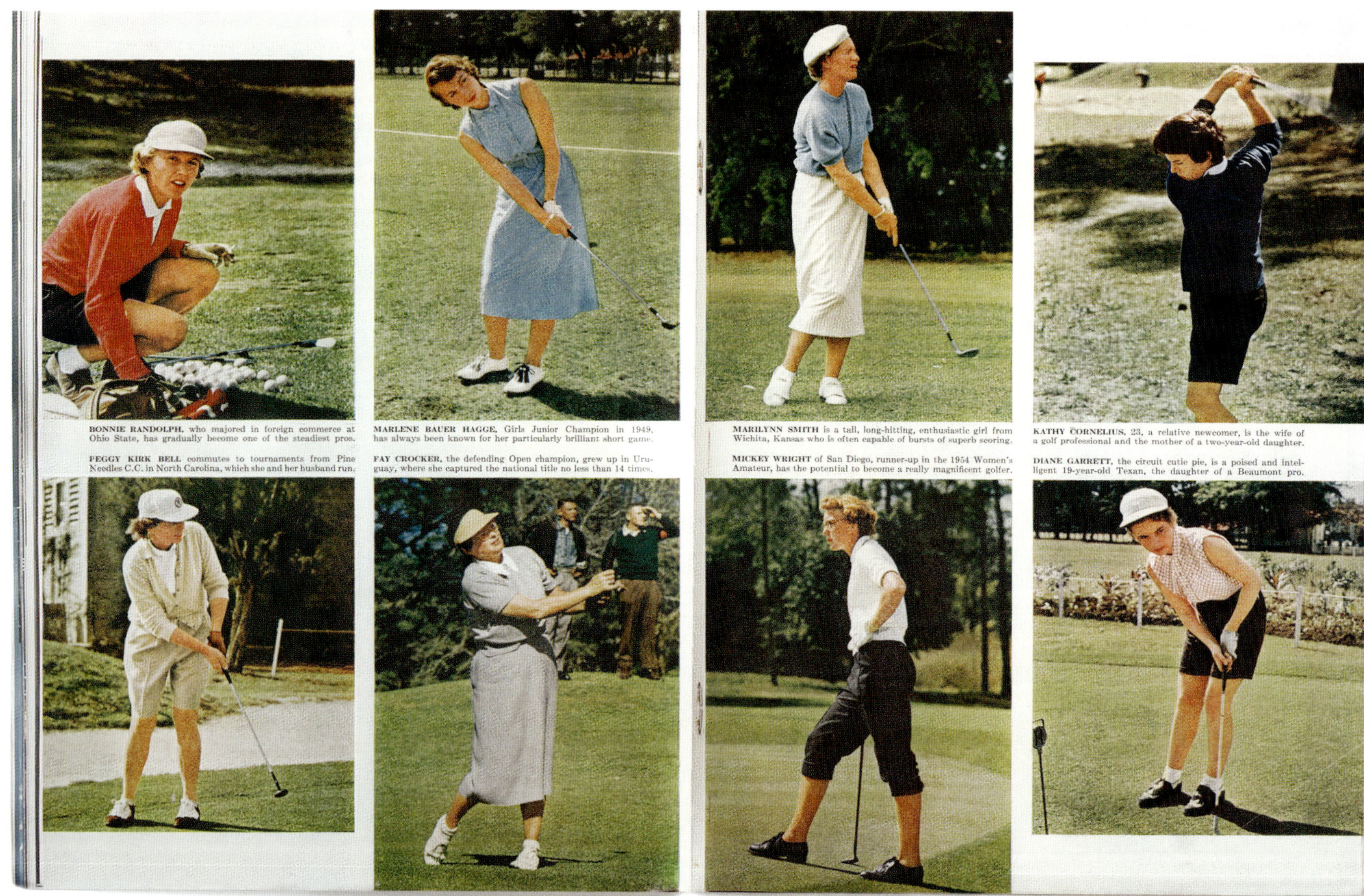

BONNIE RANDOLPH, who majored in foreign commerce at Ohio State, has gradually become one of the steadiest pros.

PEGGY KIRK BELL commutes to tournaments from Pine Needles C.C. in North Carolina, which she and her husband run.

MARLENE BAUER HAGGE, Girls Junior Champion in 1949, has always been known for her particularly brilliant short game.

FAY CROCKER, the defending Open champion, grew up in Uruguay, where she captured the national title no less than 14 times.

MARILYNN SMITH is a tall, long-hitting, enthusiastic girl from Wichita, Kansas who is often capable of bursts of superb scoring.

MICKEY WRIGHT of San Diego, runner-up in the 1954 Women's Amateur, has the potential to become a really magnificent golfer.

KATHY CORNELIUS, 23, a relative newcomer, is the wife of a golf professional and the mother of a two-year-old daughter.

DIANE GARRETT, the circuit cutie pie, is a poised and intelligent 19-year-old Texan, the daughter of a Beaumont pro.

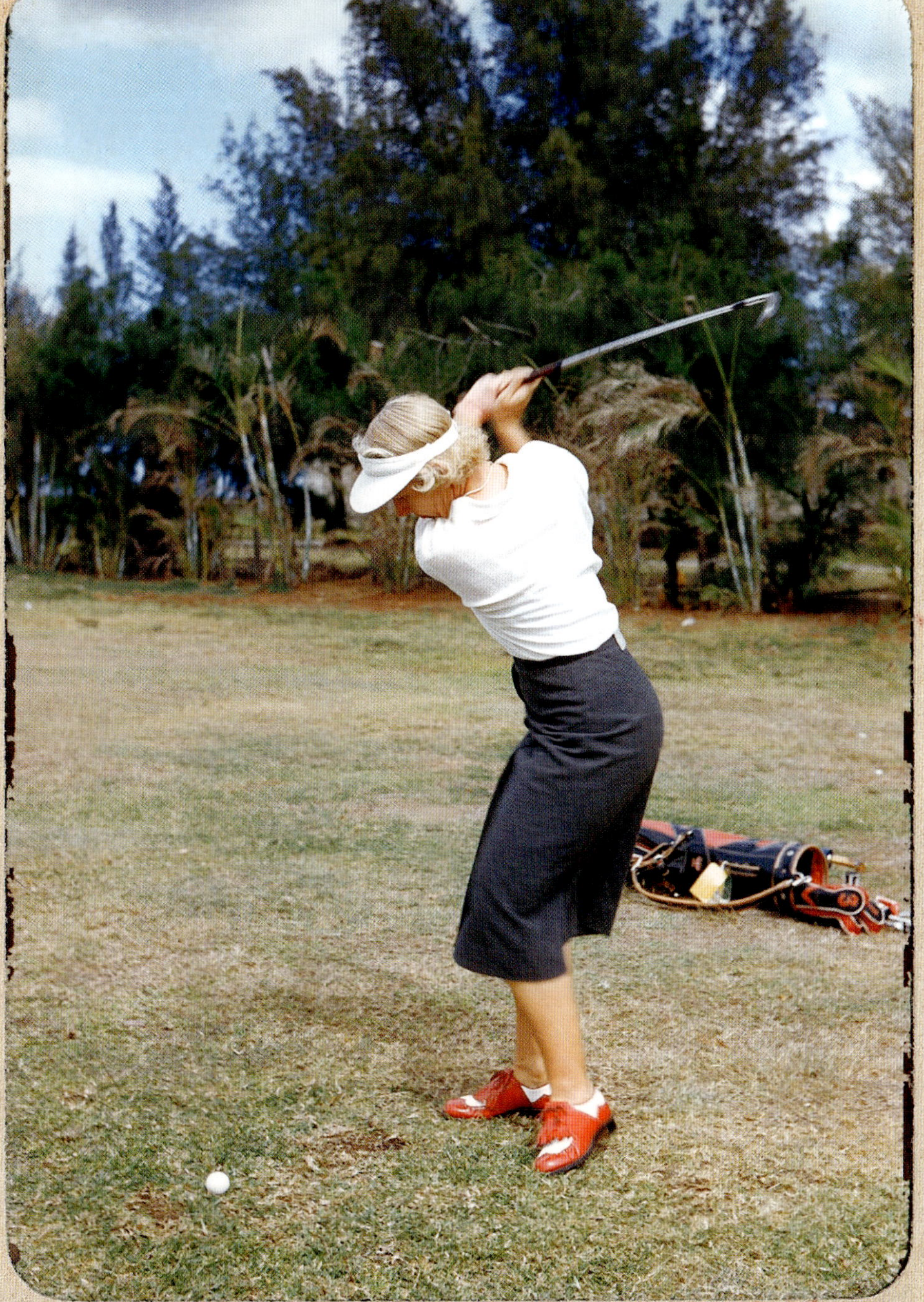

2·27·56

MADE IN U.S.A.

2/27/56

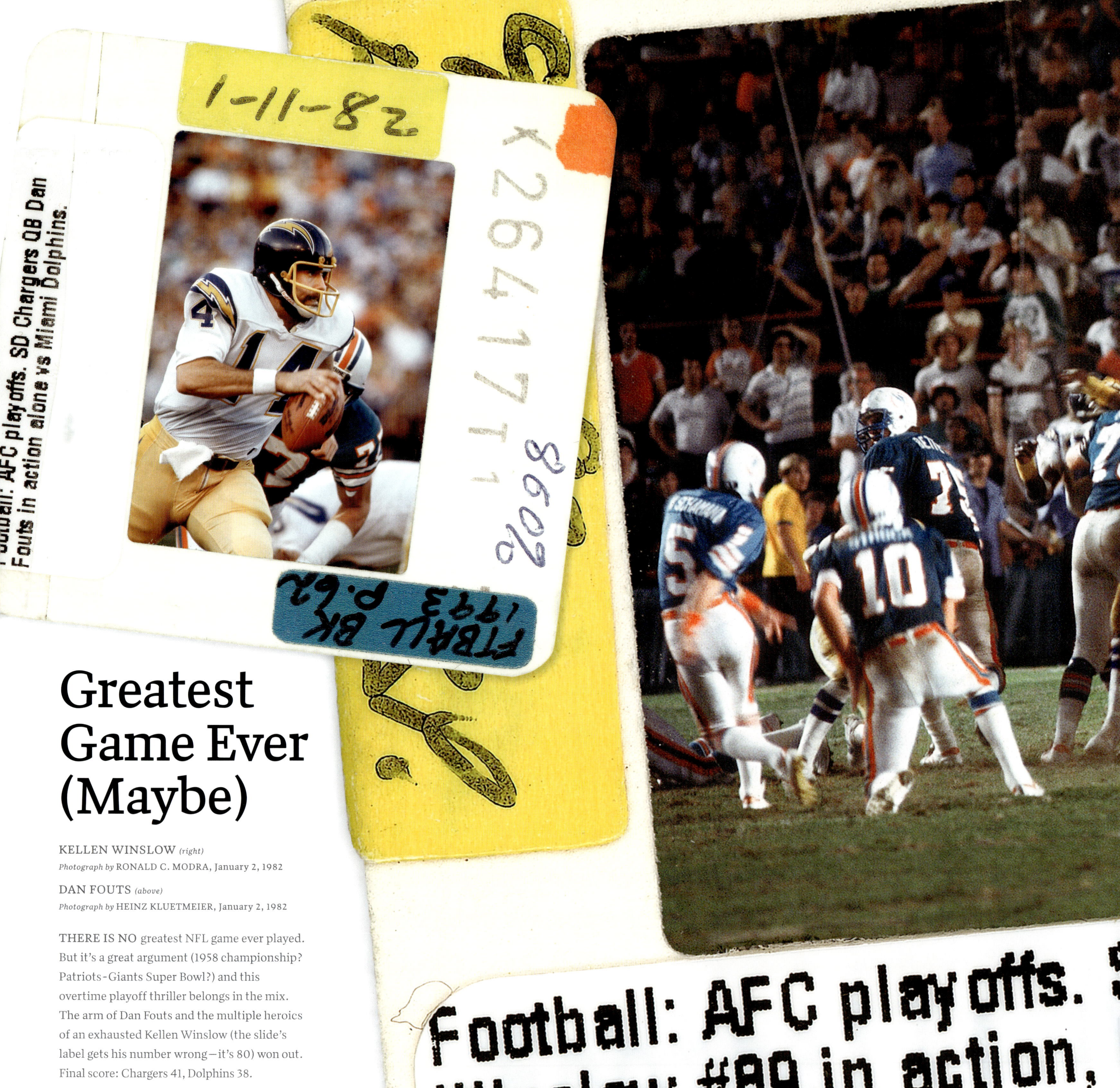

Greatest Game Ever (Maybe)

KELLEN WINSLOW *(right)*
Photograph by RONALD C. MODRA, January 2, 1982

DAN FOUTS *(above)*
Photograph by HEINZ KLUETMEIER, January 2, 1982

THERE IS NO greatest NFL game ever played. But it's a great argument (1958 championship? Patriots-Giants Super Bowl?) and this overtime playoff thriller belongs in the mix. The arm of Dan Fouts and the multiple heroics of an exhausted Kellen Winslow (the slide's label gets his number wrong—it's 80) won out. Final score: Chargers 41, Dolphins 38.

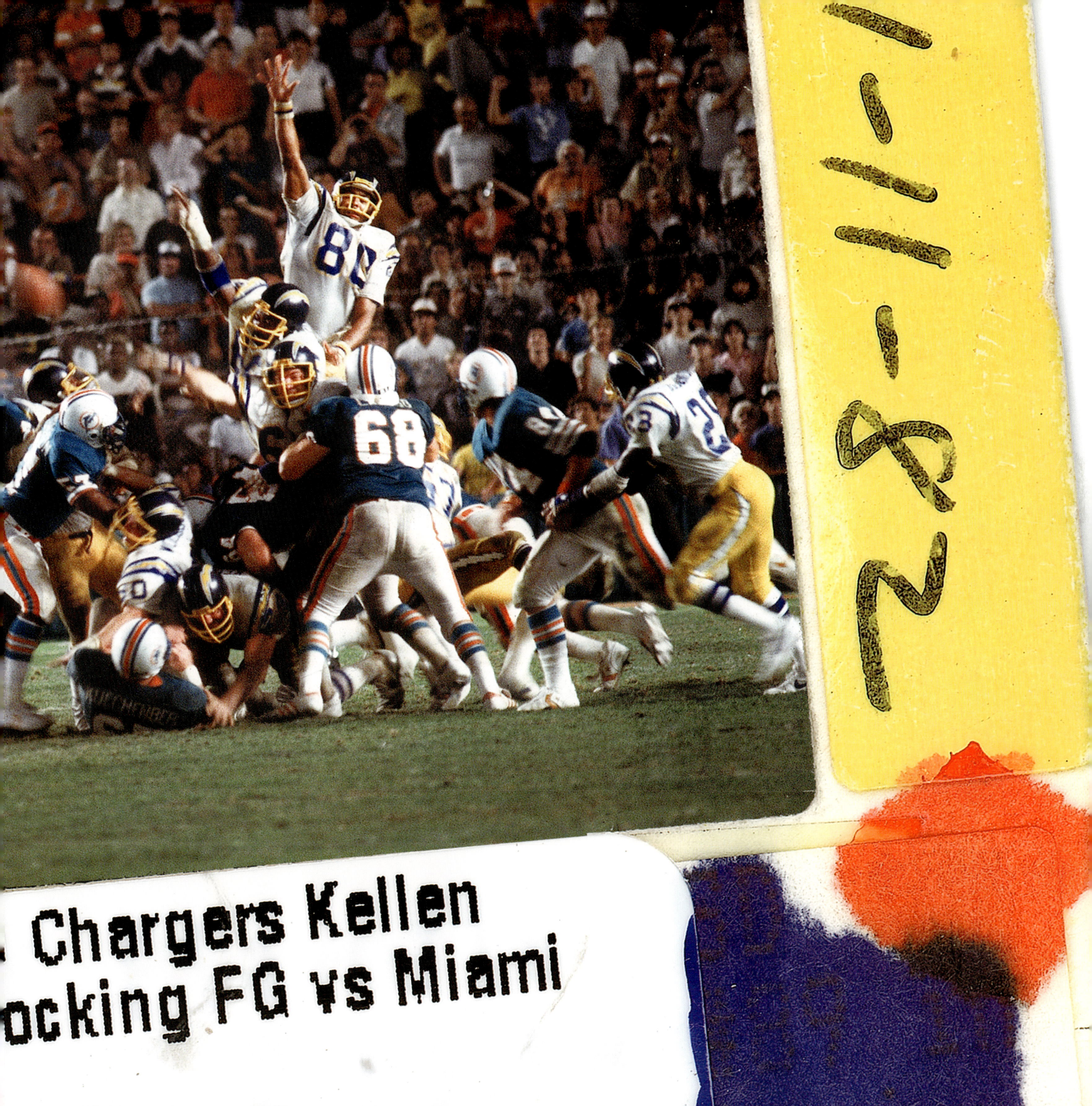
68
Chargers Kellen
ocking FG vs Miami

Fun in The Sun

STAN MUSIAL

Photograph by MARK KAUFFMAN, March 1955

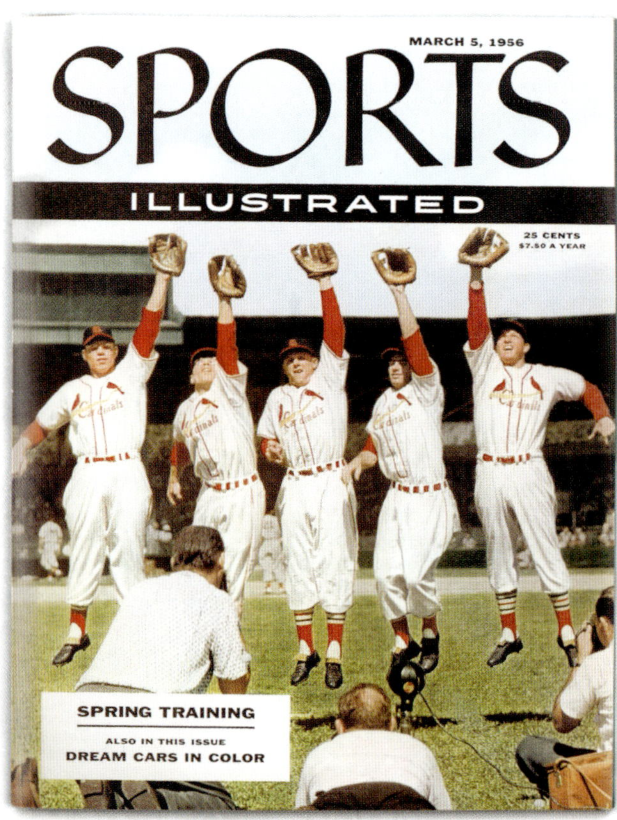

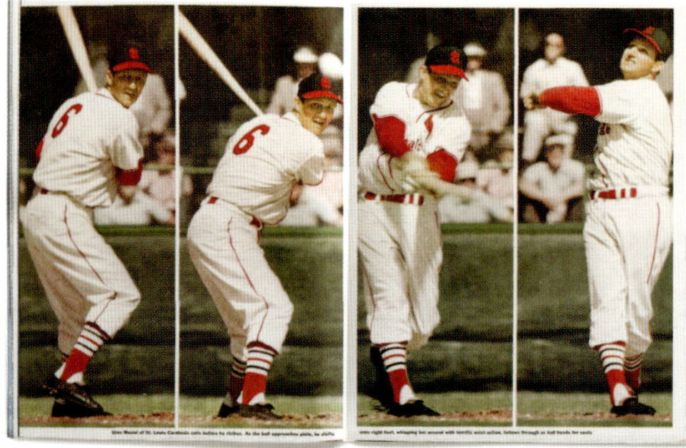

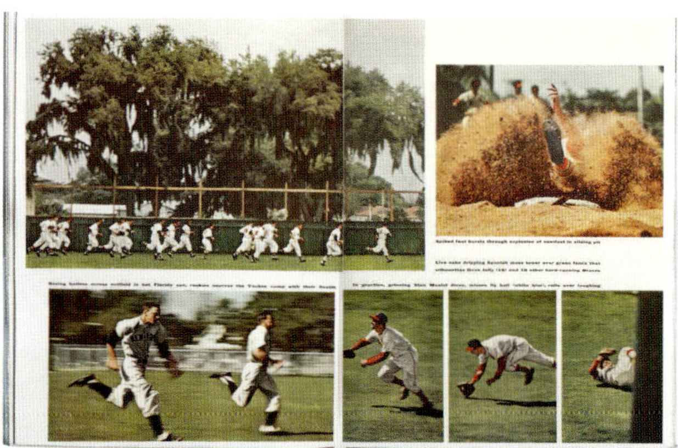

IF THE GREAT STAN MUSIAL can allow himself to roll on the ground in giddy laughter after missing a fly ball, it's a sure sign that the game doesn't count yet. Musial and his St. Louis Cardinals cohorts are still in the world of pranks, pepper and silly poses, living out the truth that no other sport has a preamble to the season quite as alluring as baseball's spring training. In this cover story, writer Gerald Holland had some fun watching the Cardinals' new G.M. try to fend off the annual feeling that, in baseball, hope springs eternal: "The new boss of the best seventh-place club in history looked across the infield at the sun-drenched panorama of young athletes. . . . He opened his mouth and almost blurted something. Then he caught himself and by a great effort forced himself to face the hard facts of the National League race for 1956: 'The Cardinals,' said Frank Lane, the realist, " 'will finish third.' "

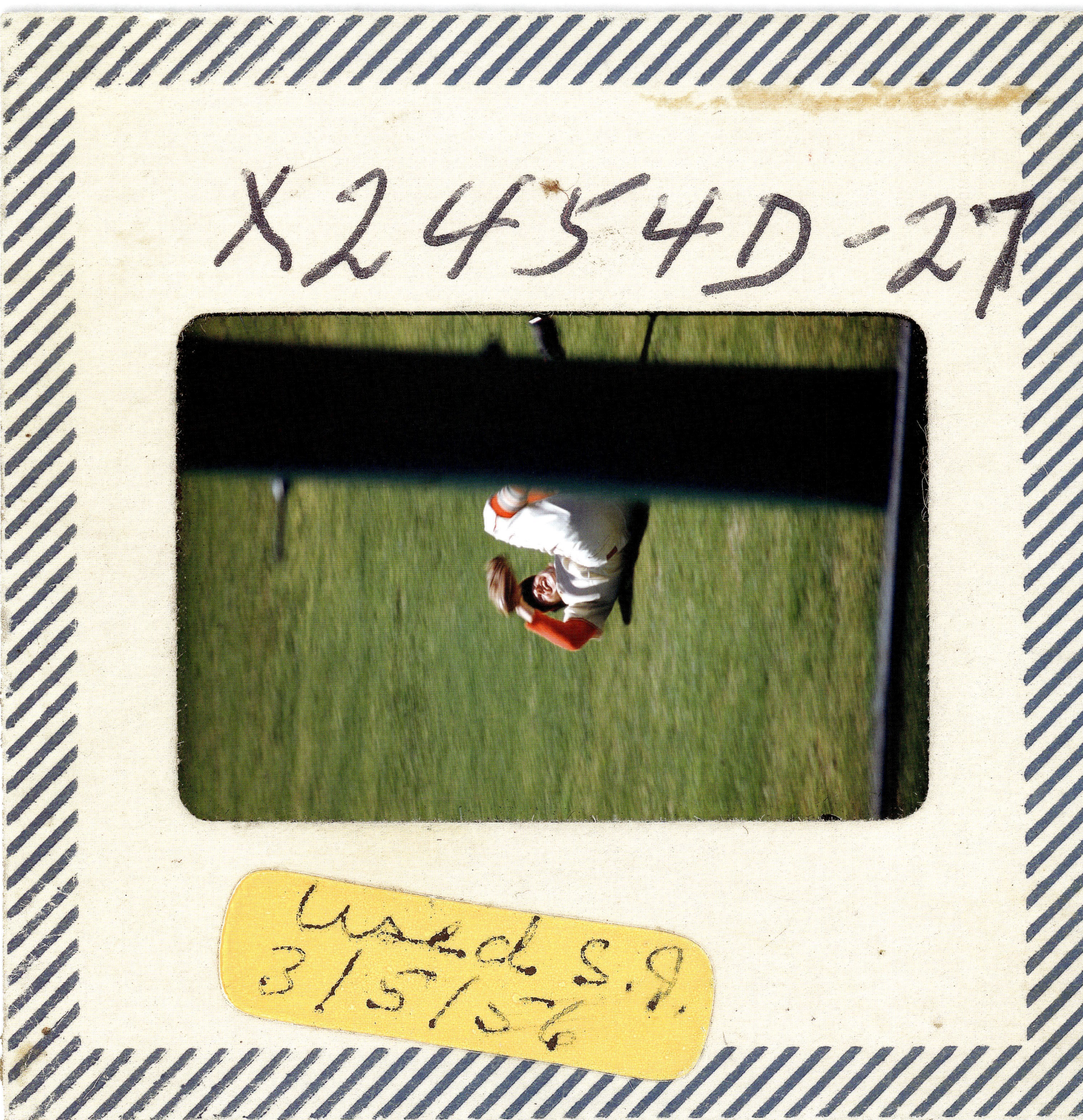
X2454D-27
Used S.I.
3/5/56

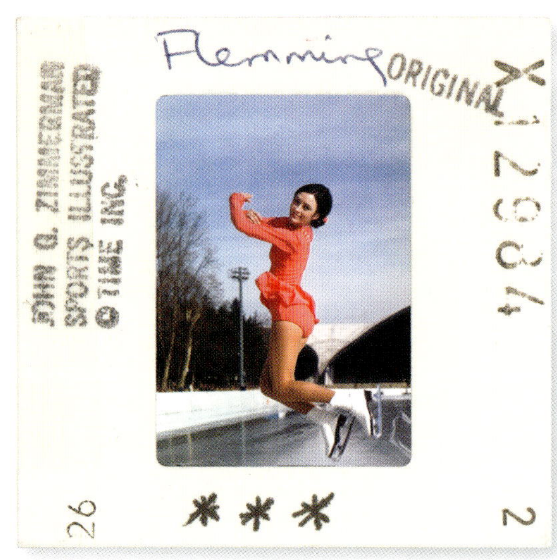

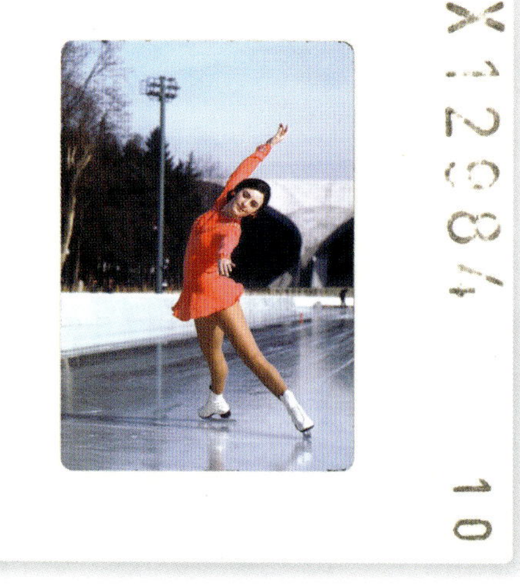

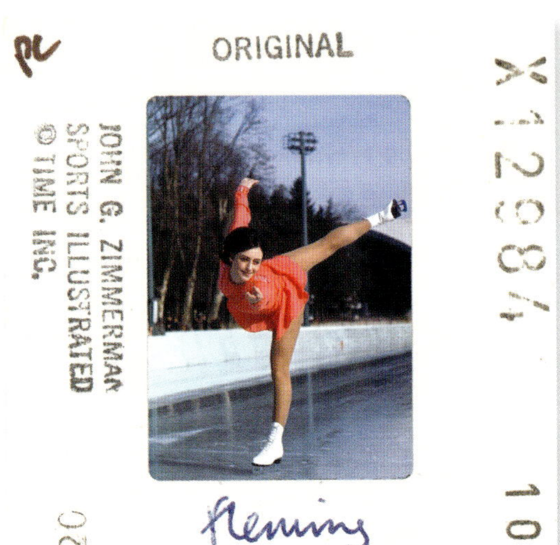

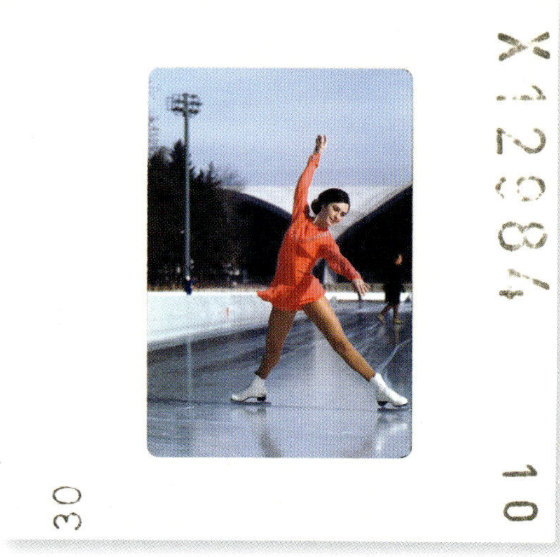

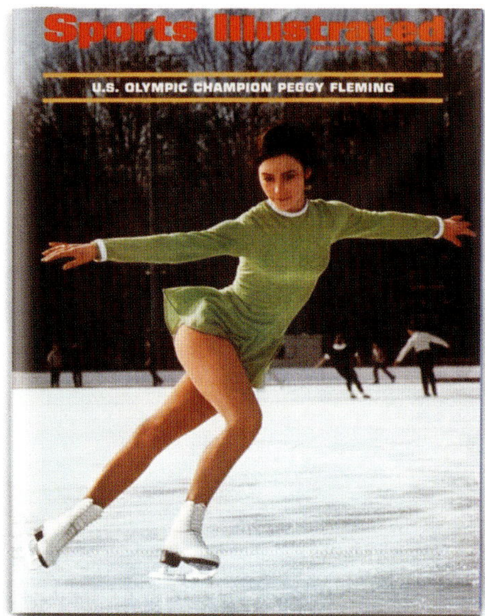

Dress Rehearsal

PEGGY FLEMING

Photographs by JOHN G. ZIMMERMAN, February 1968

PEGGY FLEMING'S 1968 Winter Olympics cover was all about having the right outfit—not for Peggy, but for SI. Headed into the skating competition, the magazine wanted to have a cover shot of Fleming ready to use if, as anticipated, she won a gold medal. But when John G. Zimmerman went to do an advance shoot, Fleming still hadn't decided which dress she would wear in competition—although she had narrowed it to two. So Zimmerman shot her in both her green and coral outfits. When Fleming gave her gold-medal performance in green, the matching photo landed on the cover, and the shots of her in coral went to the archive, never to be published.

4/26/04

Figure Skating: Feature. Portrait of USA Peggy Fleming alone during practice. Cover.

50TH Annv BK
10/1/04

JOHN ZIMMERMAN

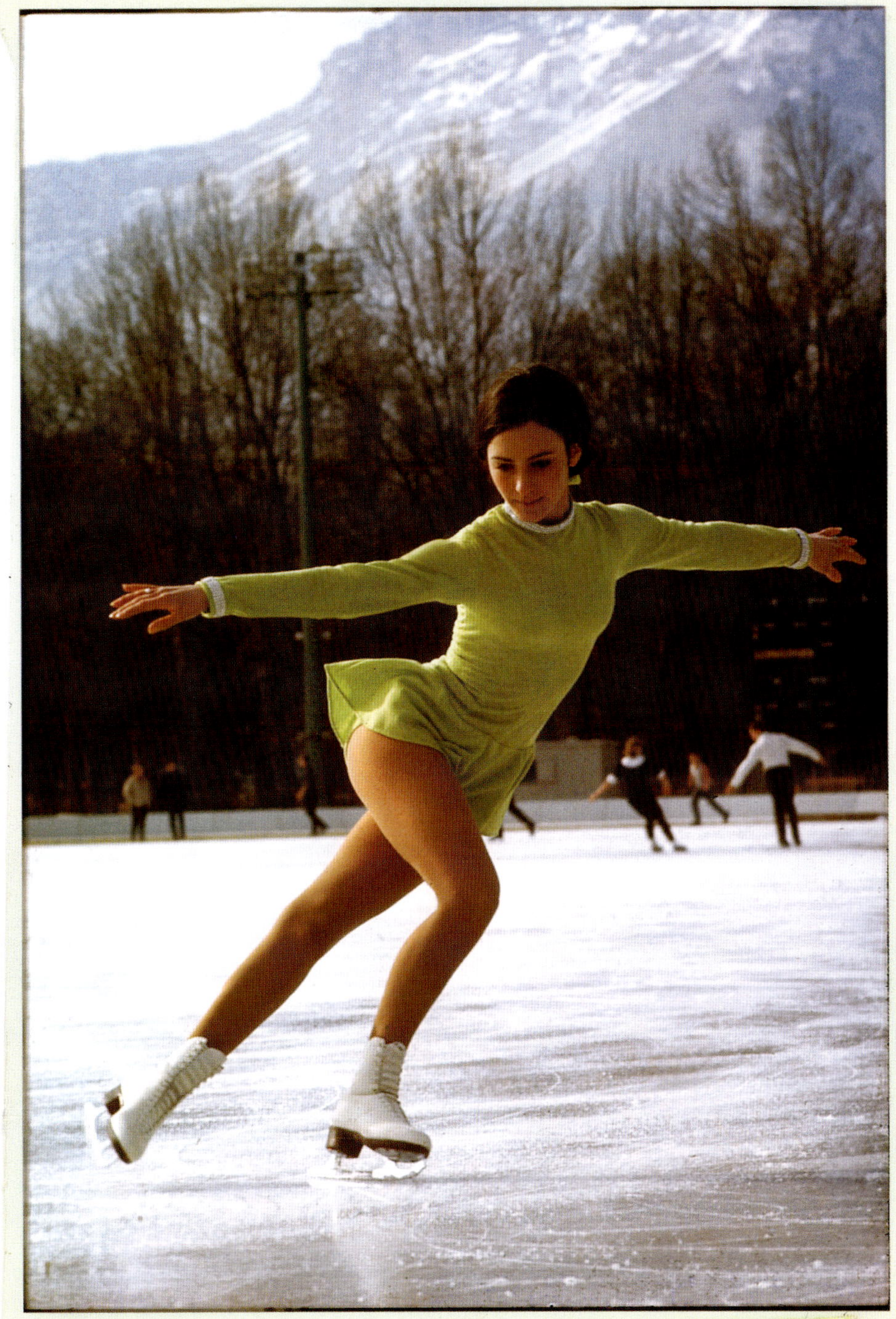

2-19-68

K22443 T1 5

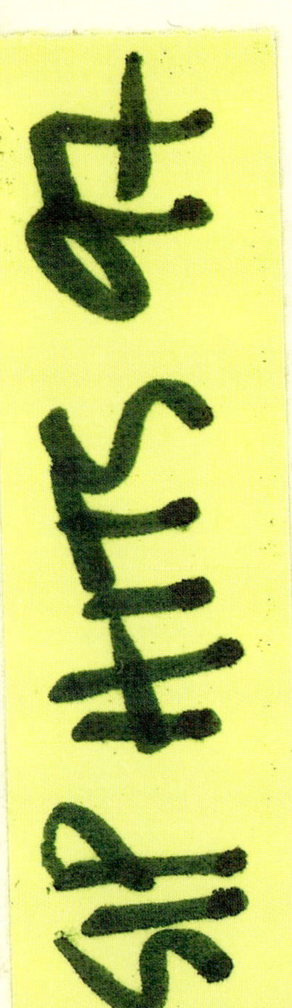

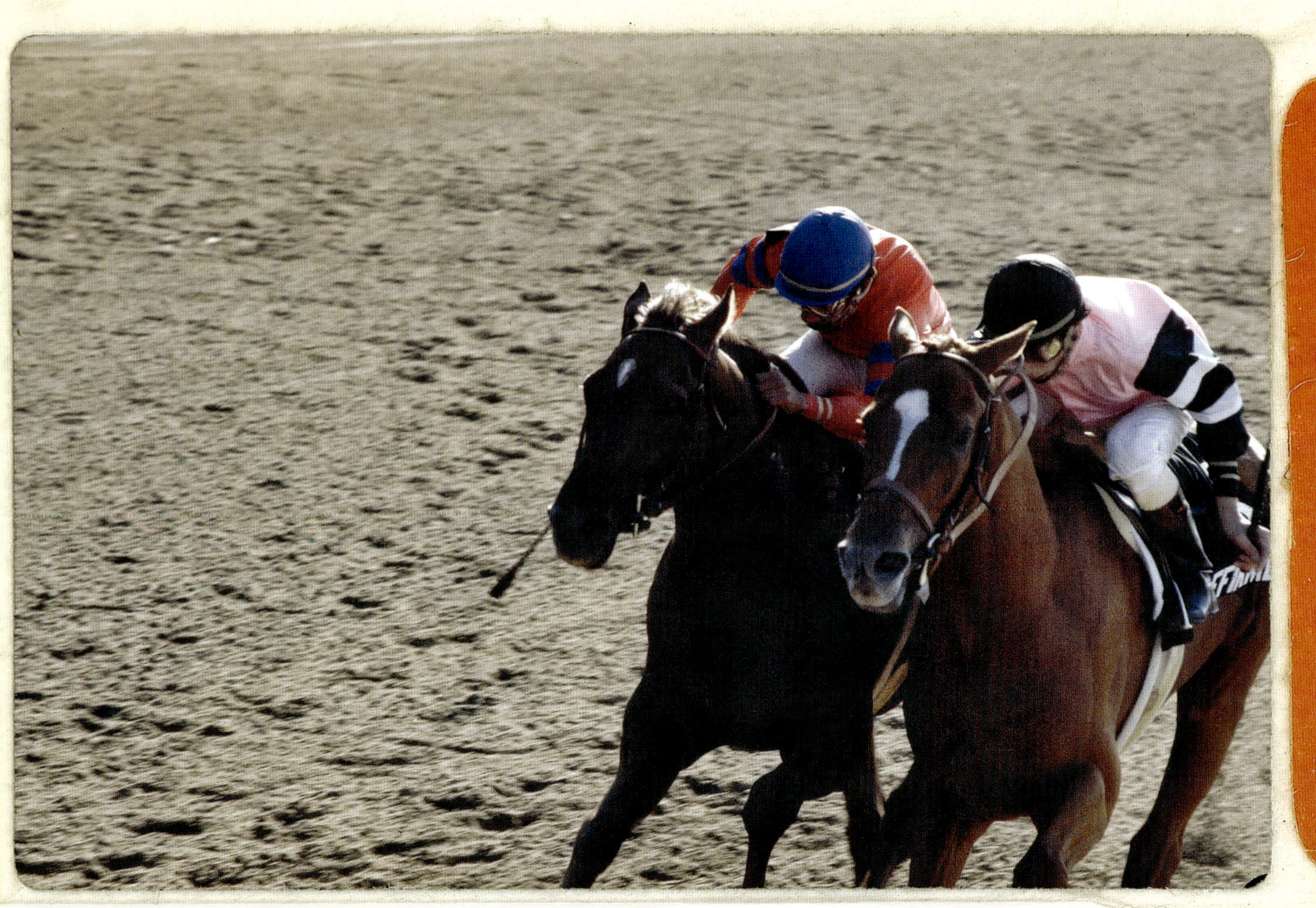

Horse Racing: Belmont Stakes. Affirmed (R) in action vs Alydar. Jockey Steve Cauthen riding Affirmed and Jorge Velasquez riding Alydar neck and neck.

The Kid and The Cover

STEVE CAUTHEN

Photograph by HEINZ KLUETMEIER, June 10, 1978

WHEN STEVE CAUTHEN RODE Affirmed, the baby-faced jockey created a sensation beyond sports. Cauthen, whose precocious skills had already earned him SI's 1977 Sportsman of the Year, presented a challenge for TIME as he gunned for the 1978 Triple Crown: how to get him on a postrace cover, given that the magazine's deadline was Saturday, when the races are held. TIME, having learned that Newsweek had a Cauthen cover planned the next week, aimed for a cover coming off the Preakness; Neil Leifer actually shot Cauthen's "victory" photo, with cigar, days before Affirmed won the race. (If Affirmed had lost, TIME had ready a cover on political cartoonists.) The yellow sticker on SI's slide signifies its later use in a custom publication—in this case, sponsored by a single advertiser—titled THE 100 ALLTIME GREATEST HITS IN SPORTS, the "hits" being loosely defined. Cauthen came in at No. 90 for his left-hand whipping down the stretch in the Belmont. It was fitting that Cauthen was in the issue: The sponsor was Jockey underwear.

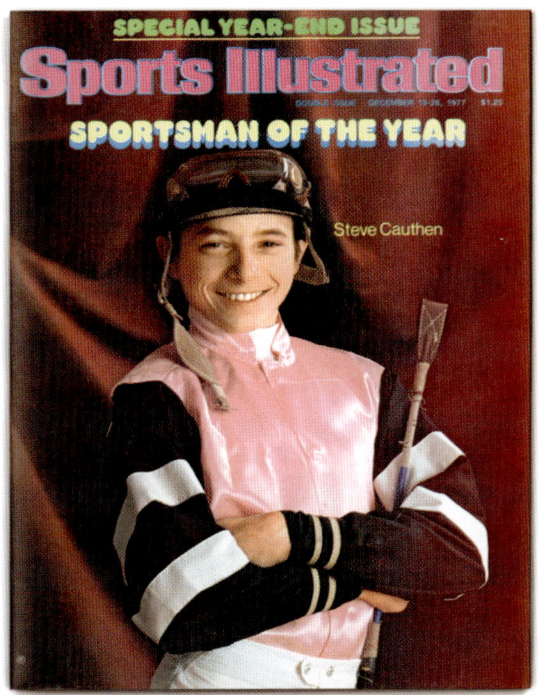

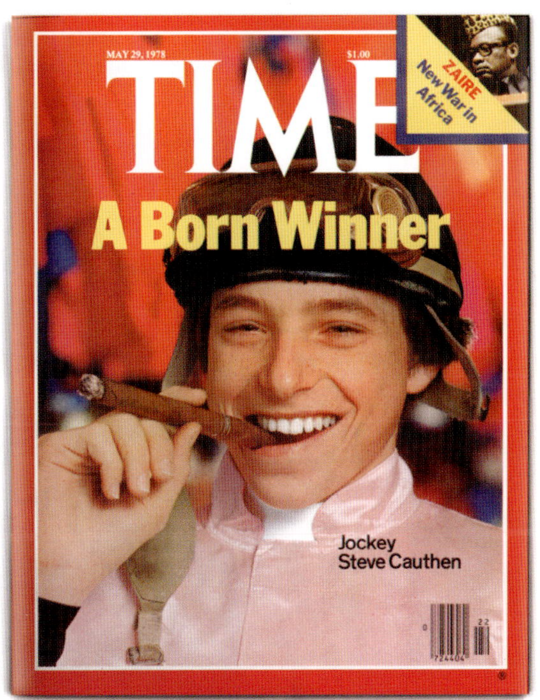

The Big Winner

DON SHULA

Photograph by AL TIELEMANS, November 14, 1993

DON SHULA HADN'T been carried off the field by his players in more than two decades, since his 1972 Dolphins finished the season undefeated. What gave this Sunday in Philadelphia a boost was that, as the label notes, this was Shula's 325th win; with it he passed George Halas to become the NFL's winningest coach.

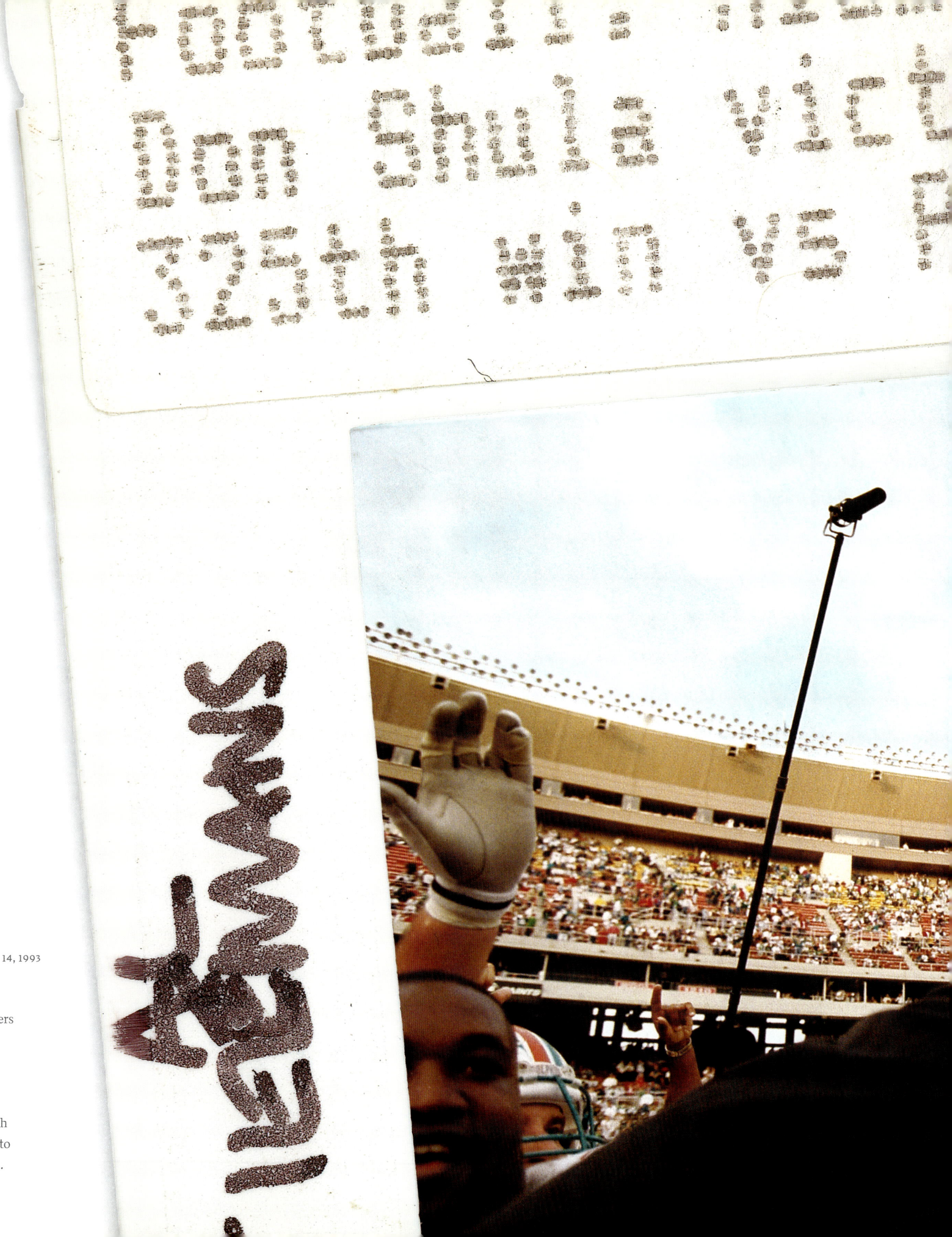

rious after
ila. Eagles;

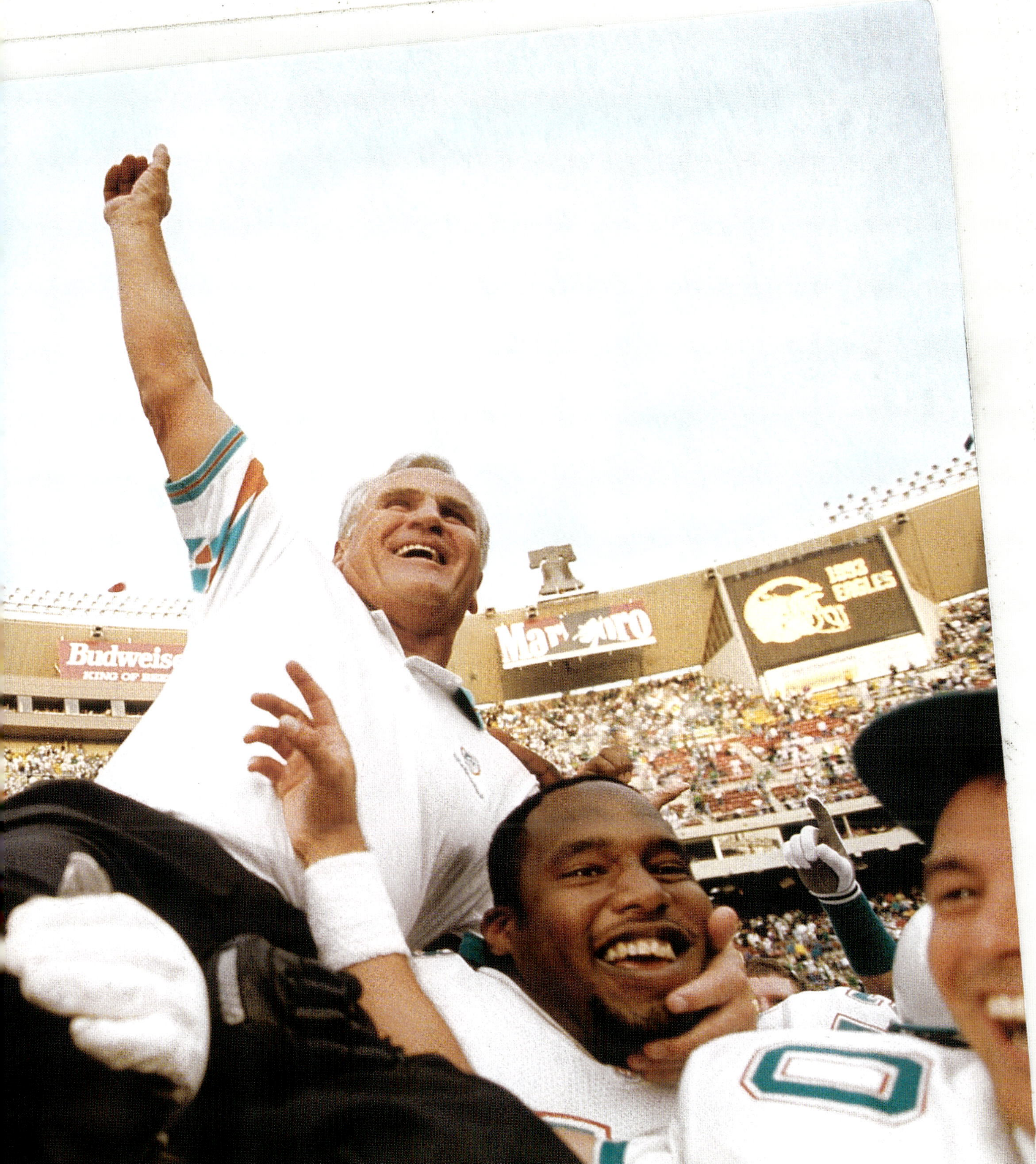

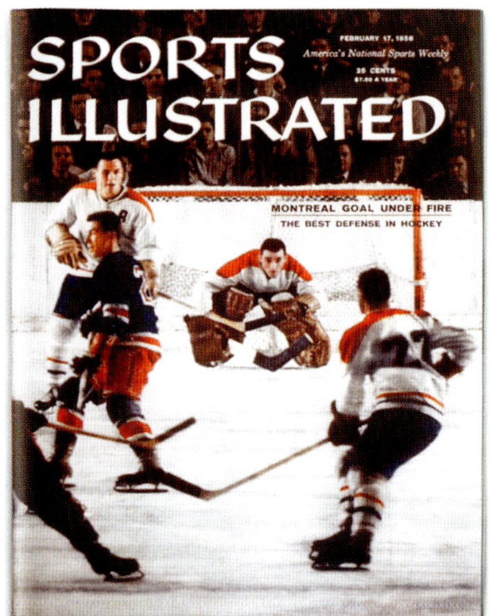

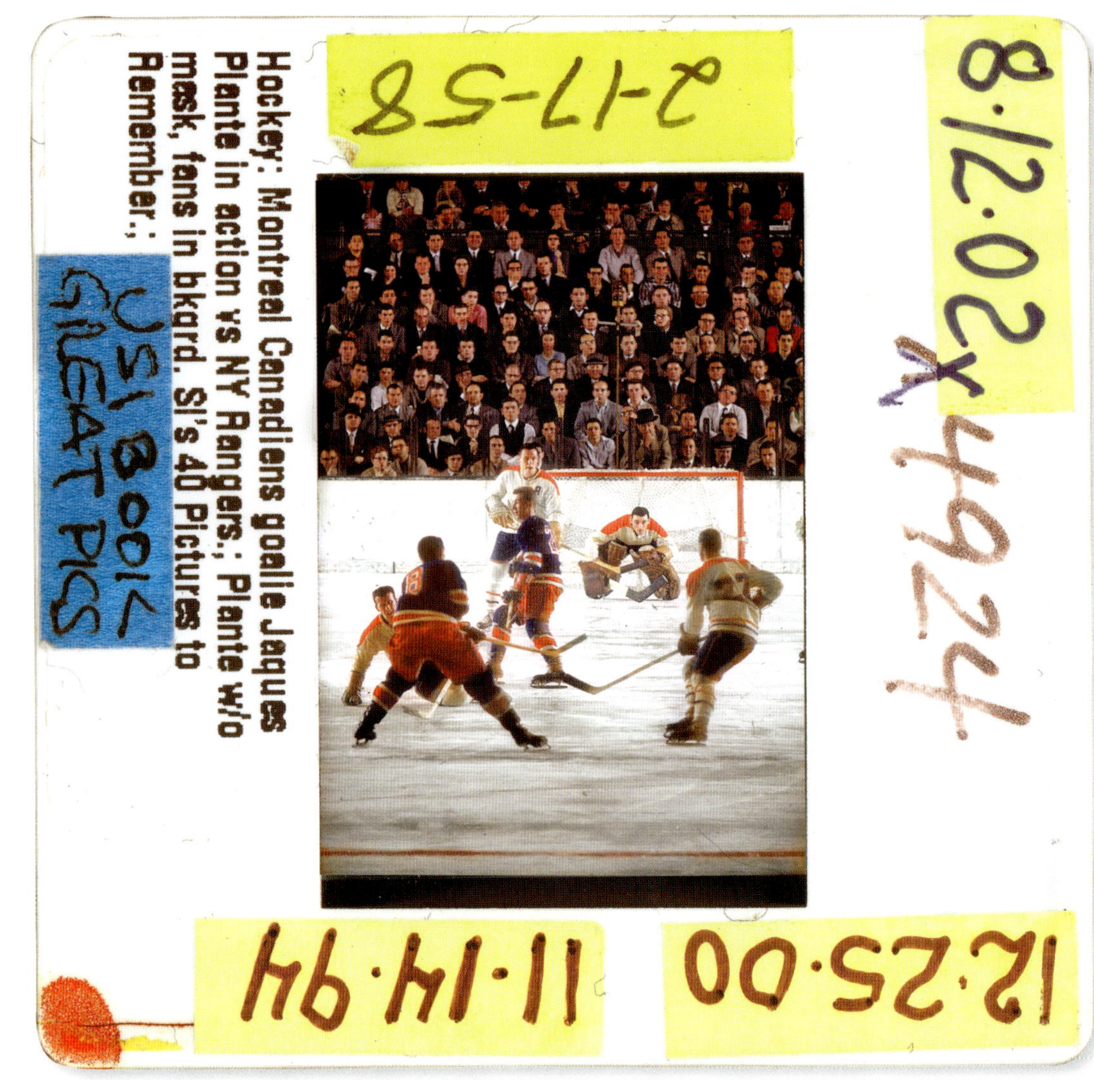

Keeping Their Focus

JACQUES PLANTE *(above)*
Photograph by JOHN G. ZIMMERMAN, December 18, 1957

FENWAY SCOREBOARD OPERATORS *(opposite)*
Photograph by WALTER IOOSS JR., June 21, 1987

THE APPEAL OF THE PHOTO above is less in the intensity of goalie Jacques Plante than in the rapt attention of the New York Rangers fans (and all so orderly! so nicely dressed!). John G. Zimmerman's photo is a classic that SI has run many times, including in a 1994 "Pictures to Remember" feature, a 2000 issue devoted to sports fans and a memorial story after the photographer's death in '02. The shot on the right, from the photo essay *One Day in Baseball*, shows men whose job it was to keep their eyes on the game: Fenway scoreboard operators James Stokes *(foreground)* and Bill Rose. Walter Iooss Jr. went inside the Green Monster to shoot the game, but was instead captivated by this view.

game; Boston, MA

06/20/1987

WALTER IOOSS, JR.

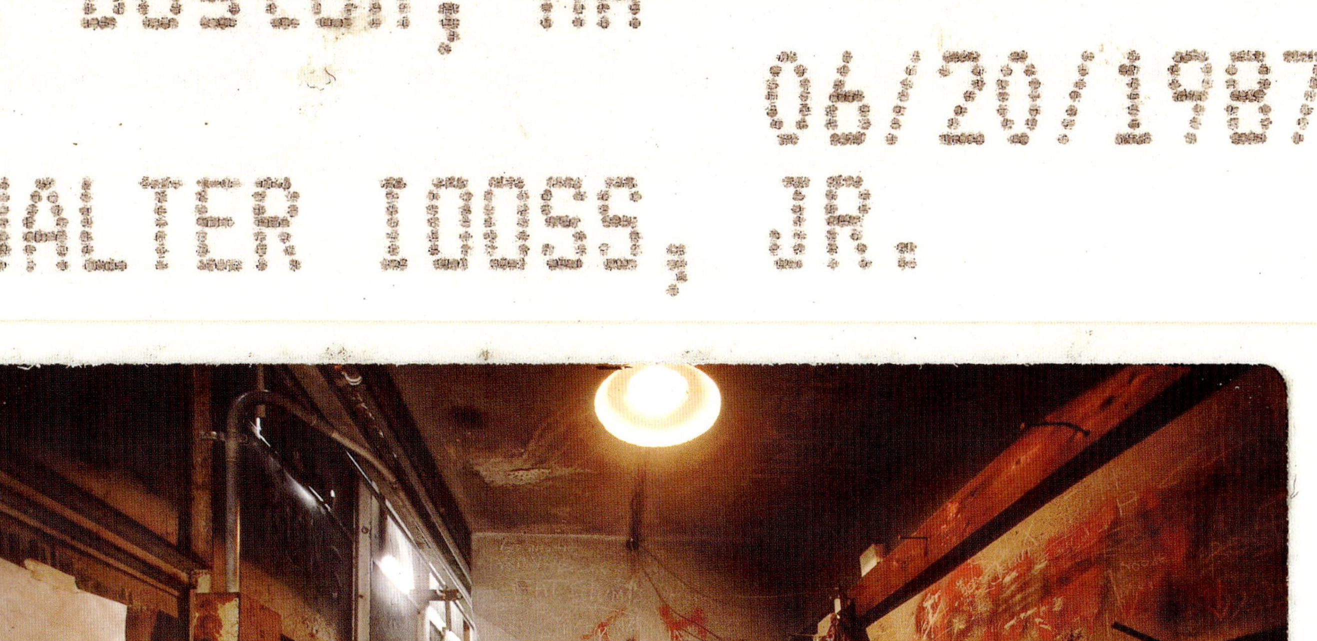

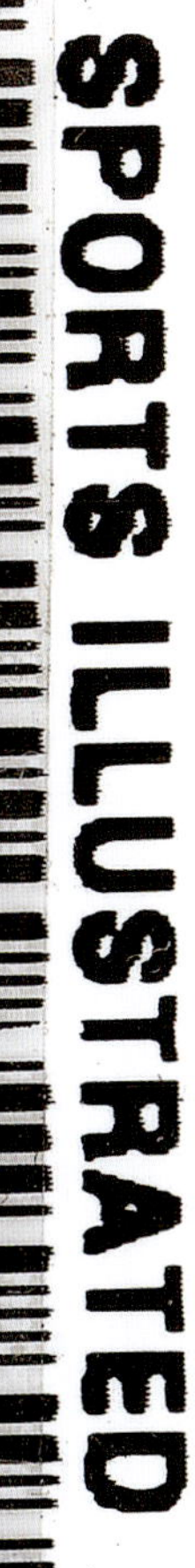

SPORTS ILLUSTRATED

PICTURE COLLECTION

ORIG

SET # X34990

124742

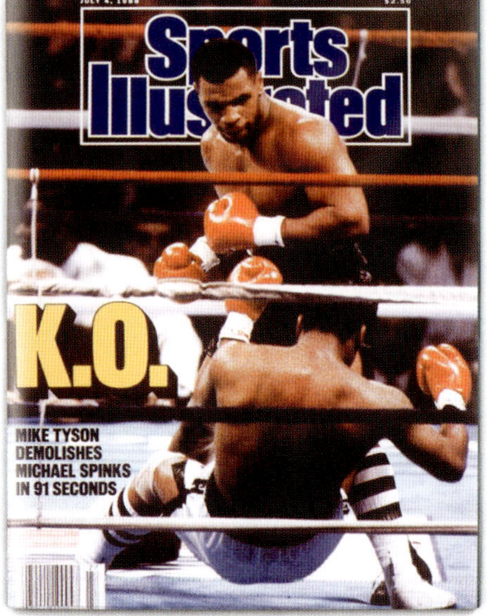

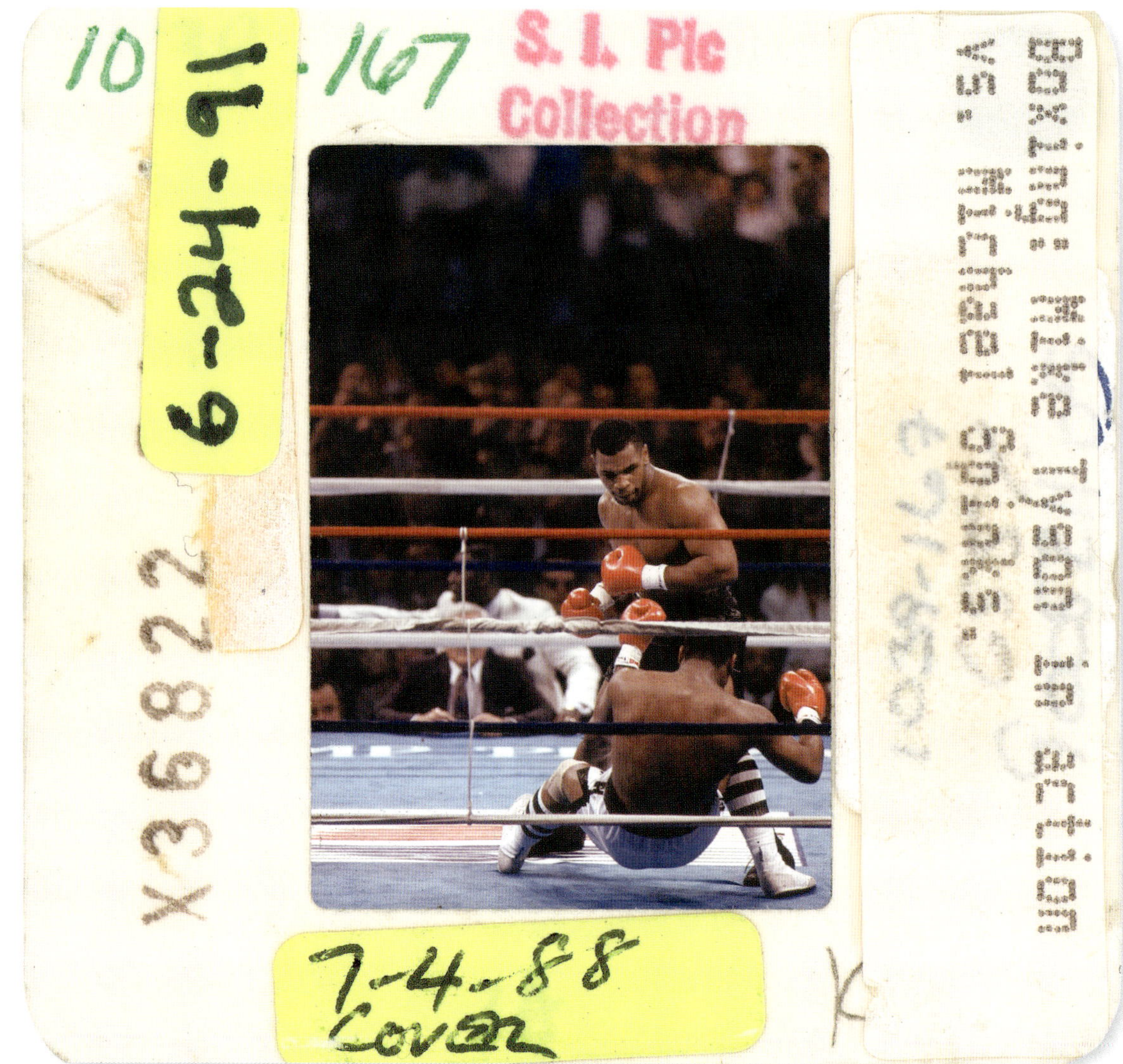

Thanks for Leaving

TYSON vs. SPINKS

Photograph by MANNY MILLAN, June 27, 1988

MOST OFTEN, a cover-worthy photo is the result of positioning: a sideline angle for Garo Yepremian's game-winning kick, a courtside spot for Boris Becker's triumph at the U.S. Open. But a little luck never hurts. For Mike Tyson's title fight, Manny Millan was set up on a platform behind 10 rows of ringside seats, worried that he'd miss a key moment if the fans jumped up in excitement. But during a long delay between the undercard and main event, the group in front of Millan left for a bathroom break. Then the fight started—and Tyson dispatched Michael Spinks in 91 seconds. Those fans missed it all, but Millan got a clean shot of the knockout punch.

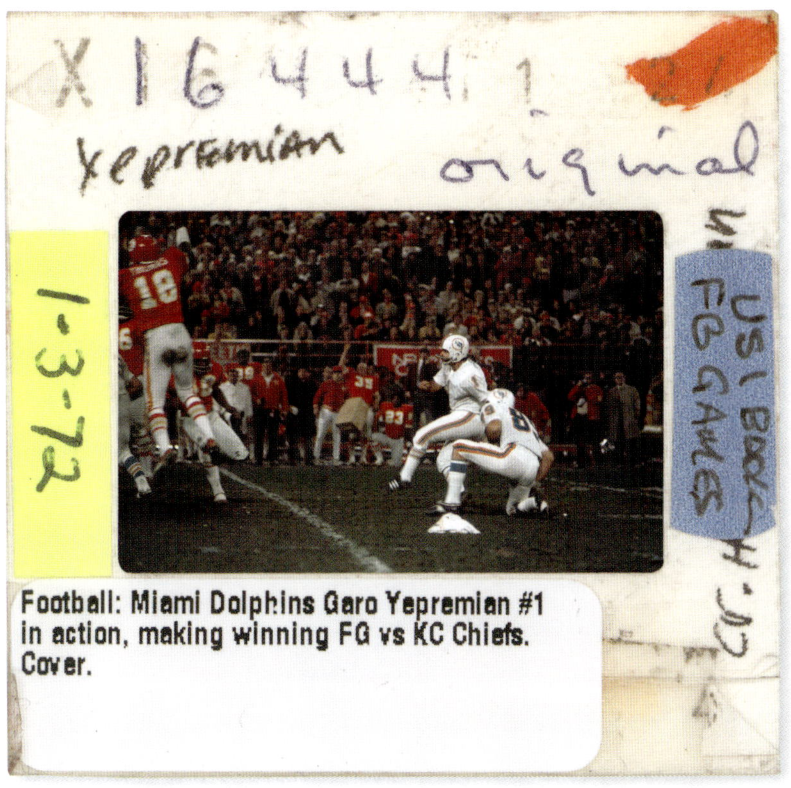

GARO YEPREMIAN

Photograph by HERB SCHARFMAN, December 25, 1971

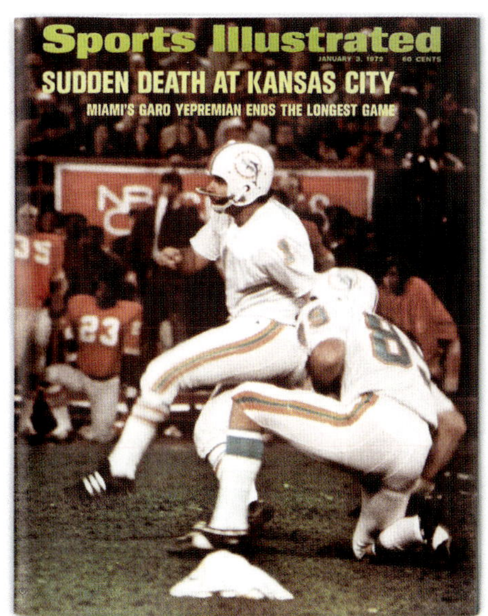

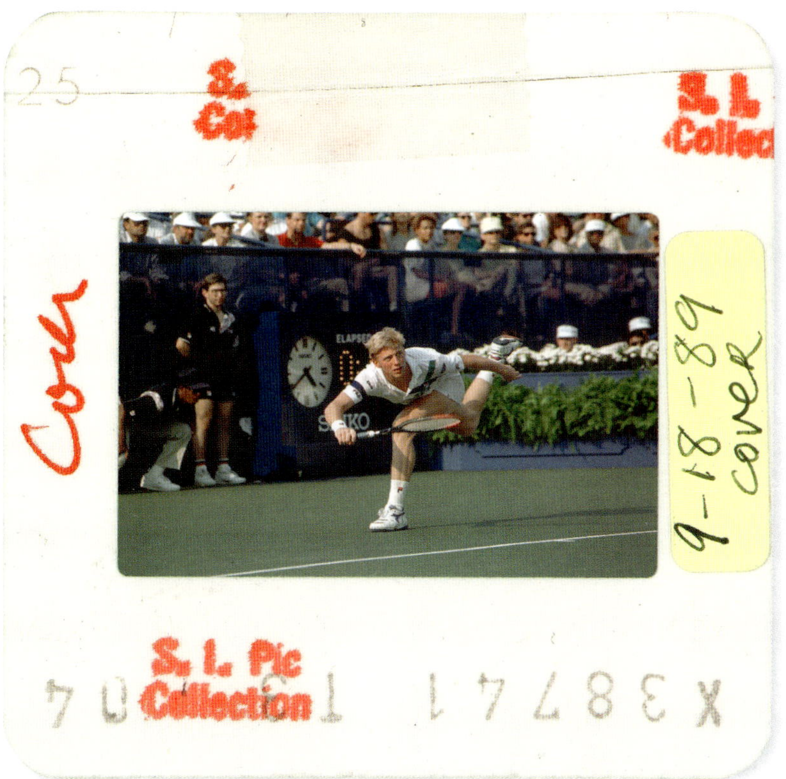

BORIS BECKER

Photograph by JACQUELINE DUVOISIN, September 10, 1989

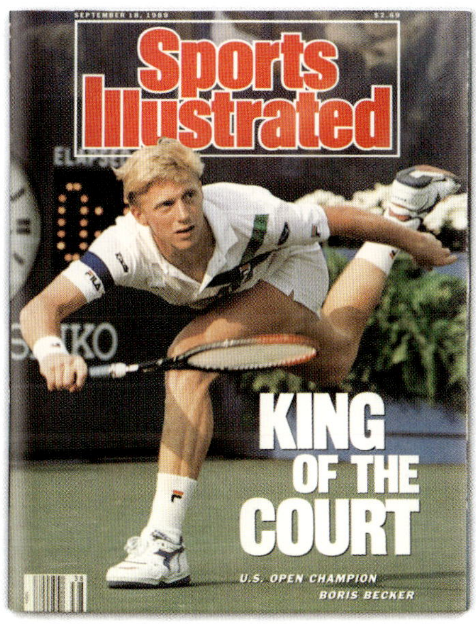

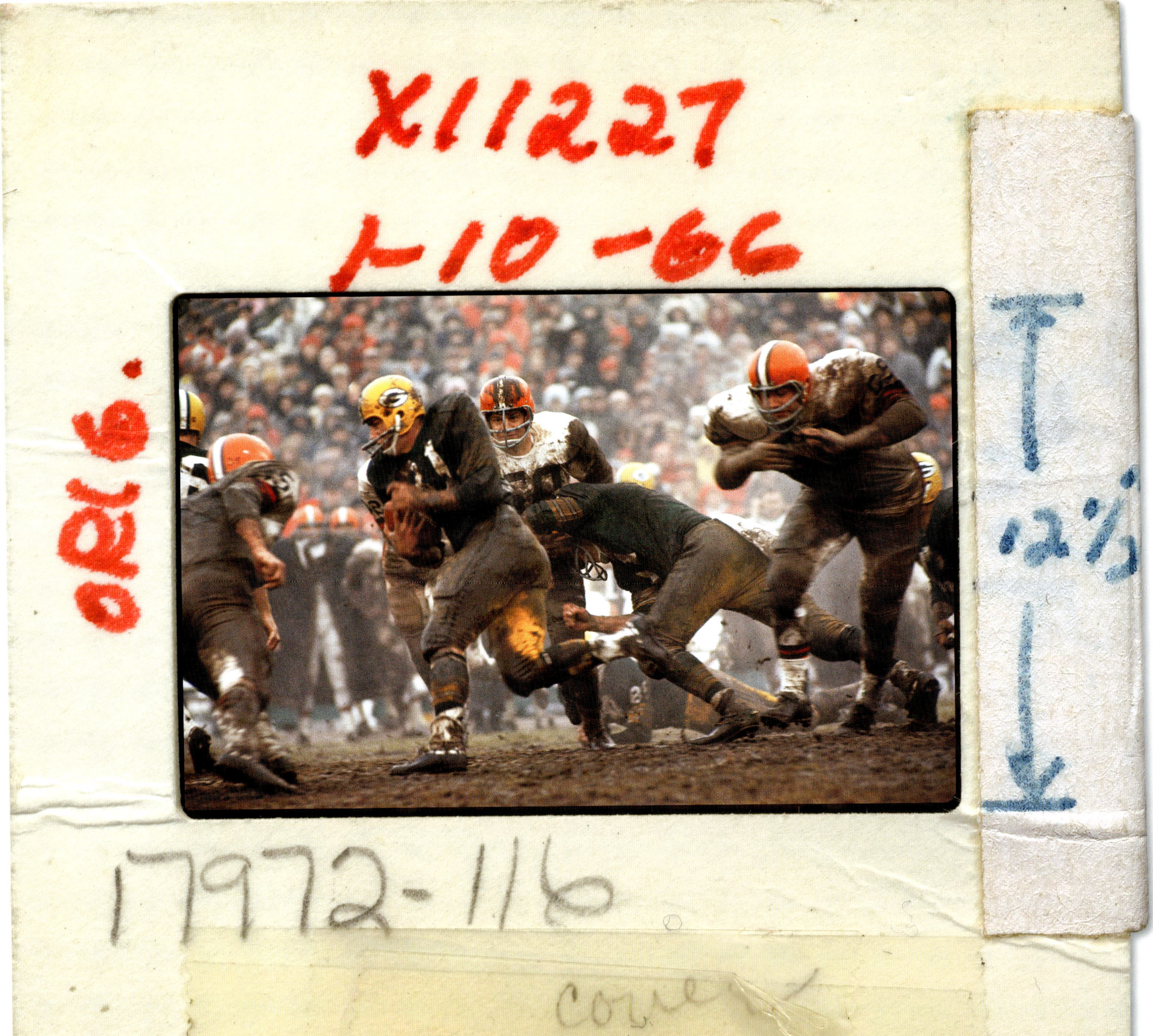

A Lovely Day For Pictures

NFL CHAMPIONSHIP GAME

Photograph by NEIL LEIFER, January 2, 1966

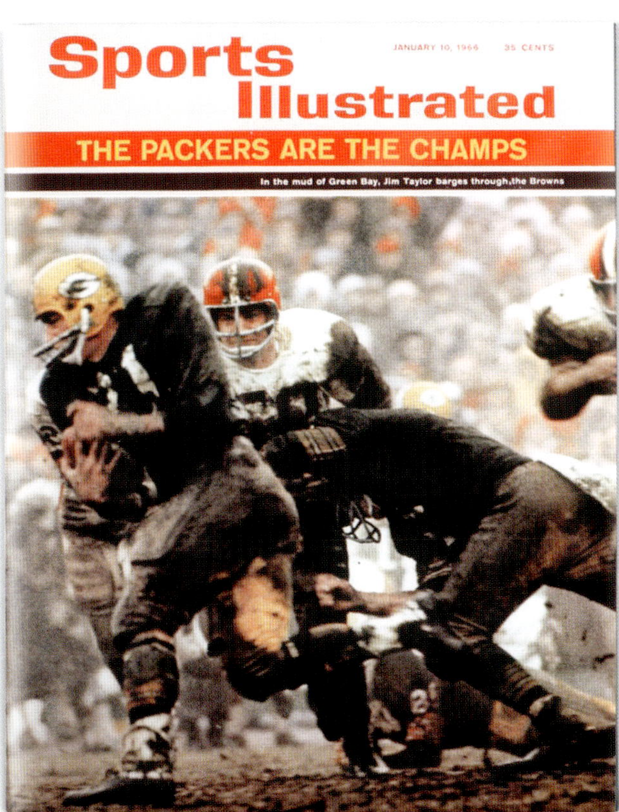

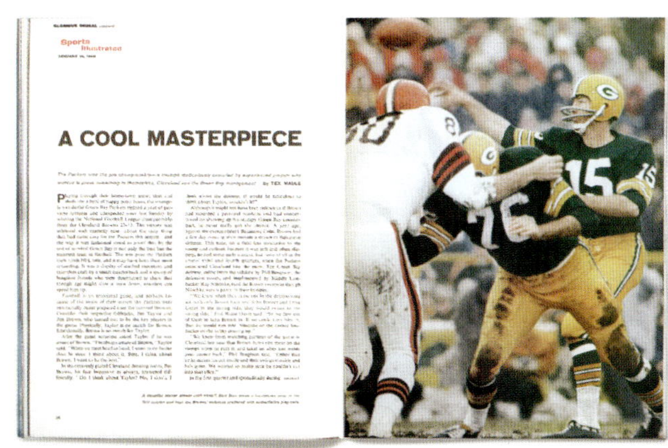

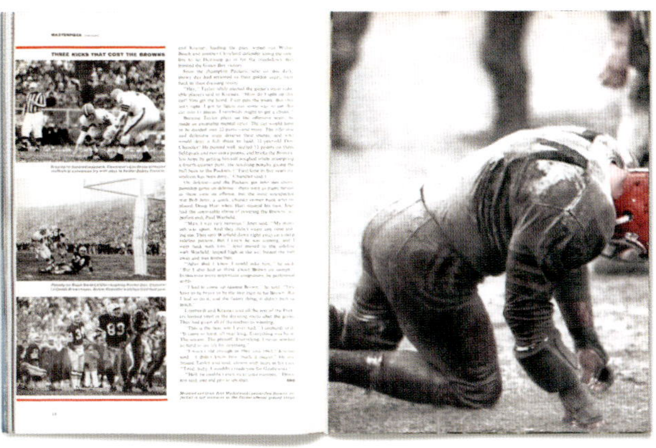

THEY ARE THE BEST OF GAMES, they are the worst of games. That, says Neil Leifer, is how it looks to a photographer when the weather turns to sleet and slush, as it did at Lambeau Field in wintry Wisconsin for a title game between the Green Bay Packers and the Cleveland Browns (two teams well-acquainted with the cold and wet). The photographer knows he is going to be out there for hours, struggling to protect his fingers, his toes and his equipment. But he also knows that as the cleats churn the turf into mud and the uniforms turn ugly, he's going to get some beautiful shots. On this day Green Bay's Jim Taylor (carrying the ball here) and his backfield mate Paul Hornung outmucked their Cleveland counterpart Jim Brown, and the Packers won 23–12.

X 8140

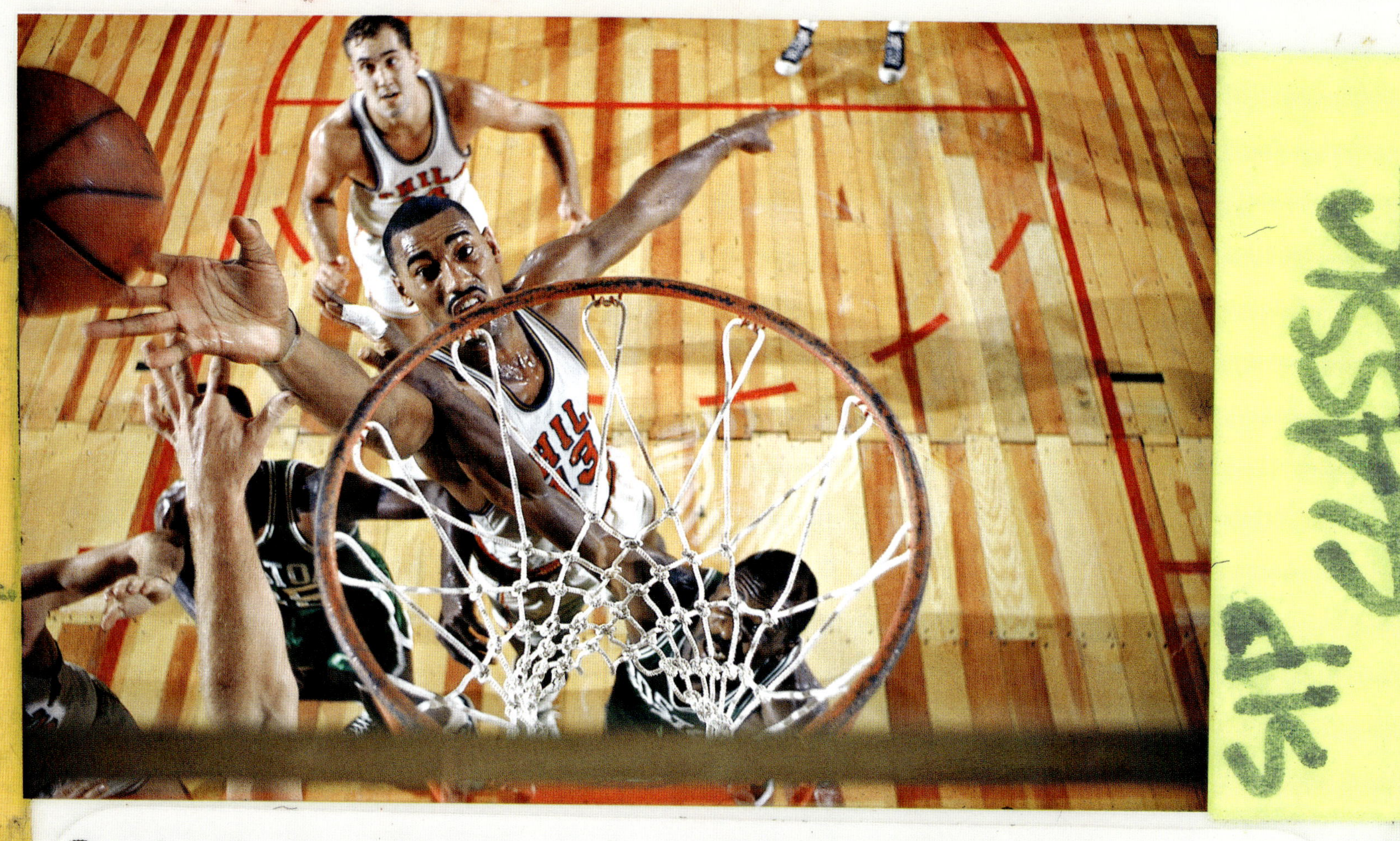

Basketball: Aerial view of Phila. Warriors Wilt Chamberlain #13 in action, scoring vs Boston Celtics Bill Russell #6. Chamberlain w. tip in.

A Higher Form of Play

WILT CHAMBERLAIN

Photograph by JOHN G. ZIMMERMAN, November 1961

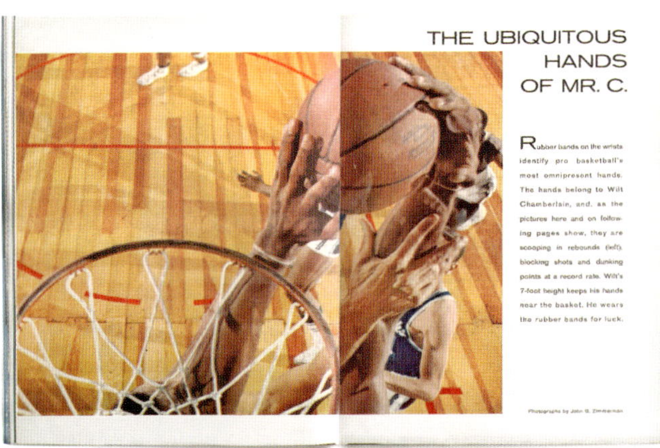
THE UBIQUITOUS HANDS OF MR. C.

Rubber bands on the wrists identify pro basketball's most omnipresent hands. The hands belong to Wilt Chamberlain, and, as the pictures here and on following pages show, they are scooping in rebounds (left), blocking shots and dunking points at a record rate. Wilt's 7-foot height keeps his hands near the basket. He wears the rubber bands for luck.

Photographs by John G. Zimmerman

SOME TELLTALE SIGNS that these photos are from another era: The Philadelphia Warriors' home floor looks like it belongs in the gym of some underfunded middle school, and Wilt Chamberlain looks like a teenager (actually he was 25). Wilt was just beginning to redefine what a big man could do on the inside. (The language setting up the final magazine spread: "Turn the page and see why it is called a dunk.") How helpless were Wilt's opponents against his assault? For the 1961–62 season, Chamberlain averaged an NBA record 50.4 points (and a not-too-shabby 25.7 rebounds). Yes, it was another era.

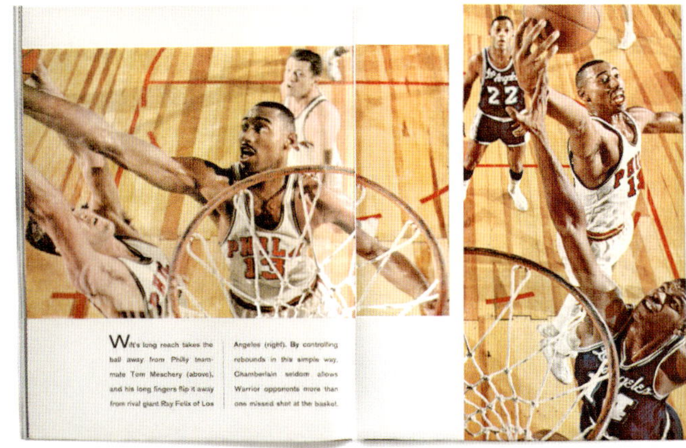

Wilt's long reach takes the ball away from Philly teammate Tom Meschery (above), and his long fingers flip it away from rival giant Ray Felix of Los Angeles (right). By controlling rebounds in this simple way, Chamberlain seldom allows Warrior opponents more than one missed shot at the basket.

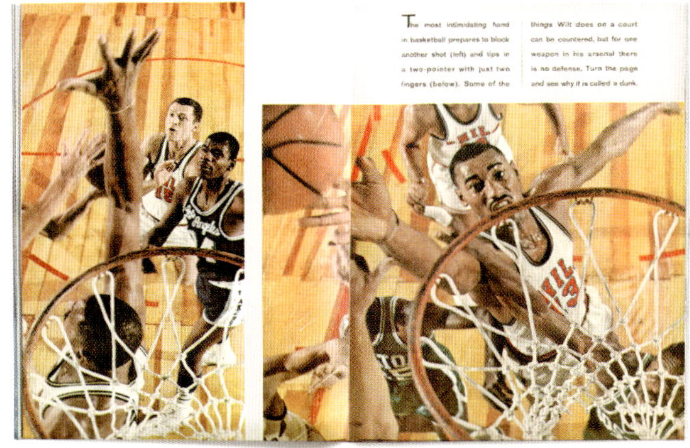
The most intimidating hand in basketball prepares to block another shot (left) and tips in a two-pointer with just two fingers (below). Some of the things Wilt does on a court can be countered, but for one weapon in his arsenal there is no defense. Turn the page and see why it is called a dunk.

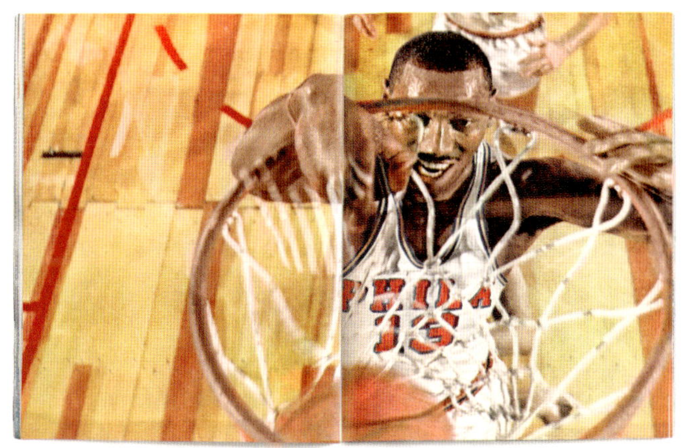

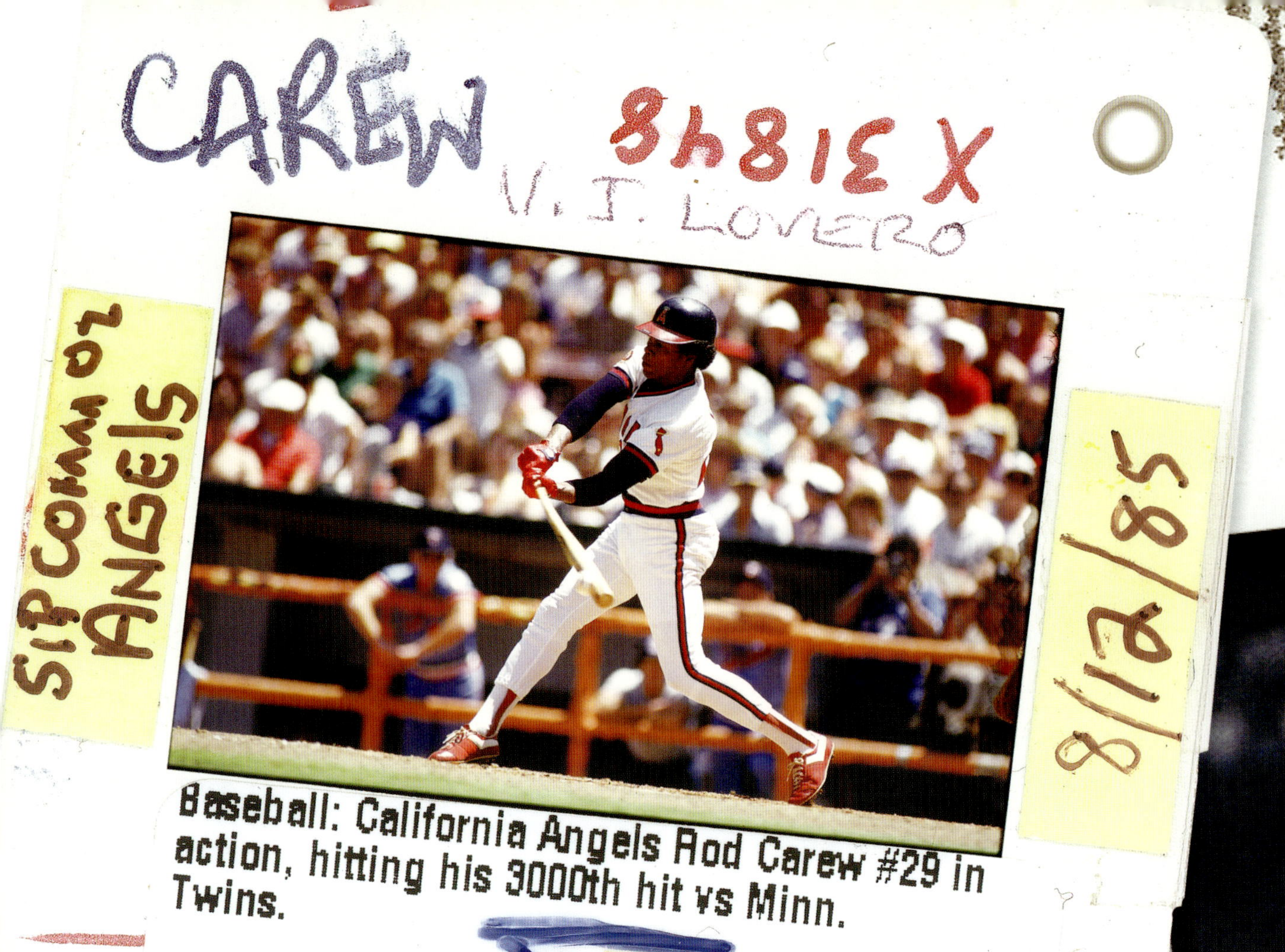

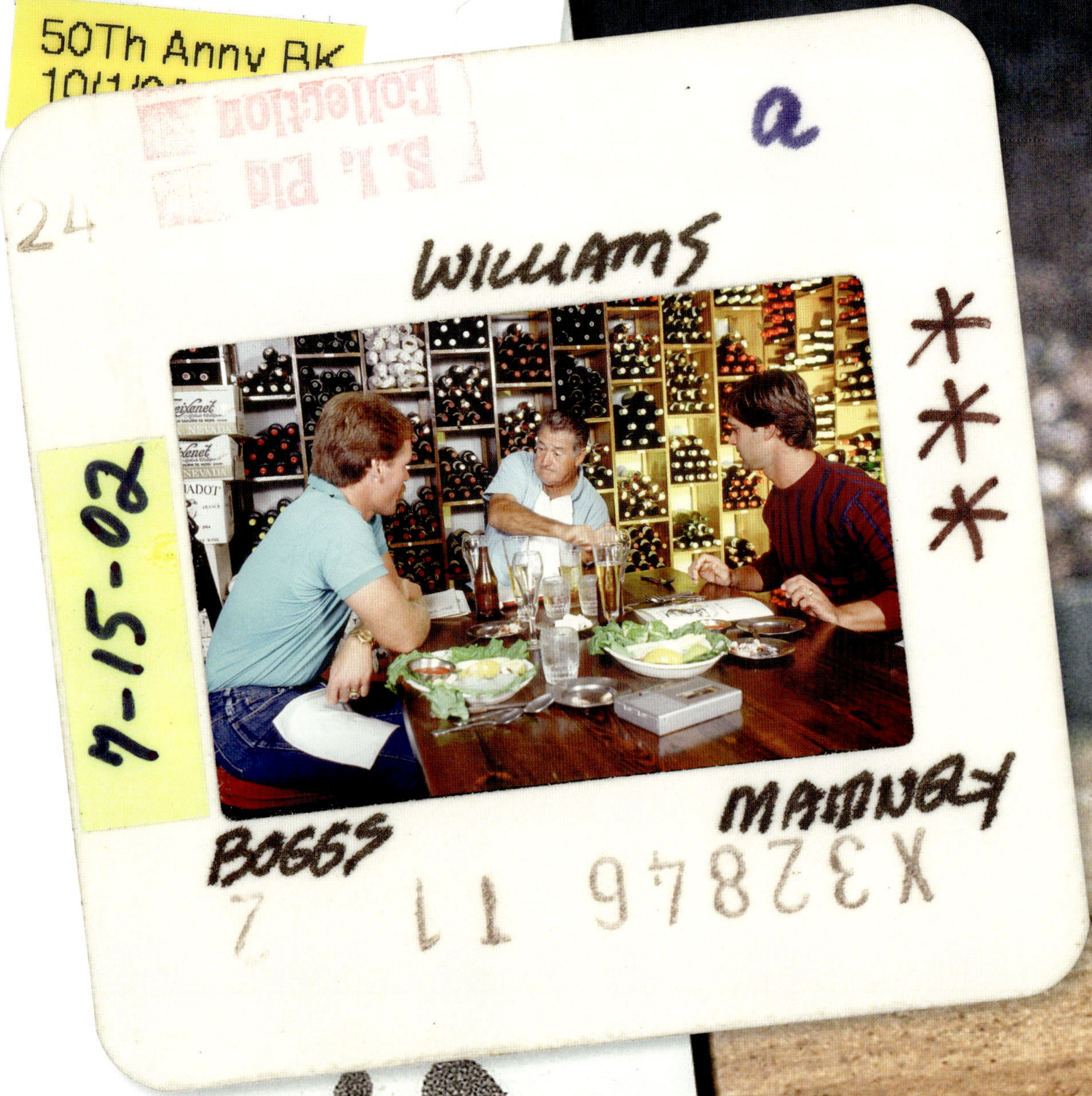

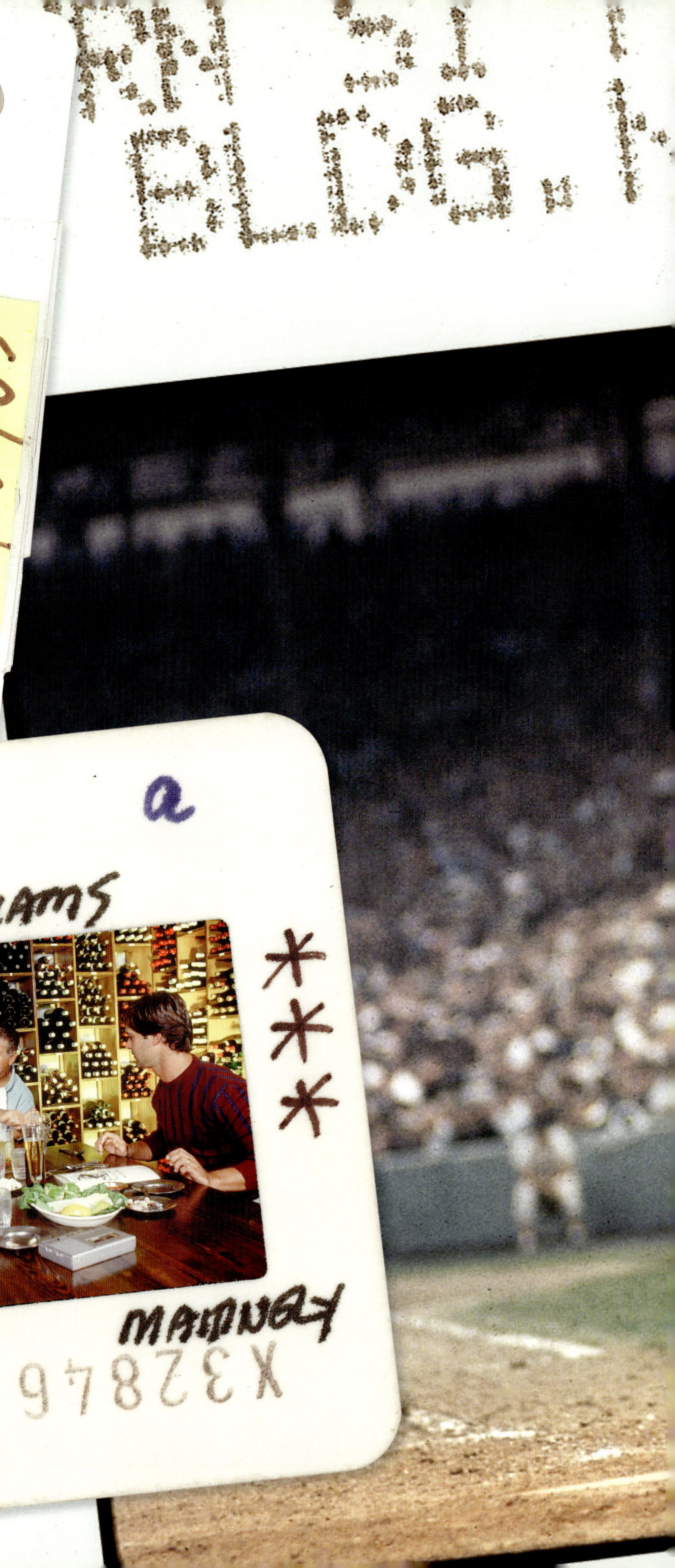

Strokes Of Genius

CARL YASTRZEMSKI *(opposite)*
Photograph by NEIL LEIFER, October 1967

ROD CAREW *(above)*
Photograph by V.J. LOVERO, August 4, 1985

TED WILLIAMS *(near right)*
Photograph by RONALD C. MODRA, March 20, 1986

ON DISPLAY, a few of the world's sweetest lefty swings: Carl Yastrzemski in the World Series and Rod Carew getting his 3,000th hit. And when Ted Williams took a break from a crab dinner to demonstrate technique, even All-Stars like Wade Boggs and Don Mattingly—also lefty hitters—had to pay heed.

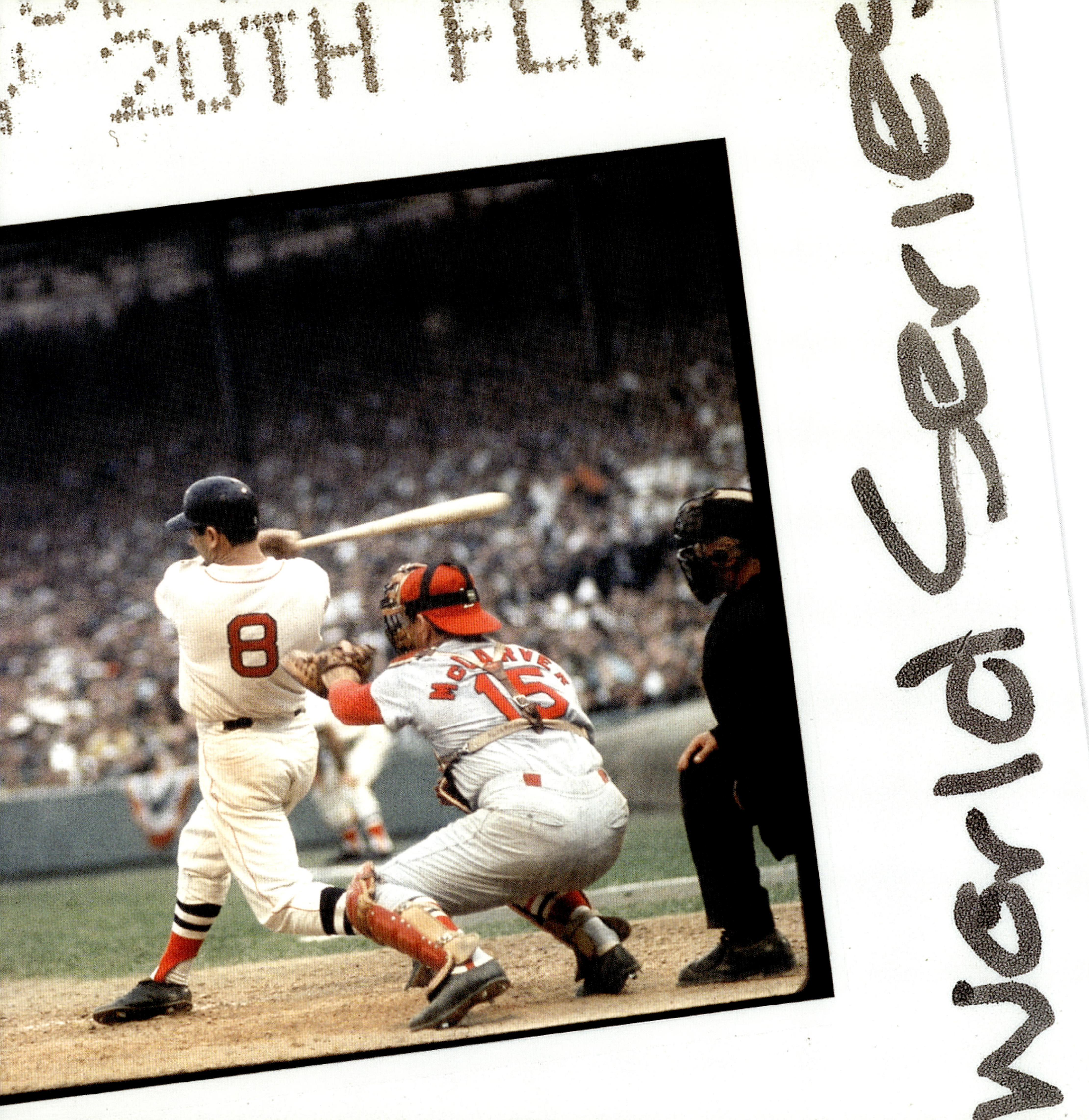

20TH FLR
World Series
8
15

In Black And White

TOMMIE SMITH AND JOHN CARLOS
Photograph by NEIL LEIFER, October 16, 1968

FROM THE REIGN of Jack Johnson, the first black heavyweight champion, to the crossing of baseball's color line by Jackie Robinson, to the black-gloved salute by Tommie Smith and John Carlos at the 1968 Olympics, to the domination of his game by "Cablinasian" golfer Tiger Woods, sports has been central to the national conversation on race. SPORTS ILLUSTRATED has been a prominent voice in that conversation, most notably with its groundbreaking '68 cover story *(below, left)* on the black athlete. Jack Olsen, the senior editor who wrote the story, reported that in interviews black athletes, who weren't used to being asked about these issues, "would start out suspicious, and in a minute or two would suddenly come a flood of words." SI did another cover story on the topic of race in '91, and again, from a diametrically different perspective, in '97.

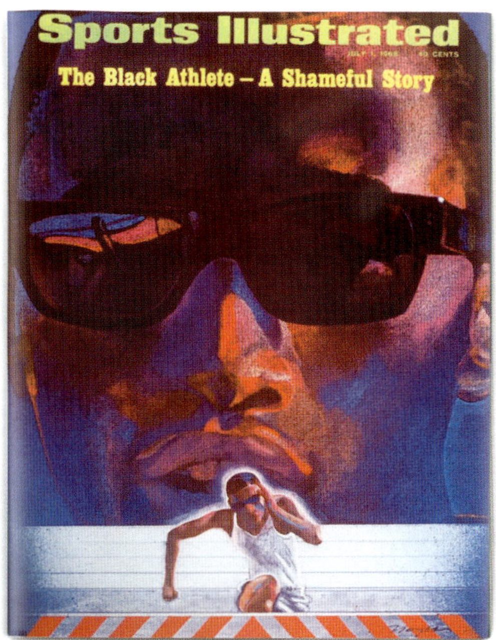

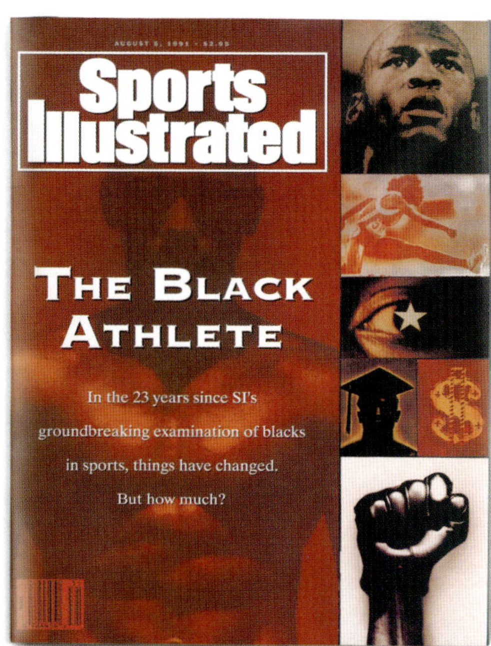

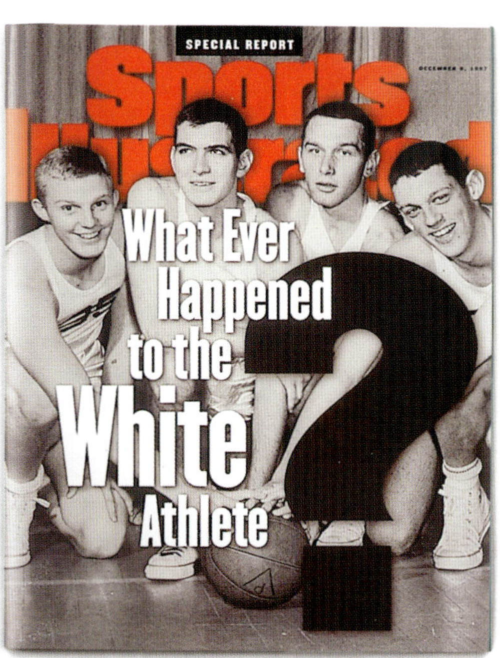

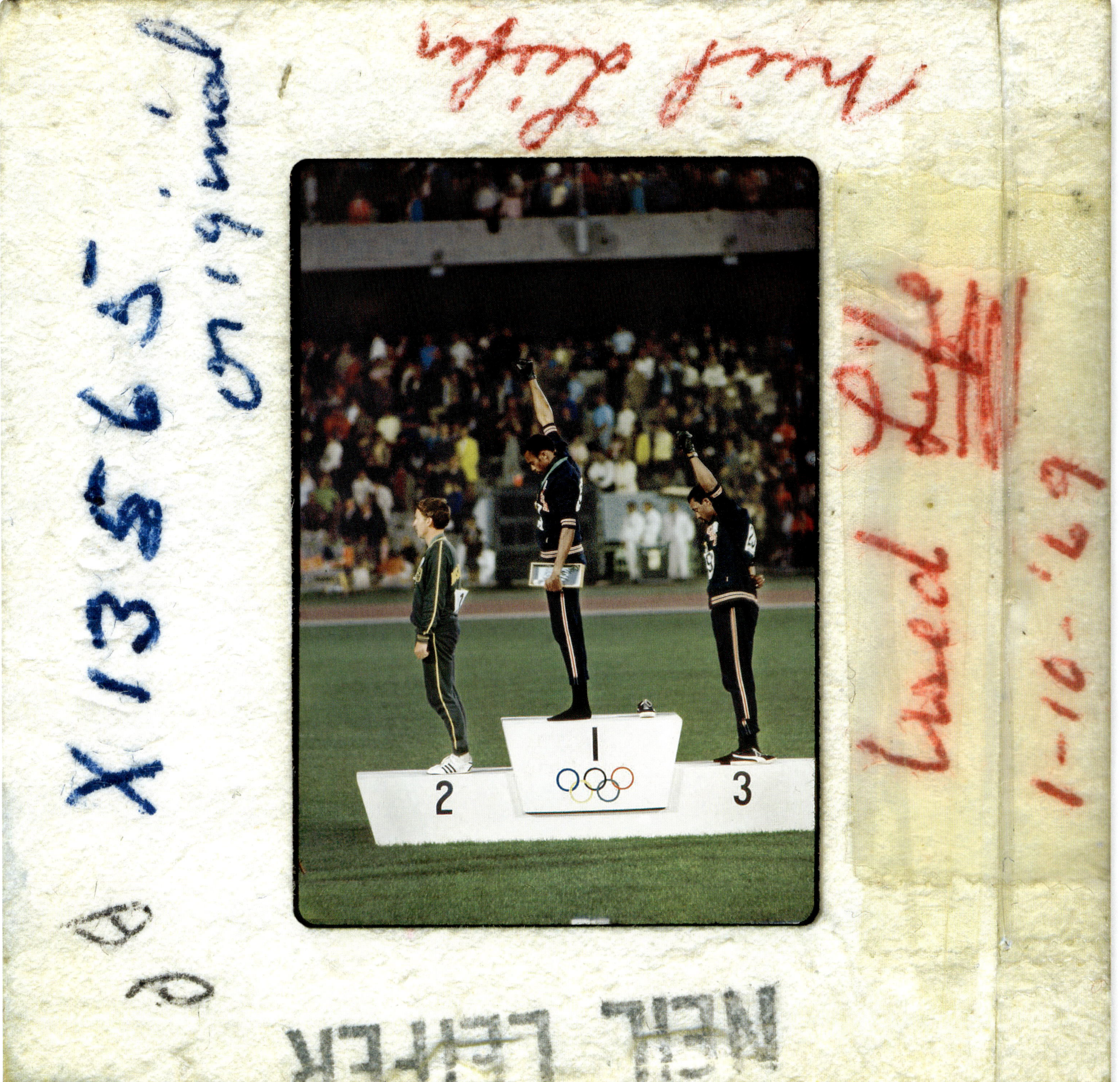
X13565
original
Neil Leifer
used Life
1-10-69
NEIL LEIFER
2
1
3

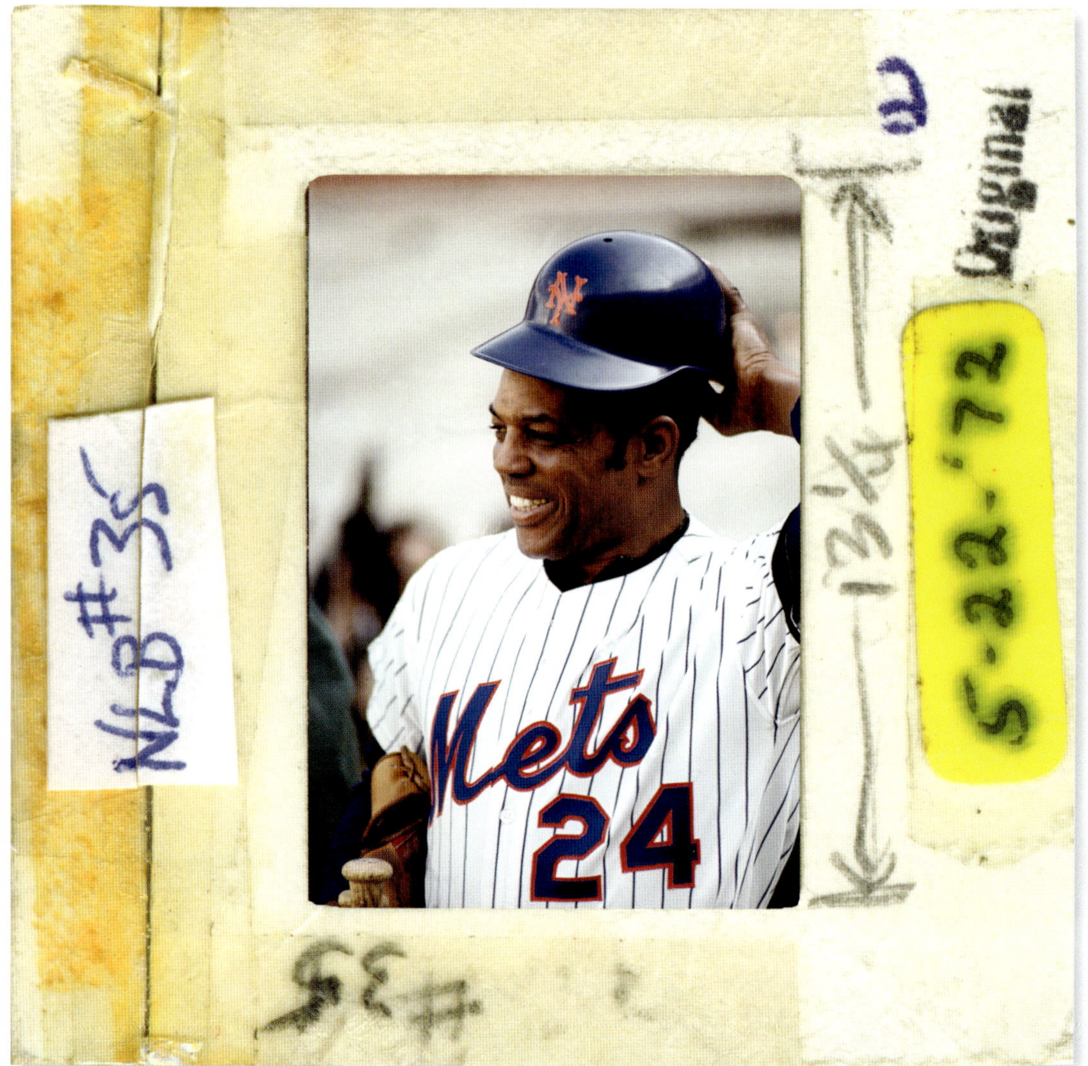

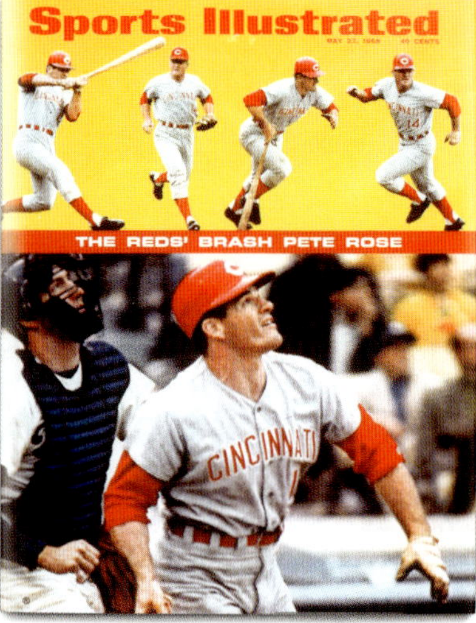

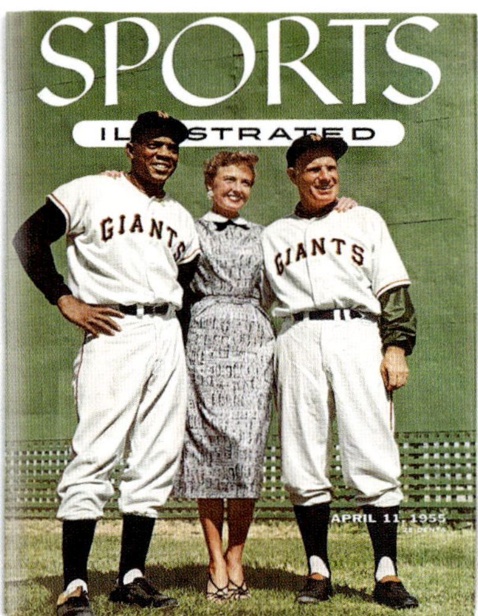

A Tip of The Cap

WILLIE MAYS *(above)*
Photograph by NEIL LEIFER, May 1972

PETE ROSE *(opposite)*
Photograph by RONALD C. MODRA, August 17, 1984

GREAT CAREERS have been charted and photographed from beginning to end in SI, including those of Pete Rose and Willie Mays. Above are the first of many covers each would occupy. Mays posed with Leo and Laraine Durocher for the 1955 National League preview; Rose in '68 was already drawing notice for being "brash," a trait that would define him through the years, as would the dirt invariably smeared on his uniform (in this '84 photo he was the Reds' player-manager). In '72, Mays had just come back to New York, where he'd started, joining the Mets for what would be a quiet two-year coda to his 20 spectacular seasons with the Giants.

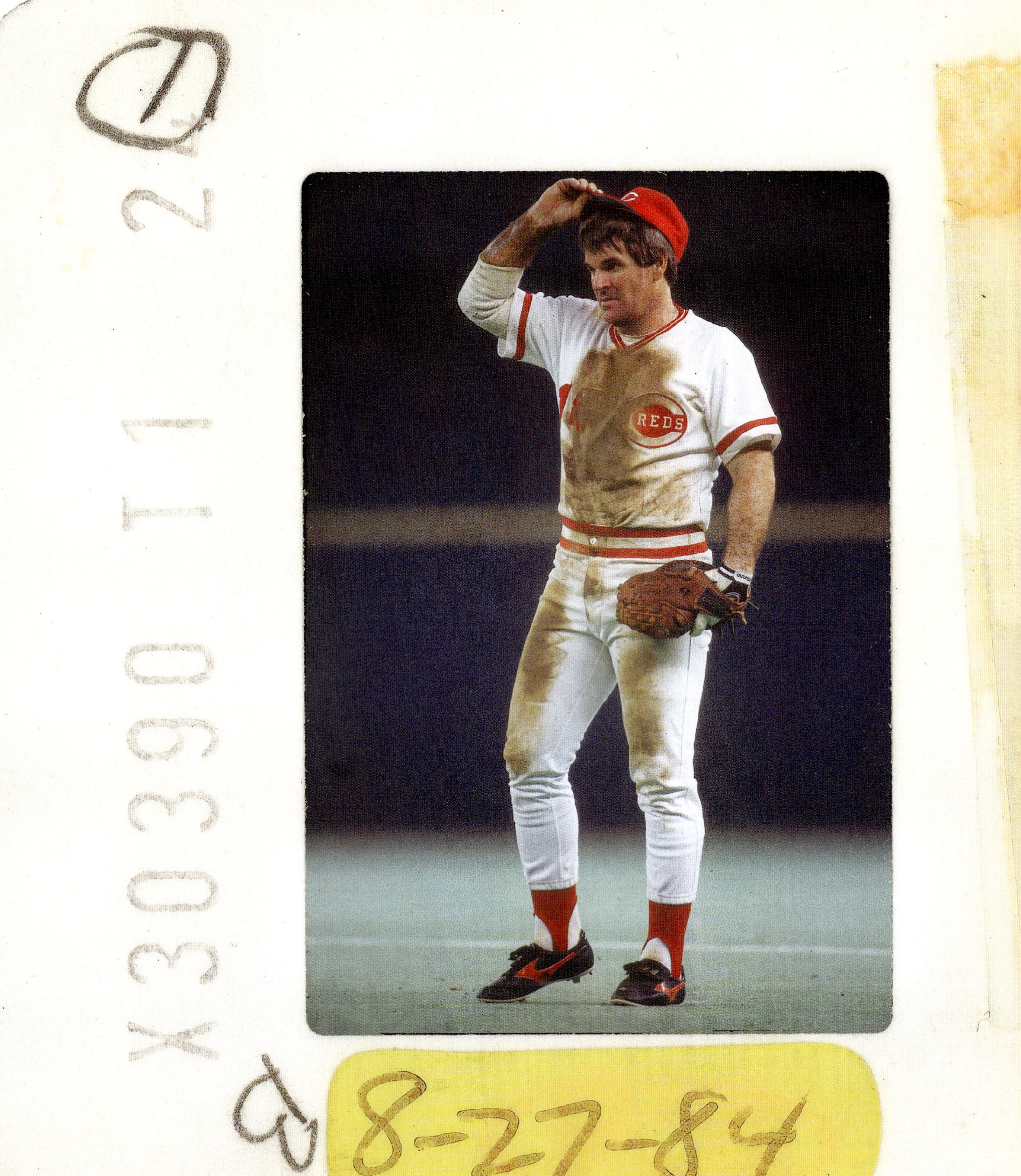

X30390 T1 2
8-27-84

7·20·98

PW

Golf: The Masters. Portrait of Jack Nicklaus alone, victorious during tournament.

2·19·96

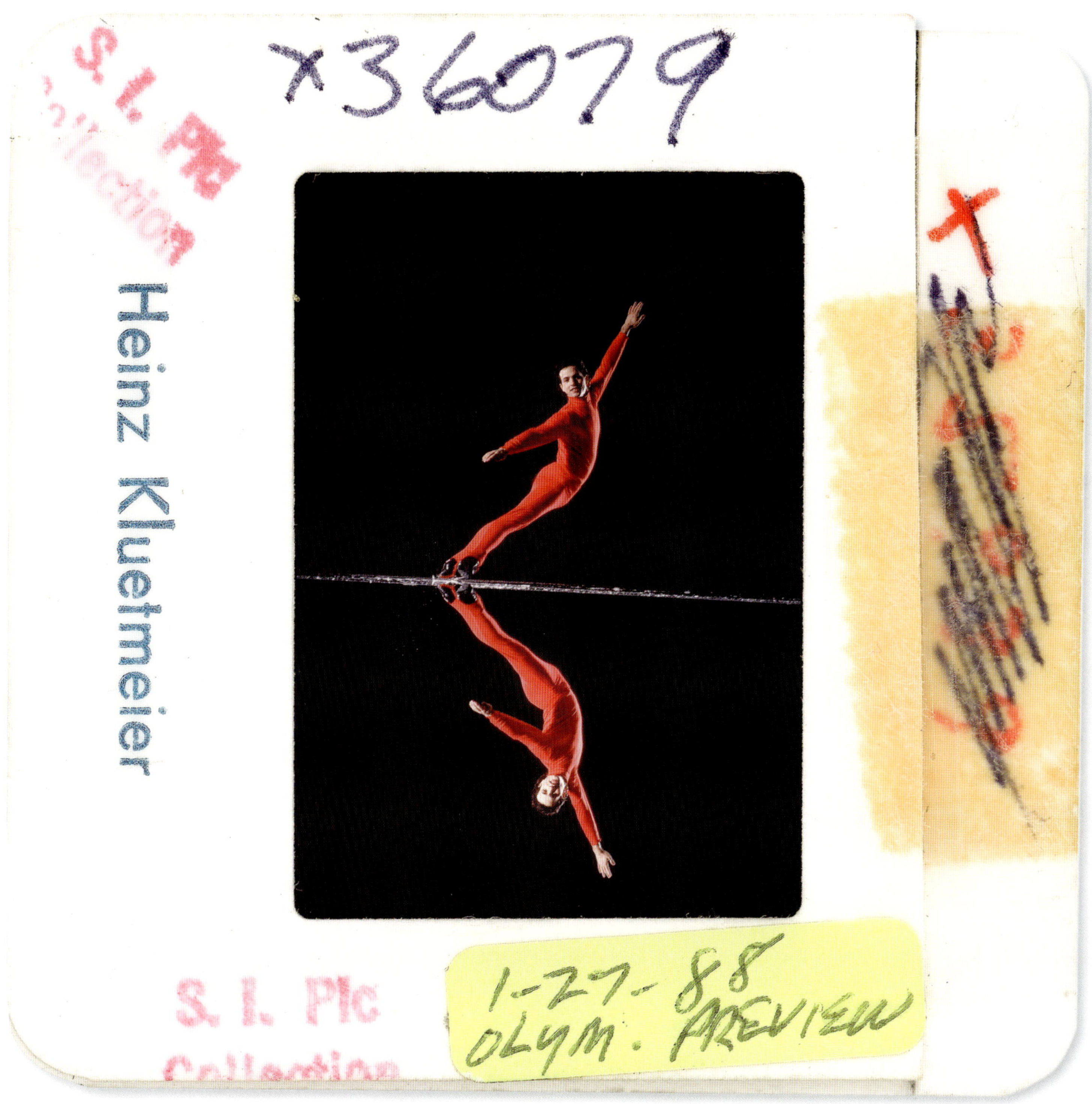

Perfect Posture

JACK NICKLAUS *(opposite). Photograph by* JOHN IACONO, April 13, 1986 • BRIAN BOITANO *(above). Photograph by* HEINZ KLUETMEIER, October 1987

NICKLAUS SHOWED his winning form in Georgia sunshine in a famed Masters triumph; Boitano displayed his in near darkness. To get the reflection, Kluetmeier set up a 3 a.m. shoot to flood the rink with water, then carefully illuminated only the elegant skater.

Together Again

MARK MESSIER & WAYNE GRETZKY

Photograph by JERRY WACHTER, January 13, 1982

WHEN JERRY WACHTER snapped this shot of the young Mark Messier and Wayne Gretzky on the Edmonton Oilers' bench in 1982, he surely had higher hopes for its use than for it to be shelved as a slide in a New Jersey warehouse and forgotten for 14 years. But that was its fate until '96 when Mess and Gretz, after years apart, were reunited as teammates on the New York Rangers and the editors wanted a shot of the two of them from their Stanley Cup–winning years back in Canada. Wachter's shot was unearthed from the archive and was run in the magazine for the very first time. The photo would run a second time in '99, in a commemorative issue for the retiring Gretzky, titled "Goodbye to the Great One."

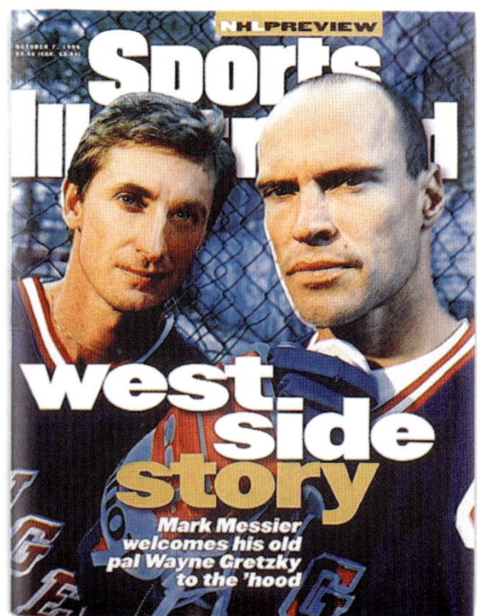

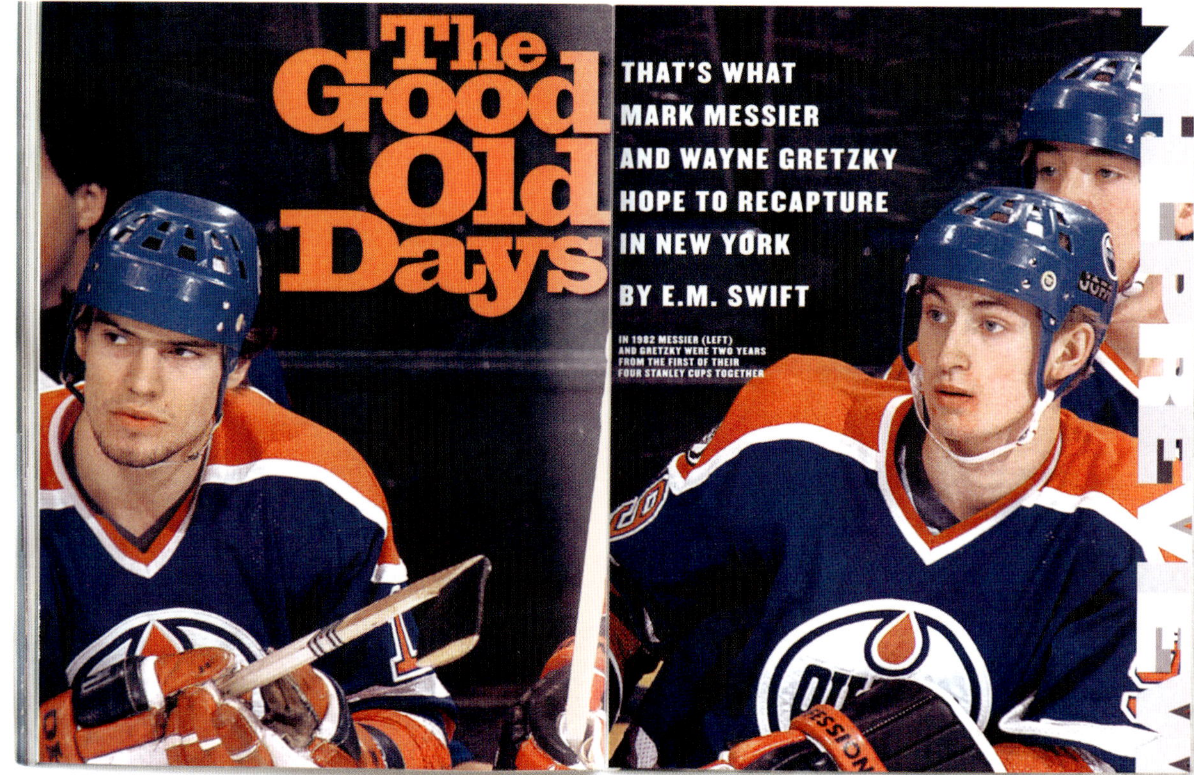

Hockey: Portrait of Edmonton Oilers Wayne Gretzky #99 behind bench w. Mark Messier #11 during game.

Location

SIP GRETZKY

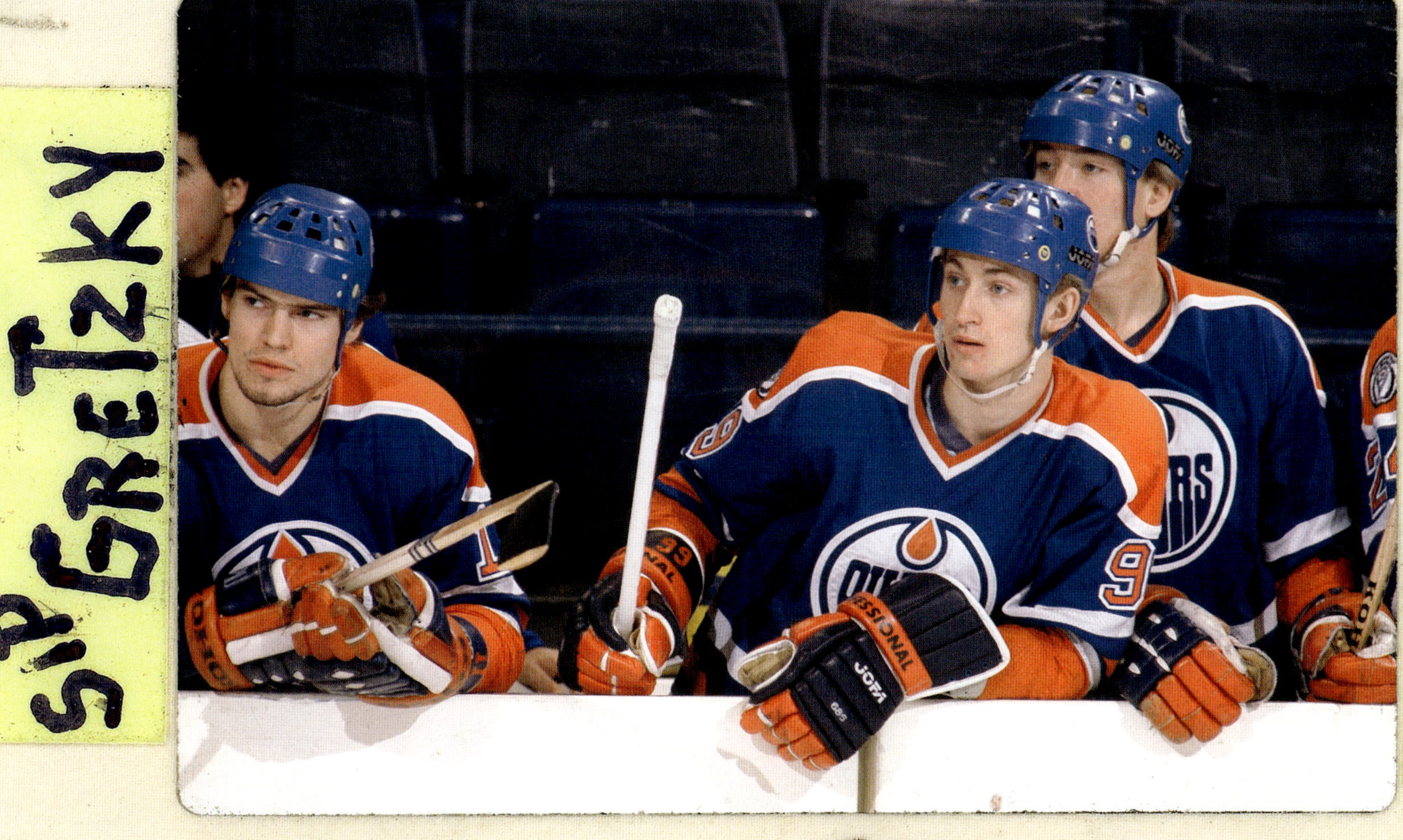

MESS. GRETZKY

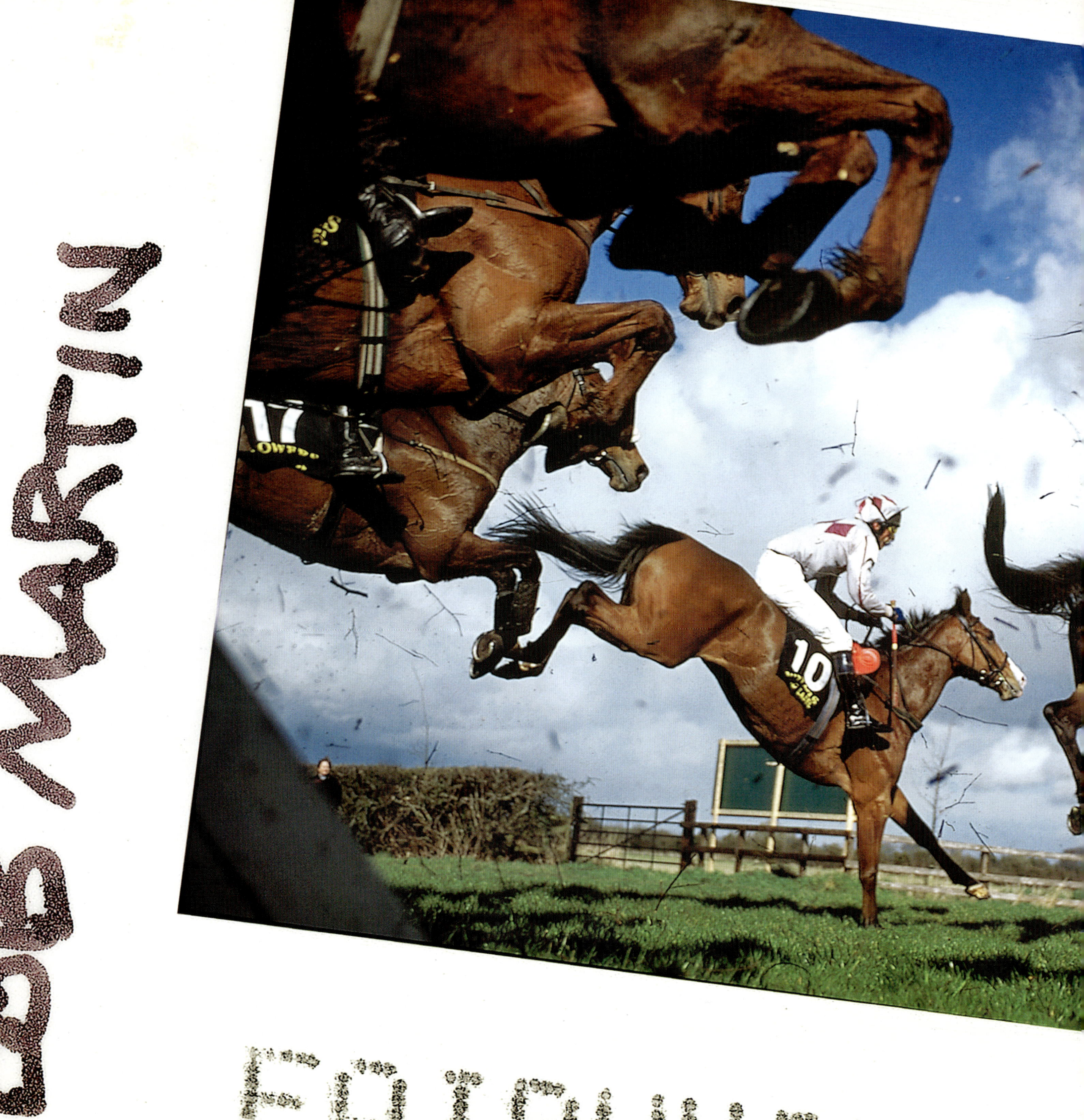
BOB MARTIN
10
FAIRYHOUSE

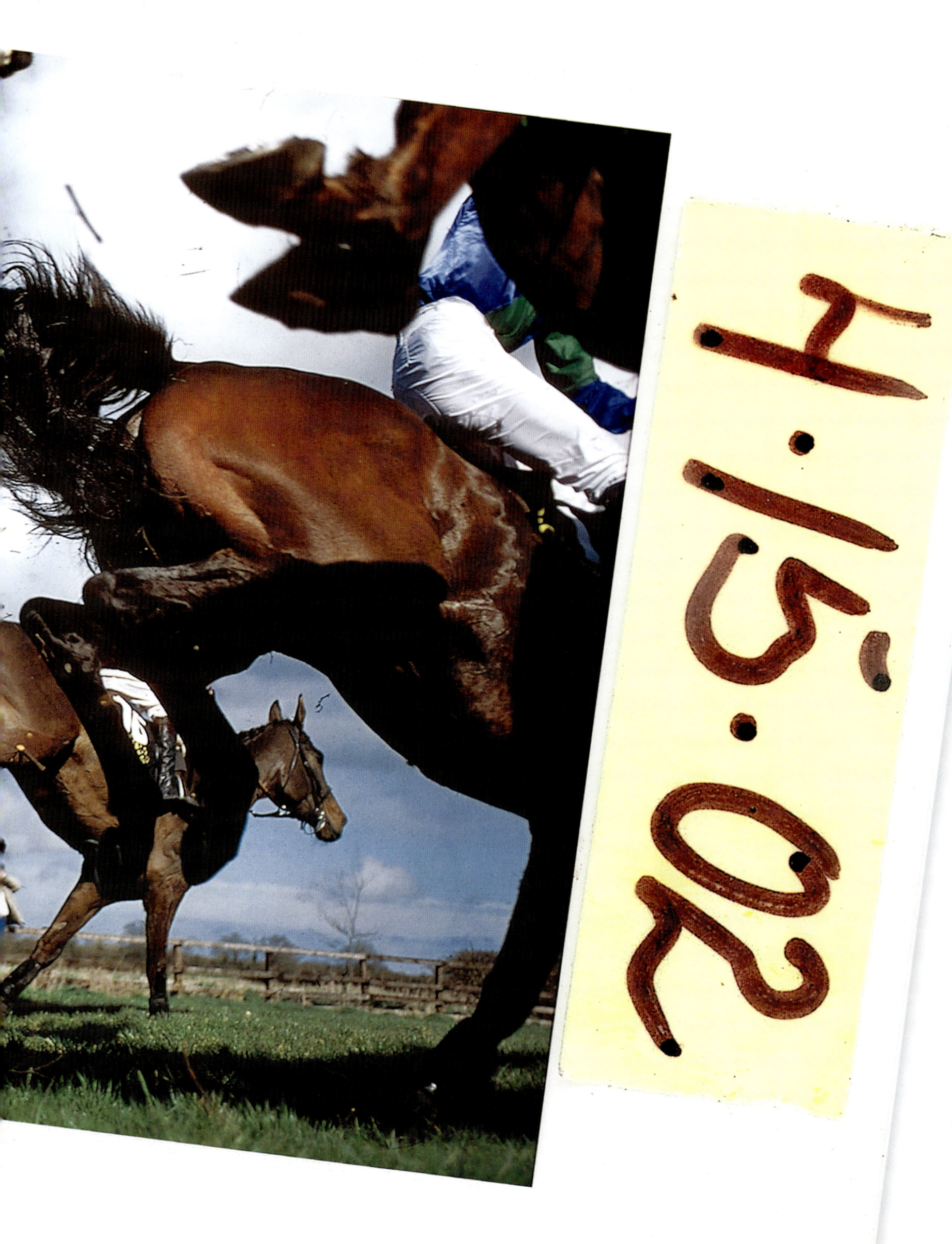

Of Hooves And Haunches

IRISH GRAND NATIONAL
Photograph by BOB MARTIN, April 1, 2002

BY EMBEDDING a camera in a jumping fence and firing it with a remote control, Bob Martin caught the underside of steeplechase racing. This unusual composition first ran in the magazine's LEADING OFF section, a weekly showcase for striking photographs, and again later in SI's 50th anniversary book.

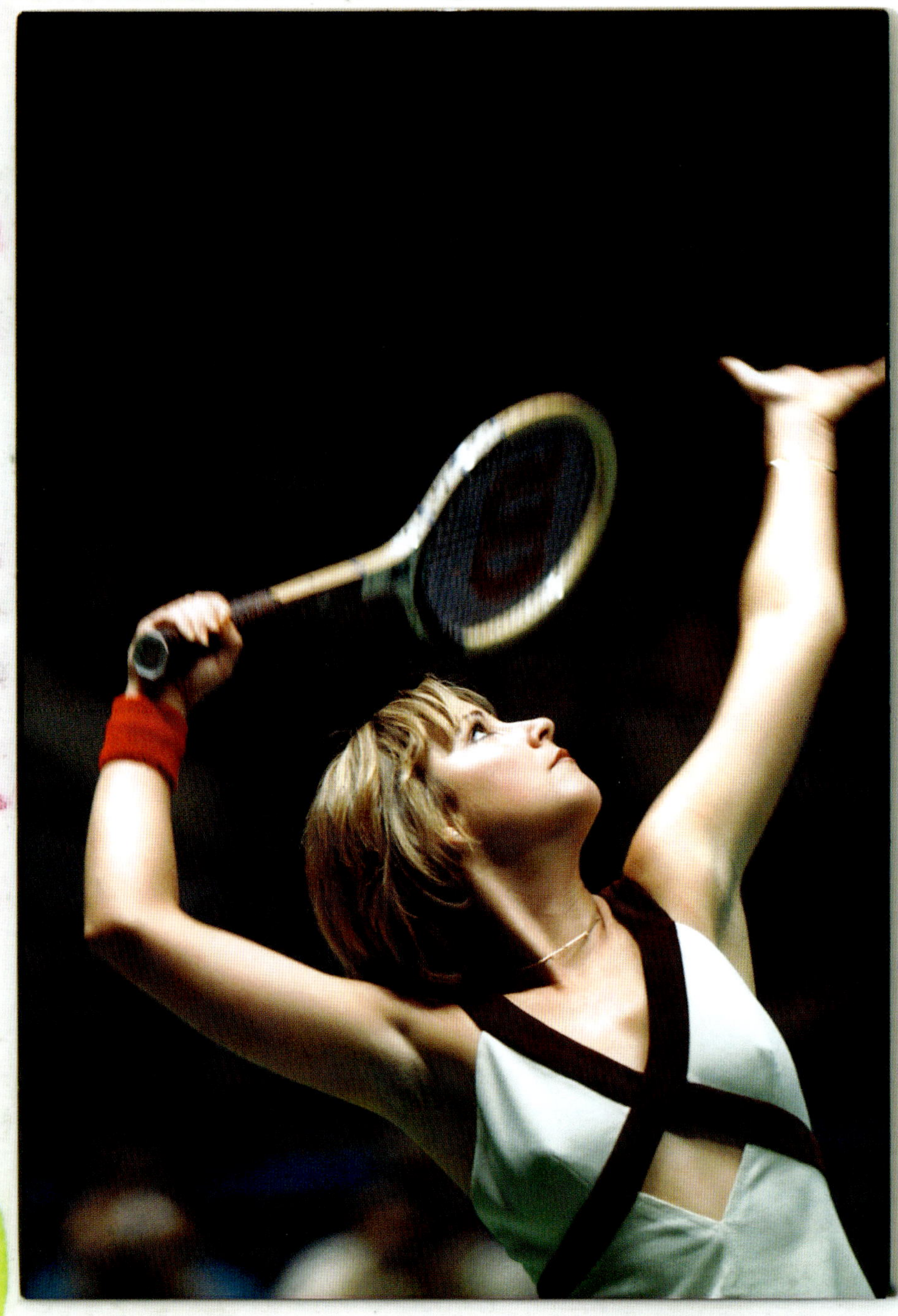

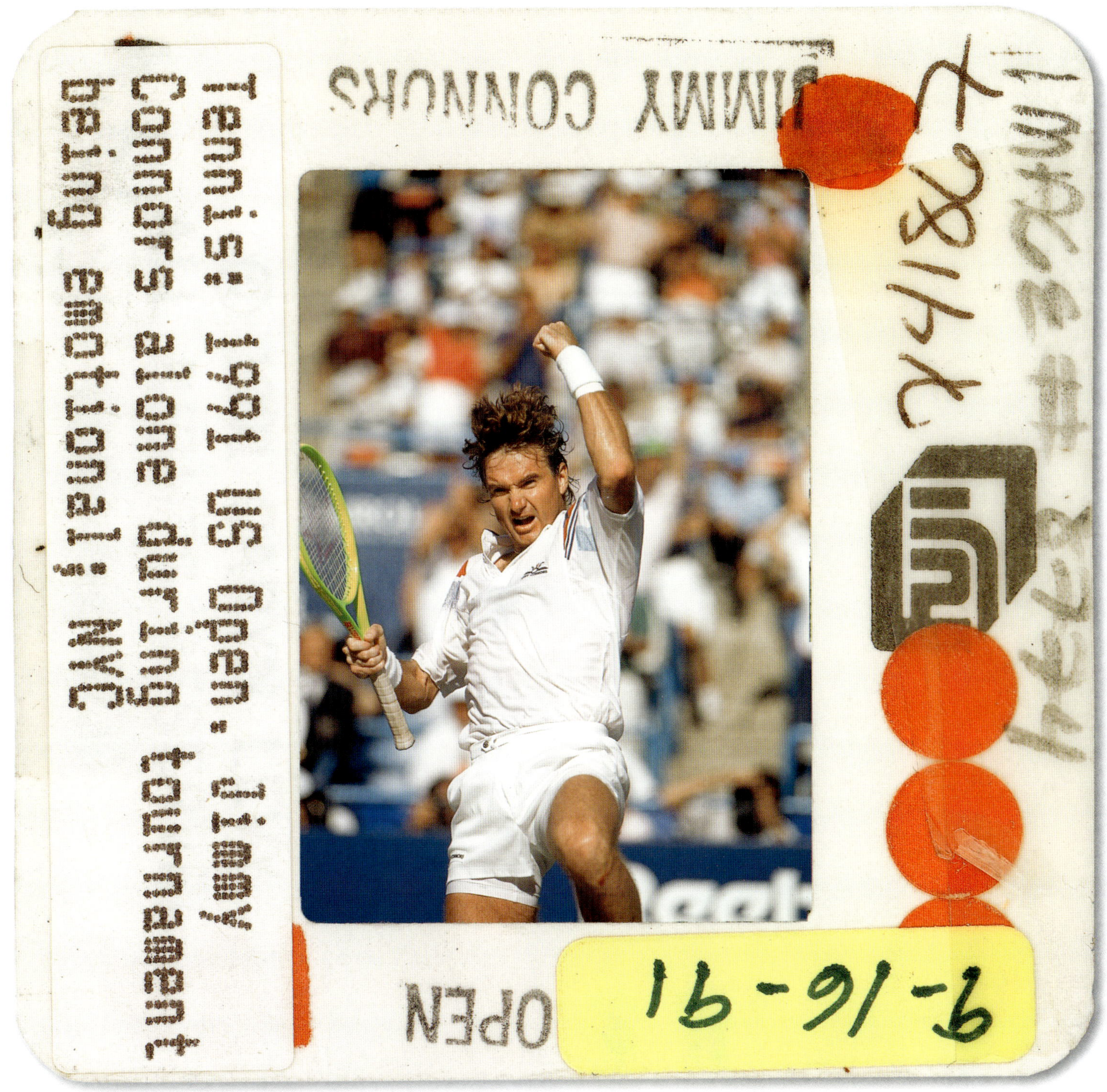

Courtship

CHRIS EVERT *(opposite). Photograph by* NEIL LEIFER, March 1977 • JIMMY CONNORS *(above). Photograph by* CARYN LEVY, September 7, 1991

HER GAME WAS COOL and crafty. His was renegade and rowdy. She was loved for being graceful. He for "being emotional," as the slide describes it. But opposites attracted, at least for a while. Evert and Connors were engaged from November 1973 to September 1974.

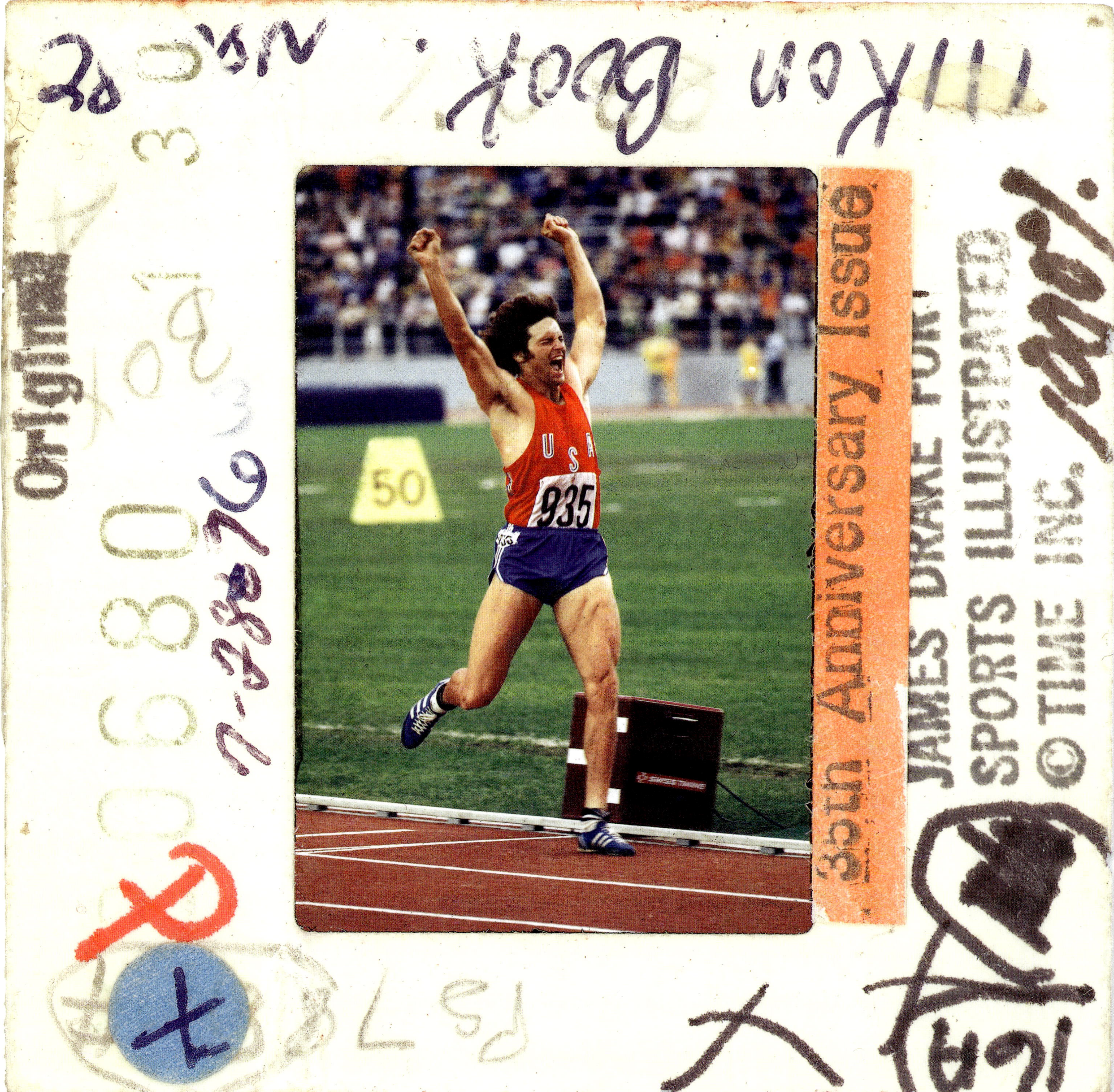

Original
7-30-76
USA
935
50
35th Anniversary Issue
JAMES DRAKE FOR
SPORTS ILLUSTRATED
©TIME INC.

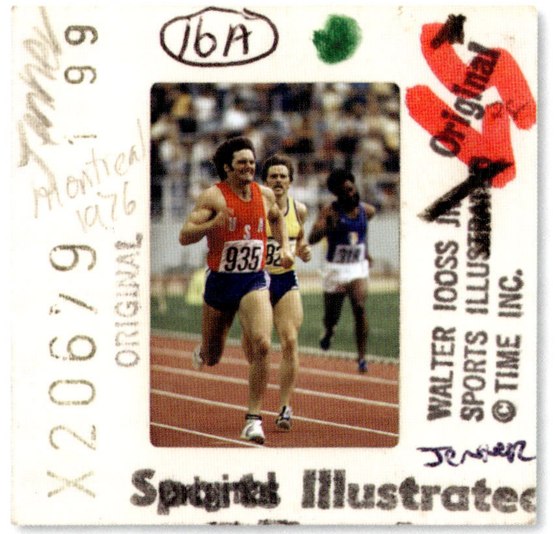

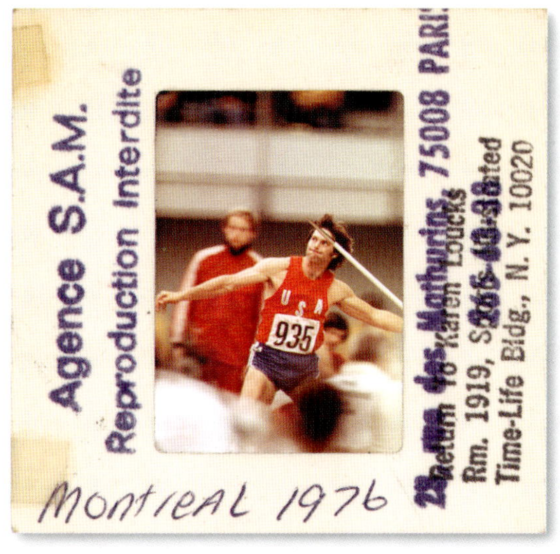

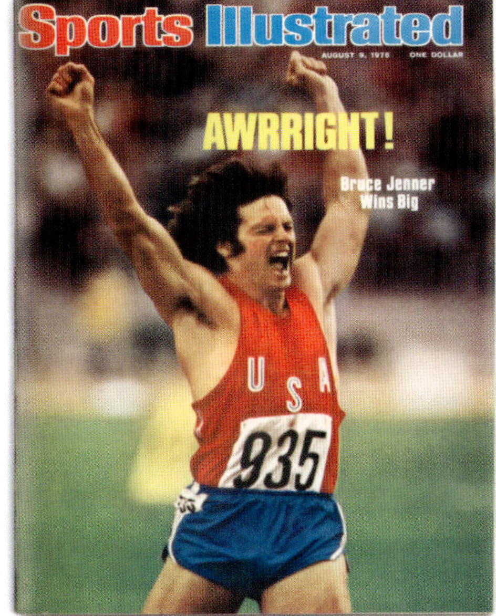

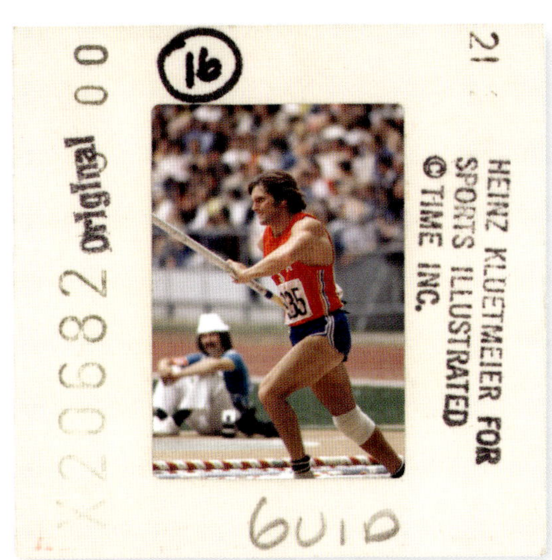

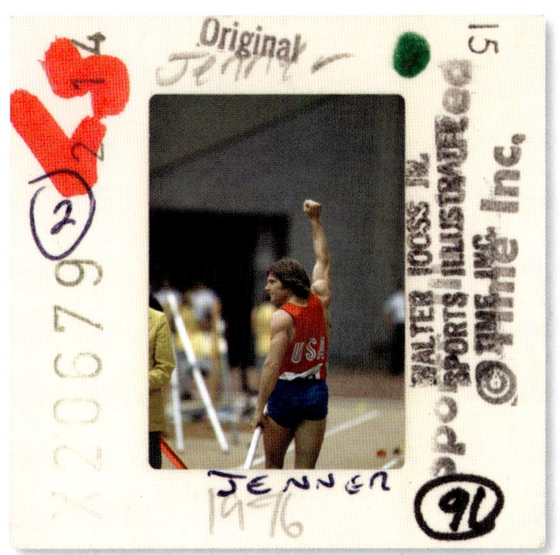

Well Covered

BRUCE JENNER

Photograph by JAMES DRAKE, JULY 30, 1976 *(opposite).*
Photograph by WALTER IOOSS JR., JULY 29, 1976 *(top left).*
Photograph by NEIL LEIFER, JULY 30, 1976 *(top right).*
Photograph by HEINZ KLUETMEIER, JULY 30, 1976 *(bottom left).*
Photograph by WALTER IOOSS JR., JULY 30, 1976 *(bottom right).*

WRITER FRANK DEFORD described Bruce Jenner as having given "a world-record performance in the decathlon and in charm" at the 1976 Olympics. (His story also described Jenner as "a handsome Pete Rose.") A testament to Jenner's magnetism: the number of SI shooters tracking him over the two-day, 10-event circuit. It appears, at first glance, that James Drake's photo of the climactic 1,500 meters event is the cover shot. But the cover photo was actually taken by Walter Iooss Jr.; the slide of it has since gone missing. Iooss was next to Drake at the finish line and the two photos are nearly indistinguishable. (Look at the *A* on Jenner's shirt.)

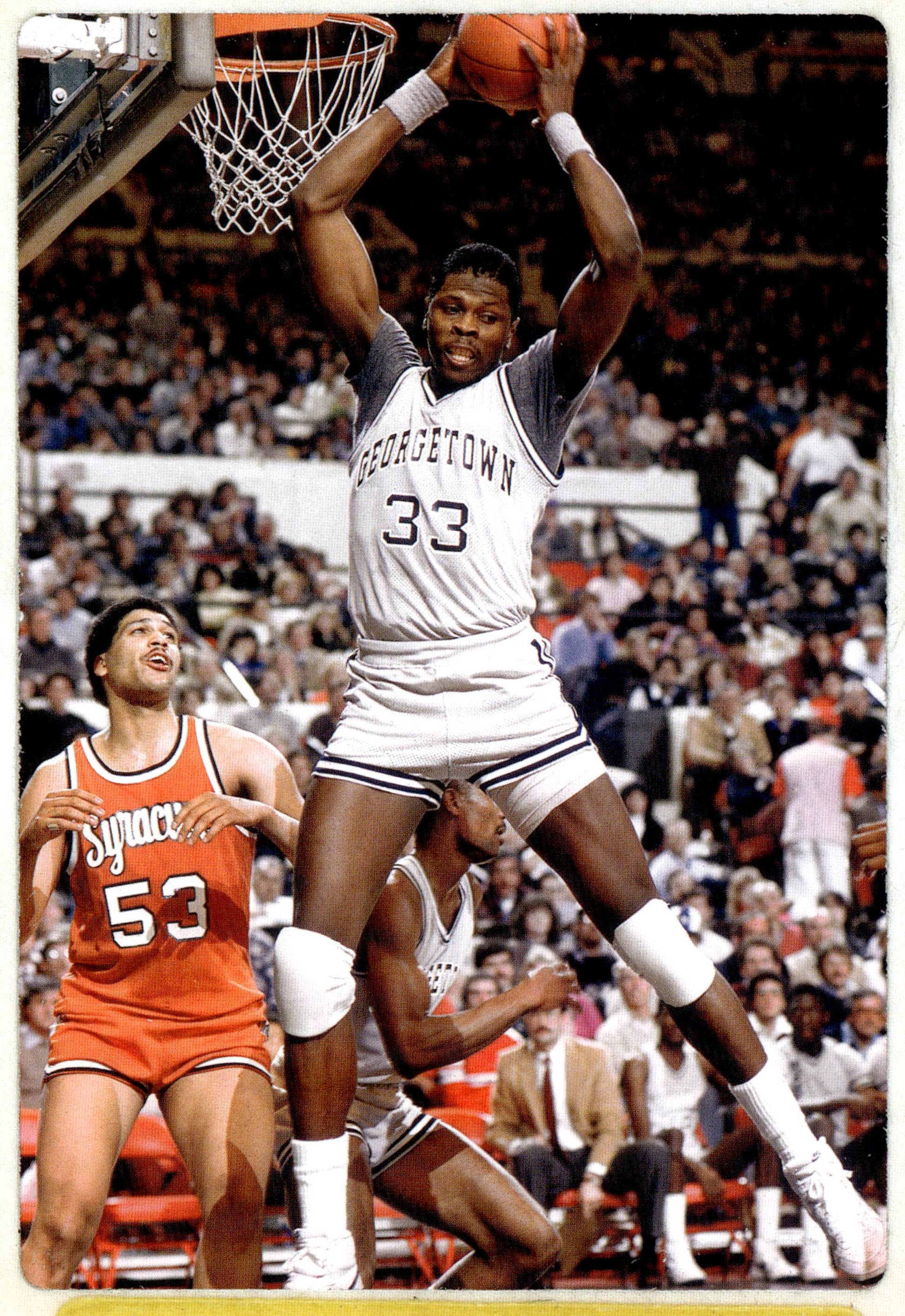
GEORGETOWN
33
53

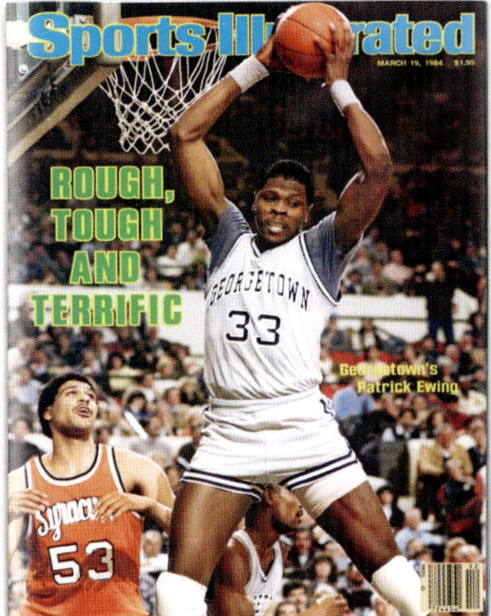

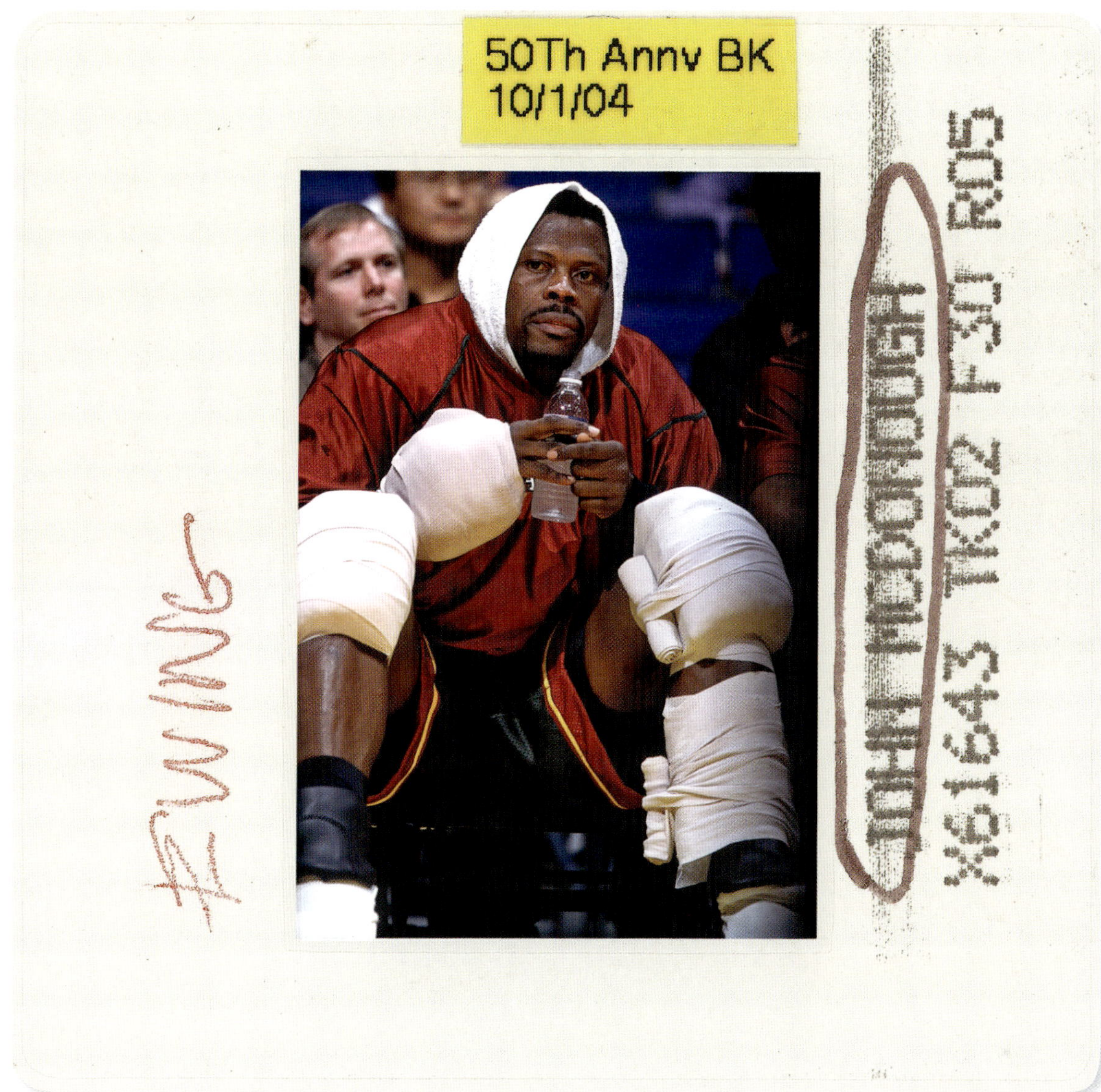

No Pain, No Game

PATRICK EWING *(opposite)*
Photograph by MANNY MILLAN, March 10, 1984

PATRICK EWING *(above right)*
Photograph by JOHN W. MCDONOUGH, October 19, 2000

AT ITS MOST ARTFUL, basketball can look like ballet. But the beauty of the game cannot hide its brutal physical toll. John W. McDonough, who has been shooting NBA games since 1976, knows this firsthand, having survived those times when a player has crashed into him while he was shooting from the baseline. ("It's like being hit with metal bars," he says.) These photos document the effects of Patrick Ewing's career on his body. As a junior with the Georgetown Hoyas, he is bounding onto the cover, the picture of pure athleticism. Years later, as he sits on the Seattle bench following 15 title-less seasons in New York, the ice packs tell the story.

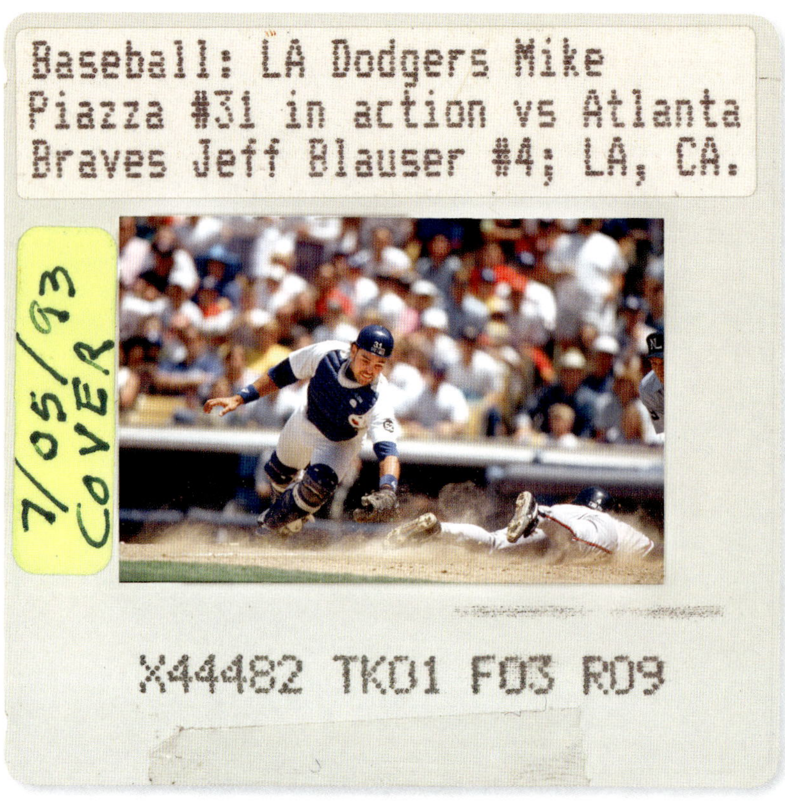

MIKE PIAZZA

Photograph by V.J. LOVERO, June 5, 1993

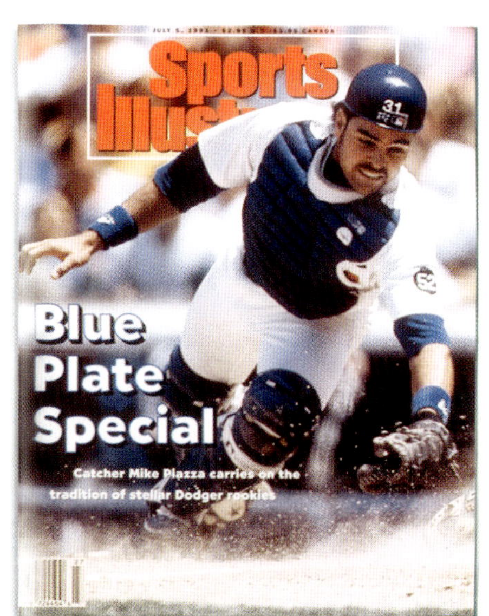

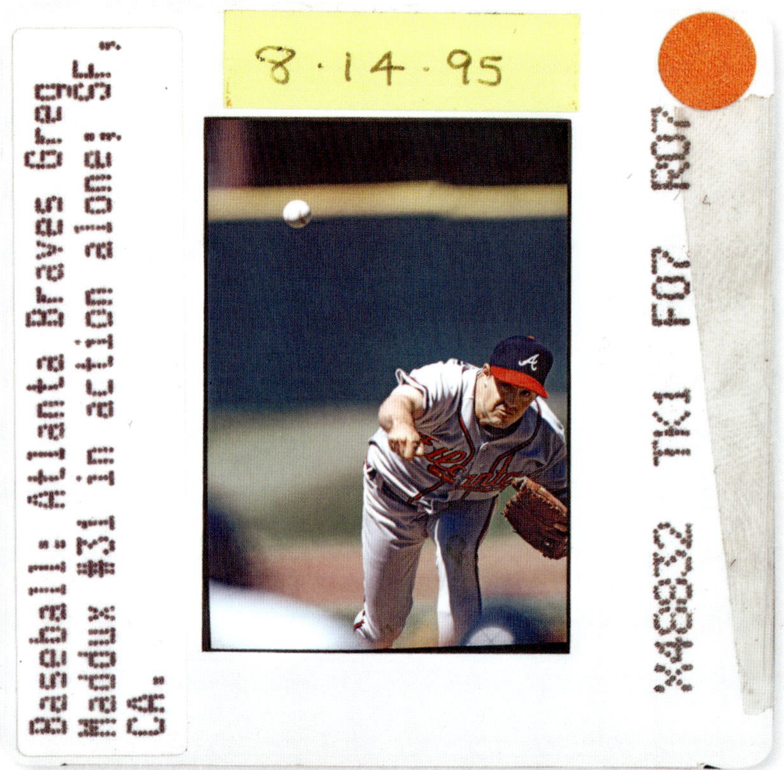

GREG MADDUX

Photograph by RICHARD MACKSON, July 29, 1995

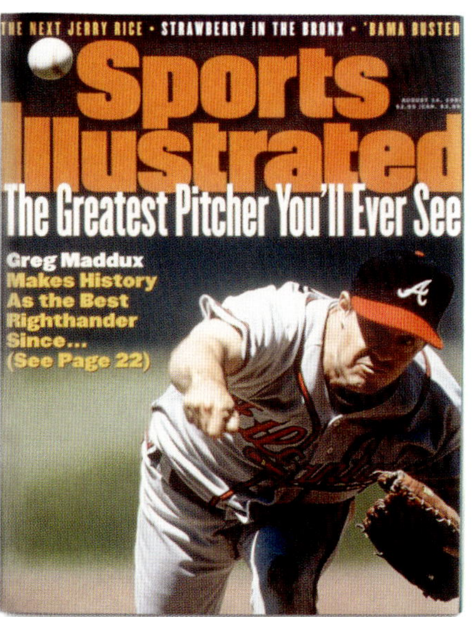

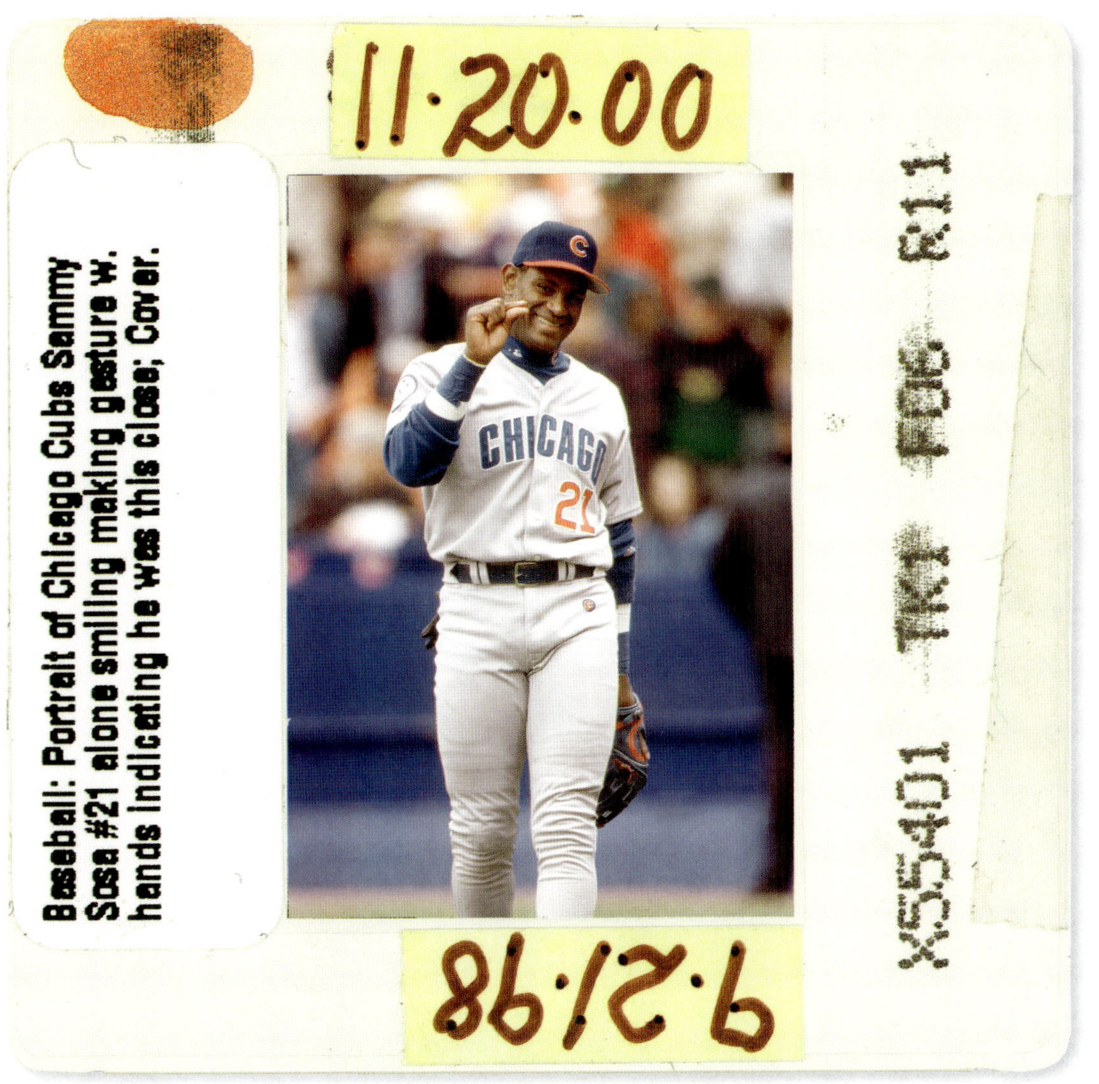

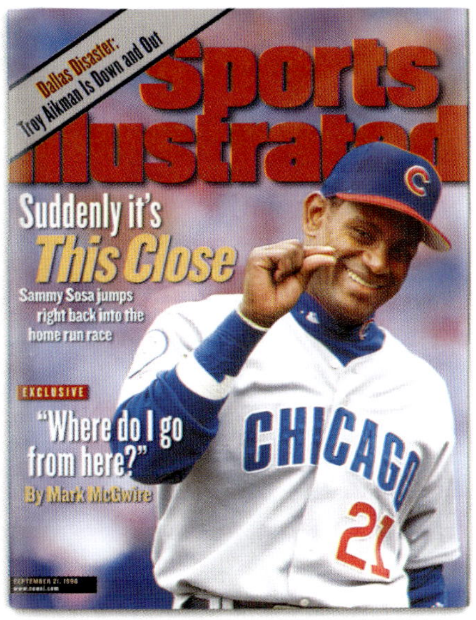

A Game Of Inches

SAMMY SOSA

Photograph by CHUCK SOLOMON, April 16, 1998

MOST BASEBALL covers, like these of Mike Piazza and Greg Maddux, illustrate their subjects in the obvious way—men at work, doing what they do best. Chuck Solomon's shot of Sammy Sosa was more a happy accident. Early in the 1998 season Solomon was hanging around the batting cage before a game, hoping to catch players in candid moments. He noticed Sosa joking with a player on the opposing team, and when the Cubs outfielder put his fingers together, Solomon got off a couple clicks. That September, as Sosa crept up on Mark McGwire in their record-setting home run race, the editors found this image and gave it a whole new meaning.

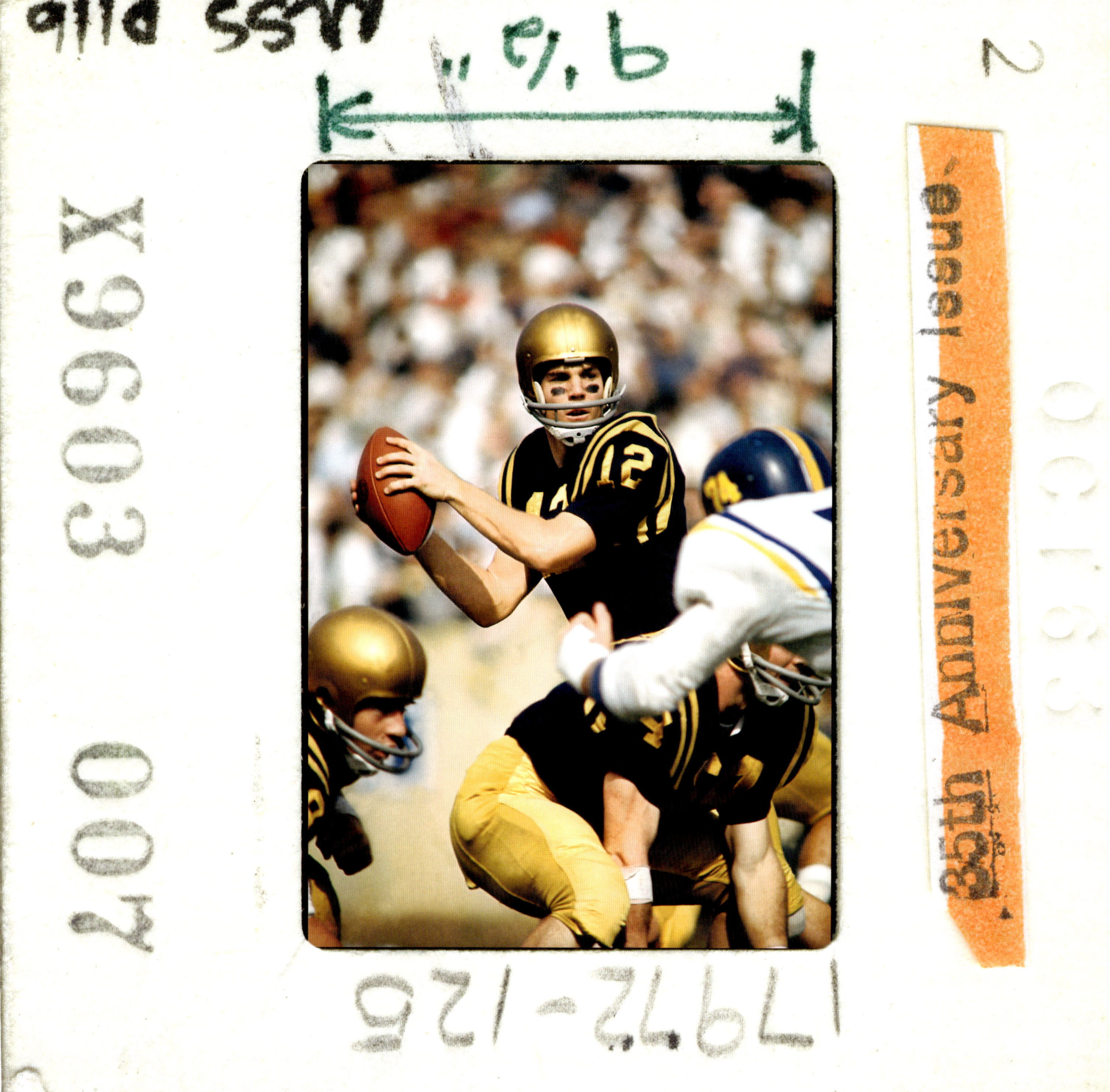

35th Anniversary Issue
12

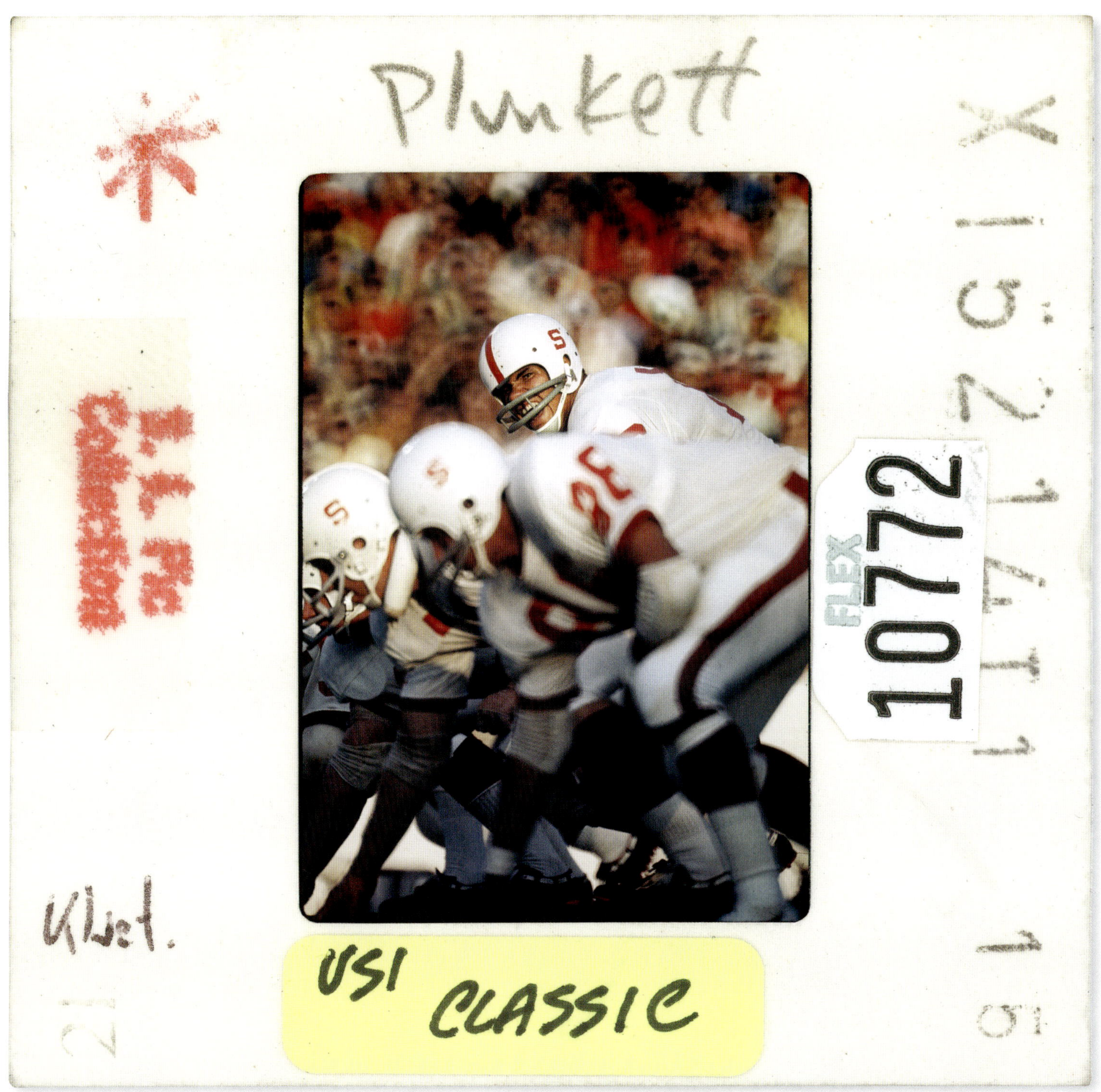

Trophy Lives

ROGER STAUBACH *(opposite). Photograph by* NEIL LEIFER, October 26, 1963 • JIM PLUNKETT *(above). Photograph by* HEINZ KLUETMEIER, September 12, 1970

THESE TWO YOUNG MEN would go on to occupy many SI slides, and had much in common: Each would win a Heisman (Staubach at Navy, Plunkett at Stanford) and become a Super Bowl MVP (Staubach with the Cowboys, Plunkett with the Raiders).

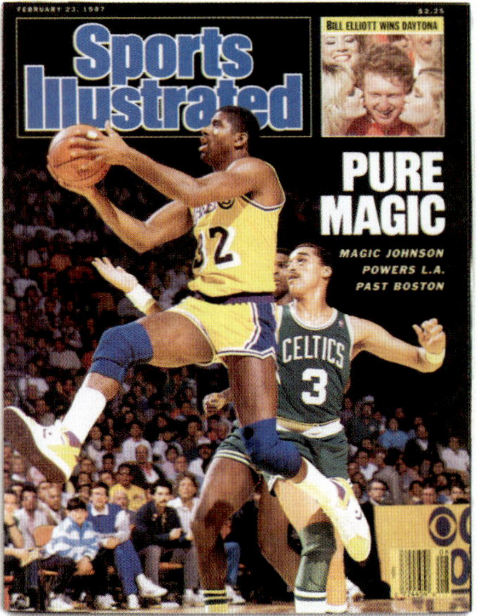

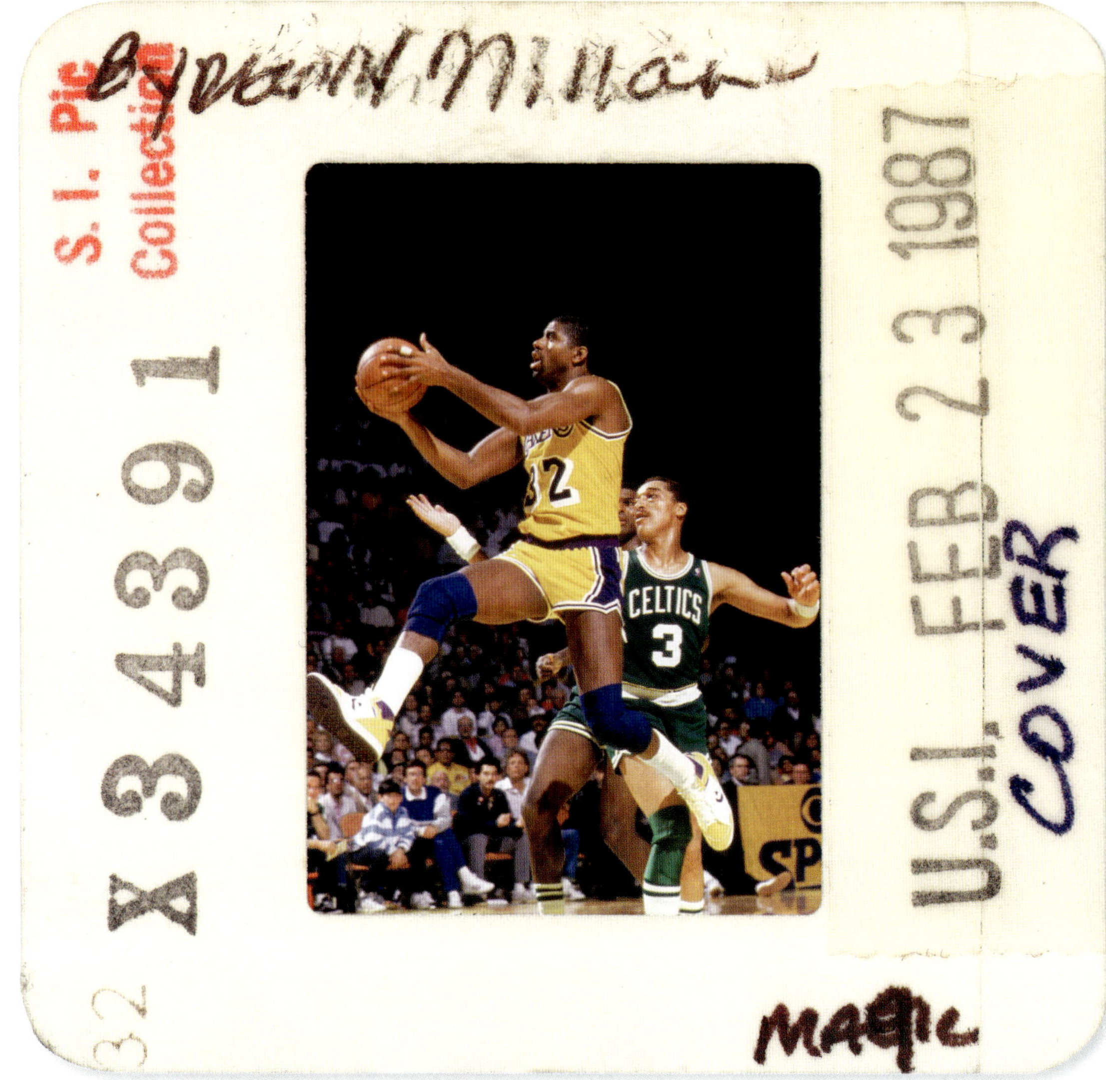

Game Savers

MAGIC JOHNSON *(above)*
Photograph by MANNY MILLAN, February 15, 1987

LARRY BIRD *(opposite)*
Photograph by MANNY MILLAN, June 7, 1987

AS THESE photos suggest, Magic Johnson and Larry Bird didn't duel one-on-one all that often when the Lakers played the Celtics. Here Magic drives by Boston great Dennis Johnson, while Bird squares off against L.A.'s Michael Cooper (whom Bird has called the toughest defender he ever faced). Even so, the rivalry between these future Hall of Famers drew fans back to a faltering NBA, and reached the point that a regular-season game between their teams rated a cover story. The Bird photo, from his third and final clash with Magic for the NBA title (won by the Lakers) ran in SI's year-end issue recalling the most memorable moments of 1987.

X34935

U.S.I. DEC 28 1987

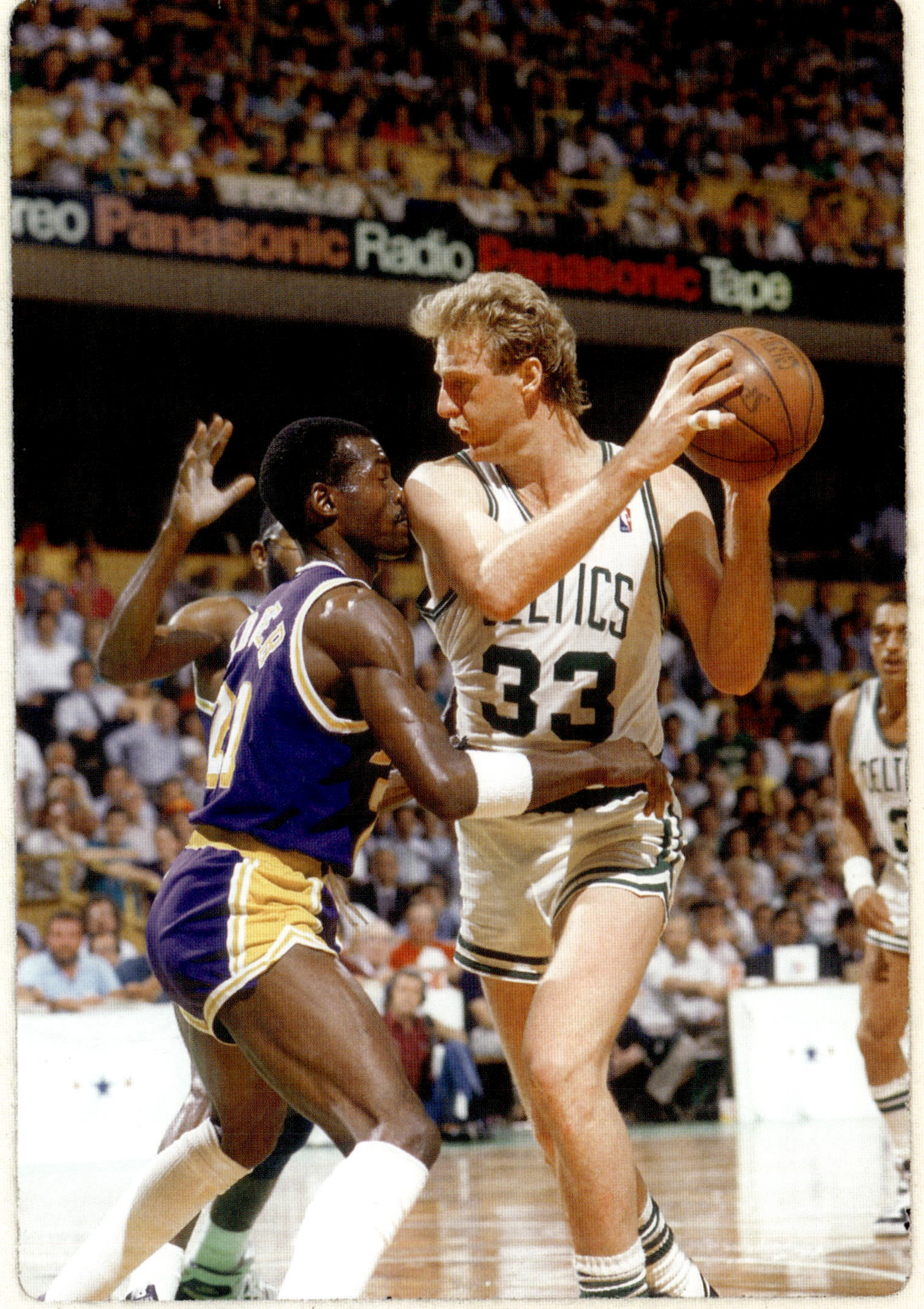

X

MANNY MILLAN
SPORTS ILLUSTRATED
© TIME INC.

87 finals

S.I. Pic Collection

AGENCE VANDYSTADT

x33368

7-21-86

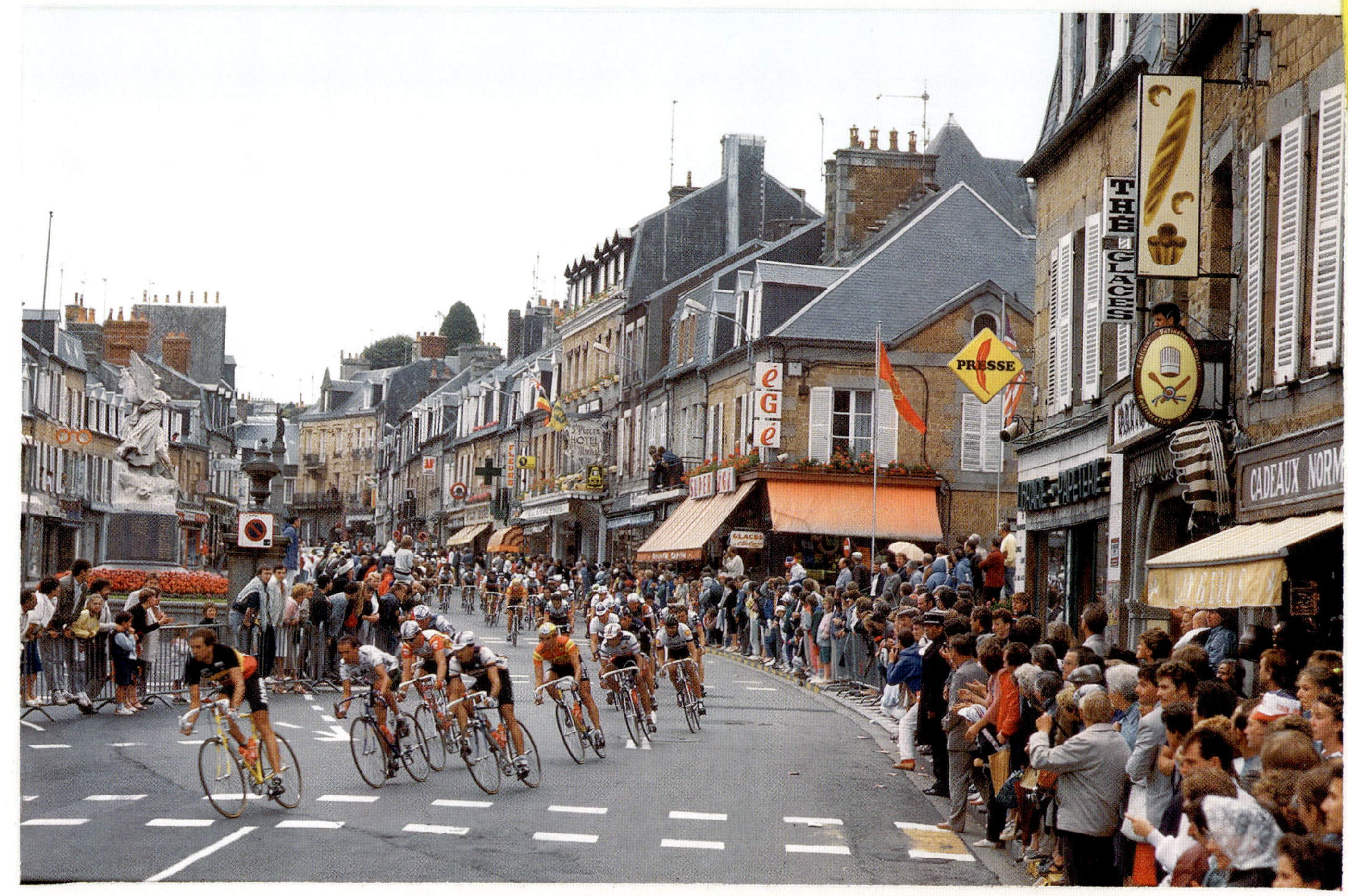

CYCLISME

TOUR DE FRANCE 1986

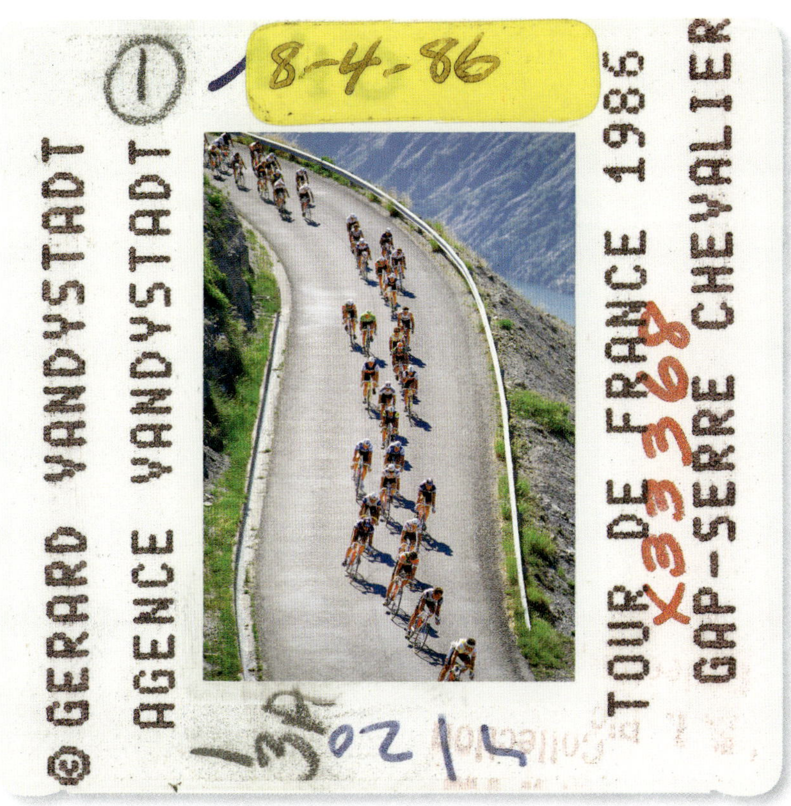

French Twist

TOUR DE FRANCE, GREG LEMOND
Photographs by GERARD VANDYSTADT, July 1986

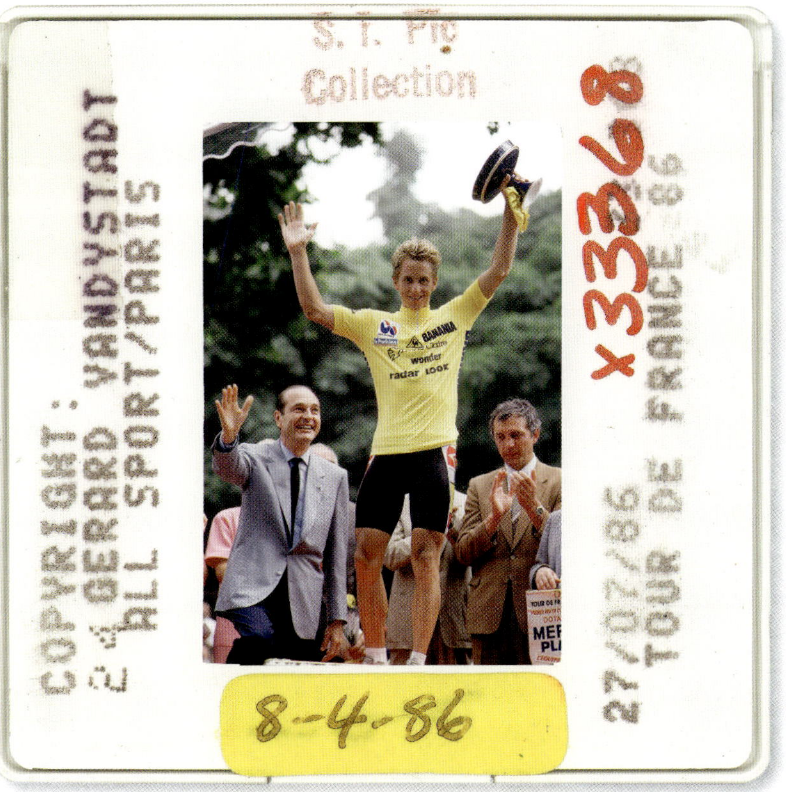

IT DOESN'T happen often, but occasionally a slide goes bilingual. In this instance, SI had employed a French photographer to cover the Tour de France; he processed the film into slides before shipping them to the magazine. The Tour, with its curves and climbs through the French landscape, is an annual source of sensational photos and perhaps the most picturesque event on the sports calendar. But the 1986 edition turned out to be a milestone event when Greg LeMond became the first American to win the race in its 83 years. LeMond would capture the yellow jersey twice more, in '89 and '90, inspiring many more Americans to take up *cyclisme*.

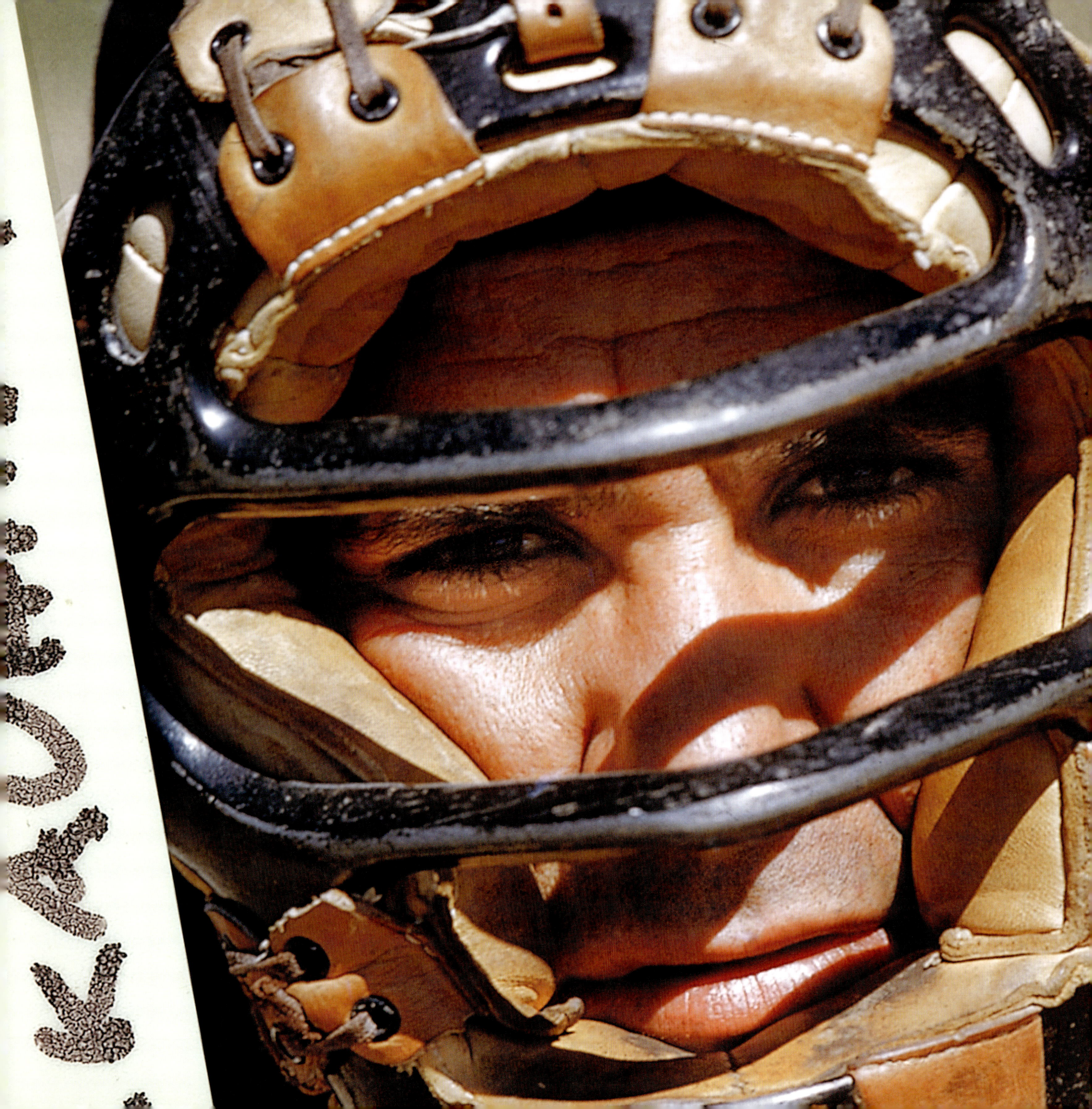

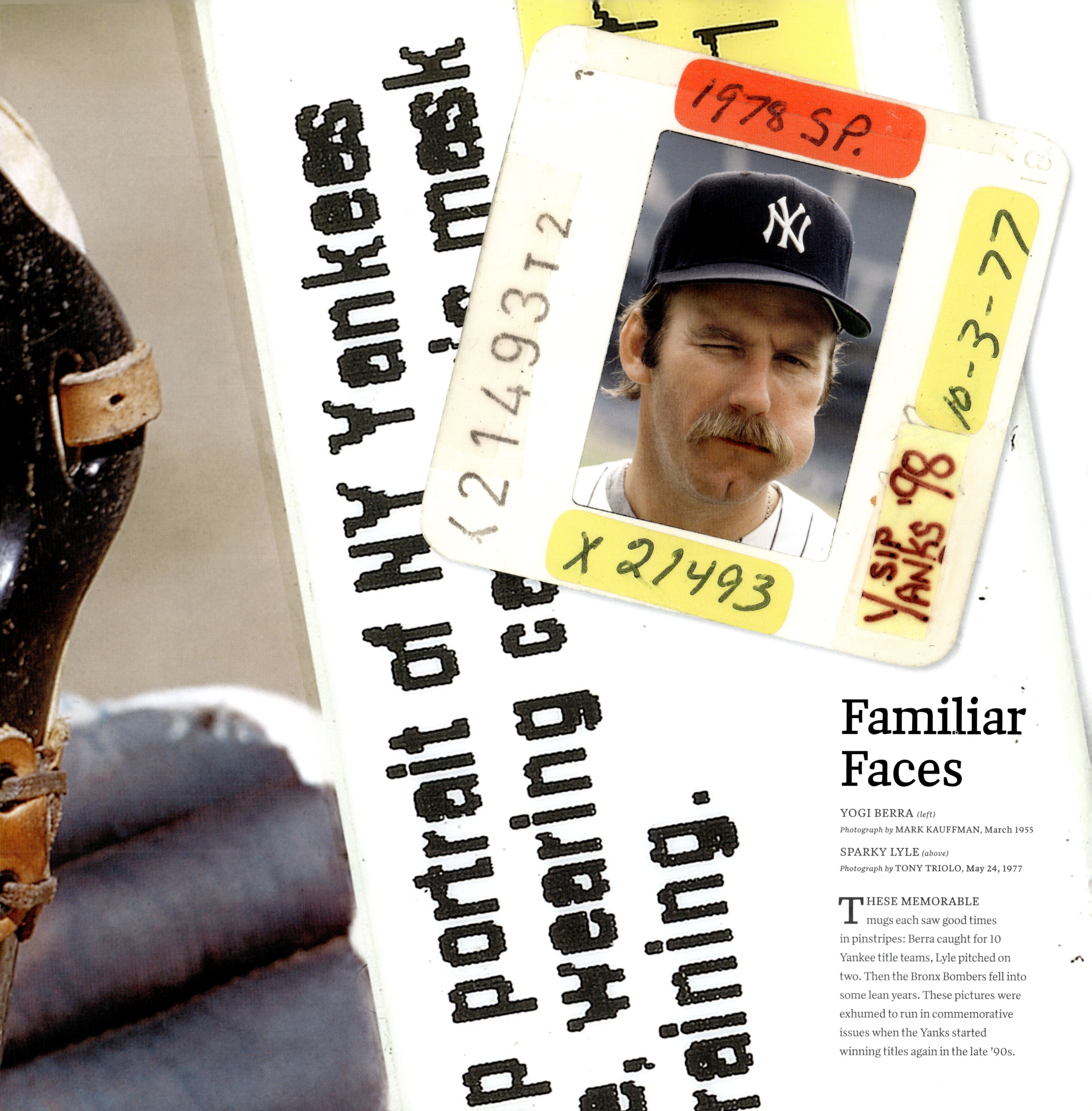

Familiar Faces

YOGI BERRA *(left)*
Photograph by MARK KAUFFMAN, March 1955

SPARKY LYLE *(above)*
Photograph by TONY TRIOLO, May 24, 1977

THESE MEMORABLE mugs each saw good times in pinstripes: Berra caught for 10 Yankee title teams, Lyle pitched on two. Then the Bronx Bombers fell into some lean years. These pictures were exhumed to run in commemorative issues when the Yanks started winning titles again in the late ’90s.

9-2-74

4/26/04

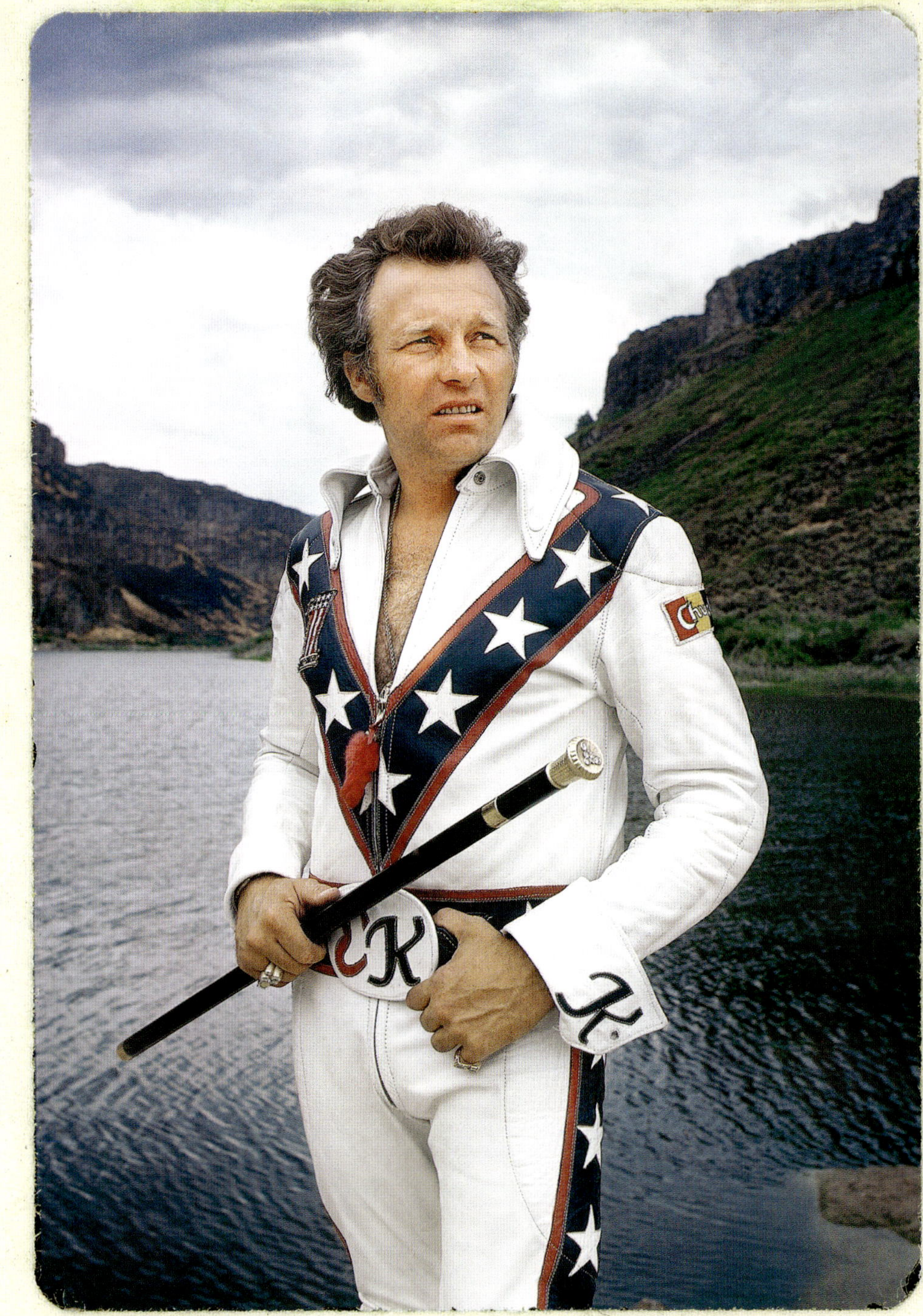

Cover 1974
X18857

SI ORIGINAL

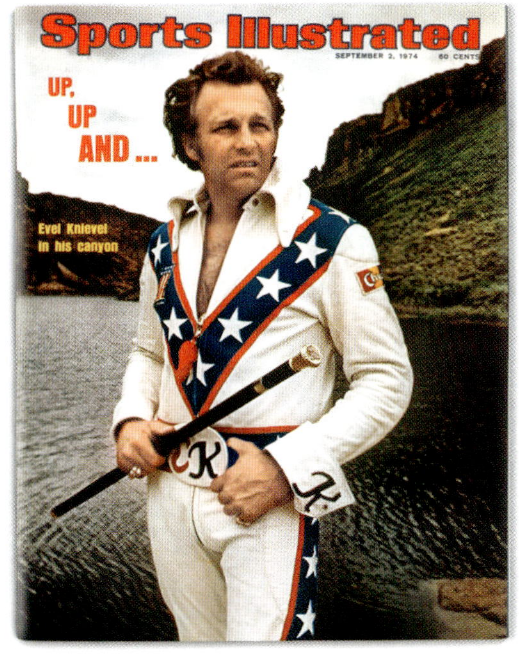

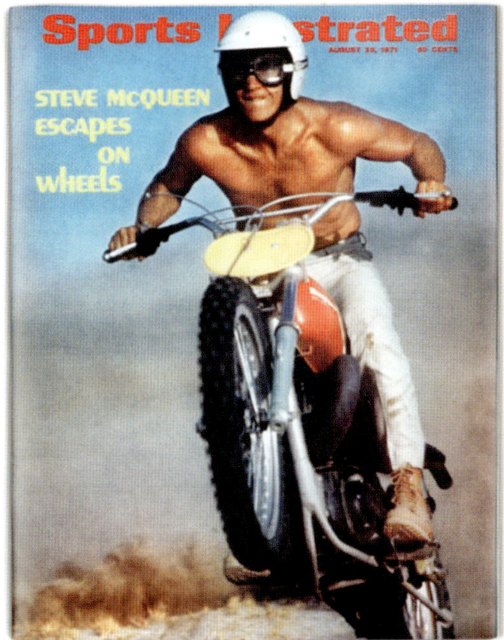

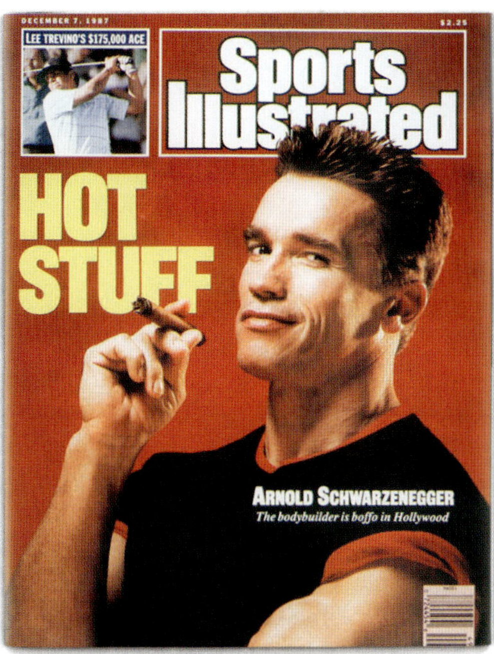

Men of Distinction

EVEL KNIEVEL

Photograph by HEINZ KLUETMEIER, August 20, 1974

WHEN ECCENTRICITY applies, SI has always been happy to expand its definition of sport. Hence the cover stories on canyon jumping with Evel Knievel, muscle-building with Arnold Schwarzenegger (before he began flexing his political muscle) or motoring around the California wild with Steve McQueen. Heinz Kluetmeier, who photographed McQueen outside Palm Springs, recalls the movie star as being a regular guy out for a good time. Kluetmeier also shot Knievel, a decidedly *irregular* guy, in Snake River Canyon before his ill-fated attempt to rocket across the river. The photo shows the course that Knievel intended to travel: The jump began at the cliff over his left shoulder, with the goal of landing on the one over his right. To see where he actually ended up—well, you'd still be looking over his left shoulder.

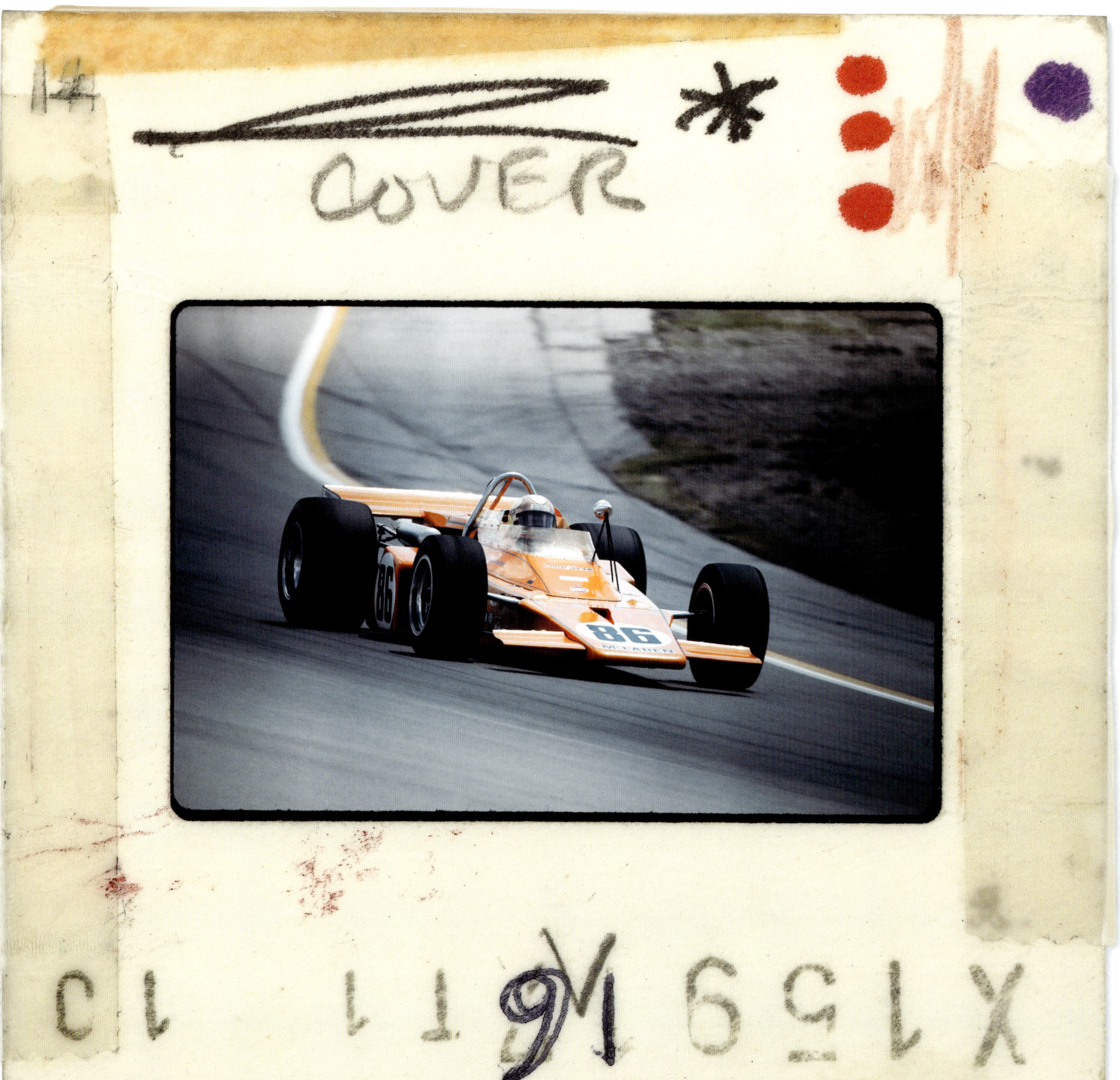

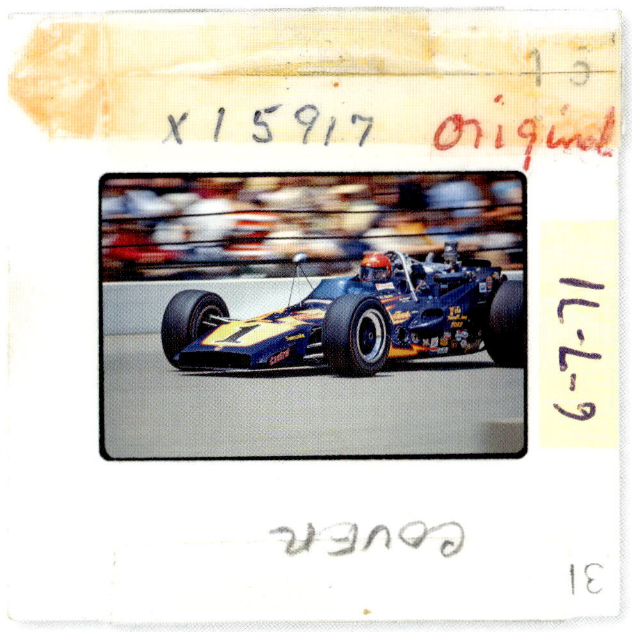

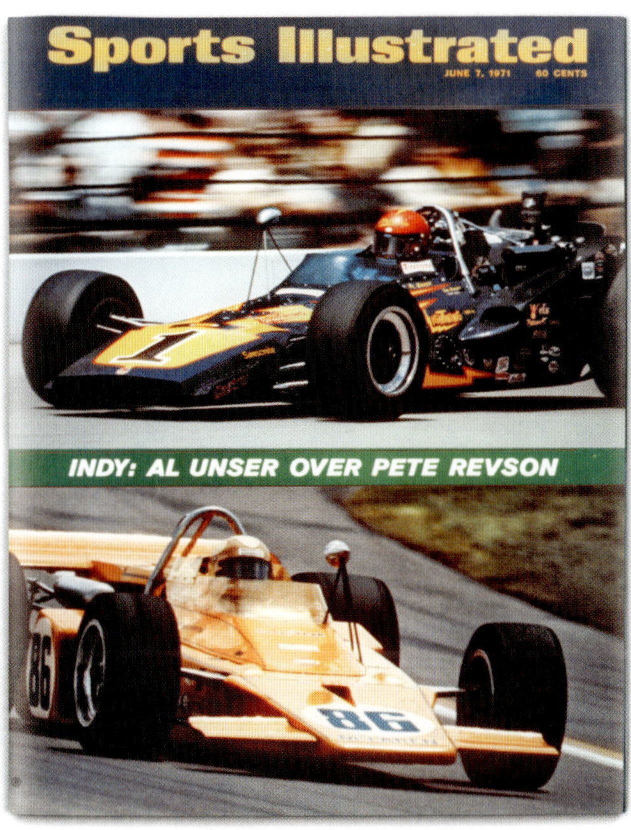

Dangerous Business

AL UNSER *(near left)*
Photograph by JAMES DRAKE, May 29, 1971

PETER REVSON *(opposite)*
Photograph by HEINZ KLUETMEIER, May 29, 1971

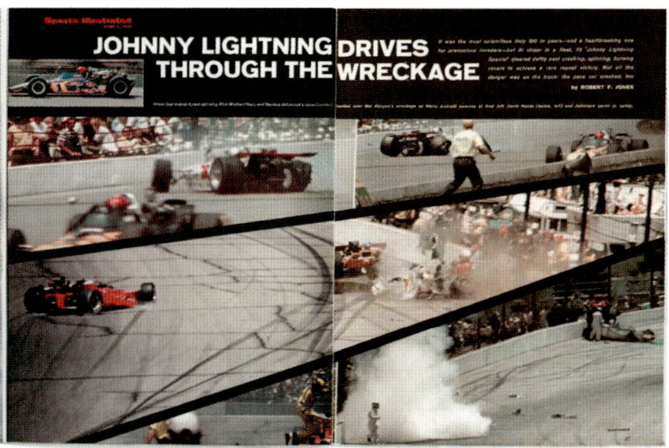
JOHNNY LIGHTNING DRIVES THROUGH THE WRECKAGE

GOOD FORTUNE is a photographer's friend. James Drake and Heinz Kluetmeier had it at this Indy 500, in ways both small and large. The small stroke of luck was that they came away with clean photos of the one-two finishers, Al "Johnny Lightning" Unser and Peter Revson, and were rewarded with a two-shot cover. But the greater blessing was that they walked away from the track intact. This race saw several crashes, including one (not shown in the above magazine spread) in which the pace car hit a photographers' stand. The SI crew wasn't in it, but one photographer was critically injured, three others suffered broken bones, and a dozen others were left bruised and stunned.

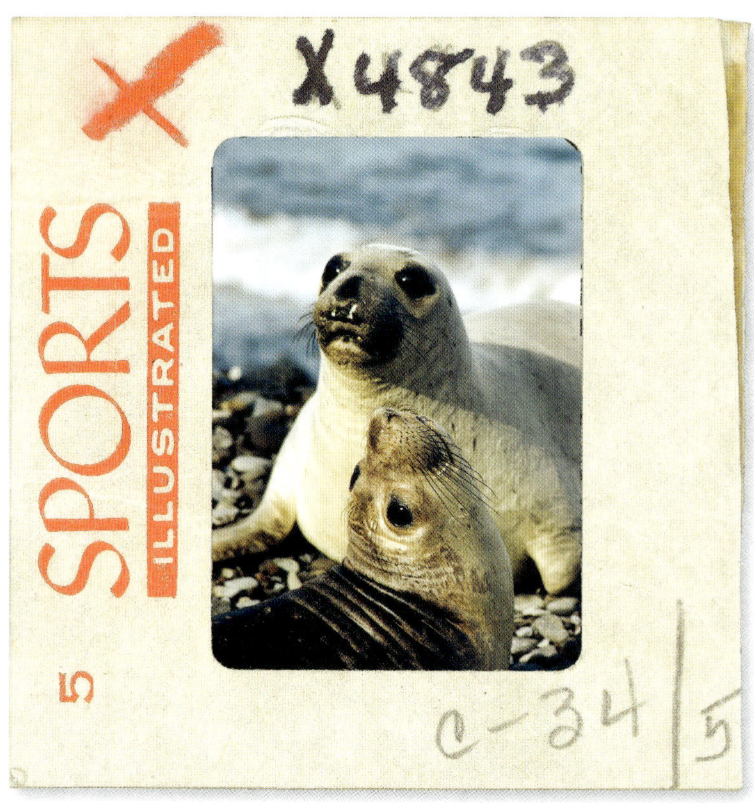

ELEPHANT SEALS

Photograph by RICHARD MEEK, November 3, 1957

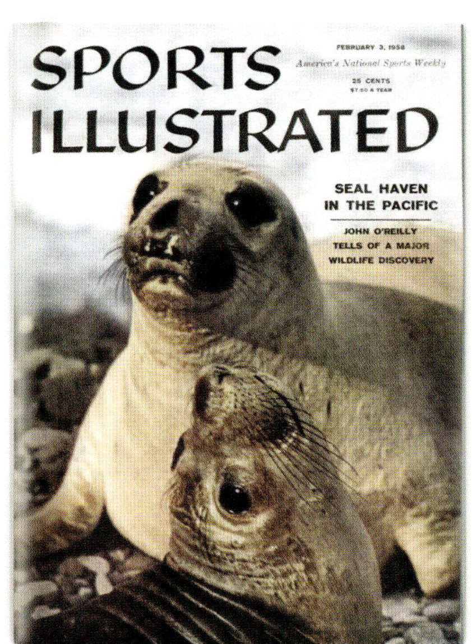

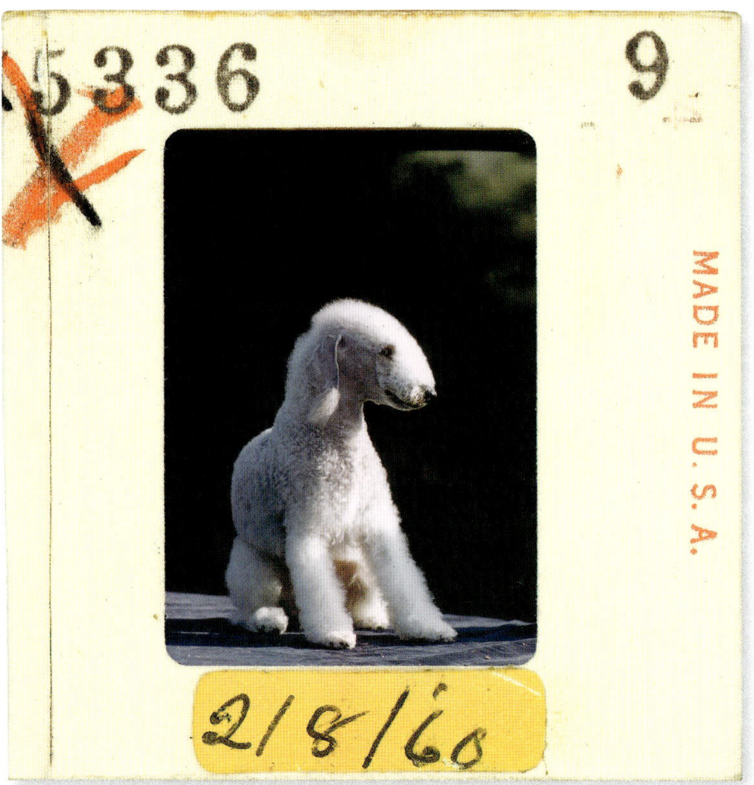

BEDLINGTON TERRIER

Photograph by JOHN G. ZIMMERMAN, July 28, 1958

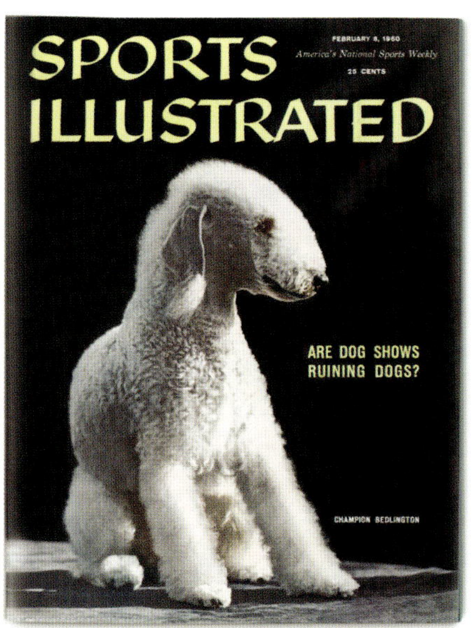

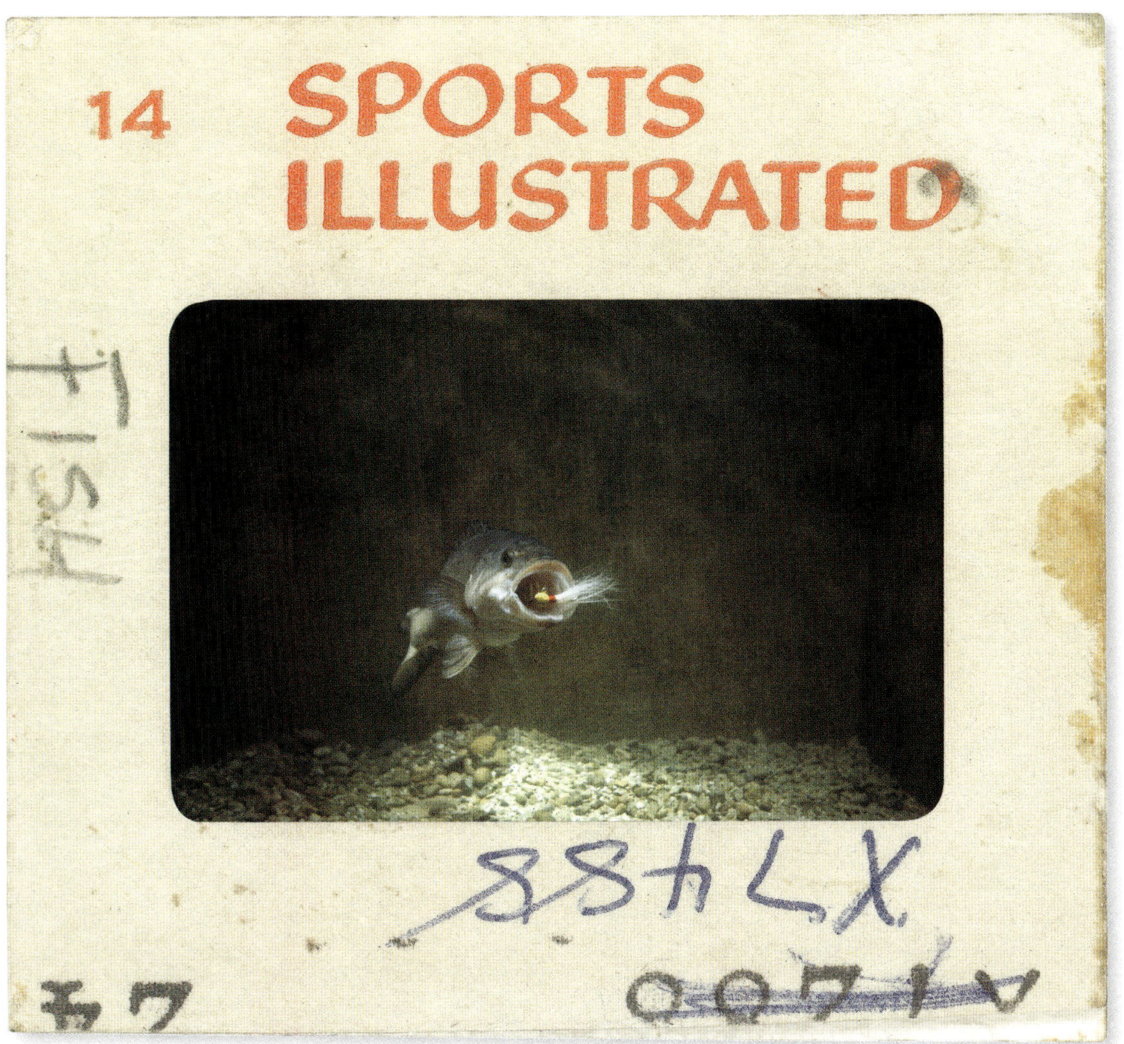

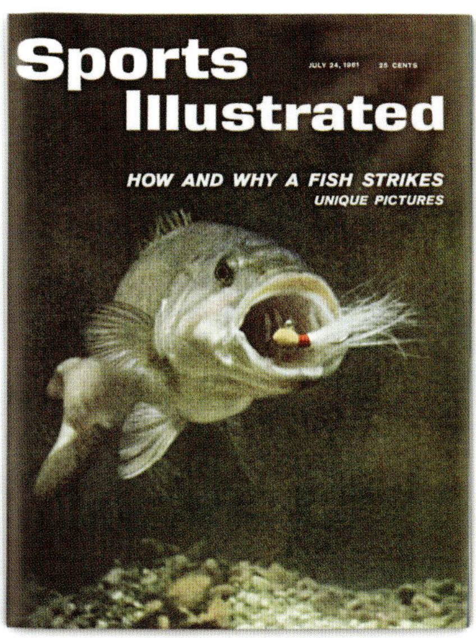

Creature Features

FRESHWATER FISH
Photograph by ELGIN CIAMPI, April 1961

IN THE EARLY DAYS of SI, the late 1950s and early '60s, the realm of "sport" was more broadly defined and encompassed both hobby and leisure. As these cover photos attest, the magazine sought many of its stories in places far from the baseball fields or the basketball courts, with expeditions in fishing and hunting (sample title: *One-Shot Paul Gets His Deer*), explorations of the natural world (*Delights of Drifting Down the Delaware*) and investigations into such hot-button issues as *Are Dog Shows Ruining Dogs?* (The story's conclusion: yes!) SI has had six dog-show covers, but none after '75 and hasn't featured a fishing cover since the '60s. And in its long history the magazine has had just one seal cover.

Credits

Miami's Dennis Kelleher was warmly congratulated after the 1988 Orange Bowl and, as the yellow tag says, the happy pair made the SI cover.

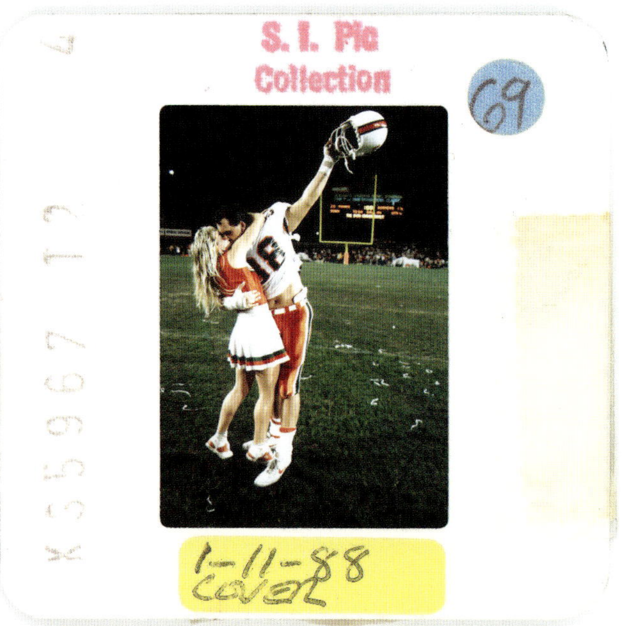

FOR THE STORIES behind the pictures in this book, thanks goes to photographers Neil Leifer, Heinz Kluetmeier, Walter Iooss Jr., Manny Millan, James Drake, Chuck Solomon, Robert Beck, Peter Read Miller, John Biever, Bob Martin and John W. McDonough. Thanks also to these valuable contributors: former SI managing editor Mark Mulvoy, writer Jerry Kirshenbaum, Howie Leifer (Neil's brother and archivist), as well as Tom Giglio and Evan Schmidt. Special thanks to SI's photo and imaging staffs, especially Steve Fine, Karen Carpenter, Jennifer Grad, Dan Larkin, Bob Thompson and Annmarie Modugno-Avila.

ADDITIONAL PHOTO CREDITS:

SLIDES AND PHOTOGRAPHS: Page 1: Neil Leifer; Page 9: Marvin E. Newman; Page 10: Leifer; Page 11: French Ministry of Culture and Communication, Regional Direction for Cultural Affairs—Rhone-Alpes region—Regional Department of Archaeology; Page 12: MGM/Photofest; Page 13: Ted Thai; Page 176: John Biever

COVERS: Page 14: Jon Brenneis; Page 21: Heinz Kluetmeier, Damian Strohmeyer; Page 28: Peter Read Miller; Page 29: Andy Hayt, Walter Iooss Jr.; Page 33: Kluetmeier; Page 36: Neil Leifer; Page 39: Leifer; Page 43: John G. Zimmerman, Leifer, Michael O'Bryon; Page 45: Iooss; Page 47: Leifer (2); Page 57: Simon Bruty; Page 60: Tony Triolo/Dick Raphael; Page 61: Phil Bath, Sheedy & Long; Page 65: Zimmerman, Harry Benson, Bruty; Page 70: Rich Clarkson; Page 73: John Biever; Page 81: John Iacono, Matt Mahurin, DPA, Rich Clarkson, Henri Bureau-Gamma, Sipahioglu-Benzakin, AP/Time Magazine; Page 83: Leifer; Page 84: Kluetmeier, Leifer/Time Magazine; Page 87: Hy Peskin; Page 88: James Drake; Page 90: Iooss; Page 93: Richard Meek; Page 96: Robert Weaver; Page 98: Robert Beck; Page 102: Boris Chaliapin/Time Magazine, George Silk, Ralph Morse/Life Magazine; Page 108: Ben Rose; Page 111: Iooss; Page 116: Iooss; Page 121: Ronald C. Modra; Page 126: Mark Kauffman; Page 128: Zimmerman; Page 131: Anthony Edgeworth, Leifer/Time Magazine; Page 134: Zimmerman; Page 136: Manny Millan; Page 137: Herb Scharfman, Jacqueline Duvoisin; Page 139: Leifer; Page 144: David Noyes, Amy Guip/Biever/Millan, Time Inc. Picture Collection; Page 146: Sheedy & Long, Peskin; Page 150: Gregory Heisler; Page 157: Iooss; Page 159: Millan; Page 160: V.J. Lovero, Richard Mackson; Page 161: Chuck Solomon; Page 164: Millan; Page 171: Kluetmeier (2), E.J. Camp; Page 173: Drake, Kluetmeier; Page 174: Meek, Zimmerman; Page 175: Elgin Ciampi

MAGAZINE SPREADS: Page 25: Heinz Kluetmeier, Joe Lertola; Page 51: George Tiedemann/GT Images; Page 57: Bob Martin; Page 58: Neil Leifer; Page 66: Curt Gunther/Time Magazine, Tony Triolo; Page 36: Herb Scharfman, Triolo; Page 77: Tiedemann/GT Images; Page 87: Robert Riger; Page 90: Walter Iooss Jr.; Page 121: Ronald C. Modra; Page 122: Hy Peskin; Page 126: Mark Kauffman; Page 139: Iooss, Leifer, Scharfman; Page 141: John G. Zimmerman; Page 150: Jerry Wachter; Page 173: James Drake, Arthur Shay (3), Kluetmeier (2)

TIME INC. HOME ENTERTAINMENT:

RICHARD FRAIMAN, *Publisher*; STEVEN SANDONATO, *General Manager*; CAROL PITTARD, *Executive Director, Marketing Services;* TOM MIFSUD, *Director, Retail & Special Sales;* PETER HARPER, *Director, New Product Development*; LAURA ADAM, *Assistant Director, Newsstand Marketing;* JOY BUTTS, *Assistant Director, Brand Marketing;* HELEN WAN, *Associate Counsel;* HOLLY OAKES, *Senior Brand Manager,* TWRS/M; ALEXANDRA BLISS, *Brand & Licensing Manager;* ANNE-MICHELLE GALLERO, *Design & Prepress Manager;* SUSAN CHODAKIEWICZ, *Book Production Manager*

A NOTE ON THE TYPEFACE USED IN THIS BOOK:
Quiosco is inspired in part by popular American textfaces used in cheap paperback novels of the 1930s. It was first drawn in 2002 for a South American newspaper by Cyrus Highsmith at Font Bureau. (*Quiosco* is Spanish for *kiosk.*) The lively details, intended to increase legibility at small sizes, also make it a dynamic choice for large headlines. Gradually the typeface has migrated north, becoming popular with publication designers of many nationalities; it is used in everything from magazines to television graphics.

12
NLB BACC

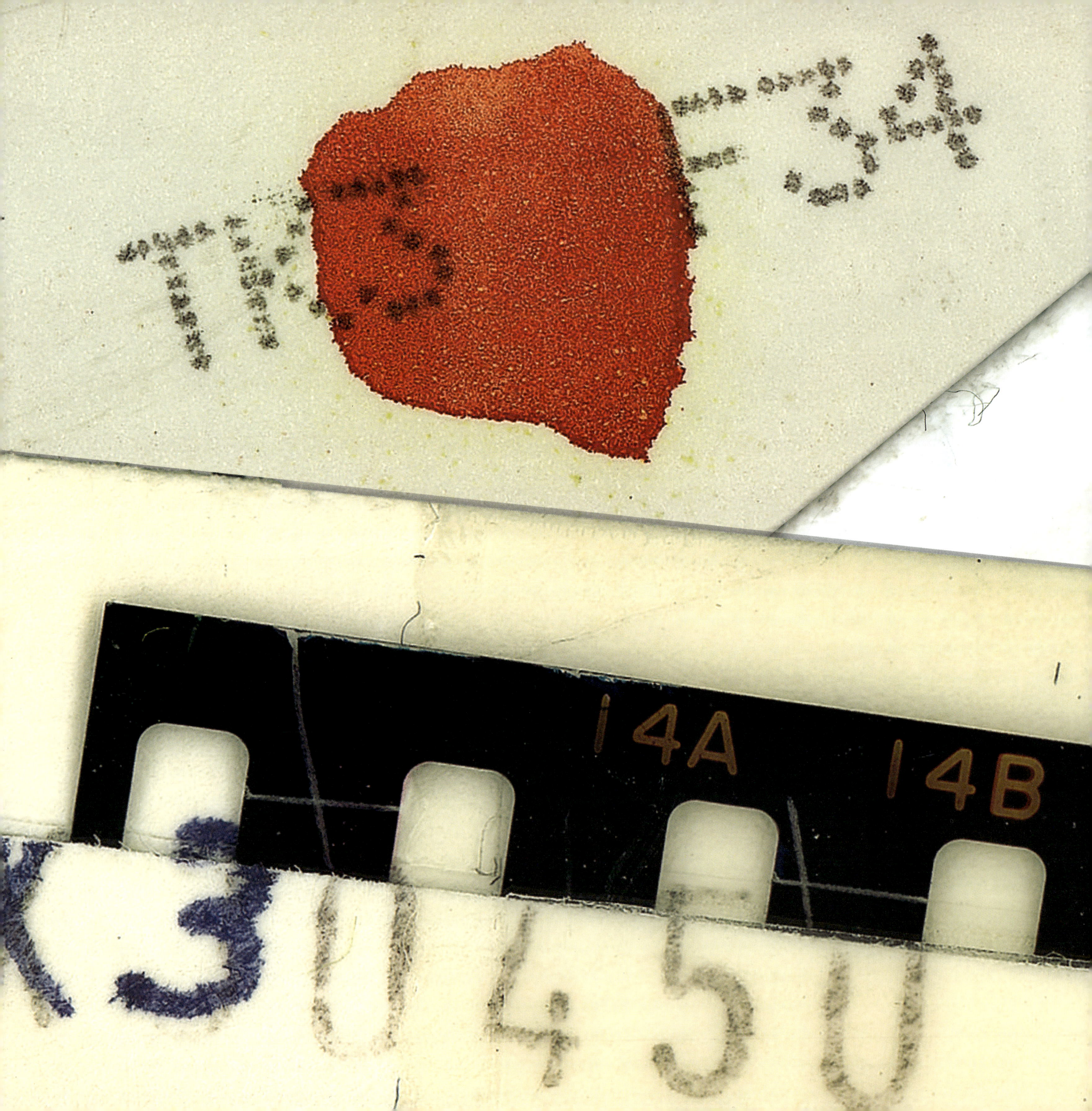
14A
14B